PRAISE FOR

From Daughters to Mothers

I'VE ALWAYS MEANT
TO TELL YOU

"Sensitive, engaging, and sometimes painful, the letters to mothers both living and dead are filled with fresh insights. . . ."
—*Chicago Tribune*

"This packed collection of missives . . . is a tribute to the unsung moments of maternity. Writers from Joyce Carol Oates to Judith Ortiz Cofer to Rita Dove gather here to address their generatrices—the living and the dead—as well as to be pictured with them in touching portraits and telling little biographies."
—*The Washington Post Book World*

"The pieces are well-chosen, with every type of revelation expressed . . . with wrenching precision. . . . Memories of one's own mother may arise and wilt the page with tears."
—*Kirkus Reviews*

"This outstanding collection of original writings gives voice to our often unspoken sentiments and reflections about our mothers. . . . The authors eloquently express universal emotions of women toward their mothers: gratitude, uncertainty, sadness, anger, understanding, and love. . . . Readers will find something of the essence of all mothers within the pages. Whether they are known as Mama, Mom, Mother, Mum, or Mommy, literary mothers (and daughters) will find the experiences related in this anthology vivid, heartfelt, and perhaps even familiar."
—Nancy Gross, *Rocky Mountain News* (CO)

"Many fine moments. . . . A sweet treat for Mother's Day."
—*Mademoiselle*

"These are beautiful letters, and that's not surprising since they were written by fine writers who are poets, novelists, essayists, humorists, cartoonists, and journalists."
—Mary Ann Grossmann, *St. Paul Pioneer Press* (MN)

"[This book] provides a moving and provocative look at the complex relationship of mother and daughter. . . . The letters . . . are intensely personal. . . . The black-and-white photos of each mother and daughter add to the emotional appeal of the writing. While many selections brim with love and understanding, there are some that express anger and frustration. . . . You can expect to shed a few tears when reading this book, but you'll also learn a few things about relationships, communication, and, most of all, love."
—*Cedar Rapids Gazette* (IA)

"This is not the stuff of Hallmark greeting cards. . . . You will not regret time spent with these writers and their mothers."
—Ann Hyman, *Florida Times-Union* (Jacksonville)

"On this Mother's Day, tongue-tied offspring might find inspiration for conveying their sentiments to Mom in *FROM DAUGHTERS TO MOTHERS: I'VE ALWAYS MEANT TO TELL YOU.*"
—*Rochester Democrat and Chronicle* (NY)

"[A] wonderful anthology."
—*Arizona Republic*

"Highly recommended . . . for women's studies, literature, and general collections."
—*Library Journal*

From Daughters to Mothers

I'VE ALWAYS MEANT TO TELL YOU

An Anthology of Letters

Edited by
CONSTANCE WARLOE

POCKET BOOKS

New York   London   Toronto   Sydney   Tokyo   Singapore

This book is for
Mary Elizabeth Brown Bower Knowles,
most complicated and blessed of women,
my mother

and for all our mothers

POCKET BOOKS, a division of Simon & Schuster Inc.
1230 Avenue of the Americas, New York, NY 10020

Copyright © 1997 by Constance Warloe
Each Letter's author retains copyright to her work

Previously published in hardcover in 1997 by Pocket Books

ISBN: 0-671-56325-4

First Pocket Books trade paperback printing March 1998

10 9 8 7 6 5 4 3 2

POCKET and colophon are registered trademarks of
Simon & Schuster Inc.

Cover design by Lisa Litwack
Cover photo © Ruth Bushman 1996/FPG International
Text design by Stanley S. Drate/Folio Graphics Co. Inc.

Printed in the U.S.A.

Originally titled *I've Always Meant to Tell You:
Letters to Our Mothers*

Acknowledgments

I thank the writers who have contributed to this anthology. Nhizoní: May you walk in harmony and beauty.

I thank our mothers, and my own mother. I have dedicated the book to them.

In addition, several editors have watched over this book at various times in the past couple of years, among them Hillary Cige and William Grose. My guiding lights at Pocket Books have been Emily Bestler, vice president and editorial director, and Amelia Sheldon, editor and repository of more minute details than anyone would ever want to know about—thanks, Amelia, for taking such care with this unwieldy project.

Along the way, others have offered encouragement and donated their time. Two former students jumped right in to help: In the early stages, Lynn Doiron was my underpaid, high-tech assistant who made the mailing lists manageable; later, Penny Wofford was my underpaid, low-tech assistant who worked the phones and sent out proof copies to the authors. Bill Thompson of Briarwood Writers' Alliance graciously forwarded packages to writers whose addresses I would never have found. Dick Schmidt, friend and award-winning photographer at *The Sacramento Bee,* has enhanced many family photos that would have been otherwise indecipherable, and we all thank him for his generosity and expertise. Santa Fe artist Kathleen Adler Harms, daughter of contributor Lucile Adler, offered invaluable advice on the cover; I thank her for her talent and inspiration. Jan Haag, Penny Wofford, Lynn Doiron, and Clysta Kinstler spent a day and a half on my front porch, copyediting eighty letters, almost five hundred pages of manuscript. I fed them well, but still . . .

My friend and former colleague Harold Schneider has lightened the load with poetry, insight, and his ever ebullient humor.

As always, my husband and friend, Roger, has walked out on that familiar limb with me, helping in ways that are both measurable and immeasurable. Among the numerous life-preserving miracles he performed, I would mention prominently his equations regarding how I would pay the authors first, wait for my advance from the publisher, and not get us evicted. In addition, he typed in many letters, made spreadsheets for tracking the thirteen items per author (a total of 1,066 pieces of stuff), and explained all this to our accountant while I sat making sounds of bewilderment. He listened as I read numerous letters aloud to him, both of us spilling tears or bubbling laughter.

My agents, Linda Chester and Laurie Fox, whom I referred to as Angels in my first novel's acknowledgment, have earned a new supernatural distinction. They are the Fairy Godmothers of this anthology. Simply put, the anthology would not exist without their out-of-this-world belief in me and, of course, the wave of their magic wand.

Contents

Contents

Introduction

Dear Reader,

The celebrity of many of the writers in this collection may have been your first attraction to this book; indeed, it's hard to deny the scholarly and literary curiosity inherent upon seeing all these remarkably gifted writers in one place, including:

Joyce Carol Oates • Rita Dove • Barbara Kingsolver • Ellen Gilchrist • Pam Houston • Lynn Sharon Schwartz • Carolyn Kizer • Natalie Goldberg • Maxine Kumin • Rosellen Brown • Judith Ortiz Cofer • Joyce Wadler • Joy Harjo • Carolyn Kizer • Susan Power • Ann Hood • Carolyn See • Ntozake Shange • Lynda Barry • Carol Bly • Susan Griffin • Connie May Fowler • Marge Piercy • Carol Shields

When their heartfelt words begin, however, you will forget their fame and discover the bare-bones truth of what they have written. Sometimes the letters have taken the form of poems, as in poet Maxine Kumin's crown of sonnets or Susan Kelly-DeWitt's waves of haiku or Enid Shomer's sestina. The various forms do not change the demands of the epistolary voice: directness, intimacy and most of all, honesty. Indeed, literary forms allow us to reach into the fire of this emotional furnace wearing the "asbestos glove" Adrienne Rich so aptly compared to art's varied disguises.

As they say in the Oldsmobile ads, "This is not your father's Oldsmobile." Well, as the editor of this collection, I say this is not your mother's anthology, either. The voices you hear are daughters' voices. But through the daughters speaking in this collection, you will hear their mothers' voices clearly.

This is also not your typical anthology. Maybe because the theme is family, the process of editing the book became a very personal experience for me. Perhaps writing our letters together during an eighteen-month period—between February 1995 and August 1996—produced a collective energy that changed us all. Whatever the magic, I find there is really only one way to talk about being the contibuting editor of this anthology, and that is to say that the book, its journey, and the writers who contributed to it have become a transformative part of my life.

The project began, as so many life-changing events have begun for me, with a phone call. On October 25, 1994, my literary agent and her associate had been brainstorming new book projects and had come up with an idea for an anthology. How would I like to edit and contribute to a collection of original letters written by contemporary women authors to their mothers? "Not an archival project?" I asked, the novelist in me skeptical of getting buried in a research project. No, they assured me. More a revisiting of a never-completed emotional cycle. I was hooked.

I thought immediately of the disappointing sentiments expressed in Mother's Day cards. So often the verses begin, *I know I don't tell you very often* . . . and then go on to express less than we want to say, not as well as we want to say it, but we buy the cards anyway. We find the cards stored in drawers and boxes at our mothers' homes, and, as we have our own children, our own collections begin to accumulate. Maybe this book could be a different Mother's Day greeting, I thought. Maybe this book could get things said that usually remain unspoken. Before I had even hung up the phone, I had suggested the title that has stayed: *I've Always Meant to Tell You.* Then came the telling.

At the time of that phone call, my mother was in relatively good health and living with her second husband in New Mexico. Since then, she has suffered vertebra fractures due to osteoporosis, moved to California, divorced her second husband, and now resides in an assisted-care center, events I was called upon, as her daughter and only child, to help her manage. I really don't know what the past two years would have looked like without the community of women that formed as this book came to life.

I can only say that as the writers began calling and the letters began arriving, I was definitely not alone. All the paradoxes of frustration and love, sorrow and joy, abuse and caring, self-doubt and empowerment, illness and health, and other issues that I had carried around as elements in my relationship with *my* mother were turning up in the letters of other writers to their mothers.

I noticed that none of the material—the lowest sorrow or the highest joy—was easy to write about. Many letters were accompanied by handwritten notes saying, "This was so much harder than I had thought it would be." I also noticed that in every letter there seemed to be an identifiable moment when the writer had "hit the wall"—a wall of intimacy, privacy or downright fear—and kept on writing. You will feel it, too, the strength of their desire to get these things said. I've always meant to tell you . . .

Carol Bly remembers her mother's valiant struggle with and eventual death from tuberculosis in the 1930s and 1940s, but she also continues the ongoing argument about social class that she carried on with her mother long after the mother's death. • Carolyn See's letter is a truth-telling benediction for anyone who has grown up in the presence of a rageful adult. • A letter/poem by Enid Shomer confronts her mother's passivity in the face of her father's abuses. • Joyce Carol Oates offers her mother a loving tribute and, with it, an elegiac remembrance of farm life. • Cartoonist and humorist Nicole Hollander offers us a circular series of communiqués to her character's mother in the form of daily phone conversations. • Suzanne Lipsett, who has no actual memories of her mother, addresses that phantom presence in a moving, deceptively lighthearted voice. • Mary Zeppa composes a compelling confession about the haunting secrets of abortion. • Joanne Meschery offers a complex portrait of her mother's life as a minister's wife in mid-20th century America.

Eighty voices blending. The cumulative effect, breathtaking.

And just in case you thought the process of writing was easier because these women are writers, it wasn't. I chose to share the following anecdotes because they reflect the distracting lives we all lead and the same hesitation we all feel when faced with the impulse to speak and the constriction in our throats that often keeps us silent:

> Hilma Wolitzer called at midnight, New York time, the night of the deadline to say she was so sad she didn't think she could write this letter. Then, months after I had received her letter, she called again, saying her mother had died. • Pam Houston called from Kansas the week after the deadline saying she hadn't forgotten but she'd been putting it off "an awful lot." • Laura Kasischke wrote from Las Vegas to say she was happily pregnant and in the midst of moving back to Michigan, but she had the letter written. • Rita Dove had to delay her letter because of a badly hurt wrist. • Five babies were born to the writers during the year and a half of this project—Ann Hood, Laura Kasischke, Barbara Kingsolver, Dawn Raffel and Susan Straight all gave birth. • Lucile Adler, a poet who is usually very concise, ended up writing a long prose collage of letters, a tribute to her mother's great courage and love of life. • Sonia Gernes, whose father had just died and she herself had just been diagnosed with cancer, somehow got her letter in on time. • Natalie Goldberg, the most famous of writing coaches, called me one afternoon to say she could not write the letter and would have to withdraw from the anthology. I said if it wasn't meant to be, it wasn't meant to be, and accepted her withdrawal. She called three hours later and said she had written the letter, she just needed to know she didn't have to! • Rosellen Brown, whose mother was still living at the time she wrote the piece, got word while at a conference in Italy that her mother had died; she decided that for her reading that night in Spoleto she had to read her "A Natural Gift." Without any printers available, she read it from the glowing screen of her laptop computer in an amphitheater looking down over a hillside to an ancient monastery. She wrote later to thank me for the catharsis of having to produce a letter she otherwise would never have written. • Finally, hardest of all to report, Suzanne Lipsett, who was among the first to turn in her letter, died before the book became a reality. She died in California, during the golden month of September 1996, after a long and absolutely

valiant struggle with ovarian cancer. Her letter to her mother speaks to all of us about the moment, and exactly what it means to speak.

My office has been populated by a roomful of women who were saying what was on their minds and in their hearts—and saying it with dignity, courage, and eloquent language. Ultimately, *I've Always Meant to Tell You: Letters to Our Mothers* is about finding the courage to say the unsayable, and then actually getting it said. I hope the telling here will bring courage and communication into your life and that of your family. Read on.

CONSTANCE WARLOE

SACRAMENTO, CALIFORNIA
JULY 15, 1996

Lucile Adler

Lucile Bloch Adler and her mother, Lucile Meinrath Bloch
Kansas City, Missouri; c. 1940

Lucile Bloch Adler was born in 1922 in Kansas City, Missouri, and has lived in Santa Fe, New Mexico, since 1950. She was married to Nathan Adler in 1940. They have two children, John Millard Adler, 1947, and Kathleen Adler Harms, 1953. Lucile Adler graduated from Bennington College. Her work has appeared in numerous magazines and journals including *The Nation*, *The New Yorker*, *Poetry Northwest*, *Sunstone Review*, *In Context*, *Inscape*, *The Indian Rio Grande*, *La Confluencia*, *Puerta del Sol*, *El Palacio* (magazine of the Museum of New Mexico), *New Mexico Poetry Renaissance*, *Poets West*, *The Massachusetts Review*, and *San Marcos Review*. Her poetry is anthologized in *The New Yorker Book of Poems*, *The New York Times Book of Verse*, *I Hear My Sisters Saying*, *The Forgotten Language*, and others. A selection of Ms. Adler's poems was tape-recorded at the Lamont Poetry Room at Harvard. Books include *The Traveling Out* (Macmillan), *The Society of Anna* (Lightning Tree Press), and *The Ripening Light: Selected Poems 1977–1987* (Peregrine Smith Books). She has recently completed a new poetry manuscript, *The Red Pear Tree*; a novel, *The Juniper Letters*; and a long prose poem, *expedition*.

Lucile Meinrath Bloch (Lulu) was born in 1894 in Kansas City, Missouri, and died in 1987. She was married to Millard Joseph Bloch in 1916. They had three daughters, Mary, 1918, Lucile, 1922, and Jane, 1926–1967.

LULU
"The bold past sashed with light."

For many years messages flew from an adobe house in Santa Fe to my mother, Lulu, and my sister Jane, and her family who lived in Cincinnati overlooking the Ohio River. The tragedy of Jane's eighteen-year-long battle with polio, and the lives that were built around it, came to light again in cartons containing my old notes, postcards, scraps of poems, and scrawled letters that were returned to me after Lulu's death in 1987.

Last summer when I found and finally dared reopen the old cartons, I realized that the untidy records they contained still offered insights into that complex household and those who loved Jane and were dedicated to her care. I have written the collage of letters that follows in honor of them all, but especially as a tribute to Lulu's endurance, profound frivolity, and courage in those long-ago dark years streaked every day by heroism . . .

Lulu Dear,

I'm home again! At my own round kitchen table heaped with old mail and yellow apples under the hanging lamp. There is a bottle of Chablis set out by N. on the table near a sprig of smoke-blue juniper berries, to welcome me. Fine gifts, but I miss you still.

That's what I want to say before I go to sleep: I miss you. Since I was with you in Ohio, the other day, I see everything differently—you, the family there; mica stones, and red sunset and mountains here. I see sickness, courage, the color of apples, motives—even your life with Jane, HRB, and Peter more clearly. I think I do.

One of the apples, with freckled yellow silk skin hiding the flesh inside, is already withered and old. The idea of Age, our ages, yours and mine, especially since this last visit, fascinates and troubles me.

LATER. I'VE HAD A QUICK SHOWER,
USED THE ENTIRE TINY VIAL OF
ARPÉGE YOU GAVE ME, AND FEEL
REVIVED.

What's left of the wine I'll sip with a fond toast to you. It's a crisp fall night outside, moonlight on the Chinese elms and the wild currant bushes by the road here. I remember the magnolia tree on the lawn high above the river where you lived so many years ago with Jane, HRB, and Peter.

And I remember the last time I saw you. You wore the heavy silver-embossed white robe Aunt Jan brought you from Morocco and were sitting all alone at the rosewood dining table, staring down from your 17th-floor eyrie at tiny black figures of skaters on the patch of snow-rimmed ice far below.

"I certainly could skate better than *that* once," you said. "And as to DANCING!"

You were right, of course. From this New Mexico landscape where the apricot trees still hold a few red leaves, I can see you dancing that last time, swaying alone near the long Fortuny curtains in your bedroom high over the Ohio River. (You were al-

ways famous for the way you moved.) But I see you first as the
furious little girl Grandmamma told us about, a pink tantrum of
ruffles dancing under the blossoming plum tree on Tracy Street
long ago. And a lifetime later in the nursing home letting me
lead you through a few steps of a dance I invented, part lurching
Tango, part slow "Blessing Way" (for which I ask forgiveness). I
wonder if you still have a copy of the poem I sent you then?

> To remain a dancer so late
> To be determined so late to stay
> A dancer is to become part
> Of the dream of an ardent heart
> Determined to dance to the beat
> Of this one dawn becoming day
> Caught by a great blush and throb
> Of laughter at such a becoming
> Such a desire to become a dancer
> In the sense of one moving, a-fire
> With effort, effortlessly becoming
> The limbs of an old tree a-blaze
> With grace and dancing still

This note has gone on so long you must be weary. Besides, I
think I hear a car on the gravel; it's sure to be N. returning, so
I'll pause to welcome him. More tomorrow.

Meanwhile, fond love . . .

NEXT MORNING AFTER FRENCH
TOAST AND N.'S GREAT DISCOVERY

Ma Chère Lulu,

I've something astounding to tell you . . . it's about the big
studio photograph N. liberated from a raccoon-gnawed carton of
treasures in our old storage shed! (Don't be alarmed, a fine new
shed is almost finished; soon we'll have a secure pine-smelling
place for storing jars of apricot preserves and mementos—like
letters, should you have time to write any, and burlap bags of
seed for the back field [where two burnished red foxes are playing in the tall grass by the lilac bushes as I write].

Well, this recovered photo is amazing, only a little stained by time, and your face, *Mirabile!* still glows above the froth of black lace at your throat. Surrounded by the awed faces of your three young daughters, all dressed in smocked silk with pleated lace-trimmed lawn collars, you stare into the dressing table mirror in the bedroom where Daddy died quietly among the fresh chintz roses.

Somehow I know the photograph was taken late on that very September evening in 1931 after his funeral. The lights along the allée of oak trees in the park across the way from our house shone (as corruption is said to do) on the faces of the three little girls watching you. And the picture shows clearly how focused we (Mary, Lucile, and Jane) were on your vivid reflection in the mirror, and on the silver-embossed hairbrush in your raised hand. Though you don't appear to be aware of us in the amber light.

(Maybe it was from then on, while our world shook and changed, that I began to print clumsy "poems" on colored paper to tuck under your bedroom door, hoping to propitiate the glamorous mother we all came later to call "Lulu." Of course we hadn't words then to describe how wildly frivolous and at the same time imperturbable you were in the face of the tragedies you told us, furiously, were routine for you.)

But I do know, almost a lifetime later, that you were dedicated to Life and aware somehow, through your every disaster, of its potential riches.

With love as ever . . .

P.S. 5:00 A.M.—THE WILD
YOUNG PLUM TREE BY THE FENCE
OUTSIDE IS SHUDDERING IN THE
COLD; A FINE FIRE BLAZES ON THE
KITCHEN HEARTH.

Odd, how little the photo in my hands reveals about you. There is in it no guessing how you would confront the demands our lives made on you from that sad day forward, little about the magical charm and power that flowed from you and made you so fascinating, made it so impossible, captivated as we were, for us to rebel against you. Certainly we were unaware then of what a force for Life you would be—especially with Jane, the youngest daughter, the shyest, the one fated to be the most cruelly beset among us. Surely you were to be honored: a gifted dancer always in your way.

With fond love,
from Daughter II

IT'S MIDMORNING NOW . . .
TIME TO GATHER RIPE APRICOTS
BEFORE THE RACCOONS STEAL THEM
ALL!

Lulu Dear,

I hate to admit it, but we're having a battle with our neighbors, the handsome family of raccoons that marches every day in a line up the road from the arroyo—Papa, Mama, and three little ones with dark masks and bright eyes. Charming. But they deserve prison sentences. The damage they've done!

Do you remember the Fall you came out here with Cathy R. to visit? How we wrapped you in a big yellow apron, gave you a wooden ladle to stir the ruddy gold mess of fruit you had helped us pick? (Yes, you were a fine worker, who laughed with the children and us as you labored.) Then you and I sat later under the apple tree outside in the patio while the fruit boiled, and talked happily about the Past. Remember? It was long before the increasingly daring raccoons got into the *latillas* in the living room ceiling. That was a disaster!

Since my last sad departure from "Cincy" the other day, I've been meaning to tell you, not only that "Distance means nothing. I hold your hand from here,"—always—but that we've been forced to call the Animal Control people. I feel cruel, but *C'est ça*; we can't go on this way.

Fond Love,
From Me Your Look-Alike
Daughter L.

LATER, AT MY DESK NEAR A CLAY JAR
OF COSMOS AND DROOPY
RUSSIAN OLIVE LEAVES—

It's time to start the posole. Instead, I keep staring at the face of the young widow—in your thirties still—and wondering . . .

about your grief when we were small; your fear of the unsettled
and dangerous future that would make such cruel demands on
you, and leave you feeling so alone and betrayed at the last. It
shows in the dark unblinking inward stare of the sorceress that
we each, in our love and fear, sensed you to be. Forgive me, it's
only a photo, dear, though fascinating.

I should tell you that over the years I've tried from time to
time to set down fragments of what I think of as your story,
"Lulu's Story," picturing first the small fury with tangled curls
and stormy eyes—the daring child who walked the weathered
backyard fence on Tracy St. as though it were a tightrope—a
weathered fence like the one near El Porvenir where you and
Daddy took us when we were little.

> only sky
> through the hole in the fence
>
> only a dark dab of child
> a pinafore
> a round straw hat
> veiled with rain
> bowing eye to eyehole
>
> then a slow movement of years
> a slow leafing of air
> till an old mind blurred by rain
> twines leaves to wear
> dancing
> over rain-soaked stone
>
> beyond the fence
> only the brilliant stare
> of the quick child
> moving near—
>
> the bold past sashed with light

That's how I think of and see you still: "The bold past sashed
with light."

With love from
your daughter, L.

NOW IT'S 5 P.M.—A TINY
SILVER PLANE FLASHES OVER THE
RESERVOIR POND AND ARROYO
IN THE LATE NIGHT.

Dear Lulu,

I spent the whole day waiting on the portal for the Animal
Control people to come set traps for those wicked (though
charming-looking) raccoons! I've been sitting for hours on this
v. uncomfortable flagstone step surrounded by a few late castil-
ian roses growing wild. (I happen to know they are mean and
stubborn; their roots clogged the road and had to be axed out
when we first bought the house.) Well, I've been studying your
picture again while I wait. There's a great pulse of light overhead,
and I feel such a sweep of sadness, I can't tell you.

You seem to be staring through and beyond me still, the
daughter who bears your name and most resembles you. Remember? I was the one with bangs. I was also probably the most
doting of the little girls who watched so long ago when you lifted
first one tear-shaped pearl earring, then a pearl-and-onyx one to
your ear, trying to choose, staring straight ahead (at yourself
only) in the mirror. Now I'm really sad.

More tomorrow,
L.

V. EARLY THURSDAY MORNING,
AFTER COFFEE, BRAN MUFFINS &
RASPBERRY JAM

Chère Lulu,

Here I am again! I've been trying to bridge the years between
the mysterious family portrait I'm holding and still studying, and
the nightmare summer of the Polio epidemic, when Jane left me
at North Station in Boston to go home to little Peter, who was
already sick. The nurse said he had a touch of "Roseola fever."

That was the last time I ever saw Jane standing upright on her
two feet (in black high-heeled pumps). Of course you remember—she had come to visit me in Cambridge after N., felled by
TB (caught in a German prison camp years before), entered a

V.A. hospital a long drive away; and she left me to go home and face the shock and trauma of her own terrible summer. I can still feel the frenzy of my rush to Cincinnati when I heard that she was sick, too, and that the sickness was Polio. In my dreams I still wait huddled with Mary on the concrete stairs outside the giant Polio Ward, still feel a kind of fear that scalded like hot lead; and dream the breathless Terror of my response to the soughing sound of respirators on the night in 1949 when I arrived to "be with" you all.

That summer erased, for a long time, everything that had gone before in our lives.

Poor Lulu, it was an era of such horror for you. Later that August, Walter, the stepfather you said you had to give us (with his two stepsons)—Walter was stricken by Cancer and died. The story of your lives together that last summer is a story of linked disasters that might have overwhelmed anyone but you. I know I was staying with you in Walter's house (in a dreadful pink cretonne guest bedroom) on the day he left for the hospital: I can see him strolling out to his car with a cocky, almost mocking salute to all of us gathered by the door.

When he died you never missed a step—you couldn't. Your hospital visits had to go on; and they did, gallantly, as you drove (fast and erratically) between Jane in one hospital, and Peter in another. Those wild drives became your unvarying routine. Perhaps it was then that you discovered you owned a private country beyond defeat.

I truly believe that as you helped Jane's husband, HRB, fight for their blue-eyed, year-old Peter, and as you began to plan what would become the long struggle for Jane's life, you redefined what courage is.

Somehow, Jane, HRB and Peter (perfectly recovered), offered what would become the design for the rest of your life, all the way to the sometimes sorrowful years you are facing now. True?

What's more, I think it was disaster that forced you all to share your lives. And in effect, their lives became your Career. Perhaps Jane's unprecedented need saved you. True? Do you agree? Possible? Yes?

> With love and admiration
> from your middle daughter.

JUST WASHED MY STRAIGHT AND
WISPY HAIR, AND WALKED DOWN
TO THE RIVER THROUGH THE WILLOWS
WONDERING ABOUT ALL OF US.

Chère Lulu,

Looking back it seems to me now that after WWII, my life, and sister Mary's life and settling down, were too remote for you to focus on, distracted as you were by death (Walter's) and protracted illness (Jane's years in the respirator). Though you did try to visit the grandchildren in St. Louis and those running wild through the wild grasses here. And once you flew to Paris. Once to the Orient. And, I hardly dare say it—but you must be lonely sometimes—dear Lulu, pretend you give me your hand . . .

> pretend you give me your hand
> pretend we go out
>
> early
> to hear the mourning doves
> in the field
>
> pretend you trust me
> so much you believe
>
> their clear voices
> rinsing the bare field
> in the early morning
>
> cry
> as I promise they will
>
> Rejoice Rejoice
>
> old friend dear one
> thin pancakes wait
> in the copper pan
> inside

Yes, but Jane's life! Jane's life, lived for eighteen years in that respirator, directed yours, of course, and all of ours, even mine to some extent. And during those eighteen years, as you told me, you "lived only for her and for her family," always setting the stage, filling the rooms of the house you all shared, with flowers, light and color; and at a certain level, directing the drama, joined by friends and relatives, joined by the great-hearted nurses, and by your aristocratic Cordon Bleu, Elisabeth, whose cuisine made your household even more famous.

Yes, I think Jane's extreme need was a sort of terrible gift to you; your devotion becoming her small family's long and difficult reward. Poor Lulu, you couldn't be praised enough! You truly did earn medals—for valor—but there was anger, too, of course.

When it all became too much you despaired and called me and I did try to come. Though I flew again and again to the house over the river, I know it was never often enough; that no amount of listening late at night as you poured out your rage against the tragedy you tended could console you.

Oh, but I was so tired those times! Because by day I had sat for hours perched on a high stool beside the respirator mirror that reflected Jane's slightly Asian (I told her) hazel eyes, perhaps describing for her the wild iris fields we had explored at Cajilon, or listening to her tales of your exotic ménage, and of her own struggles, very private, very dark, secret and sad. Yes, they were. I can't begin to tell you how guilty I have felt for not being there with Jane and with you, more or always. Nevertheless, it's time here to find N. and the children.

> You must hate my saying:
> "I must go now"—but I must,
> and I send love as ever. Your
> daughter, L.A.

NEXT DAY. IT'S NEARLY DARK AND
I'M INDOORS; WEARING THE RED
STOLE N. GAVE ME FOR MY
BIRTHDAY.

Bonjours, Lulu,

It's all over now! It doesn't matter anymore that I can't understand the Past; the Animal Control men have been and gone. They brought cages and there are traces of blood on the flagstones still. Oh Lord, time to heat some lentil soup and a loaf of the French bread N. baked. *En Avance!* I am upset about this!

I think there's half of a leftover lemon pie, too, with a graham cracker crust made from the superb recipe I found on a can of Borden's condensed milk. I think we tried it once long ago when you were here? I think you were seriously polite about it and smiled a lot. But Lulu, the children loved it. The children? Yes, remember them? How they tried to take you exploring on the path through wild grasses and wild white morning glories to the river gate under the cottonwoods, and on? But how you, in the most charming way, said no; though you took off your pearls with the dark sapphire clasp, handed them to an awed K. to hold up, just for a minute, against her little five-year-old neck, and then asked J., in a vague but admiring way, if he had ever climbed to the top of that really huge old tree near what you kindly called "the garden."

In return, the children, slightly awed by their Grandma's elegance and charm, invited you to visit (what I knew was the inaccessible place) where a raccoon family lived, in the arroyo near a trickle of rusty water from the Reservoir pipes. Raccoons?, you asked, delight and horror on your face. Perhaps later, dears, you murmured. Well, the children vanished as (you were aware from experience) children will. J. and K. barely knew you, but then neither did N.; and as for me—

Bonne nuit chère
Maman

AND NOW A GOLD MORNING!

Last night I dreamed I saw you dancing still with K. on the black brick floor of our living room. K.'s long light hair is flying, and you both are laughing. You are teaching her the Charleston. She tells me how wonderful it was, learning to dance from you. I'm glad you and she had that time together.

I don't know how often I came to "Cincy" over the years. But I do remember our hours-long phone talks between trips, and your pleas "for just a tiny visit because Jane has been having such a bad time lately; she's sad, I think. She *needs* you." Or,

"We're giving a little party, and I need your help, dear." Sometimes I came; sometimes when florists arrived, I was there with you to rearrange their flowers; while Elisabeth with dear red-headed Marcella and a staff of assistants prepared and set out marvels on silver platters. Jane in her room decided on silk or chiffon scarves with nurses Dottie or Gladys's help; she watched, her eyes cold, I thought, while gold or jeweled pins were set in place on the matching pillow slips. Exhausted, her white face peers out at me still from the overhead mirror, worldly wise eyes telling me . . . "Stand back . . . Stand back . . ."

> Later I dream we watch
> dancers
> crowned with peach buds
> march on satin club feet
> through the sand
>
> a woman shaped like a fir tree
> wound with green wind rolls by
>
> streams of faces
> nostrils like black silver
> sniff the cold air
>
> tracking the dancers
> on their way to the mesa
>
> to praise? to protest?
>
> climb with us
> past floats
> trimmed with unborn lilac
> and clacking cockroach shells
> past gargoyles and clowns
>   dragging
> a painted saint on wooden wheels
>
> to the flat mesa top
> where black goats crop
> below the hawks' pas de deux
> this raw May day
> help us retie all the green ribbons

> stand back   stand back
> let the dancers clump on their way
> to protest or praise
>
> cold day
> so many crowns in bud
> all that pain all that joy
> parade without end
>   hobbling by

Late at night, wrapped by N. in a crimson trousseau quilt, my eyes on our apple tree outside the hall window—night after night I listened to the heartbeat of your household.

You reported that "Dottie was really angry, and she said . . ." "Gladys told me . . ." "Jane closed her eyes and wouldn't speak to me . . . wouldn't listen . . ." "And HE supported her!" "I try so hard but they turn on me! Nothing I do, NOTHING, is right." "Tell me, advise me; I'll listen, I'm desperate—tell me where I have gone wrong? Am I wrong? What should I do? You know I live only for them, don't you? If only you were here!"

"Lulu dear," I answer over and over night after night, seeing it all, wanting to say . . . not daring to say and so give more pain . . . Sometmes N. would bring me tea or a little bourbon in a battered silver baby cup. And once, when you called after your Fountain of Youth party, the time all the living and dining room furniture was removed, carpets covered with canvas, sand put down, palm trees fixed in place, a fountain installed, and a monkey borrowed, I think, from the Zoo—one of your greatest triumphs—I called out to N. and we took turns laughing and drinking bourbon from that dented cup.

Oh, Lulu dear . . . Poor dear Lulu, I was never much help to you.

(It was only years later, after Jane's death, that the nursing home sent a moiré-covered box full of penciled notes in your distinctive script, and I saw and felt the force of your anger against heartless daughters—especially me—and the uncaring world.)

Often when I visited, you wore a rosy cashmere robe and regaled me with tales of those who truly loved you—noble great Elisabeth, creator of the superb Sole Veronique; devoted Cathy

R., your heart's kindest daughter, and various doctors, hairdressers, and old suitors. What you really felt so late was Betrayed, Forgotten, and except for Cathy R., Alone and Angry. She and kind nurses kept watch over the brightly colored pills and the vodka, and helped you arrange your collection of crystal boxes. But Jane herself was absent and had been for years, her long, slow drama ended.

After Jane's funeral on the long flight home in the 707, I dozed for a while—over Kansas, I think, and woke to look down on a red neon heart-shaped CAFÉ sign blinking in the dark below; there, in its on-again, off-again light, you stood, dressed in the raspberry wool Chanel suit you wore at her funeral one September afternoon among the red and purple flowers that banked the terrace outside her room. The scene had been beautifully planned and arranged ahead, as usual, by you—even to the white church steeples I was convinced you alone had set in place, bright and distinct, across the Ohio river on the Kentucky shore. You looked calm, stricken, and Proud. Now, in your extreme old age, watched over by grandson Peter after HRB moved away, life has been lonely. Bitter and lonely.

Often you speak vaguely about the two bad daughters who deserted you, leaving you alone to tend Jane, who was a saint (as I believe she was), while I, like Mary, the eldest and most beautiful daughter, would not (could not bear to?) stay. There was no reply possible; I felt in your presence that I had indeed been "bad"; I had mastered guilt early. I was used to it, however, and would own it almost cozily forever.

On one of my last visits with you at the nursing home, you sat for a long time in silence. Then, with a glance at me somehow both baffled and sly across your vodka and tonic, you said, with horror, "We aren't friends, are we?"

I explained that I was only a daughter, but the one who had been named in your honor.

"And where is Jane?" you demanded. Then vaguely, "Is it Fall?"

I say *I* am here still, it is Spring, the magnolia must be in flower, but Jane is dead.

"Well, I did my best for Jane," you said, very clearly. "For you and Mary too—my very best."

I truly believe that, and more; your best was a marvel; a mysterious blend of your every talent. Your most vigorous gifts were called into play—you organized rooms, colors, views, nurses, staff, suave sauces, chiffon scarves in an endless battle for more elegance, more gaiety and color around the giant respirator where Jane lay watching her guests, her doctors, her flowers, her sustaining husband and blue-eyed son in the mirror over her head. And I believe it was in large part you who planned that the mirror would always reflect for Jane the garden end of her room, the broad river beyond, and the Kentucky shore.

"No one knows how hard I tried to give you everything, or how like me you are," you persisted. When I didn't answer gratefully enough about my genes, you took fire.

"No one listens to me," you mourned. "No one knows how like me you are! You get everything from me!"

> "I leave an heirloom—rage—
> my presence in your blood
>
> though I forget your name
> you once were part of me
>
> I want at last to give
> a cruet or a tower
>
> whatever daughters claim
> who never understood
>
> the slur of silk like flame
> on flesh that was not theirs
>
> I want at last to move
> a rouge rag over love
>
> or with a paste of tears
> and curdled silver milk
>
> polish sullen years
> till flowering vines appear
>
> on épergnes of old age
> though I forget your name
>
> I nestle angrily
> untarnished in your blood
> You inherit me"

Lulu dear, you are right—only it's not simple rage, nor merely guilt that I've inherited—It's a reckless sense of joy in the face of almost anything.

Love again
and as always

TODAY AFTER A HARSH STORM EVEN
GRANDE DAME THE FIR TREE SEEMS
DISCOURAGED.

Dear Lulu,

No blue, black, and white magpies are flying to their heavy nests in the fir tree branches. There's a mountain of wash to be seen to and I'm hard-pressed by friends. When I feel this weak and powerless, I think how relentlessly you pursued your goals—love, laughter, caviar—even in the face of tragedy, perhaps especially then. And the power in your slight body is still great. Why couldn't I have inherited your strength at least? Once you were as elegant and full of laughter as a fountain—why couldn't you have willed all that style to me?

Well, in the mirror that held us all so long ago, I recognize you still, dear Sorceress, a force sometimes somber, sometimes brilliant; but alive for "as long as ever I live."

With love—
Your Daughter L.

P.S. Tomorrow I leave Santa Fe to bring you a white-banded basalt rock from K., an eagle feather from J., and a great embrace from N. and me.

Lulu died on September 13, 1987. Now, almost fifty years after the family photo was taken, I wished I could hold Lulu again and whisper to my Old One dying and fearful of dying, who was almost but not quite too afraid to dance with me by the silk-covered bed near the last—whisper to her over and over again, "It's all right to go now . . ."

How terrifying when, for the first time ever, my mother obeyed me.

For her funeral I wore the thin beige wool dress she had urged me to have fitted properly, and borrowed her pearls for courage and reassurance, feeling that she might have approved of me even if, especially if, I looked a trifle pallid and gawky with pain as I read in her honor:

Black sapphire on her hand
We sing
Because she was
And is and yet will be
Part of the lullaby
Darkened or lilting grace
We must learn to face
When shadows robed in white
Rustle at our door
With ampoules on a tray

Lullaby you are
The face that we compose
In spite of what we know
So we in turn can face
The dark we learned from her

Give us the heart to bear
A lamp that sings at night
across a breast of snow.

Amulet
let her wake
one time again to dream
the flaunt of rose-ribbed silk
and pale persimmon light
that dressed an afternoon
trailing in to meet
love long ago at home
her power still alive
and beauty satisfied
in a gold past smocked with gold

then croon the fire down
lie if you must lie
until she lies at peace
draped in a gown of song
and rich soft folds of stone

Lulu,

I can't stop writing you! Only yesterday I wanted to tell you
about the silky skinned yellow apples I found in the wood bowl

on the table when I came home—how young and fresh they looked. And you'll never believe this, but when I glanced out our bedroom window this morning I saw a tiny black-masked face peering out at me from the apricot tree—and then another. And then yes (!) a new family of black-eyed raccoons came climbing down the trunk to cross the road and head for the rocky arroyo—They're home again!!

Love As Always—
Lucile II

Andrea Barrett

Anne Jensen, Tucker Barrett, Andrea Barrett
Concord, Massachusetts; April 1957

Andrea Barrett was born in Boston, Massachusetts, in 1954, grew up on Cape Cod, and now lives in Rochester, New York, with her husband. She is the author of the novels *Lucid Stars, Secret Harmonies, The Middle Kingdom,* and *The Forms of Water;* and of *Ship Fever & Other Stories,* a collection of short fiction, which won the 1996 National Book Award for fiction.

Anne Tucker Jensen was born in Buffalo, New York, in 1931, grew up in New Rochelle, and lived in New England and elsewhere before moving to Florida. She has three children, three stepchildren, and seven grandchildren.

Blue Dress

Dear Mom,

I know you remember this picture. Your father-in-law snapped it on Easter Sunday, 1957, at his home in Concord; we were there, outside that pale blue house with the raspberries in the back, and the poodle prancing through the field, for what should have been one of the ritual Barrett family gatherings. Except that it hadn't gone as planned, and everyone was angry. This was your husband's family, not yours; and although you'd dressed up your two children (Heather would not be born until 1958), and dutifully brought us to your in-laws' house, my father failed to show up for dinner. From the golf course, where he'd gone to play in a tournament, he phoned to say he'd been delayed. In the future this would come to seem like part of the ritual, after all; in the future lay stormy times, divorce and remarriages, complicated changes and lives that could not be foreseen. You were twenty-six years old that Sunday, Tucker was just about to have his first birthday, and I was two.

Was it an accident that my grandfather caught here a picture of the woman he, and everyone else, wanted you to be? Blue dress, so proper and elegant; high heels that kept you from running; smooth face concealing your thoughts. Captured, you appear in this minute to be focused entirely on your children, tied

21

by us to a life that seldom suited you. The shadow stretching behind you looks like the mold you were forced into, resisted, and soon enough escaped.

But here's what I've always wanted to tell you—that I'm *glad* you escaped. Now, in my fortieth year, I find myself more and more grateful that our lives weren't lived as this picture suggests: that you didn't "behave," that you didn't allow yourself to be shaped for very long by the expectations of your family. What I want to thank you for is for bolting (even though I hated it then) and for reinventing yourself so constantly over the years (even though I've resisted some of those reinventions). The example of your life has suggested to me that it might be possible for a woman to follow her own path and carve out her own life.

When I was sixteen, several years after my father and step-mother won custody of us and relegated you to the role of a weekend mother, your decision to leave the Cape and create a life on a wooden sailboat with your new husband, Niels Jensen, seemed outrageous. When, tiring of your watery wanderings, you came to anchor on St. Croix and decided to live there for a while, your children and stepchildren balked; when you re-turned to live for a few years on the Cape we all believed—wanted to believe—that you'd settled down at last, and we were grateful. But no sooner had you planted your gardens and fixed the fences than you suddenly decided to move to some acres of land in rural New Hampshire.

I learned a lot from watching you and Niels build a home with your own hands, and populate the landscape with chickens and goats and geese and rabbits, ferns and fruit trees and orchids—a little Eden, made and held against all odds. What taught me the most, though, was when you abandoned it. Something in me has always longed for stability, permanence; it seemed inconceivable that, having worked so hard to build that homestead, you'd leave it just when it was done. But that was the point, you told me then; that it *was* done, that there was nothing left to do but to maintain what had already been brought into being. And that was boring, you were bored.

You sold that land and that house and almost everything in it, cast off what couldn't be sold (including almost all the remnants of our family history, your parents' belongings and the memen-tos of your earlier lives; there are good reasons why this photo has come to me not from you but from my grandfather's albums, salvaged by my aunt), and set off on yet another life. For the next seven years you and Niels would have no home but the RV in which you crisscrossed North America, moving every two weeks from one campground to the next and carrying only what would fit in that tiny space. On your peregrinations you would stop, periodically, wherever Tucker and Heather and I were living, wherever Niels's children and then grandchildren were making their homes. Two Siamese cats kept you company. When you pulled into our various driveways they howled, then howled louder when you pulled out.

For those years you arrived, then disappeared, with a rhythm that followed the seasons. What kind of a life was this? I often wondered. (During those years, I continually thought whatever life I was leading was the one I would lead forever; and was continually proved wrong.) Sometimes it was hard for me to see that you were not in search of a life but actually living one—rich and full and complicated. With each year's periodic visit, you brought overt news from the rest of the world to your more settled children, and also the covert news that life is movement, not stillness; process not stasis.

What your itinerant life taught us was that nothing is permanent, nothing lasts; that there is no value in things; that life is where you find it and what you make of it; that friendships made on the wing may nonetheless be true. That what sustains us are connection, love, imagination, and courage. What you taught me, most of all, was not to be afraid.

I wonder, now, how you took those first hard steps. Perhaps, once you left your children behind to make that leaky boat your home, all the subsequent shedding of homes and lives seemed easy. I know that nothing was easy, later, after Niels died and your shared wanderings came to an end. None of us expected that you would want to hit the road alone after that; as none of us expected that, tiring of your solitary drives and moves, you would come to rest three years later in a little trailer park in central Florida.

Once more, as you have always done, you give every appearance of being settled—potted plants on the patio, a storage shed out back, new curtains and a tabletop grill. Everyone in that trailer park knows you, as you know them; and in that dense web of connections and bowling leagues and weekly bingo games someone else might see permanence. I see you making a home—yet again, yet again—where you've landed for this spin of the wheel. Where will you go next? I wonder. And will I ever learn the secrets of your remarkable adaptability? Meanwhile I write—each new book, each new story—always with difficulty but without fear, because of you. When I head off in a new direction, when my interests shift and I set sail for new lands, you are who I follow.

Much love,

Lynda Barry

Lynda Barry was born in 1956 and lived on the same street in Seattle throughout her childhood. She began drawing comics in 1977 while attending The Evergreen State College, and her comic strips now appear in over fifty newsweeklies nationally. Nine collections of her comics have been published, along with a novel called *The Good Times Are Killing Me*, which she adapted into a play. She is an illustrator and writer for numerous national magazines, continues to paint, and is a commentator on National Public Radio. Her contribution to *I've Always Meant to Tell You* in the form of a comic strip "will have to do as far as photographs go."

WHEN I WAS LITTLE, I LOOKED JUST LIKE HER. WE HAD THOSE DRESSES THAT MATCH AND ACCORDING TO MY MOTHER, THE PEOPLE WHO SAW US SAID WE WERE WONDERFUL. THEN I HAD TO GET GLASSES WHICH MY MOTHER HATED BECAUSE IT SPOILED MY LOOKS. THIS WAS A LONG TIME AGO WHEN MY MOM'S EYES WERE PERFECT AND MY DAD WAS STILL WITH US.
MY BABY SISTER MARLYS WHO MY MOM SAYS WAS BORN WEARING GLASSES. AND ALSO "CHUBBY"

"YOU GOT YOUR FATHER'S LOOKS. THE BOTH OF YOU." SHE SAYS TO ME AND MY SISTER WHEN SHE GETS IN THAT ONE TALKING MOOD ABOUT HER MISTAKES IN LIFE. AND SHE TELLS ME I HAD BETTER GET BUSY WORKING ON MY CHARM. "WELL, BE GRATEFUL YOU DON'T HAVE A WEIGHT PROBLEM." SHE SAYS, THEN LOOKS STRAIGHT AT MY SISTER.

Meg Belichick

Meg Belichick with her mother
Stratford, Connecticut; c. 1976

Meg Belichick was born July 29, 1967, in Youngstown, Ohio. She is a sculptor and artists' book maker living in Brooklyn, New York. In 1995, she was awarded fellowships from both the National Endowment for the Arts and the New York Foundation for the Arts. She also received an artist book production grant from the Women's Studio Workshop in Rosendale, New York, for the production of her artists' book, *Miss Gowanus*. The original text for this book was selected as a semifinalist in the 1994 Open Poetry Contest and has been published in an anthology of the National Library of Poetry. Her books and sculpture are in the collections of the Whitney Museum, the Brooklyn Museum, the New York Public Library, and the School of the Art Institute of Chicago. Her work has been exhibited at the National Museum of Women in the Arts in Washington, D.C., the Art Museum of Santa Cruz County in California, the Hunter College of Art Gallery, Lombard-Freid Fine Arts, and the John Weber Gallery in New York City. Her mother has asked not to be named here.

As If I Am You

I am writing this story from *your* memory, Mom. It's not much of a story, only an isolated memory that stays with me since the night you told it to me. It just sticks there, a Post-it in my brain.

I find myself writing this as if I am you. I can see it all from your description of the simple turn of events. I don't know what makes *me* any more able to put your memory into words than you could recount some memory of mine—except that you would always be you playing me, your version of me, which is much more like you than I will ever be.

The setting is Grandma's kitchen that I remember from my childhood. There are five chairs in the kitchen painted thick with white paint: three small narrow spindly ones and two with wide curved backs and decorated seats that leave marks on your bare legs in summer after sitting on them at lunch.

You are standing on one of the spindly chairs pulled sideways up to the sink, drying a breakfast plate. You are wearing brown corduroy overalls like the ones I was wearing in that dream you had where I was trying on all of the overalls I used to wear when

30

I was little and showing you how small they are on me, how I've outgrown them. Now it looks like me standing on the thin white chair. Me, playing you as a girl.

I am you, drying the dishes as my grandfather turns the pages of the *Bridgeport Post* spread across the gritty flowered oilcloth. One leaf of the table is propped up with a shim. The napkin-holder-girl I bought for Grandma on Mother's Day at a school fair stands in the center of the table next to a chipped Pyrex butter dish. A china figurine of a girl in braids with full skirts, her hands have been broken off and glued back on with wood glue that has dried dark brown. Grandpa fixed it with that glue he used for everything when it broke. There is a space cut into the back of her skirt for paper napkins, but it is empty now.

Someone taps at the window behind the shade pulled down on the back door. The ice man is here to deliver. I lower myself from the chair, holding one cream-colored plate with two hands. I steady myself with my side pressed to the white painted steel cabinet. The buttons of my overalls scrape the metal ridges and porcelain lip of the sink on my way down, making a sound like loose change in the bottom of the washing machine. I push back the lock and open the door.

The ice man carries in a block of glistening ice held with giant tongs.

"Morning, sir," he greets my grandfather who stops reading the paper.

My grandfather turns to me then and says, "That is *not* the way you dry a dish." He is sitting five feet away from me with his wooden leg sticking out across the worn brown linoleum.

I remember that you wallpapered this kitchen and painted all of the molding maroon when we lived here after you got out of the hospital. You put a piece of clear plastic over the wallpaper behind the sink to protect it from water. You wanted to replace the old fake brick flooring with something new, something brighter; I don't remember why you never did it. Maybe we moved into our own house by that time.

"You are not to touch the clean dishes with your dirty hands," my grandfather is saying. "Hold the plate under the dishtowel with one hand and use the other end of the towel to dry the plate."

In the story I am cleaning up the kitchen after everyone has gone off to school and work. Being careful not to disturb him, I am cleaning the table around my grandfather, who is reading the paper. I am washing and drying the cups and saucers and plates. The ice man arriving unexpectedly has scared me. It makes me nervous not because of what I am doing now but because of what will happen later when the kitchen is clean and four chairs are set back around the table and one into the corner by the stairs.

I do not know what happens afterward. You told me that naptime was when it would start, but I have no details in my memory, none from yours. I have only the shame and embarrassment, the stiffness in my body, a lock on my spine.

I want to tell you that I was not there, but I wish that I could have been. I wish I could have been your big sister or your mother. I would have protected you, sent your grandfather to a hospital or a jail. You could have colored pictures at the kitchen table until lunchtime. I would have made a picnic. We could go for a walk down to the beach.

Meg

Anne Bernays

Doris Fleischman and daughter, Anne Bernays,
about age nine
New York City; c. 1939

Anne Fleischman Bernays was born in 1930 in New York City. A Barnard College graduate—where she was campus correspondent for *The New York Times*—she worked in publishing before moving to Cambridge, Massachusetts. She's published eight novels (among them *Growing Up Rich* and *Professor Romeo*), one textbook (for fiction writers), and many essays, articles, and book reviews. Bernays has three daughters and five grandsons. Married to biographer Justin Kaplan, she goes by her birth name. Bernays and Kaplan are coauthors of *The Language of Names*, published February 1997.

Doris Elsa Fleischman was born in 1892 in New York City. A Barnard College graduate, she worked for the *New York Herald Tribune*, then for Edward L. Bernays as a partner in his public relations firm, where she did most of the writing. She married Bernays in 1923; they had two daughters and six grandchildren. For most of her life she was "Miss Fleischman." She died in Cambridge, Massachusetts, in 1980.

Dear Mother,

Less than a week before you died in 1980—that's fifteen years ago by now—I sat in the kitchen of a woman I hardly knew and told her that I had never said anything to you that I thought you didn't want to hear. Like a lot of my statements, this was a stretch. When I was a little girl and sufficiently heated up, I used to scream at you that I hated you. Obviously this was something you didn't want to hear and was, like my later remark, an exaggeration. But there was too much truth in it not to sadden me when I admitted to this stranger that I was always on my guard with you.

Since then I have two times embarked on a memoir (twice contracted for by publishers and twice withdrawn) that turned out to be something other than what I had intended for it, namely, a dazzling piece of work. Writing about my childhood in New York City—an overprivileged little girl if there ever was one—I began to understand the enormous price you had paid for the sake of being a married woman.

You were a feminist, a Lucy Stoner as those women who kept

34

their so-called maiden names were called way back in the early part of this century. I think there were about two dozen of you, all told. You were a public and a private feminist. You wrote articles about feminism; you also made me introduce you to my schoolmates as "Miss Fleischman," which embarrassed me and confused them. But you were your husband's slave. What a paradox! You did whatever he told you to—and he had an opinion on just about everything. He made all the major and a good many of the minor decisions about where our family lived and what style we were to assume. You preferred the subtle and the outwardly modest; he bought houses big and pretentious enough to accommodate a dancing school. You read novels and poetry; he never read anything but books that threw light on the management of group dynamics. He chose your friends, he kept you within calling distance. If there had been beepers back then he would have had one implanted under your skin like a pacemaker. I can remember only a few times when you went off and did something on your own, like going to the three-day Bach Festival in Bethlehem, Pennsylvania, once a year. Before I married, you said, "Remember, Annie, that when you have a fight with your husband, he's always right." This is one of the saddest pieces of advice I was ever given and it still bothers me. I followed it for the longest time until the day, years after I was married, that I recognized it as a dose of poison. But capitulation was the way you sustained your marriage. You were—and this had to be a conscious decision on your part—his creature entire. (You see, I have become a literary person, which gives me permission to reverse normal word order.) I didn't know it then; I've only learned it through trying to write my own life. Isn't that odd?

Yours was a marriage in which both people were obscurely but profoundly miserable, the man because he was a thorough egoist and also couldn't keep it in his pants and the woman because she allowed her husband to be cruel to her. The poignancy of your life has to do with your conviction that you were so unattractive (this was one of your favorite words) that no other man would ever look at you. And the irony is that you were, at the very least, presentable, with large questioning eyes and a heart-shaped face. You were also incredibly strong and independent before you met your husband; it was as if he knew you had to be broken and trained like a circus tiger in order to perform the tricks he wanted you to display and, in doing so, reflect the spotlight back on him. Do you think I'm being too hard on him, now that he too is dead at, for crissake, one hundred and three years old?

If you were still around I would say all this to your face; I wish I'd been brave enough while you were still alive.

With much love and some trepidation,

Annie

Carol Bly

Carol McLean (later Bly) and her mother,
Mildred Washburn McLean
Duluth, Minnesota; 1940

Carol Bly was born in Duluth, Minnesota, on April 16, 1930. Her most recent book is *Changing the Bully Who Rules the World*, an anthology of stories, poems, and essays connecting ethics, stage-development theory, and communication skills (Milkweed Editions, 1996). She is the author of short story collections: *Backbone* (Milkweed Editions, 1985), and *The Tomcat's Wife and Other Stories* (HarperCollins, 1991), winner of the Friends of American Writers Award; and essay collections: *Letters from the Country* (Harper & Row, 1981) and *The Passionate Accurate Story* (Milkweed Editions, 1990), winner of the Minnesota Annual Book Award in Nonfiction. Her work is widely anthologized and has been included in several Pushcart anthologies. Three of her stories were made into *Rachel River*, an American Playhouse prize-winning film. She lectures, teaches, and conducts workshops nationwide. She is presently a teacher in the University of Minnesota's Master of Liberal Studies program (spring quarters 1995–96). The mother of four children, she divides her time between St. Paul and Sturgeon Lake, Minnesota.

Mildred Washburn McLean was born in Duluth, Minnesota, in 1890 and died there in 1942. She was educated at Wellesley and spent nearly all the rest of her life in Duluth or in Tryon, North Carolina, where her parents had a second home. She married C. Russell McLean of Duluth, then struggled with tuberculosis until the time of her death. Streptomycin came too late for her. Her interests were reading literature aloud to her children, playing the violin, and listening to serious music; she was also a sharp, serious bridge player.

My Dear Republican Mother

My dear Republican Mother:

If you came back to life so we could talk, I would want it out between us, first thing: is it or is it not all right for human beings to live on nature's old pecking order, which we usually call the "class system."

Oh—pecking order! In everything from hawk's-eye weeds to alpha wolves to *E. coli* bacteria to Ivy League graduates. Inherited in wild creatures' genes, inherited in human beings' capital and childhood expectations. Then, in both animals and people, taught to the young as if it were a virtue.

That is where we would have our quarrel. You were impassioned about three activities that scarcely catch the eye of less privileged people.

1. Privileged people teach their young that the pecking order—or class system—is immutable and therefore as right as need be. It is right in the way that trees and water and stars are right.
2. Privileged people exert early discipline in courtesy and careful workmanship upon their young.
3. And privileged people teach their young the various loves of culture: love of nature first, because that comes nearly automatically to children anyhow; love of beauty in art and music second; and, finally, the love of literature and philosophy—story as scenarios, thinking about honor and ideals, amiably talking about ideas, in bits and pieces if not in whole systems.

When you died of tuberculosis in 1942 I was only twelve, but you had taught my brothers and me as many of your expectations as you could. We took it from you that we had a right to some leisure hours spent in astute card play or reading. We took your early training in table manners. When introduced to adults we were to step forward and shake hands firmly. We were not allowed to simp or giggle the way the other girls in my Brownie Scout troop did. Because you were always ill with the most dread disease of the 1920s and 1930s, you were unable to show us much beauty in nature at firsthand but you did your best: you gave us little lectures on the beauty of nature. You gave us those words, used the abstract words in ordinary conversation—beauty, glory, nature—words my pals in Brownie Scouts heard only in Sunday school and church. You read aloud to us as much as you could without coughing up sputum or breaking the doctor's orders about overdoing it.

Streptomycin came too late to save your life. The doctor dictated intervals at which we children might visit your bedside on the third-floor screened porch. We were not to hang about too close to you. We were allowed to hug, the face turned away from your germs, but kissing was chancy. Sometimes I was allowed an afternoon nap on the other twin bed in your porch. The Duluth foghorn gave out its half-funny, half-pathetic groan at intervals in the summer. You explained to me that fog is not just fog but something dramatic and beautiful. How wonderful mist is, you told me. You told me about England's "season of mist and gentle fruitfulness." Like many patients with lingering illness, you had the knack of making first-rate mental pictures. You made me see the long, red-hulled ore boats on Lake Superior. You made a little scene for me, of the captain and mates peering through their glass-castle windows at the fog. The ore boat masters and mates weren't the only ones, you said dramatically. Odysseus had the same problem. In my recollection, you were wobbly about Aeneas and Vasco da Gama but you were keen and fulsome on Odysseus, Sinbad, and Magellan. You had by heart, paraphrasing, the best fog scenes of Dickens, in *A Tale of Two Cities* and *Great Expectations*.

Since you couldn't take us children to museums, you *talked* about art. Even then, when I was ten and eleven, I felt you were trying to give me some invisible kit that would come into my mysterious use later, the way the gifts of Norns and flounders and other half-wild mentors are never of immediate use to the pilgrim who receives them.

In the family scapegoat system, I was scapegoated to be "creative"—that is, artistic. You authorized the maids to add my crayons and construction paper to the shopping list for the corner store.

After your death, I am the one of the four children who was given your Grand Tour scrapbook, with its black and white postcard photos of great paintings and sculpture from Munich to Rome. Whatever that trip abroad in 1913 meant to you, a year after your graduating from Wellesley, I remember your emphatic way of telling me about the shiny postcard-pictures. You talked about art as if love of art would disappear in a midwest dairy field or a forest unless you stood up for it. You told me to look for the amazing little dots of light in Corot. What Turner was good at was gigantic, sweeps of sky and diffused light over the tiny activities of mankind with its beached dinghies and struggling ships.

And music. When you were well enough to come downstairs to dinner, you put on records of Brahms, your second favorite to Wagner. The drop-down 78s tore around unevenly like airplanes doomed in flat spins, but they spun out the unmistakable, gallant sounds of Brahms. You taught my brothers and me that it was just barely all right to love the second movements of things, because all children loved second movements of symphonies, dolefulness and gentle wistfulness being accessible even to inexperienced listeners. Ideally, you explained, one listens for and then loves the *development*. I hated the "development" of themes, and I disliked your explanations about the requisite sonata structure of first movements. Like my youngest brother, I preferred Tchaikovsky's Piano Concerto No. 1 to all else, and only part of its first movement, the theme later made into a song called "Tonight We Love." Long after you died, your sister Hope told me that your true love was Wagner, and that what I supposed was your "grand tour" of Europe had been discreetly intended as a trip to Germany to see if you were musical enough to . . ."—Hope always stumbled over this part: musical enough to *what?* At bottom, I expect, she meant musical enough to leave the upper middle class with its drinks-hour rhetoric and languid expectations in order to be a serious person.

Apparently you were not musical enough to leave your social background. You returned to America, and married, and raised a family until you died. But how could anyone other than a genius be musical enough to leave the half-idle, half-industrious life of privileged people? How well you presided over your little alpha wolf kingdom, with the amiable feelings of entitlement, the gentle manners, the complacencies—telling the servants in that complacent tone, "O yes, thank you so very much, Toini—do set it down right there, will you? Thank you so very much, Marie. That's perfect!"

I felt dread at the tone you took with the maids. Yet how should an ill person thank someone for kindly, briskly, doing the needed errands? Certainly I wouldn't have been happy with the 1990s informalities. "Hey, thanks" doesn't do it. "I'm like, I'm glad you brought that bundle of skeins over" doesn't do it. You said aloud "Thank you very much indeed" when what you meant, innerly, was thank you very much indeed.

But I wanted you to resemble the other Brownie Scout mothers of my Glen Avon Troop. Why *wouldn't* you use their informal language? You seemed so obstinate. All I wished was that you would occasionally call things *goofy* and if only! if only! you and Dad would *putz around* and tell my friends' parents you putzed around all weekend and had a *fun time*. I'd have been gratified if you had left off using expressions like "lame duck" and "dog's breakfast," too. There was such harshness in your metaphors. Once we were hanging around the fireplace: someone had come to dinner. My brothers and I were listening; the adults, glasses in hand, were talking. I heard you say of some family, "Well, the boy seemed all right, but the girl was a lame duck!" I grew confused, wondering if you were describing a brother of mine and me. My Scout friends' mothers never talked about any child, boy or girl, as a "lame duck."

You read to us from Dickens, Louisa May Alcott, Jane Austen, and Shakespeare: that reading, and reading aloud, gave the formality to your everyday expressions. Shakespeare added approximately 3000 words to the English language: he didn't subtract them, as modern American culture has done. When he needed a word, he apparently made up the word—the very opposite to what we do now. If the Brownie and Girl Scout parents spoke informally and inchoately in the 1940s, Americans are twice as inchoate now. Ironically, we are today much more precise about our emotions than a half-century ago, but only in the psychotherapeutic sense, not in narrative description. I expect you would be horrified at how we have reduced our vocabulary to one word in five or six. For example, the word *uncomfortable* now means not only sleeping on a lumpy mattress but also, figuratively,

1. morally offended or outraged,
2. uneasy about a possible outcome of a motion or vote just made,
3. suspicious of whichever strangers have joined us at this meeting,
4. aware of having just this moment betrayed one's own values or our own socioeconomic group, and finally,
5. fearful lest what we just did in this room may be advantageous for us but disastrous for invisible and countless others.

Perhaps we have this word *uncomfortable* now because in the 1990s Americans have so much to be uncomfortable about. In your lifetime, neither Democrats nor Republicans needed to feel uncomfortable about much foreign policy. In your lifetime, the

CIA was still in its Boy Scout preversion, the OSS, a legitimate intelligence agency coordinating the terrifying war with respect to Occupied Europe. You did not know, because ordinary educated citizens didn't know, that both the Nazis and subsequently the British invaded Norway not just for seaports but for the "heavy water" (H_3O) plant at Rjukan—the major material of atomic bombs. You had been dead three years before our own country, not an enemy, dropped atomic bombs on human beings. So your time was more "comfortable," and you exercised the right to use strong language.

You died at the height of American patriotism, in 1942. You were either ignorant of or in impressive denial about notable sins of commission and omission of the United States between 1781 and 1942. You did not know or chose not to be conscious of the fact that the National Guard fired on striking autoworkers and coal miners. You probably barely noticed Kristallnacht and didn't focus on the fact that the United States did nothing about it. In your lifetime, lucky people, even though educated, were not expected to *double think* the morals of the country. Genuine intellectuals were critical enough of the United States, in the 1920s and 1930s, goodness knows, but not half-intellectuals—people of privilege with some taste in the arts and the habit of discussing things over drinks. A more or less educated, intelligent woman in 1942 might well worry about the safety of one or another of her sons, but she didn't have to feel "uncomfortable with" disastrous, oddly boyish policies on the part of her own country.

You practiced courage about your long illness. If you lived now, I think you'd be brave enough to look at the bad ways the world goes around and be more than "uncomfortable with" them. You might no longer vote Republican. You would be willing to look at tough facts of the moral kind, and suffer. Besides, I need to be tolerant. If it were 1860, I bet neither you nor I, if we were white, would have put up a decent objection to slavery. I may well have just slid along with others of my background—the very quality I didn't like in you.

From 1978 to 1981 I finally learned to grow up and look straight at bad news. Like most children who spend more time with maids, teachers, and Scout leaders than with their parents, I knew how to make use of mentors. Psychotherapy suited me. My psychotherapist showed me how to eject a good many old family lies—a great relief—what the poet Denise Levertov called, in her poem "Modulations," "the luxury of unlearning old lies." I learned that one must name the evil if one thinks something is evil, because identifying evil is vital to life, whereas denying or shamming in order to preserve a familial relationship with the perpetrator of evil is a psychological version of suttee.

Naming evil was unfamiliar to me, as it was for nearly all people brought up in the liberal arts. People of my background were expected to be tactful, polite enough to follow an argument, alive to beauty, and entitled to center themselves in their class mores.

You and I would start our conversation here. My psychotherapist was cross at me for not "coming to closure" with my anger toward you. "Nonsense," I told her.

"Oh, but I wish your mother hadn't died so that you and she could come to closure!" Chris exclaimed.

"I don't wish that," I told her, "because she was a bully, and although I may be a bully as well, I will always feel the bullying in her. What good would come of our talking about her bullying? She had such a way of bullying us children if we failed some ideal of hers! She would even bully us over whether or not we had a daily bowel movement. She bullied any of the maids who spoke in the least plaintively. She bullied anyone who interfered with her expectations." I waxed quite rhetorical, as fools do during first and second and even third sessions with psychotherapists. (Later, of course, one settles down to being simple, telling the truth, and learning what one can.)

"Nonetheless," the therapist said, "I wish you had come to closure. I don't mean denial," she added carefully. "I mean closure."

The least I can do, then, is write this letter. I shall list some of your marvelous virtues, my dead mother.

You had physical bravery. In the Great Duluth Fire, you took your car again and again into the downtown area to pick up people. You drove them, hanging on the running boards, out Woodland Avenue to a safe area.

You never, not even once, complained to us children of your struggle with tuberculosis. When my eldest brother was two you caught TB from your father. Then you had three more babies at intervals your doctor prescribed. You raised all four of us despite coughing spells, despite constant fear of a spontaneous pneumothorax (collapse of one or both lungs), in constant fear lest we children show up positive on the Mantoux tests. You spat up phlegm and blood, trying not to let it happen in orthodontists' offices or railway dining cars. You went through occasional, appalling pain. You had to endure bed rest, on the sleeping porch in summer and fall, alone, without Dad, on the third floor, and long stays in sanitoriums in Minnesota and North Carolina. Your doctor, in his wretched 1930s wisdom, did not allow you to breast-feed your children. A hundred times I have thought of you with pity as I freely nursed mine.

A third virtue, one presently endangered in our species: you were a thoroughgoing mother. You weren't well enough to do housework. You couldn't do the cooking—cooking, the classic arbiter of motherhood. From your bed, however, you *could* mend and knit, provided Toini or Marie or one of us children brought you the wood-handled knitting bag and your mending box. All this equipment lay on your breakfast table, once the blue Wedgwood breakfast set had been carried away on its tray. You wove elegant khaki patches onto my brothers' knickers, and taught me, too—seriously, as if I were an apprentice. How much I appreciated that! Apprenticeship is one of the dearest roles of childhood, not just watching Dad or Mother, but being taught a hands-on trade. I didn't much mind your conscious superiority: your mending *was* better than ordinary women's mending. You made that clear. I didn't mind because I was being initiated into the superior women's group. Any child can be corrupted that way. Hand sewing, making oneself do it well, not loosely, may be a thousand ways different from Hitler's Landswehr or Jugend training, but the same psychology operates: children will exert themselves harder than is agreeable to them if they feel they are being groomed to do better than others.

I swore I would knit all of my children's mittens someday. I would patch their clothes. I found you nearly godlike, sitting up in your silk bedjacket, with your balls of yarn about you on the white counterpane. The counterpanes—a piece of household goods I have never had in any house of mine—had little alternate columns of seersucker and plain weave. They were always utterly white, because the maids washed them twice weekly in very hot water and some bleach, to kill the TB germs.

First-rate menders, you told me, wove the patching precisely at right angles. The warp and weft must cross over and under one another at 90 degrees, or the patch would look like a dog's breakfast. The implication, as with everything you taught me, was that one must hold the fort of the elitist view against the mediocre work of the many. I couldn't argue with you. The other mothers of my Glen Avon Church Girl Scout troop did patches on my friends' clothing that did look like a dog's breakfast. Crafts enthusiasts often have a tinge of contumely about them. I didn't like your superior attitude, but that doesn't mean I didn't catch it myself. As Marianne Moore said in "In Distrust of Merits," we are not good enough for our vows.

You were a first-rate conversationalist, somewhat stuck in conventional male-affirming legends. As I look back on the kinds of stories you chose to tell and read to us children, I suppose you would be a prize 1990s Joseph Campbell buff if you still lived. You took seriously the Nordic legends that Thorstein Veblen referred to as "theological underbrush." You told me about Odysseus's making the crew tie him up against the female seductions of Scylla and Charybdis. You skipped a little lightly past the virtues of Freya, because you were a tomboy and preferred the regressed Alberich and beautiful Siegfried. But like most tomboys, you admired fierce motherhood—fierce motherhood often meaning the protection of young spirits from the ignoble or separatist fathers. It was the mother lion and wolf whom you admired, not the philandering male. You repeatedly reminded us children that Siegmund first learned about disinterested love from watching wild mothers and their kits or cubs in the German forests.

You were brave about your palpably approaching death. You had longed to believe in an afterlife but couldn't. Your parents had been agnostics before you. I wish you had read outside the conventional canon of Wellesley graduates in literature: you might have come across Jens Petter Jakobsen's great novel, *Niels Luhne*, the book that Rainer Maria Rilke carried around with him. The last sentence of the novel is: "And then Niels Luhne died—the difficult death." I knew that you had pathetically inquired of your Wellesley friends for any spiritual hope they might offer. One of your classmates, a Buddhist, sent you a prayer book. I have it and am saving it to read when I am dying of something, to remind me of both her kindness and your classy bravery.

I want to list more of your virtues, but I can't. Not only was I twelve years old when you died, but I had by then spent several winters away, with relations in the South. You wrote me any number of witty letters—the usual fare of sanitorium patients' letters—stories of patients who received boa constrictors in postal packages and the like. My aunt made clear to me that you were "a terrific correspondent, with your witty narratives" but I felt chagrined: I didn't always get the point of the irony. I was too young, or not bright enough, for your wit. I felt grateful, but underqualified.

And a low reservoir of enmity lay between us from when I was less than eight years old. I blame it partly on the cowardice I had when I was a little girl, and partly upon your unswerving espousal of the two-class system—nature's pecking order dressed up as a logical entitlement of Hill School and Asheville School and Abbot Academy graduates to feel superior to others, without their necessarily doing a lick of work to change the world.

My cowardice: my brothers, but not I, since I was the youngest and the only girl in a gender-role-oriented family, were trained for sturdy character. It was they, not I, who obeyed our father's admonishment: do not say or do things that "would worry Mother." I constantly sneaked up to the third floor to worry you with one or another woe. You always responded to me kindly enough, but at the same time I saw your hand creep out over the counterpane, feeling for the little globe of your call bell. You rang for a maid to fetch me away again because of the doctor's orders about "complete rest and fresh air." I was disgusted with myself (as were my brothers) about my persistently worrying you, but I couldn't keep clear. If daughterhood is an addiction, I had it. Even as I flung myself up the forbidden staircase to your sleeping porch, I knew I ought to stop and tell myself something along the lines of "Just shut it up, you silly clot [language from the admired E. Nesbitt]—have pity upon your mother, not upon yourself for once!" But I couldn't. My interest was for myself.

When you cried out one night, the youngest of my brothers rushed up the stairs from our bedroom floor to the third-floor sleeping porch crying, "I'm coming, Mother, I'm coming!" He was only twelve or thirteen. He had great sweetness of character.

(One in our series of maids had told me that he was the best of us four children, and it was a real shame that we others weren't so unselfish as he.)

Instead of going up to you then, I hovered at the bottom of that flight of stairs. I did not want to see my aging mother screaming. My heart was engorged with cowardice. I felt then that I would never live down such a cowardice. Because I was too cowardly to do what seemed to be expected, I was angry at you. What right had you to be ill, anyhow? I knew, intellectually, that you had not voted to have tuberculosis. I knew better, but still exclaimed to myself: Why couldn't someone else's mother be sick and mine be well? "Not in my backyard," we would call such feeling now. I was a nimby.

My being a coward, however, did not make you an angel. For one thing, you were more anal-retentive than any other human being I have seen in sixty-five years of life, or even any of the personae of the classic 1950s jokes about anal-retentive people. None of us, not you nor Dad nor, of course, any of us children nor the maids, knew any psychological theory. Norman O. Brown had not yet written *Love's Body*, the definitive book on *excrementum* as a spiritual reality. As late as 1970 my middle-class father still jeered at Freud without having looked at any of Freud's work. Of us four siblings, I am the only one, in fact, who has taken seriously any post-Freud philosophers of psychology.

You were stuck on whether or not each of us had had a bowel movement or not. The last time you ever interrogated me on the subject, you sat on the toilet seat cover in the children's bathroom, asking me if I had had "a movement" that day. In our family all movements, excepting those of Brahms's, Beethoven's, and Tchaikovsky's symphonies and concerti, were bowel movements. The first time I heard the expression "the movement of the clock" I grinned filthily.

"But if not this morning, surely yesterday?" you said, nearly pitifully.

"No," I said, wielding the innermost weapon of a child against intrusive parents. Whatever else parents can do to us, they cannot make us move our bowels if we decide not to.

You frequently reined in the loose, Virginia Woolf-ish collars of your dressing gowns; surely, having such modesty, you could have acknowledged that others might value theirs.

"Darling," you said, "surely the day before yesterday? Surely you had a movement the day before yesterday?"

"No," I said.

"No *what?*"

"No, I didn't, Mother."

Next a surprise—and one of the most memorable moments of my childhood. You broke into tears. Your weeping was quiet but it went on.

Then, for the first time, I began to forgive you for intruding on my privacy. My heart went out to you, although I still balked, braced, motionless on my short legs before you. For the first time I felt compassion that you were ill, constantly ill, always ill. Just in that moment I realized a certain truth as well: the family tradition of saying "when Mother gets better . . ." was only a ritual of denial. As I watched you cry I realized you would soon be dead. And for the first time I felt how your illness had its harsh claws hugely, deeply in your body. I realized how horrible it was for you: in that moment I stopped merely resenting that you weren't a vivacious member of the PTA who, like other mothers, would chair a scary stall at the Washburn School Hallowe'en Party. I got the point of your suffering for the first time.

So I ordered my stiff tomboy legs to make the two steps forward to kiss you—not to be kissed, but to give a kiss, in pity.

But then you said, "Now see what you've done!"

I stopped.

You looked right at me and said, "Now . . . you have made Mother cry!"

I don't blame you for passive-aggressive manipulation. One can't blame people for behaviors not yet even identified and classified as bad in their generation.

The maids—a string of them from before I was born in 1930 and onward—came from farm towns like Aitkin, Flatwood, Moose Lake, all within two hours' driving time of Duluth. Generally awfully nice girls, they would start working for us at 14 or 15 or 16. They worked for our family two at a time, one doing most of the cooking and the other doing most of the housework. They both served at dinner and they both spent all day Monday doing the family laundry and Tuesday ironing clothes and mangling the sheets. Their sleeping room, between our basement level and the first floor, was so damp that if one of them left a cup of coffee overnight, a gardenlike moss greened it by morning.

The maids made our breakfast, sent us off to school, and saw to it we bathed at night. Except for dinner, which was always planned by you, our meals were the maids' choices. We had their love of soft white bread, Spanish rice, fried Spam once Spam was invented, macaroni and cheese. When you were staying in the sanitorium and Dad took his dinner with you there, the maids dropped all the rib roasts and Yorkshire pudding and roast leg of lamb off the menu: we crowded around the kitchen table, eating meatloaf and hot dogs and hamburgers, which to this day symbolize to me affectionate nourishment with no double messages.

Of all the maids, I was especially fond of Toini. One day she moped at the kitchen window. Some clothes were boiling in a Hi-lex solution. The dog, Bruce, lay with his jaw leant against a stove leg. The kitchen smelled of steam and dog. Toini looked out over the gravelly driveway. She said, "I feel blue." Her uncle had died. I had to guess what feeling *blue* meant, since it was new to my vocabulary. I raced up to you although we had been told not to bother you at that particular time. "Toini is blue," I reported.

"Blue!"

"Toini wants to go home to her uncle's funeral."

You remarked, "Toini will have to pull herself together."

One maid, however, was vicious. Inez used to spank my brothers in the basement-stairs landing: she felt safe beating them there because they wouldn't cry. But she took me down to the cellar and into the fruit room, since I shamelessly screamed. My designation in the family, remember, was just Artistic or Creative, not Strong of Character like my brothers'. Inez locked me in position across her lap. Then she swung away at me. Inches from my face on one wall of that fruit cellar stood our family canning, spaced along the white shelf paper. I could see the jars' wire springs, the fading labels in my grandmother's elegant script. Gooseberry Conserve, 1934. Currant Jam, 1936. Apple Jelly, 1936. When I was married, my good-hearted mother-in-law offered me all her old canning jars, but they had those steel clamps. I bought my own Ball self-seal tops and rings instead.

Once Inez was at me so long I had trouble breathing. From the other end of the basement hallway, we both heard my father's car on the gravel coming into the garage. I escaped. I expect Inez was glad enough to see me go, too, so she could scurry upstairs to the kitchen and pretend to be helping Marie with dinner. "One of these days," Marie told her (as she reported to me years later), "you're going to get caught! You'd better watch out!" Marie did not inform on Inez to my parents, however, because young hired women's mores did not then include making interventions. Loyalty to colleagues is a basic mammalian behavior. In lions, we call it species loyalty or pride loyalty. In human beings it has several names: old-boy or old-girl network, Cabinet loyalty to the president—moral developmentalists sometimes call it Stage II behavior—a kind of live-and-let-live philosophy within the tribe. Whistle-blowers are people who have overcome such pack psychology.

I tried to explain to my dad.

"Oh, no, Dear," he said. "I know that wouldn't happen." Then he added the usual refrain, "Try not to worry Mother with it."

One day the police caught up with Inez. Inez had stolen from The Glass Block and other Duluth stores, using various employers' charge accounts. I was delighted to hear that she was going to jail. Perhaps they would beat her. Children are not clear about what the police can or cannot do. I had no idea that in the 1930s Southern police did indeed beat black people but not white people. I did not know that Northern police clubbed people, but generally only picketers, not women in domestic service. I did not know that the National Guard had been called out to fire on striking autoworkers and striking miners—but I had a romantic idea that with luck, the police would beat Inez. At the same time I should have preferred that she were arrested for child spanking rather than charge-account theft. But of course I didn't know that in the 1930s mild child abuse was not a crime at all.

Dad had a scrupulous businessman's hatred for crooks, especially for crooks who had got the best of him.

"Well, she should go for being mean to kids," I said.

He said, "I don't suppose that she was ever mean to kids."

I reminded him about the fruit cellar beatings.

"Oh, I don't suppose anything like that happened, Dear," he said.

* * *

One spring, when you could still travel, you and I took the overnight train from Chicago to Duluth.

I loved the train's departure. It was early afternoon between Chicago and Evanston. The train ground away fast against its bearing surfaces and flanges. We were on a neatly made elevated track above the slums. Coal smoke from our engine sank down and stroked people's sheets hung to dry between backyard shacks and tenement hooks. Children my age glanced up at us.

"Do people like living there?" I asked you as we sat opposite each other in a Pullman section. My heart was full of the usual happiness of riding trains. I knew the drill. After a while we would go to the dining car—not easy, since you sometimes coughed up phlegm during meals and other people would glance at us. We would sway left and right with the other diners as the train lurched along, and lift our heavy forks and knives with the Chicago and Northwestern logo engraved into their silver. My white napkins were as heavy as a whole sheet. While we were gone the porter would make up the car into its sections of berths, upper and lower. We would have two lowers, with their magical dark green beize curtains, each a little bed as secret as the bed of Scrooge.

North of Evanston, our train passed long strings of slatted carriages behind which animals were being taken south to the stockyards. On a previous trip, I had asked you about those animals. "They do not know they are going to die," you said gently. You seemed nearly equable. There was no edge to your voice as there was when one asked about poor human beings.

"You must listen for the clunk clunk clunk of the wheels going over the rail-section ends," you said with a wonderful smile. "That is the characteristic sound of trains." You explained that the rails were not abutted end to end because the iron must shrink and expand.

Because you taught me to love that sound, I have paid attention to it on trains from Oslo to Geilo, from Fredericksstad to Berlin, between London and Audley End, Essex. Sometimes, even, on especially worn sections of the Interstate 35 between St. Paul and Sturgeon Lake, Minnesota, my car wheels would go thunk thunk thunk over the separated road sections. Nostalgia would awaken in me a good two or three minutes before I identified the thunk thunk thunk of the tires. You got the point of beautiful moments no matter how trivial. You said, verbatim, *treasure up whatever lovely moment comes along*. You were not a fool: you knew better than most that death comes, welcome or unwelcome. What's more, death sends its lieutenants, sickness or degeneration, out to forage ahead, blatantly to take stock of us when we are only minding our own business, raising our families on a diet of Dickens and *The Boy Scout Manual*, on Louisa May Alcott, on lonely agnosticism. You were a dab hand at taking happiness in such swift small shafts as fell upon you.

So I was happy in the train. I looked out over the train smoke and hundreds of shoddy backyards going by. Most of my mind glowed with anticipation of sleeping in my Lower that night. Only absentmindedly did I ask: "Do those people like living there?"

You said, "You know better than to ask a question like that."

Perhaps you meant that I was tactless. If the rich once start imagining how the poor feel about the slums or other depredations of the world, the rich will have traded in complacency for consciousness, and who of them needs that? As Dickens pointed out, any good club secretary knows enough to dispatch a servant out and around the front of the building to banish any starving bums who might be pressing their noses against the leaded glass. "Gentlemen, God rest you merry," the carolers say, "may nothing you dismay," not "God wake you up to civic awareness, Gentlemen . . ." Any *real politik* teaches that when the poor do exercise the grace to "pull themselves together" (as you wanted Toini to do), then others can enjoy their pleasures the more fully.

I felt angry with you. In the very next moment, I had drunk the potion of immunity you offered. I actually congratulated myself on being someone who deserved to travel in a train, as opposed to someone who deserved only to live in slums. Years later I read Chekhov's remark that seeing others in pain gives the rich a "flutter." I felt that extra fillip that afternoon.

At the same time, I knew that was foul. I felt the foulness of it, and delighted in it, the way children who have spent dozens of mornings in Sunday school delight in busting their first streetlight. Or the first time they enjoin their friends to bully some kid at recess. There's a good deal of fun to evil. A question to pose bomb setters and militia sharpshooters: was it rather fun—to plan, to anticipate, and then to pull it off?

I suppose I shall always feel disdainful of your bullying, small scale though it was. It did some early career-decision-making for me. Your bullying turned me from drawer-of-pictures to writer-of-stories. And then your rudeness about my first story sealed my devotion to writing, not drawing.

At nine I wrote a novel called *The Adventures of Hilary Mel-wheel.* Melwheel was a hero of the American Revolution, but he was beaten by his parents when young. My novel consisted of two sheets of typing paper, each folded in half, torn along the folds, then folded again into quarters. I had common-pinned the signatures together through the spine. There is no joy like that of having made a book, so I took it up to show you.

You amiably began to read aloud. "And then they wiped Hilary," you read aloud.

"Whipped," I corrected. "They whipped him."

"You want two *p*'s to shorten the *i*," you said. "And you need an *h* after the *w* to get the *whuh* sound in *whip*." Your Wellesley B.A. had been in English.

You read on. Like Hitler, Melwheel was a battered child who rose to amazing leadership. On page two you found another beating. "Then they wiped him again," you read aloud.

Before the middle there was another wiping or whipping. Again you read it aloud as "wiping."

I did not say to you, "Since you know my intentions, you might have the generosity to pronounce the word as I intended it pronounced." That would have counted as opposing Mother, a subset of the forbidden "worrying Mother."

Later I decided that you bullied out of fear for our family status. In the last winter of your life, we visited you at Nopeming, a TB sanitorium near Duluth. We children stood outside in a $-20°F$ wind; the nurses wheeled you to a window so you could talk to us. My brothers were brave about the cold. They told you whatever adventures they could think of from their basketball games, their prep school and college life in general. I huddled, shamelessly, and had to be told twice, sotto voce, by Dad to stand up straight and smile at you and not keep turning my face out of the wind. There was your face, glowing and roseate with the typical low-level fever of tuberculosis, your head and chest swaddled with extra blankets so you wouldn't catch cold. I knew it was better to be loving than to be craven about freezing feet.

Then you said, "O no, Carol! Not glasses! You don't wear those glasses all the time, do you?"

I did, because that was 1941 and I was eleven, typically the age at which American children get nearsighted, but not then in such numbers as they do now.

I had been taught not to lie. "I am supposed to wear them all the time," I said.

"But you don't really have to wear them do you?" you exclaimed. And then you added, looking more at Dad than at me, "No one in our family has ever had to wear glasses! It must be a mistake!" I recalled, with dread, your calling some little girl a lame duck. Wearing glasses might not be so bad as being a lame duck, but it sounded something like.

I did not see you again. The war took one brother into V-7 training, another eventually to Camp Devon and Fort Bragg and to what was called "the European Theater of Operations." The youngest went away to school, and I to my aunt in North Carolina.

Nothing in your life led you to drop your class ideals. But who is purer than all her or his peers? If I lived in 1860, how do I know that I would make a substantial objection to slavery? I might slide along, white and entitled. If 1995 were 1942, the last year of your life, perhaps I would be a Republican, too. Perhaps I would deny any American history that was dishonorable. If this were 1942, I would probably be as simple and proud as I was at twelve, proud that Americans were going to defeat Germans.

The peculiar, complex wisdom of the 1990s, family-systems thinking, was not even thought of when you were alive. How could you possibly have guessed that ways would be worked up to help family members treat children with respect, not irony, while empowering the children to notice and call evil evil when they see it.

But that was then, as the social workers say, and this is now. Why should a woman of sixty-five beat her head against her long-dead mother's politics? How absurd it sounds! As Somerset Maugham said, if one "loses one's temper at every human folly one will live one's life in a constant state of ire."

Maugham was not a change agent, however. Whether or not one wants change lies at the bottom of most quarrels between mothers and daughters. If children do not butt their heads against their parents' class values, then those class values will keep fattening through more than the proverbial seven generations. How we all wish that German children of the 1930s had butted their heads against their parents' class values! Coming to one-on-one closure with a mother is chicken feed compared to the old and the young working for change.

If we each deliberately list our dead parents' virtues, then, without indignation, list their failures next, and then—most important of all—list *those evils they neglected to countermand in their time*, then we can drop a good deal of the schtick about roots. We can look forward instead of backward.

I shall always take exception to your complacent feelings of entitlement. If I were a painter I might have forgotten all such quarrelsome stuff, but writers are writers: they lean toward philosophy.

At our best, we writers keep in mind how mysterious a mother is! Anybody with the skimpiest character would recognize the fortitude of a parent like you, who took such pains to do what you could for us children. Between fits of coughing you taught me how to work hard with my hands and to love beauty and to get a kick out of small moments. You did all you could not to let any of your children make a dog's breakfast of their lives.

Carl

Sally Ryder Brady

Back: *Francis C. Ryder (father)*, *Dorothy Childs Ryder*
(mother)
Front: *Joan Ryder Wickersham (sister)*, *Sally Ryder Brady*
Miami Beach, Florida; 1943

Sally Ryder Brady was born on May 26, 1939, in Boston, Massachusetts, and "spent most of my lucky childhood in the Cape Cod village of Woods Hole. My mother and father wove a safe nest for my older sister and me, one from which I've been able to dive into many dangerous pursuits: the theater, writing, teaching, and scariest of all becoming a mother, four times in five years." She has published a novel, *INSTAR* (Doubleday), and two volumes of *A Yankee Christmas* (Rodale). Her stories and essays have appeared in *The Boston Globe, House Beautiful, Good Housekeeping, Family Circle, Woman's Day, New Woman,* and other publications.

Dorothy Childs Ryder was born on May 8, 1912, in Middleboro, Massachusetts, "and lovingly raised with grace and wisdom by her grandmother. She knows how important mothers are, and even as a data analyst who specialized in underwater sound, the sounds she treasured most came from my sister and me. We always came first, and still do."

Standing in Two Places

Dear Mummy,

Here I am, midway between you and Sarah, midway between mother and daughter. I am both; I am fifty-six. Except when I'm with you. Then I might be ten again, or twelve, still feeling like a kite on the end of a string. This place is confusing: when I'm with my mother I'm younger than my daughter. But standing here in two places at once gives me a brand-new view of love. And guilt. Let's take love, first.

Take tiny Sarah, slick with birth, and me, limp with a fiery, overwhelming love before I'd ever even touched her, before I'd uncurled a single tiny finger, or seen the sheen on the soles of her feet. No lover has ever known a passion such as this, eclipsing everything, everyone, even eclipsing pain. Yes, over the years this passion has tempered. But threaten one hair on her head and my love floods fast, as blinding as the day she was born. Sarah knows this. She can see it in my eyes, hear it in my voice, and when she does, I sometimes see her stiffen against it, and retreat.

But I scan my memories for a time when I felt something close to this passion for you, Mummy, and, this is hard to say, guilt creeps in. I hear my own accusing whisper. "You never loved your mother, no, not the way you love Sarah." I need to prove this is not so.

I remember with aching clarity a night some fifty years ago. You'd listened to my prayers, tucked me in, kissed me, and turned out my light, left my door ajar. I am lying here in my dark room, watching you put neatly folded stacks of sweet-smelling towels and ironed pillowcases in the linen closet. You are humming, the way you do when you put away the laundry. You are waiting for Daddy to come back with the baby-sitter so you can go to a party. I like it when you go out together, I like your pretty high heels and the way they sound, I like your perfume, and the way your earrings catch the light. But tonight I feel something new, a terrible and shocking grief that builds, minute by minute, climbing up my throat.

How can you leave me, when I love you so much? I want to shout this at you. I want you to stop and hear me. I love you. I love you when you hum out there with the lamp and the laundry. I love you so much it makes me cry and now my pillow is getting wet. I hate loving you this hard because if you leave me, if you go out with Daddy, maybe you won't come back. The car might crash, you might die, you might never come home to me.

But I never said any of this and you did go out with Daddy and you did come back. And now I see that what I thought was love for you was really a child's self-love, a self-centeredness coupled with fear. Nothing at all like my love for Sarah.

So I look some more—surely there must have been a time when a deep, selfless well of love for you lifted me high. You have certainly always been at or near the center of my changing life, even when I've wished you weren't. I remember how I used to love it when you watched me show off on my new figure skates, or came to the third grade operetta to hear me play the triangle. I remember how proud I'd feel when you brought valentine cupcakes to the whole classroom, or when you drove us on field trips and made us all laugh—did you know everyone always wanted to go in our car?

"Your mother is so pretty," they'd say. Or "so nice" or "so much fun."

As I grew older, and went off with my friends to sleep-overs, parties, dates, holidays, as soon as I came home you would always sit me down in the living room and say, "Now, start at the beginning. You got in the car and . . . then what?" You would listen for hours, alert to every nuance and anecdote. I loved that. But once again, I wasn't the one reaching out to you. You, as usual, were reaching out to me.

There is one time, though. I think I was thirteen or fourteen. A golden autumn day when we had taken a picnic to the riverbank, just the two of us. We'd finished eating, and without really thinking, I began to construct a fairy-size log cabin from the tiny twigs scattered at the base of the sycamore tree. I knew I was much too old for this, and yet I didn't feel embarrassed. You were stretched out close by in the sun, half asleep, half watching me, a comfortable mixture of attention and privacy. Time slowed and the moment stretched, no barriers between us, nothing to break the silvery thread connecting us. And even though I keep this moment right here, in the brightest part of my heart where I can drop in and find it easily, I have never told a soul about it. I haven't even told you, until now. I've never said thank you.

Here's why. I'm afraid. Afraid you'll say "What? What afternoon? I don't remember any picnic, any log cabin." If this moment that is so perfect to me means nothing to you, won't that devalue it? Make it worthless? You see how frail I feel next to your power? How powerful I know your love for me is?

Which brings me to guilt. For half a century you have lavished your love on me. In return, I've been a fairly dutiful daughter— that phrase carries a pinching truth—dutiful, tightfisted, that's me. Because I have not returned your incredible, limitless love. At least, I have not returned it to you. And this feeling leaves a varnish of guilt.

Yet when I look at Sarah, and feel my eyes well up, and that sappy, lax smile spread across my face, and a breathy pride push somewhere between my heart and my throat, when that happens to me, I see in her eyes the lacquered glisten of a similar guilt. Sarah knows and I know, too, that she will never love me the way I love her. But does she know that it's okay? I must tell her. "Don't worry, Sarah," I'll say, "you'll pass the same blistering love down to your daughter. That's what we do, we just hand it down and down and down, and it's all right." I want to say this to Sarah, just as I've wanted you to say it to me.

There is something else I see about mothers and daughters. Not love, exactly, and not guilt either—I'm not sure just where this fits. You made sure my childhood was rosy and secure, my teeth straight, my education excellent. That's what we mothers do. We want the best for our daughters. We want them to be better than we are—smarter, prettier, richer, happier. Better mothers. And if we succeed, and our daughters more or less fulfill our expectations, then they usually also leave us behind. This seems unfair. My self-confidence, my place in this shifting world, my sense of who I am and what I can accomplish, these are all the result of your love and attentiveness. You guided me as if I were a kite, carefully playing out the string until I stabilized. I can see your upturned face right now, radiant, watching me soar.

So it is, I hope, with Sarah and me. I want her to be better than I am. When she wears a too-short skirt, paints her eyelids gaudy blue, dyes her shiny hair a lifeless yellow, I nag her. I don't mean to, it just pops out.

"Mom." I hear the impatient edge to her voice, the familiar words. "You don't understand."

But I do understand, just as you understand when I flaunt an excessively liberal view or dress in baggy ethnic clothes or swear like a sailor. Ironic, isn't it? I still struggle to be something else, something more than just your daughter, and at the same time I work to make my own daughter more like me. And more than me, too.

Sometimes I can feel myself looking up to her, to Sarah, another kite, flying high above me, caught by the wind. I hope she has her own golden riverbank memory tucked away where she can find it. She doesn't have to tell me about it, or say thank you. It will belong to her the same way mine belongs to me. What's important is that she have it, safe. I look down and see your face below me, raised to watch and wonder at my flight, just as mine is lifted to watch Sarah's. Just as Sarah one day will look skyward and hold on tight, when her own daughter catches the updraft and sails toward the sun.

Thank you for listening, again, from the beginning.

Love,

Sally

Jill Breckenridge

Josephine St. Clair Breckenridge and Jill Breckenridge
Pasadena, California; August 1977

Jill Breckenridge was born in Boise, Idaho, on October 23, 1938, nine years after the doctor told her mother she would never be able to have children so she needn't worry about birth control. Jill's published works include *Civil Blood,* a novel in poetry and prose about the Civil War, and *How to Be Lucky,* winner of the 1990 Bluestem Award for poetry. She is at work on a novel.

Josephine St. Clair Breckenridge was born August 12, 1907, in Silver City, Idaho. "Her father was the town banker. The family moved to Boise when the bank went broke after one of the many silver crashes. Mother was a beautiful, spoiled, only child. Later, she had the sleek look and feisty temperament of a flapper. She once confided to me, 'I never had an unhappy day in my life until I married your father.' She died June 9, 1980, of throat cancer, just two years after my father's death."

The Horoscope Promises Me a Mother's Gift

"Your mother has a lovely gift for you;
she's grateful for all you've done."
—Joyce Jillson's Horoscope
for Scorpio, 1/25/92
Chicago Tribune

YOUR MOTHER HAS A LOVELY GIFT FOR YOU

Mother, one of your first gifts was this story: You are galloping
across the Idaho desert, dressed in skin-tight jodhpurs, trying to
outrun a pregnancy you don't want. You are too beautiful for a
swollen belly, and you never had one because you liked vodka

more than milk or meat and potatoes, so you weighed the same
at eight months, when I was born, as you did before I entered your
belly to gallop with you, riding the waves of a stormy sea, rocking
and rocking in that silky water. Mother, your gifts to me were put

together with so little faith that anything could end well, they
unwrapped themselves before the holiday. Twice-used ribbon
uncurled, wrinkled paper relaxed to expose gigantic slippers,
or a sweater in red, my worst color, breasts swollen with

sewn-on poodles. One year, a blouse blazing with a rhinestone
Eiffel Tower. How those gems glittered in my bitter eye! During
a national knickknack craze, a pair of green ceramic frogs. *Look
underneath*, you wrote on the card, and I did, the daughter you

referred to as *Miss Priss*, to get a laugh from your friends when
I walked through the room where you played your boozy game
of Canasta every week. I looked and found, in bass relief, sculpted
genitals, green, but clearly human, on their undersides. Although

I never learned to like the water, I learned how to fight, my weapons
the stamina of youth and lethal words, bullets that exploded after
they hit their mark. A sullen teenager, I wore makeup like a shield.
When you said I *looked cheap and hard*, I shot back, *You should talk,*

Wrinkles, referring to the mask of pancake makeup you wore, a
failed attempt to cover the ruins of a once exquisite face. After my
father died, after moments with you more tender than ever before,
the next Christmas, a large box arrived. I put it under the tree in

its brown paper, knowing that sometimes your gifts weren't
even wrapped. But maybe this year, it would all be different.
Our five children gathered around the tree as I opened the box.
Inside, my dead father's clean, but clearly used, socks, his

handkerchiefs, and his cache of seventeen disposable razors.
In the bottom of the box, you laid an apron for me, the daughter
who, unlike you, loved to cook, an apron embroidered with a crazed
woman locked in a cage. Under it, the words: *Can't get out of the*

kitchen! Of all your gifts, Mother, only the frogs got a laugh,
not at the time, but later, when I began a family tradition with
your son, my only brother. After Thanksgiving dinner at his house,
I hid the green changelings in the nearly stripped turkey carcass.

Not discovered until his wife broke up the carcass for soup, the
frogs brought on shrieks of protest, then laughter, then phoned
threats of retaliation. For years, back and forth between us,
we passed those family heirlooms. They crouched under mounds

of giblet dressing or squatted beside jellied cranberry sauce,
until, one year, they disappeared. The poodles, the Eiffel Tower,
and the woman caged in the apron are long gone, but those obscene
frogs are hidden in one of our two houses, both inhabited by other

families now, raising their own children, recording their own brief
histories of beauty and battle. Somewhere, in one of those houses,
two green frogs are waiting to be found, years from now, by a family
baffled by cryptic green relics of another family's off-color history.

SHE'S GRATEFUL FOR ALL YOU'VE DONE

I've known women who apologized every day of their lives for being
alive. I've known others who burned themselves to ash, chose depression or disease to light that cold seductive flame. So, I'm
grateful to you, Mother. You taught me to fight, not quit. You

showed me the strength of a good offensive. I'm grateful, too,
you had no final words for me the day you died. Called to your bedside, frantic I'd arrived too late, I found you propped up on a pillow.
The nurses said you'd insisted on sitting up and *putting on your face.*

For your deathbed, you wore heavy pancake makeup, eye shadow,
and the dark red lipstick you wore even to sleep. Your gorgeous
gray hair was styled, every wave in place. But by then, the cancer
had stolen your voice. Grief mixed with that familiar regret

swamped me—another missed chance to finally get it right. But
later, I saw this too as a blessing, preventing you from giving me
the gift of your last words. So now, I invent your words, Mother:
Go in peace, my daughter, you who I gave the little I had to give.

THE MOTHER'S GIFT TRANSFORMED

This disturbing gift you willed me, Mother: your combative vision
of our past and future. Stretching behind and before me are thousands
of mothers who embrace their daughters with insults or admonitions:
Just don't get smart! Why are you so uppity? Who do you

think you are? the mothers shout as they pound the girls with
looks, with words, with dishrags and belts. *Just who do you think
you are? Not much,* the girls could answer, *Not much,* but, caught
in the curse, they shout back insult for insult, aiming their words

to inflict the most damage. Now, years beyond the war, one side
of the battle dead and buried, I give you the gift of my vision, Mother.
In this vision, I stop the mothers, arms raised to slap or punch, halt
the daughters before the words leave their open mouths. I declare

a truce, and begin this uneasy peace with a gesture: A mother and
daughter—so alike, so different, it doesn't really matter—are
together in a small kitchen. It is stuffy and hot, not the kitchen
from the women's magazines they once dreamed about, an aqua

kitchen, where even the white appliances were smiling. The girl
sweeps a lock of hair from the sweating forehead of her mother,
as the woman bends above the stove, stirring a pot of soup too
thin to feed a family of four. The mother stops stirring, covers

the soup and sits down, beckoning to the daughter, who laughs,
blushes, then protests, *I'm too old to be rocked.* But the mother
pays no attention and rocks her a long time, and then the daughter
stands and changes places with the mother, whose turn it is to

protest, but the daughter will hear none of it, and rocks the mother, and rocks and rocks her, and that is where this vision ends, with warmth and the steady movement of two fragile humans, arms wrapped around each other, humming, a song without words.

Your daughter,

Jill

Rita Mae Brown

*Julia Ellen
Buckingham Brown,
mother of Rita Mae
Brown
The cat's name is
Mickey.*
Hanover, Pennsylvania;
c. 1948

Rita Mae Brown
Hanover, Pennsylvania;
c. 1950

Rita Mae Brown was born in Hanover, Pennsylvania, on November 28, 1944. Taking birthday control pills and still raising hell.

Julia Ellen Buckingham Brown was born March 6, 1905, in Carroll County, Maryland. She died in Ft. Lauderdale, Florida, on August 13, 1983. I told her Florida was God's waiting room.

11 SEPTEMBER, 1996

Dear Mother,

Remember that sandwich loaded with mayo that I made for you when I was eleven? It wasn't tuna fish, it was cat food.

Remember the time Little Terry peed into the holy water? I talked him into it.

Then there was the time the truck rolled down the hill. I let off the emergency brake. However, I didn't mean to do that so it's not as bad as the above.

What about the time your lipsticks were bitten in half? Boy that stuff tastes awful.

Dropping tiny ball bearings into the cake batter before you stuck it in the oven was a cheap shot. I thought the devil's food cake was a present for Aunt Mimi, how was I to know we were going to eat it?

Remember when all the foxhounds rioted out of the pen, raced into the hollow and smashed Mr. Wolf's still? I wanted to hear them sing. I had no idea the still was down there.

And all that scandal about me being gay. Well, shit, Momma, I'm not the only one in the family, I'm just the only one that tells the truth.

Did you die to get away from me?

I guess I'd better live a long time because you'll be waiting for me at those pearly gates—to get even.

Love,

The Kid

Rita Mae Brown

Rosellen Brown

Blossom Brown and Rosellen Brown, *age ten*
Glen Oaks, New York; c. 1949 or 1950

Rosellen Brown was born May 12, 1939, in Philadelphia, Pennsylvania. She is the author of nine books, including four novels, the most recent of which are *Civil Wars* and *Before and After;* three collections of poetry; and a book of short stories. Her most recent publication is *Cora Fry's Pillow Book,* a sequel to her 1977 novel-in-poems, *Cora Fry.* She has been married since 1963 to Marv Hoffman. They have two daughters, Adina and Elana.

Blossom (Lieberman) Brown was born in 1904 "somewhere around the Jewish High Holidays but who knows exactly when?" in a now-disappeared shtetl in the Ukraine called Chashvata. She emigrated to New York via Baltimore when she was about seven; an eager reader, she gave herself the middle name Josephine in honor of Alcott's Jo; married to David H. Brown in 1927; they had three children, the youngest of whom is Rosellen. Though she worked as a secretary before her children were born, she would tell you that they were her greatest achievement. She lived for the last twenty-some years of her life in Florida, where she died on July 31, 1995, after this letter was written.

A Natural Gift

Dear Mama,

It's a little discouraging writing to you these days, when your mind is like a sea dotted with the tiniest green islands of memory. I'm not sure anymore what you are hearing. I'm not sure, either, what matters: the depredations of age call everything into question. Nothing I can say about it is original—how the losses make our active, striving years more valuable at the same time that they lay over everything a dense veil of futility. How I've never felt humbled by anything the way your slow dwindling has humbled me and made everything seem, yes, Ecclesiastes had it right, vanity.

So, adding up the "totals"—accomplishment, achievement, all the *a* words, starting with *ambition*—feels a little beside the point. You are here. You are what you are just now. A minute, since you've passed 90, is as short or as long as it was years ago when you were the girl in the photo with that butterfly of a bow in your hair or the young woman with a baby in your arms. No longer remembering that past—and without much future—this moment, the present, isn't what it's cracked up to be. My brothers and I swim into your line of vision and out again. We seem to visit your awareness the way we visit the city you live in, intermittently, leaving almost no residue behind.

There isn't a lot unsaid that I feel needs saying now, and I suppose that's lucky. We never worked up a long list of recriminations, voiced or unvoiced; I never even "rebelled" in the true sense of the word—not all in a rush, visibly (by which I mean audibly!), insisting that attention be paid my grievances. As my life defined itself, I only drew away my absolute loyalty; my eagerness to agree with you, defend you to others; your sufficiency as arbiter of my taste and my desires. Early on, I think, more protective than defensive, I felt enough of what it was to *be* you, your vulnerabilities clear to me and unthreatening, that I didn't enjoy hurting you. In fact, it cost me something to cause you pain, just at the point when a lot of my friends loved to turn the knife in their mothers' flesh. I don't know why I didn't feel the need; maybe I should have, maybe I'd have grown up faster? Too late to wonder.

But the "differentiation" accomplished itself willy-nilly. How could it not have come about when I lived a life so different from yours? You, Russian born, the poor girl who had to go to work after the eighth grade, at 14; who took courses at night school, always hungry for the education you couldn't have; who, once your first baby was born, never went to work again—the common immigrant scenario. I, the middle-class girl of my very different generation, who also did the expected, with your blessings: college, graduate school, travel. The values were yours, their fruition mine. You never understood why the women I grew up with, at least those who had children (and what was the matter with those who didn't choose to have them?), needed to work outside their homes, or even why as a writer I had to work *in* mine, my children nearby but never, from your point of view, sufficiently tended. You thought it was wonderful that I wrote and published and won prizes but you searched, always, for proofs of my maternal derelictions. I remember once, angry, telling you that I wouldn't let you take pride in my achievements if you wouldn't respect what it took to accomplish them.

It was not your experience to need such accomplishments for yourself, however. Even though it was clear to me that, given your energy and acuity, born in a later generation you'd have been right up there with the high achievers, I've never been able to make it very clear to you that if you send women to college, they will likely want (either early or late) to use their educations in the world. You didn't have the tools to understand that—with some notable exceptions, we are only the children of our times.

But here's the crazy thing: You should have been the writer in the family.

You are the one with the most audacious talent, the ability to leap, to make undreamed-of connections, to work your way through the most complex and rewarding syntactical branchings. (Eighth-grade educations were worth more in those days.) Your writing's got rhythm, vision, smarts—I use the present tense: it's too painful not to. I've never seen a natural gift like yours, though all of it went into letters and, for one short period, into a volunteer organization newsletter whose editorials you sweated out as if they were meant for the Op Ed page of *The New York Times*.

And you—you disparaged that talent as, I finally learned, you disparaged so much in yourself, and I don't know why. When it came to your remarkable verbal gifts, the first and easiest thing was for you to bow in deference to my father, who had a fine way with light verse. He published letters to the editor on political controversies and clever poems in the New York newspapers around the time of the end of World War I, and he sent you marvelous, witty love poems. Supple and funny but never profound, they were crowded with what we always called the "50-cent words" of a self-taught man who also never went to high school (though few would have guessed it) but who grew up on the formal rhetoric of the early century. "Oh, Daddy's the one who can write," you'd say, laughing, "not me." But always, when you said "Who, me?" so dismissively, I could see your eyes shine with a kind of wonder, a hunger for praise, a delight at the compliment. You loved it that I, your writer-daughter, could insist on your serious talent, but you never took it in, never made it part of yourself. "I always had such respect for the real writers, the ones I read, that I never allowed myself to think I could do what they did!" you'd say. "I was never deserving . . ."

Nor were you deserving, in your mind, of a lot of things. Once, I remember, though I can't recall the specific thing you were speaking about, your eyes filled with tears as you told me how you never thought you had the right to—and here my memory fails me. (The memoirist never admits to a forgotten climax to a story, but I'm no memoirist.) It may have had something to do with daring to go to the head of the supermarket line with a single stick of butter—something like that, some instance of a poisonous, self-destroying modesty that appeared to come down over your whole being like a sack that closed around you and wouldn't let you breathe. I remember thinking that my own, and my own children's, lack of boldness began right there in that panicky self-obliteration.

I asked you why you thought you didn't deserve more—in the small claims and the large, I meant—and you couldn't tell me why. One of your sisters, you always said with awe, was very intelligent, the other very beautiful, but in spite of that you were your father's favorite and the only one of them who really lived a fulfilled and relatively happy (though extremely sheltered) life. Why did you think you deserved so little? What did you miss along the way of ego-strengthening self-respect that builds daring the way early fluoride builds strong teeth?

If your unschooled adolescence made you self-conscious, I never saw that; most of your girlfriends also lacked formal schooling. I often wondered if your shaky, even willful, reasoning would have been disciplined by a longer education. Your lack of trust, for example, in scientific method led you into bizarre assertions about how the body works—you treated cause and effect, when it suited you, as a casual, even a foolish, fiction. But that's not the kind of mystery one ever solves—there are no controlled experiments to answer it.

You liked to describe your self-effacement as too scrupulous an overvaluing of others—those you knew and those distant luminaries like the writers you didn't dream you could emulate. Fortunately for me, I am not so scrupulous and have written in the face of a lifetime of my betters, innocently clamoring to join them. But the mystery, Mother, that has already disappeared into the diffusion of your memory, is not so much why you never had the will to use your talent—there are plenty of people who are good at something: dancing, singing, puzzle solving, high jumping, yet have no desire to put it to formal use. But you, whose will was always so vigorous, who kept our family moving and harmonious in a hundred ways, why did you feel you deserved so little for yourself?

Your timidity, though you seemed bold, I suspect, to others, made you a Mrs. Bridge, the Kansas City matron in Evan Connell's devastating novel—a woman who shivered at the need to make choices, indecisive, prey to the opinions and accusations of others with or without merit. You lost sleep over every purchase—we used to laugh at the memory of having found you once at three o'clock in the morning, sitting halfway down the stairs considering a chair you'd just bought—and, of course, it went back to the store the next day. More painfully, you took to heart every unkind thing anyone ever said to you and harbored it close to your heart, guilty beyond anyone's defending.

The paradox of ambition, of course, is that no one can maintain with perfect certainty what it is that will make us happy in our lives. By my standards, you could have used your enormous gifts to more satisfying advantage. Yet you—you continued to insist—you insisted even recently in one of the brief remissions of the sleep you seem to be practicing for the longest sleep of all—that one of your greatest accomplishments was simply having me, as if I were the pot of gold at the end of the rainbow. That claim of me as your greatest accomplishment had to have been one of the best gifts any mother could have bestowed. I grew up on this story that you loved to tell and retell: How, after you'd given birth to two boys and desperately wanted a girl, your doctor bet you a bottle of champagne that I'd be your girl. How, coming up out of the anesthetic they used so prodigally back then, you heard the nurses murmuring, "Oh, Mrs. Brown loses!" How you struggled through the mists of semiconsciousness to remember that this time losing meant winning. How, joyously, you put it all together and knew you had your girl. That story was like a fairy godmother's blessing on my head, and it protected me all through my childhood from the slightest envy of my older brothers.

Eyes misting over, you whispered this now-mythologized tale to me from your bed when I saw you last time. (It alternates with the set-piece tale of how you met my father one bewitched weekend in the country and then and there changed your name from Bertha, which had been the corruption of your Yiddish name, Blume, to Blossom, which was its far more palatable translation.) How dare I try to define for you what ought to have been your need, your satisfaction? I suppose I should be grateful for the writing gene, and the family gene, and the will you used on so many other things, but which I've combined with your love of words and made my work life. If I wish you'd had both, family and work, it's because, loving and admiring you, I wish I could have seen what you'd have made of your intersection with the world. The wish may be anachronistic, but I can still think it would have been a good encounter.

Meanwhile, how complex you continue to be, even in this limbo without much memory of what you've said three minutes ago. When we were settling you into the nursing home where you live now, after another confrontation with your many incapacities, I said to you without much hope (two nurses standing at the foot of your bed introducing themselves), "Mom, while they're here, do you have anything you want to ask them?"

And you, gazing out the window, not at a loss for words or for syntax more complex than most can handle at the height of their powers, said contemplatively, smiling a little, "Well, I don't suppose I can ask them if it would be possible for anyone to make a sky lovelier than that!"

No, I said, I guess you can't. What a writer you would have been, Mama, if you'd wanted to, or dared to, or, like your stubborn daughter, needed to be one.

With all my love,

Posey

Elizabeth Brundage

Elizabeth, Richard, and Joan Silverherz Brundage
Maplewood, New Jersey; December 3, 1961

Elizabeth Brundage was born December 3, 1960, in Newark, New Jersey. She is a graduate of the Iowa Writers' Workshop and received a James Michener Fellowship for her novel, *Lily Stone,* which was nominated for the Editor's Choice award at Pushcart Press. She has published fiction in several journals and is currently at work on her second novel.

Joan Silverherz Brundage was born October 10, 1932, in Rockville, Connecticut. She grew up on a tobacco farm in rural Connecticut. She received her B.A. from Connecticut College, where she majored in government. She divides her time between New Jersey, Connecticut, and Palm Beach, taking her grandchildren with her whenever possible (". . . so you'll take them out of school for a week or so!")

Thicker Than Blood

Mom,

Yesterday Dorothy brought over the dollhouse furniture from the farm, and I opened the box and took everything out. I haven't touched those things for over twenty years, but I remember them vividly, and the girls were so excited, setting all the little pieces out on the rug—a table here, two chairs, the four-poster bed, the bowl of apples, the porcelain dachshund—their little hands carefully designing an imaginary life, which is what I would do, too, upstairs at the farm, in the big back room where your dollhouses were kept. There were two houses, a strapping metal Colonial and a shabby cardboard Cape. The Colonial was deluxe; it had a stone terrace, French doors, a bird bath. In the Cape, life fumbled along. The windows were puny and the pink curtains I'd fashioned out of construction paper were dingy compared to the flowered drapes in the big house. I preferred the reckless Cape. It whispered stories to me. Things happened in the dark crooked rooms. The families had troubles, just like our family did, and I could empathize and feel sad and try to fix things. I could make order out of those imaginary lives in the midst of Richard's chaos. These days I have to remind myself about what we went through together, the alarming reality of our past with him, and the larger tension of what will happen next.

When I look at pictures of you and Daddy those first weeks after you got Richard, you are the image of the eager new parents. It was 1957. Richard sits on your hip, a beautiful roly-poly baby, no trace of his churning legacy. He had a difficult beginning: pulled from the quivering flesh of his birth mother, a fifteen-year-old German immigrant with a complicated past. Her own mother had abandoned her when she was six, which must have made her decision to give up her baby very painful. She stayed in the home for unwed mothers for three weeks, caring for the baby boy who would soon become your son, then willingly surrendered him to the State, where he was placed with a foster home to await his adoption. It took over two months, and he was transferred twice. He was so sick at the time just before the adoption that the authorities almost reneged on the transaction.

Before entering your lives, your son already had a wounded past that no amount of money or affection could heal. The wound still bleeds. All his life he has felt it, he has tasted its blood, he knows the pain by heart, but he has no idea how to heal it.

You and Daddy have your own pain.

What was it like having a son who was so volatile, whose violence was so irrational? He was your son, but not your blood, and how did that feel, waiting with such anticipation for a baby, and then getting him?

All this talk in the media about the poor biological parents in search of their "natural" children—making the adoptive parents out to be the villains, the *thieves!* How many times did you wish in the deepest part of you that you could give Richard back? Maybe it would have been more appropriate for him to have been raised by his birth mother, who betrayed him from the start with a careless pregnancy. You can see her maternal handiwork in his face, in the impenetrable darkness of his eyes—born lacking something essential—an emotional disability that no nurturing could fix. And how unfair for us to assume he would grow out of it; how unfair—*unjust*—to have an expectation that he would be able to live a decent, successful life.

Was I afraid of him? You bet. What effect did he have on my

life? The fear of him, of what he might do, all the pain he caused you and Daddy, his violence, chipped away at my ability to trust people—men in particular. I would have made an incredible detective. Sometimes I even fantasized about becoming a cop, because I know I'd be good at it. Going into his room as a kid, snooping around, finding things that made me shake. Dope. Condoms. Bullets. Learning to anticipate his behavior. The menacing ease of his machinations, his convoluted rhetoric, his bizarre strategies of manipulation. Not stupid. The intelligence may be there, but whatever the brain requires to use it properly is not.

How does *she,* the woman who designed him, imagine him in her lonely private moments of reflection? Can she picture his flawless baby skin riddled with tattoos? Does she see his wiry body, infiltrated by twenty-three years of heroin abuse? not to mention the cigarettes and alcohol. Can she imagine eyes as black as the devil's, savoring a deep and vicious longing for something he cannot define? He was flawed from birth, a botched recipe, yet you had no warning. All you had was your expectation, that this *gift from God* would amount to something, that he would have the ability to benefit from all you could give him. Almost immediately that dreamy motherly complacency dissipated. You could see he wasn't right. He couldn't listen, couldn't take direction. Kept hurting himself, almost deliberately thrusting himself into chaos. When you talked to your pediatrician, he told you to *stop being a Jewish mother!* After all, Richard *looked* normal.

When you and Daddy decided to adopt another child, the social worker didn't think you could handle it on account of Richard being such a challenge. I can only imagine how that must have made you feel. Somehow, by some miracle of fate, they let you have me. I have always felt lucky about that. I have never, *never,* felt cheated for not having my biological mother raise me. In fact, my adoption day, January 4th, has always had more importance for me than my birth date—I believe it was the luckiest day of my life, and I'm grateful for it. I never felt that my being adopted was a big dark secret, because you and Daddy were always so open about it, and as problems deepened with Richard, there was no pretending he had come from the two of you.

I remember the smell in our house growing up, stale pot and

Lysol. I remember the girls staggering down the stairs in their halter tops, their tight pocketbooks full of Parliaments and birth control pills and Seconal. Jethro Tull blasting on his lousy stereo, *Sitting on a Park Bench,* the tweeters twitching. And me, this cloudy pubescent, trying to clean up his mess. My hands trembling, loading your wedding crystal into the dishwasher, strangers in the house, dogs shitting on the living room rug. That time we came home from the beach, he was passed out on the stairs, almost dead. He even said something, muttered something, *better take me to the hospital, I'm about to OD,* that's what I remember, and then Daddy putting him in the car, a blue Country Squire I never wanted to ride in again, him passed out in the back on the blue vinyl, and your troubled face watching them pull away. I remember driving that car myself, home from my dance classes when I was a senior in high school. My sweaty black leotards. The cigarettes I'd smoke on my way home, the windows open. I was consumed with Richard. Wondering where he was, I was terrified of him. I think the clandestine smoking was a way of speaking his language, of trying to get over to where he was and seeing how things looked. My experimentation with drugs in college was about that too. I always tried to see things from his side, but even at my lowest there was too much light for that.

I used to lie awake at night thinking he might come in and kill us all; I was in high school, my room out front. I used to listen for him. I felt that I had a keen sense about him. I felt I knew him, knew what he was capable of, and that that truth was too much for you to bear. I couldn't fall asleep until he was in bed, till I could hear the thick surrender of his breathing. That always took a while. He might vomit in the bathroom. He might cook something downstairs, eggs and toast, four o'clock in the morning. I may have been distracted in high school, I realize now. He was always there. He was everywhere. He haunted my days; he still does. And yours. Although you tell yourself you're beyond him, you've got him under control. You don't. You will never have him under control.

Do you remember when I invited Richard to my home for Thanksgiving dinner? It was Scott's and my first year in the house, and Richard seemed better at the time. He had the truck, he was making money. He'd gotten married. I wanted to let him know that I was willing to let go of the past. So I invited them. And they came, not because they too were hopeful about bringing closure to our family, but because he wanted to see what we had that he didn't. He wanted to use the experience to hate me even more. We all pretended that things were fine, having them there. We all sort of floated through the day, dizzy with memories, a little frightened. I knew they were getting high. They kept going out for walks. Coming in with their eyes watery and unfocused. Talking slow. So much going on inside their heads—their little secret—the swirling queasy pleasure of heroin that made them feel like they were above us, like they had the answers. Telling me his eyes looked strange because he was tired, he'd been on the road for days. The lies on his tongue, like fungus.

After they left I told myself that I never wanted to see him again. I didn't want him near my children. Hannah, who was four at the time, asked me endless questions about him. Even with her limited experience, she knew there was something frightening about him, something she wanted no part of. He was a freak to her, with his tattoos and cigarettes and wild expressions. His laugh, its guttural lunacy. Her fear made me wonder about myself at her age, just the beginning of our wild ride with him.

Three weeks later my birthday rolled around; I turned thirty-three. I decided it was time to find my biological roots, and his as well. So I wrote to the agency for my nonidentifying information. They told me they couldn't give me his, but in a few months they'd send me mine. It was a very personal thing, making that request. For somebody as curious about life as I am, it amazed me that I still had this mystery in my life, this remaining kernel of circumstance that defined me in some way.

I remember the day my information came in the mail. I was trembling as I opened that letter. I was thirty-three years old before I knew anything about my biological past. Reading over the information I felt this intense sense of relief. My biological mother had been a reasonable woman, not somebody who'd been careless, who'd abused the pregnancy knowing she'd be giving me up. She'd lived in a home for unwed mothers and had a healthy pregnancy. It helped knowing I was half Jewish, since I look so Irish, and that has helped me so much in terms of identifying with our religion and encouraging the children to identify with it. And knowing that she was young, that they were students, justified her need to move on with her life, to put the pregnancy behind her. There is a certain amount of comfort in knowing that they were good people, hard working, and that she, like you and me, had a good relationship with her mother. And that her decision to give me up was a pragmatic one. She had good qualities, and it is likely, of course, that I inherited some of them.

But you are my mother, and I can't imagine anyone else being that for me. And I can't imagine ever being without you because for all these years you've kept me going, you've kept me on track, in the most giving selfless way, and you have shaped my vision, you have provided me with a perspective of the world and my place within it. You've inspired the courage within me, to not be afraid to speak my mind, to see things clearly, to know the truth. All the things you do for me that you know I appreciate but sometimes don't thank you for. Whenever I'd come home from college, and even now, there's always a little something waiting in my room, a new nightgown, a new sweater, a Clinique gift, whatever, and it makes me feel special; it makes me feel I'm still your little girl, even though I have all these adult issues in my life—the house, the mortgage, the children, my marriage, our cars, my work, the bills, the TV, the changing world . . . I'm still your little girl and I still like playing outside and getting dirty and being held and told that everything will be all right. I don't know how the world has gotten so big and tough and ugly and I don't think people really like it this way, but they don't know how to change it or stop it from spinning so fast, and I look at Hannah and Sophie and I wonder what it will look like here on this planet in twenty, thirty years, and that's like swallowing a bone—no matter how much water I drink, it's still there.

There is the past and there's right now and then there's the amazing realization that we are expendable, and that we won't live forever, and that one day we will die, you will die, and I will die, and no matter how much I can intellectualize that, it's still frightening, it's still painful. It's hard for me to accept the fact that I may have to be here on this earth without you one day.

I sometimes look at my children and think, what will happen if I die? What will happen to them? Who will care for them the right way, the way that I do? Only you. And what if you're not here?

We go out to the farm together, you and me and the girls. Driving down Pinny Street, I notice a calm come over you. You're going home. You describe your dreams of this place as if you are always trying to get back here, to get home. As if your mother is still in the kitchen, making blueberry blintzes. As if your father is in the corral, roping a horse. As if your sister is doing handsprings on the grassy front lawn. As if you will find yourself, an awkward teenager in a G. Fox dress, walking in your mother's garden, knee-deep in snapdragons. We are always children when we go home, no matter how old we are. It is here that I watch the child rise within you, your brown eyes bright with excitement, your hands empty, free. You move with the jaunty ease of a schoolgirl, remembering when the fields were shaded with cheesecloths, those enormous tobacco leaves lifting in the wind.

The farm remains loyal to our memories. The old white house with its crooked black shutters, sitting up on the hill as if it's been waiting for us. I imagine your mother's ghost at the window on the second floor, pulling aside the dusty curtain, smiling when she sees us down on the lawn. I know this is where she's returned to; they're both here, Hannah and Sam, and I can almost hear them whispering.

I have always loved the mystery of this house, the dirt cellar full of snakes and bristling mousetraps and Sam's old tools. The smell in the air of saddle soap and sawdust. And the attic with its trunks of costumes and twisted shoes. It is here in this house that I first heard voices inside my head, hissing like insects, urging me to write.

Your grandfather bought the farm in 1915, when your father, Sam, was just a boy. His father had started out in the liquor business with a gin mill, but then prohibition came and he moved his family to Connecticut to grow shade tobacco for cigars. The farm flourished, and it quickly became Sam's favorite place on earth and would remain so to the end of his life. Everybody in Ellington knew The Silverherz Farm, and everybody admired Sam. While his brothers had gone to college, he'd stayed on the farm. I remember his cowboy tricks, standing on his horse, his rope whirling through the air. He liked a good meal, your mother's beef and barley stew, and he liked his salt and butter. He took naps every day, listening to opera on the radio. He knew his way around a piece of wood. He'd hold that wood in his hands like a human organ, carving until it was right. He was a tough character with a gruff exterior, and although he was sensitive, he rarely expressed tenderness.

Grandma made a tough choice, marrying Sam. She was a city girl, college educated, and she liked nice things. She had sky blue eyes like the best kind of weather, but there was a great storm hovering. She had things in her past that were mysterious, things she kept to herself. You told me once that she'd been in love before Grandpa, but the man had jilted her for a woman from high society. I don't think she ever got over it. It must have been very difficult for her, living so far out on the farm after the excitement of the big city. I remember her hands, large for a woman's, and her big turquoise rings. She used to sit out on the front porch with a fat biography on her lap, dozing in the shade. *You can't talk to the trees*, she'd tell me. I think she was lonely, and he controlled her, and I think her revenge was Alzheimer's. She retreated into that murky place, that reckless bumbling darkness where her pain was a shapeless blur of little significance.

I know you miss her. Deep down you may resent her for leaving you the way she did. Willingly retreating—that's the part that gets to you. You used to snap at her, you used to say, *Stop doing that, Mother!* She twitched her shoulder and it drove you crazy; it meant she was getting old and she would leave you soon. She'd go out and sit in Grandpa's truck, waiting for someone to take her somewhere, a restaurant that had been closed twenty years before. She used to call me doll baby. *Put a little lipstick on, doll baby!* Once, at the beach—I was maybe six or seven—I was sick and she took care of me. She used to go into the bathroom to take her tub; she'd be in there for hours. I remember visiting her in the Hebrew Home. She was on the top floor, closer to heaven, I used to think. I remember sitting with her in the hall when she didn't even know who I was, watching the nurse feed her with a spoon, raping her disinterested mouth with some orange shrimp slop. The silence in the car afterward, driving away, the tears in your eyes. *Let me go,* she whispered to God one night. *Let me go!* No matter what, we die alone.

We drive to the cemetery to see her, to see them both. A lovely place, with old sweeping trees and crooked stones. It is not a scary place, but a quiet field overlooking a dairy farm. I can tell you feel comfortable here, and peaceful. This is where you will come when you die, and this is where I want to be too. We watch my daughters dancing on the stones. Spinning on the soft grass. Singing with their sweet small voices. And from way down deep, the spirits hear the girls dancing—they are smiling in their silence.

I worry about being without you. I cannot even imagine it. You're my *mommy!* The same girl who grew up in that big white farmhouse. The same girl who felt awkward, or beautiful, or estranged, or victorious. I don't always know how you feel. I don't know what you do with your bad memories of Richard. I know you don't like them, you don't like feeling sad. I hope you don't feel guilty; you shouldn't. I think you appreciate the fact that you can tell me anything. I know you have always appreciated my honesty with you. I wonder what you don't tell me.

I have always told you almost everything, only holding back things that might upset you, or make you worry about me, things like drinking too much at a party, or being depressed about a decision I have made. I love my life. I have always loved being me and you have always let me. I love being free. I love my thoughts. I love making a story in my head. I love my books. I love just holding a book. I love the thin shiny poetry books on my shelves. I love the salty smell of the books in the library in Clinton. I love bringing a library book to the beach and getting sand in it. I love the way pages go soft in humidity. I love all those words churned out on the page. I feel grateful that I am smart, and I am happy with the way I look. Sometimes I wish I had more courage. I wish I could just go out there and chew people up; maybe I'd be more successful. But of course I can't. I have been loved by many people, I think, and, perhaps even admired, and that feels good. I think I have probably frustrated some of my friends, but they rarely express this to me. I am sure that I have caused you to worry about me once or twice.

Sometimes I wonder, am I crazy? My head is full of people. My emerging characters. Wanting air space. I fell in love with writing when I was about ten years old. I just wanted to write. I was desperate to write. I remember staying with Grandma Lucy and reading *The Outsiders*—I must have been in fourth or fifth grade—and I thought, wow, I want to do that. I remember writing a story emulating that book because being Richard's sister was hard, and I thought I had an insight about him that others didn't and that I should write about that.

Then I got older and I fell in love with the atmosphere of writing, of being a writer. Once, at the beach, I wrote a poem on Sam's old manual typewriter, up in my room under the small yellow light. I loved the orange glow, the deep black of the night outside, the wet salty air. You always made me feel good about myself, made me feel that whatever I did was all right, even wonderful. That I should go out there and try things. God, I hope I can do that for Hannah and Sophie. Because it's tough out there. It's complicated. I just hope I can be half the mother to them that you have been to me.

Mom, I just want to live a good life. I just want to give and be appreciated and I think that's what you want, too. I want someone to say *you're doing a great job, you're on the right track, you're an incredible woman!*, but nobody does, except for you. I know my moods trouble you. My darkness. I think you know it's there. You've tasted it. You've read my work. And maybe you don't like it, which is only natural, just as I don't want to believe there's darkness inside my daughters. Yet I already see it, I know it's there, as valuable to them as their beauty and light. I feel a responsibility in my work to put down the truth. It is nasty and ugly and bad smelling as it can be. People don't like it. But it's necessary. It's what writers do.

You tell me you admire me for sticking with writing after all the hard work, the rejection. You shake your head, you say *it's hard to keep failing*. Those words cut deep because I don't see this process as failure. What many people, including you, don't really understand is that writing is not a choice I have—it's a joyful affliction. I live with it like a terminal condition, like a blessing. The writer in me is the best person I know. She is my strength, my terror, my passion, my trembling child. She is the whole truth. It's hard to wait for success, yes. It's hard. But success is not what drives me to write.

I've done things for you, Mom, that you don't realize. I married before I was thirty. (I remember you calling me out in L.A., urging me along. I was twenty-five. You had read some survey from Yale about women who don't marry in their twenties, how their chances of marital bliss dramatically decrease with age.) I got pregnant by the age of twenty-eight so you could have the grand-children you wanted.

But my writing is my own; it's not for anyone else. I write because it is my way of trying to make this world a little better, even if that sounds corny. I don't give a fuck if it sounds corny. It's a way of making clarity. Some days are better than others. And it's not just when I'm sitting at the computer, it's all the time. I am *always* writing. It's not about just writing, just being this woman—married to a doctor—who happens to write. Writ-ing is the blood in my veins, the air I breathe. It's the way I think, the way I lie awake at night, listening to the wind in the trees, the chimes, the gypsy moths drilling the screens. It's the whirl in my heart when I hear an ambulance, the prickle in my throat when my daughters cry. It's the way I look at the sky, the way black clouds will suddenly fill with sun. It's about our wonderful house and the things inside it that tell the history of our lives together. It's the people I see every day, the cops, the women waiting at the bus stop, the guy in the wheelchair who steals hubcaps. It's your face and your sister's face, and the memory of your mother's face. It's the memories I have of Richard's vio-lence. It's the way I see my husband, how I fell in love with his long arms and rushing blue eyes. It's our daughters, how they lie side by side on the living room floor, how they hug each other and hold each other and laugh with each other. It's their hands, making order in a flimsy dollhouse, moving tables and chairs and couches and bowls of fruit, putting the people here and there, inventing them. It's the look they get when they've accom-plished something, when they're proud of being exactly who they are.

It's not always pretty. Often disturbing. But it's mine. It's my voice, and I thank God I have it. And because of you I am not afraid to use it.

I love you.

Elizabeth

Lillian Castillo-Speed

Jennie Castillo, at her mother's house on Concord Street
East Los Angeles; 1946

Lillian Castillo-Speed, at the house on Concord Street
East Los Angeles, California; February 1950

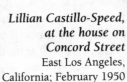

Lillian Castillo-Speed was born on February 15, 1949, in East Los Angeles. She is the coordinator of the Chicano Studies Library at the University of California, Berkeley, and is also the head of three ethnic studies libraries on that campus. She is the editor of the *Chicano Database on CD-ROM*, the *Chicano Index*, and the *Chicana Studies Index*, as well as the editor of a fiction anthology, *Latina: Women's Voices from the Borderlands*, published by Simon & Schuster in 1995. In 1996, she was named Librarian of the Year by REFORMA, the National Latino Library Association.

Jennie Castillo was born Jennie Guzman on March 17, 1930, in East Los Angeles, to Petra Guzman, a native of Zacatecas, Mexico. Jennie married Richard Castillo at age fifteen, a boy she met when she was eight and he was eleven. In La Puente, a suburb east of Los Angeles, they raised five children. Her husband of forty-seven years died in 1992; she continues to live in the same house on Lassalette Street in La Puente.

Ordinary Gifts

JULY 15, 1995

Dear Mom,

I'm thinking about those boxes of snapshots you keep in your closet. Of all the black-and-white ones, my favorite is the one of me standing in a short white dress and big white baby shoes, my hair really short because I am too young for it to have grown yet. It must be my first birthday; I have a very big smile and there are big white rectangular boxes all around me on the grass, big shapes to widen my eyes and slick paper and ribbon to crush with my baby fists. Nothing more. The questions over the years have been: What was in the boxes? Whatever became of the contents? There were probably gifts from Quela, Cuca, and Lola, and maybe from Grandma and my namesake, your *comadre*, Lily.

But I am curious about what *you* chose for me and wrapped up for me to open and to know that I had received something we adults know as a "gift." A one-year-old would have learned to expect good things to come to her without the barrier of gift wrap or the occasion of a birthday. You buy something beautiful for your baby. Maybe it's something that has colors she's never seen before. Maybe it creates sounds utterly new. Or maybe it's a sweet chunk of watermelon from which you've obsessively removed every seed. In any case, you know that you want it for her because you want everything for her. Do you take it out of the shopping bag and hand it over? Yes, of course. Countless times you do this and rarely think about it afterward. These are the secret, unceremonious gifts from parent to child whose message is: "Stick with me, kid. There's plenty more where that came from and I'm the one to get it for you. Don't count on anyone else to be this nice to you for no other reason than the mere fact you exist." But wrapped gifts are different. You wrapped paper around what? A doll? A dress? You gave it to me for my first birthday, and that was the day you started teaching me about the social side of things, that I would have to look to others besides you for the give and take of life.

But I am sure that the gift I've always meant to tell you about is one of yet a different kind, and it is full of mystery for me. Remembering that photograph of simpler times helps me sort out the madness of that record-heat week when Dad died. It will be three years this August. You'll probably be glad to know that this gift has taken me into spiritual considerations. I'm sure that is not a trade you would have made—Dad's death for your daughter's finally admitting that there may be more to things than what logic lets us grasp—but there it is.

What is so thrilling and hopeful is that it was so ordinary. It happened a few months before Dad died. The three of us, Dick, and Nathan, and I, were sleeping at your house in the bedroom I always use when I visit, the one that has a window on the front door. It seemed like the middle of the night when for some reason I half awoke and actually never fully awoke until the next morning. But in that semiconscious state, I heard Dad getting ready to leave for work.

It was a Sunday morning and I vaguely remembered that I had tried to wait up for him the night before, but we finally went to bed before he made it home. And now, here he was, already leaving again! It was still dark. From the window I could hear the front door opening with that screen door that always bangs if you don't catch it in time. I had only one drowsy thought: I had to say good-bye, and if I hurried I could. If I hesitated it

would be too late. Later on that morning the three of us would
have to make our 400-mile drive back home. Carefully I moved
away from Dick and tried not to let the too-soft mattress bounce
me along. Even more carefully but still hurriedly I placed my feet
where they wouldn't step on Nathan. He was spread out on some
blankets next to the bed. I don't know if they woke up, but there
I was in the long flannel nightgown you loaned me, finally getting to the front door.

Dad had his clipboard, his baseball cap, and his keys, everything he needed to open up at the Western Hills Country Club
restaurant and start the day's meals. You were there, too, standing by the door with an expression that remains a mystery to me.
Did you think I would make him late? Were you jealous of that
quiet morning time that I had interrupted? Were you impatient
with my sudden concern when it seemed that I didn't have many
conversations with him anymore? I put your face in the background to think about later. I went up to Dad and gave him a
kiss with some difficulty because of the cap, and then a hug, and
murmured that I just wanted to say good-bye. He said a few
words in Mexican baby talk to the effect that I looked like a
sleepy little girl, and that's exactly how I felt. I was no longer a
wife, mother of a teenage boy. I was just little Lily again. Funny
how quickly that transformation came and then went as I hurried back to bed and took a look out the window as Dad's Ford
Escort backed up and his headlights briefly lit up the dark street.

I didn't think about this incident again until later, as I was
trying to get comfortable enough to sleep in a hard chair in the
waiting room of Queen of the Valley Hospital. Dad's heart attack
had brought us all there to wait, taking turns to see him. By the
third day we knew that he had also had a stroke and that was
why he didn't talk to us. We could only talk to him and hope he
understood, while he could only stare back. On the fifth day of
our vigil, on Friday at five o'clock, he was gone. It was as if he
had made it through one more work week. All of us children
had tried to say good-bye to him. Berty was especially desperate
because she had not had a chance to reconcile with him. She had
held his sins more tightly in her heart than the rest of us and
now had no way to release them. She had lost the chance to
regain her father before losing him. As I tried to sleep in that
chair on one of those nights, I wondered why I had been so

lucky. Not only had Dad and I said good-bye to each other, but for a moment we had returned to that state of unconditional love, back to a time when he was the world's finest man. As the world's finest man, he had always made sure a dog could get a drink of water, usually from his cupped, knife-scarred hands, and nothing had been more delicious than his famous clam chowder. As the world's finest man, he had never left us unprotected.

Who or what decided I should have this experience, this gift? Why me? Whom do I thank? Was it so there could be at least one soul at ease among us who could handle all the death and burial details, including calling a priest from St. Joseph's to give the last rites? Why couldn't it have been Berty, who needed that experience much more than I did? All I know is that I was compelled to pull myself out of bed and get to the door before Dad left that Sunday morning.

As you know, I never had that Catholic gift of absolute faith. But that other gift came from somewhere, I suppose, and for some reason—I'm not sure. But maybe the kind of gift I'm trying to tell you about doesn't need a reason. You taught me about gifts and the human reason for them, but this thing that happened and that I haven't tried to explain to you before is pretty much incomprehensible to the middle-aged skeptic I've become. Maybe by the time it's my turn to die, I will have figured it all out. Until then, I hope I can just have the good manners to accept this gift and say thank you. I thought you'd want to know . . .

Love,

Lily

Judith Ortiz Cofer

Fanny Morot and Jesus Ortiz, wedding
Hormigueros, Puerto Rico;
1951

Judith Ortiz (Cofer),
age two, birthday party
Puerto Rico; 1954

Judith Ortiz Cofer was born in Hormigueros, Puerto Rico, in 1952. She is the author of *The Line of the Sun,* a novel; *Silent Dancing,* a collection of essays and poetry; *Terms of Survival* and *Reaching for the Mainland,* collections of poetry; and *The Latin Deli: Prose and Poetry.* Her work has appeared in *Glamour, The Georgia Review, Kenyon Review,* and other journals. She has been anthologized in *The Best American Essays, The Norton Book of Women's Lives, The Pushcart Prize,* and *The O. Henry Prize Stories.* She has received numerous prizes and fellowships and is currently an associate professor of English and Creative Writing at the University of Georgia. Her most recent book is a collection of short stories, *An Island Like You: Stories of the Barrio* (Orchard Books, New York, 1995).

Fanny Morot Ortiz, born in Hormigueros, Puerto Rico, in 1936, is the mother of two children. She lived in the United States as a Navy wife, with Paterson, New Jersey, as a home base. She returned permanently to her hometown in Puerto Rico after the death of her husband in 1976.

Querida Mami

For years you have been revising your life,
rearranging the furniture in familiar rooms. Now
approaching sixty, you can only see
a fragile house of porous bone
you can no longer trust to give refuge
to your vital spirit. The betrayal
of pains that cannot be explained
by a day of woman work, alarms you. You turn to me
for words that will make a difference.
What have you given me, Mami?

Images for my art, always at the edge
of my daily self, claiming their place in a poem;
impressions of our hours together.
They do coalesce into art,

95

if we subtract our separate struggles
from the purified memory of us once
in innocence, mother and child. We were perfect
for days at a time. You may recall, the moving scenes
now ingrained in a fresco; the primary colors
grown subtle with time, Mami.

This too: your memories, passed into me
through your blood, or perhaps
in your salty breast milk I rejected
before I could take in all I would need
to fully understand the old stories of you before me,
of a lovely girl with a mane of thick black hair,
a blanket desired by a determined suitor
who needed to wrap himself in it
and never face the light.
He wanted to climb into a tower
where the untouched princess waited
for the one who would transform her
with his kiss into handmaiden
and pliant consort to a melancholy man.

The dreamer you married at fifteen
saw me and many other children
swimming like guppies in the black pupils
of your eyes, and you fell into his dreams for a while.
Jarred half-awake by the pealing of bells
the day before your wedding you cut your hair
close to your head like a helmet of curls.
Is that why you did it, Mami?

I can also see a young woman,
still soft and plump from childbirth
leaving a hospital with her second and last child
in my receiving blanket, having sealed
her body's gates to other lives forever.
You were then only eighteen
and I was two. Already you knew how not
to get trapped by life—as well
as the exact price you had to pay
for the escape.

Now you think it is all behind you.
The woman's battles you call *la lucha*,
as well as the surges of power
that sustained you through the good
and the bad days of *la vida;* the man you loved
more than he dreamed you could, still unable
in the end to understand the gift
of your not-giving yourself complete
to anyone, is dead. You want to know
if it can all be shaped into a life like a book.
At least as difficult as your question
is making art, like assembling a puzzle
in your head from the memory of its shape, Mami.

I know only this: the meaning is in the making.

Sometimes my childhood comes back to me
in flashes like those hidden messages
we are not aware we receive, that come
not through our eyes, too slow to assimilate
the strobing particles of meaning as light,
but directly into the brain, mainlining
the memories into our synapses.
Amniotically connected,
you are always with me, present in my blood
and in my skin cells, now rearranging into patterns
you'll recognize. I do not think about you
each day, nor do I often take the time to consider
how we inhabit each other like nesting dolls,
each fitting so neatly within the other, yet free
to stand on her own. You have given me
this you-in-me,
and our connection is as natural as a mother
taking her child's hand at the dangerous intersection,
not stopping to think
everything it means.

Te quiere,

Wanda Coleman

**Mrs. Lewana Evans and her children,
Wanda (Coleman) and George**
Los Angeles, California; c. 1948

Wanda Coleman, née Evans, was born in Los Angeles, California, in November 1946. A former contributing editor for the *Los Angeles Times Magazine,* she was the first Fletcher Jones Chair of Literature and Writing, the Department of English, Loyola Marymount University. Her books in print from Black Sparrow Press include *Imagoes, Heavy Daughter Blues* (Poems and Stories), *A War of Eyes and Other Stories, African Sleeping Sickness,* and *Hand Dance.* A chapbook, *American Sonnets,* was published by Light & Dust Press in 1994. Her autobiographical *Native in a Strange Land* appeared from Black Sparrow Press in Fall 1996. She was a recipient of a literary grant from the National Endowment for the Arts, 1981–82; a Guggenheim fellowship in poetry, 1984; a Literary Fellowship in Fiction from the California Arts Council, 1989.

Lewana Evans McDaniel was born in Hennessey, Oklahoma, in June 1920, and has lived in Los Angeles since 1943. She is the revered mother of four children, including Wanda. She has eight grandchildren and two great-grandchildren. The former domestic, aspiring journalist, and retired seamstress has recently remarried and lives happily in South Central Los Angeles. She presently edits and distributes the *Hennessey Old Timer's News-letter.*

DEAR MAMA: Words Having Failed

Come on, Mama—

Let's go back. Return with me, thirty-odd years ago, to another of our shared instances, which today seems brutally relevant to my present gropings, current state of contentiousness, utter disorganization and chronic exhaustion. I'm worn out by wishes. And I'm factoring you into the yawns and nods. It's about time I expressed this aspect of my woeful frazzle to you, since mine is a particularly driven anxiousness which exaggerates my watchdog nature as I strive to be there for you every effing moment. And yet I must serve my own impossible agenda, too. Now that middle age is breathing down my corset, I'm so emotionally in arrears, so starved for strokes, the merest self-examination/IRS (internal revenue soulsearch) taxes me severely.

You see, Mama, I've yet to effectively manage my girlchild

compulsion to be understood and appreciated. It's grown up big, dark, ugly and demanding. Yet I live better by it now, Mama. I've settled into it, like smelly foot-soiled mules as I flap around in my house of melancholy. Rather, I sweat under it, like a pair of too-tight stretch-alls straining at the thighs. The nonacceptance fits, but not without pressure. And when I'm not careful, the slightest wrong step causes those synthetic fibers to snap and send me, and those around me, spinning.

Talking about it.

No hugs. It's enough to be near you. In case I'm needed. For you, Mama. Always. For you, no silliness is too silly. No weight too backbreaking. (Except during Papa's final slip into end-stage cancer, those last hard months when your panics, generating phone call after phone call, would reach into and snatch me out of the haze of sleeplessness. I'd throw cold water at my face, struggle into street clothes, and wear out my tires on that worrisome trek to and from the Emergency Room. Once, when I had shut my eyes for a three-hour nap, the phone rang. I had been up two days without a wink, working against a deadline. Mama, I had just finished the project and collapsed onto the bed. When I groggily awkwardly lamely tried to explain myself, you screamed then banged down your receiver in my ear. After you hung up, I passed out of consciousness. I called you back later, sought and was granted forgiveness for that momentary glitch in my vigilance. It was evident that I couldn't have woken up to save myself. Oh, Mama, when I lose you I'll lose my only true witness!) These days, I repeatedly push myself beyond myself even as I berate the lateness and smallness of my achievements, and curse my failure to do major damage—that is, to make significant amounts of all-American cash. Yet, I'm most pleased when my accomplishments make you proud and you broadcast the news throughout the family.

Which means, I can never say no to you except in bad health or danger. Because . . . in my midteen years, in the 1960s, it was even more impossibly difficult to maintain my self-esteem under the constant all-pervasive barrage of rejection and race prejudice. I was always too something. Too black. Too nappy-headed. Too fat. Too uppity. Too bookishly smart for anybody's good. The National Forensics League was my ego's salvation. Original oratory was my forte. I was one of six high school students of African descent from our South Central Los Angeles campus who chose to compete in the public speech and debate society's national program of high school competitions. We were considered oddballs on our campus famous for athletes who escaped poverty through intramural sports.

Remember, Mama? Nobody but our parents ever saw us off or cheered us on. Preparations started Thursday or Friday for the one- or two-day tournaments. Sometimes you'd leave work early and pick me up at school. When we got home, you'd plow through the old cedar chest for scraps of material to patch into something wearable. Or, finding nothing suitable, wearily shop for fabric. As usual, I'd fix dinner while you napped. (There were four of us—me, George, Marvin, Sharon—but I, being the oldest, was your helpmate. I listened to your complaints about your job. I quietly closed and guarded your bedroom door, shushing my brothers and sister, when you had a crying jag. I loved to surprise you with a sparkling spotless room, from venetian blinds to waxed floors, when you came home following a tough experience. I dutifully picked your corns and filed down those calluses, by-products of cheap shoes. I hated washing and ironing the laundry, but, nevertheless, learned the proper temperature for each type of cloth, how to damp iron, even how to properly fold dress shirts and perfect-press pleats [I spent my high school prom night ironing the leftover wash in front of the TV console. No boy in my graduating class dared ask "the professor" out. Today, in my own household, I never touch an iron except in an emergency. Everything goes to the cleaners.].) When dinner was ready, I'd set the table. Then I'd wake you up at the appointed time, and you'd get up and groggily pick over the meal I'd cooked. Or I'd serve you on the couch, setting up a TV tray, where you'd relax and listen to the evening news. Me and the kids would eat at the table. Afterward, I'd put a choice plate in the oven for Papa, clear the table, and draft my brother George to towel the dishes after I had washed them. I would wipe the table and sweep the floor. George would empty the trash. While the kids played outside or watched television, you and I would lay out the pattern for my new outfit on the dining room table and cut the cloth. You'd spend almost all of Friday night, leaning into the power Singer, sewing. You'd work nonstop, with only a minute's break to say "good night" to the kids. I'd stay up late to assist you, remove straight pins and refold pattern pieces. I'd bring you a glass of ice water if you needed it. Between spates of memorizing my speech, I'd read the instructions aloud when your eyes "got tired." If the pattern was difficult, and you made a mistake, I'd help you snip and pick out the fine stitching. When I became bleary-voiced, you'd send me to bed.

Those exciting Saturday mornings, we'd get up early. Most times you'd never slept. I'd try on the dress or ensemble. While I packed my lunch, you'd pinking-shear and hand stitch the hem or cuff the sleeves. Then you'd fry my nervous, damp, fresh-washed kinks with the straightening iron—all for me to "look fresh 'n pretty" for the tournament.

But pretty took considerable labor in my joyless sun-filled ad-olescent days, when the standards of youthful beauty were exem-plified by Sandra (*Gidget*) Dee, Connie (*Where the Boys Are*) Francis, and Annette (*Beach Blanket Bingo*) Funicello. Your insis-tence that I be well dressed gave me desperately needed confi-dence. I was big and dark and ugly in a world that did not value me. My pleasant face was a perfect marriage between you and Papa. I had paternal grandmama's eagle eyes, a medium nose, an average mouth with lips of medium thickness; being overweight had been a problem since third grade. My broad-shouldered Wa-tusi upper torso, from Papa's side of the line, was awkwardly thrown off balance by the Hottentot fullness waist-down, from your side of the line, and you made me wear a girdle. Food—greasy junk and between-meal snacks—filled the chasm created by peers who rejected me because, although they too were col-ored, I was the third-darkest girl on campus. And of the three, I had the worst grade of hair, blessed with Papa's recalcitrant naps instead of your beautiful, long, glossy black silks, Mama. Eating, and sometimes we ate alone together, made the loneliness less lonely.

Once I was completely dressed for the day's series of bouts, had arranged the folder containing my speeches, and filled my purse with tissues and cologne, you'd give me fifty cents or a dollar for soft drinks. The house would still be asleep when we pulled out of the driveway.

Repeatedly, we six—two boys and four girls—from John C. Fremont High, went up against our predominantly white, better-educated student peers from richer Southern California schools.

Sometimes our plaintive oratory, culled from the speeches of Clarence Darrow or dramatic excerpts from *The Robe*, shamed bigoted judges into rewarding us with certificates, medals, or trophies. More often, those Saturday nights, we returned discouraged and empty-handed. Mr. Newsom, our White coach, did his best to rouse team spirit, and urged us to think ahead to the next tournament and beyond—but we knew he was only one man, powerless to combat the indomitable racism that repeatedly denied us victories. On those unforgettable evenings, our stunningly unfair losses rendered us tearless—stymied anger and sadness were the palpable terrors that rattled around in our silence as we journeyed homeward on the big, shiny yellow-orange bus.

We knew we had been failed.

Mama, it meant *everything in the world* to see our raggedy old Rambler sedan hugging the curb on San Pedro Street, halfway up the block; to find you, sometimes half-sleep, waiting when the school bus hissed to a stop. "I tried, but . . . ," I'd say—and somewhere in the moodiness, during the drive home, you'd manage to ignite the fuel of Mr. Newsom's words. True victory, you'd say, was in knowing I had done my best against unbeatable odds.

"Everyone wants to win, but draw or loss, fight to get on top. And if you must lose, go down fighting."

Your words were salve for my wound.

Now, in this present, whenever you've summoned me, that scenario, and those words, has replayed itself on my heart, silencing grumbles and tendencies to be contrary. Memory drives my sacrifice of time and money—there's no such animal as spare time in my jungle—to return to the home I've never lived far from, to do my best for your benefit: to interpret the law and complex legal documents, to accompany you on doctor's visits, to scratch your dandruff, to sit outside surgery during operations, to clean your house, to recommend the appropriate professionals to deal with the problem, to take you shopping for groceries, to rub your back, to pick up church dinners, to study the contraindications of your medications, to interpret confusing news reports, to accompany you to funerals, to take you to an occasional movie or concert, to drive you wherever else necessary, to hurry over after midnight when an intruder is trying to break in and the police haven't gotten there yet, to attend your church for special occasions, and to take you to visit my children, your grandchildren.

Mama, mama.

It's time I closed this particular episode from our overlapping pasts. Like always, Big Girl's gotta run. Like someone sings in the song, hard luck and trouble remain my capricious companions. Sleep deficit and an anemic pocketbook dictate my erratic lifestyle. And there's ever so much of the long-neglected I've always promised to catch up on. But I felt the imperative to make this time to reminisce. So please don't let me forget to say "thank you" before I go.

Over these three tumultuous decades, I've borrowed, begged and haphazardly developed ways of resolving the multitude of conflicts and disappointments that continue to shape this trial I call my life. Thus far, I've found the strength to prevail. And although I'm not and never will be what you'd call happy, and although I'm not and may never be what I'd call satisfied, I'm capable. I'm dealing with our society's bloody difficult, demeaning, and damning demands. I'm fighting. To win, of course. But draw or loss, I'm fighting.

Much much love—

Wanda

Lynn Doiron

Lynn Due (Doiron), her mother, Opal Marie Due,
and brother, Randy, at the River Ranch Dairy
Mira Loma, California; 1956

Delores Lynn Due Doiron was born on January 11, 1947, in Upland, California. A recent top-ten finalist in the *Ann Stafford Poetry Prize* competition, she won the Bazzanella Literary Award in both fiction and nonfiction while obtaining her B.A. in English at CSU Sacramento. Her work appears in various literary magazines—*Catchword, The American River Literary Review, Messages from the Heart*—and has been accepted for future publication by others, including *The MacGuffin*. The mother of 3 children and grandmother of 2, she now resides in Shasta County, California, in a house she and her late husband, Alphonse, constructed from hand-peeled logs.

Opal Marie Due was born Opal Marie Ivy on October 15, 1925, in Batesville, Arkansas. She arrived in Ontario, California, via the long route from the old "home place" near Batesville. When she was a young girl, Opal worked her way with her parents, Tom and Elsie Ivy, and her sister and brother through the crops in need of harvesting, until they put away their traveling tent, cots, and hand-sewn quilts to settle amid the citrus orchards and grape vineyards of Southern California. She dropped out of high school as a sophomore, citing "too shy" as the reason, and, at 19, married William Harvey Due. At 20, she gave birth to Delores Lynn; at 24, William Randolph; at 32, Debra Jean; and at 34, Donnita Ivy. Before her death in 1991, she was known as "G.G." by her great-grandson, Alphonse L. Doiron. She died in the log house built by Lynn's family. She died with children, grandchildren, great-grandchildren, brother, nephew, and old family friends in attendance. She was much loved and greatly admired for her courage, humor, and giving nature.

Letters to Mama from Cottonwood

HOUSE THE COLOR OF CHOCOLATE

1

After noon on Sunday, Mama: delicious sounds—
   a splat of apple against the wall,
      your *shusch!* of Dad's teen brother's

almost-got-you guffaws. Delicious sights—
   Curl of red peel in your hair,
      Quiet! finger pressed to lips

then your final missiled wedge,
    and uncle skulking off,
        bits of fleshy MacIntosh juicing

down his cheek. He passes Dad
    who naps under tented newsprint
        on the sofa, brogan-booted feet,

calf-manure crusted, extend over upholstered
    arm. Headlines rise and lower
        with his ex- and inhalations.

Before he stirs, paper sluicing to floor,
    all the kitchen walls will shine—once again
        glossy as egg-whites in our house

the color of chocolate. Then you'll run
    the vac, working out in a radial star,
        suck up straw loosed from his shirt,

dull flakes fallen from boot soles,
    while singing some honky tonk song,
        humming between known words.

    2
A honeybee—distracted from patches
    of purple clover clouding a field of alfalfa
        across our drive—spirals down

in uneven loops to inspect roses outside
    your window. Hesitant, she selects blooms,
        packs pollen on over-burdened hind legs.

She has no notion
    of me as I watch
        from behind the glass.

    3
For a time you helped me sound
    hard words, allowing me the throne
        of your lap. I held my book, furred and hard

and green on the outside as unripened peaches,
    and read from *Honey Bunch Helps on Wash Day*.
        And sometimes I squirmed, waiting for Monday,

our Wash Day, and the place between
    breeze-caught sheets billowing from wire lines
        where you would hang them with wooden pins.

And I—from my make-believe table
    between cotton walls—would serve tea
        to imagined friends whose spirits lived

inside Teddy and Susie, a doll with no hair,
    and watch your silhouette bend to the basket,
        and listen for the snap of towels.

4

Once wisps, loosened free from long braids,
    swung up my cheek, then skittered to rest
        light as a daddy-long-legs spider dancing

the face of her web—I slapped at the tickle
    and sounded out so-*puh*, just as you had,
        your lips so close to my ear.

You had no answer
    for soap's silent *a* I tried long, and short,
        and *app*le-like to include.

5

Before sundown Daddy brings cuttings
    from the fencerow of sweet peas and you
        arrange them in a clear mayonnaise jar

and center the jar on our table.
    We survey our bouquet and tell each other
        how fine, really pretty, very good

then you ask if I've yet culled the roses,
    reminding me of spent blooms, how plucking these
        allows room, spurs bud regeneration.

And I unhook my toes from chair rungs,
    unfold arms from chin-cushion position
        where I studied crowded pea stems—how

they bunched and crossed; how air beads
    clung in tiny, clear pearls then broke and popped
        all along ridged green, vanishing.

6

In the night I dreamed of many bees burning
    circle-8's around one browning rose
        and inside the rose,

next to its heart, a worker bled
    amber beads over legs too heavy to budge—
        coffin and contents, all dying.

7

Now, Saturday afternoon—a buzzer sounds
    cycle's completion. The dryer door groans
        open and, from the porch, fingers pinching

corners while her chin presses percale middle edges
    to her chest, my daughter-in-law calls
        to her son and daughter

who buzz around me in my adirondack chair
    on trikes and bikes as if I constitute
        Start and Finish.

Remembering the asylum of cotton walls,
    I smile, then consider hard words, learning
        to sound, unexplainable silencing

and the spirit of you, not imaginary,
    not housed inside a bald doll, flashes past
        on her trike: "Mama! Grandma!

Look! See me? I scored!"
    And brother, training wheels gathering speed,
        giggles "almost-got-you, Missy!"

as your seed continues. Vining heart, mind,
    the good of our days, a bunching of delicate pastels.
        I pack each memory on feathery hairs

of my heart, Mom,
    and write them here for you,
        the worker, who enabled me to bloom.

A MONDAY COAT

1

Mama, when you melted into the old rocker cushions
    like a tapered white candle
        into its holder, I had to peel

your arms from the wood arms, carefully
    rolling them up and in, as I lifted you
        inch by inch. You winced

when hair follicles pulled free and
    stuck to the smooth oak arms. I continued
        to fold. So tedious when

2

everything's stuck. Evenings now, I sit
    in the rocker, stroking the hair on its arms
        and think of how nicely I managed

the shoulders, squaring them up
    with pins, tucking your elbows in
        and of how my fingers pressed all

but one of the wrinkles
    out of your chin. I'm glad I didn't
        do as requested—you asked me

3

to shear the arms. You wanted a Monday coat
    woven—a coat for me to wear
        made of hair. As it is, any

time I like, I can sit inside your arms.
    When the mood suits, I take you
        down off the shelf,

untie double-knotted strings
    around the JC Penneys shirt box
        shake the creases and pins

from your folds,
    and am born
        all over again.

Rita Dove

Rita Dove, her mother Elvira Dove, and her brother
Tommy Dove in the backyard
Akron, Ohio; c. 1954

Rita Dove was born in 1952 in Akron, Ohio. She is the author of a novel, a verse drama, and six books of poetry, including *Thomas and Beulah*, which won the 1987 Pulitzer Prize, and most recently, *Mother Love* (W. W. Norton, 1995). Ms. Dove was Poet Laureate of the United States from 1993–1995. A Commonwealth Professor of English at the University of Virginia, she lives in Charlottesville with her husband and daughter.

Elvira Dove was born Elvira Elizabeth Hord on April 14, 1924, in Akron, Ohio, where she has lived all of her life. The oldest daughter of working-class black parents, she sang in a family gospel group as a child and graduated from high school at the age of sixteen. She is married to Ray A. Dove and has four children, all of whom are college graduates.

Little Song for My Mother

Dear Momma-leak-ins,

Remember when I first addressed a letter this way? I was in college, away from home for the first time, and on an impulse fired by equal parts of nostalgia, misery, ebullience, and daring, I wrote the new salutation at the top of a fresh piece of stationery—in ink, so there was no turning back. After I'd mailed the letter, I had a rush of panic: What if you found it demeaning? Or childish? I needn't have worried; you loved it, though it made fun of your height (5 feet flat) and was, of course, a juvenile thing to do. Now that I'm 43 years old, with an adolescent daughter of my own, I realize that no mother is ever insulted if her child behaves like a child towards her!

But this is different; this is supposed to be the letter I never wrote but meant to write. The topic implies that all those other long-distance communications—from undergraduate years and graduate school as well as the hundreds of notes, birthday cards, postcards, and telephone calls since—were merely small talk, half-truths and subterfuges. There's an aura of estrangement clinging to the title of this book, a mood of longing and regret. So why did I agree to the "assignment"? Perhaps because I believe in the journey and discovery—maybe, if I sat down and tried to write such a letter, I would find out what it was I never told you.

Today I was burrowing in the attic, gathering suitcases for an impending trip overseas, when I came across a carton of correspondence and memorabilia from 1974, the year I went to Germany on a Fulbright fellowship. Somehow a packet of letters I had written home had slipped into my things. How wide-eyed I was, how naively confident! Here's an excerpt from a letter begun on December 6, Sankt Nikolaustag, and finished three days later:

> Sorry I haven't written for a while, but studies are getting more attention than usual this week. On Wednesday my class (the "Taugenichts" seminar) got together at a beer cellar. The purpose was to become more acquainted so that the class discussions would become less self-conscious and be livelier. I think it worked! We stayed up till 2, talking . . . by that time I was half asleep. It's funny—I can stay up all night if I'm dancing or having a good talk with a small group of friends; but all they did from 12–2 was drink beer and discuss "the function of literature."
>
> But, alas! The time has come for assiduous study once again—it is Monday. I'm getting ready to go to the library and slave until about 7 P.M., then come home and cook dinner. I've been having a lot of dreams lately, and you're in almost every one of them . . . so you see your spirit reaches across the ocean. I've even started keeping a dream book.
>
> Mommy, mommy mommy . . . Send me some more pictures of you . . . I've pasted all the family photos on my wall and I want more. Everyone thinks my family is beautiful (of course, I always knew it).

What can one make of such a sickeningly sweet relationship? Tolstoy said, "Happy families are all alike; every unhappy family is unhappy in its own way." But I think happiness also has its gradations, in niggling worries and regrets. For instance, although my childhood was nourished by books and punctuated by fascinating tidbits pulled from the parental storehouses of learning—Dad trying to teach me logarithms at age eleven, or the countless times you marched into my room announcing that it looked like "the wreck of the Hesperus"—I never stopped to think about where that knowledge came from, especially in your case. Okay, what if you would occasionally phrase a question in French or stop in the middle of making dinner to exclaim, "Is this a dagger which I see before me, the handle toward my hand?" You were Our Mom. A Housewife. (We said "homemaker" in those days.) What more was there to know?

Your story. A shy little girl who loved to read but whose most vivid memory from school was the acute shame felt when a teacher read *Little Black Sambo* aloud and the class snickered at your bright blue-and-white striped dress, salvaged from a coat lining. I knew that you had skipped two grades and graduated when you were sixteen. What I didn't know, until I was married with a house of my own, was that you had been offered a scholarship to Howard University, which your parents turned down for you because they were afraid of what could happen to a sixteen-year-old girl in the big bad city of Washington, D.C. Besides, what use was college to a marriageable young lady? So you entered business school, worked as a seamstress to help with the family finances, met my father over Ping-Pong at the community center (and beat him, too!) . . . but there the story stops.

I wish you could have taken that scholarship—but I'm so happy that you didn't, because to have that wish come true would have meant no Ping-Pong game—and therefore no Rita. You would have gone on to college, you would not have met my father, and I and my siblings would not exist—simple as that. Even if we were to suppose a situation where you had gone to college after marriage and had the same constellation of kids, I still would not have become exactly who I am today. You would have divided your energies between home and career, you would have been more protective of your time (as I am with my daughter) . . . and I would not have grown up with the exhilarating and liberating confidence of a child to whom all is open, a confidence and assurance borne, in part, of a childhood taken for granted.

What I regret most is my inability to write about you more directly in my poems and fiction. I've written poems about Dad's roses and telescope and carpentry, how he drilled us in flash cards and struggled against discrimination as a young black chemist. But your trials, as a woman and as a black woman, have been a quiet knowledge to which I've borne witness in poems and prose, mostly without direct acknowledgment. Up until this year, the only mother of your generation I had written about bore no resemblance to you whatsoever; Belle King (whose daughter is the protagonist of my novel *Through the Ivory Gate*) is a demanding, love-starved woman who can't relinquish her painful memories. In fact, part of the driving force behind the poems in *Thomas and Beulah* was the hope that writing about your parents would enable me, eventually, to write a poem for you. Only now, many years later, could I write that poem:

PRIMER

In the sixth grade I was chased home by
the Gatlin kids, three skinny sisters
in rolled-down bobby socks. Hissing
Brainiac! and *Mrs. Stringbean!*, trod my heel.
I knew my body was no big deal
but never thought to retort: who's
calling *who* skinny? (Besides, I knew
they'd beat me up.) I survived
their shoves across the schoolyard
because my five-foot-zero mother drove up
in her Caddie to shake them down to size.
Nothing could get me into that car.
I took the long way home, swore
I'd show them all: I would grow up.

It didn't happen exactly like that, of course. You parked the car out of view, and I felt no mortification getting into it afterward. I wasn't even that worried that the other kids would think me a sissy because my mother had to step in—I was actually proud that you had cowed them, and I learned an important lesson that day about righteousness and conviction as equalizers in a confrontation. For the sake of the poem, though, emotional tension is necessary—and that tension relies upon the ambivalence of the victim. I think you know that, and understand why I bent the facts. But I also hope you recognize the form of the poem (you liked to quote Elizabeth Barrett Browning's *Sonnets from the Portuguese,* too!) and remember that a sonnet is, most importantly, a song of love.

Your daughter,

Rita

Tess Enroth

*Tracy Low McElwee with her daughters, Tess (age one)
and Mary (age seven)*
Delano, Minnesota; Fall, 1926

Tess Enroth (Theresa, "Treasie" as a child) was born in Minneapolis on August 20, 1925. She grew up in Minnesota, beside clear blue lakes, where the Northern Lights and the Milky Way light up the night. After living in other states and on four continents, she has found her home in Oregon. Her poems, short stories, and articles have appeared in anthologies and literary journals such as *Cottonwood, Lake Effect, Poets On,* and others.

Theresa Marie Low McElwee was born July 27, 1892, in Minnesota. She was called Tracy and for a few years taught in one-room schools. She married Frank McElwee, who built roads, and they brought up daughters Mary and Theresa. In 1958 they retired to California, where she grew gardens of sweet peas and violets. She died January 31, 1966.

I'm the Mother

An early memory: I am tired after an evening of splashing in puddles and running barefoot in the cool grass. My weary efforts to undress falter, and in one easy movement, my mother draws me up onto her knees and settles me against her soft warmth. She lifts my dress over my head and then, as she washes my feet, recites a poem about going "to bed by day." I know the boy in *A Child's Garden of Verses,* his "land of counterpane" and his rope swing hung from a tree. And like him, I'm certain all's right with the world, for I am enfolded in my mother's all-encompassing love.

Now I lie awake. My bedroom is dark but for a strip of light on each side of the window shades. It is only the back porch light, not sunrise. My body aches from having slept without turning, and I pull myself up on an elbow and reach for the lamp switch. Down the hall the night-light casts a glow on the hardwood floor near the bathroom door, and I decide not to turn on the lamp. I can see that the white comforter has slipped to the floor on one side, leaving half the bed uncovered, and the sheet is icy. I shiver. I like a window open no matter what the weather, yet the room feels airless, and I gasp for breath.

Inside the fiberglass cast, my bone marrow is molten metal

surging from ankle to knee. I look at the clock's glowing digits, hoping I've slept four hours, hoping it's time for my pill. I see it is past three o'clock but can't remember when I had the last one. The medication does things to my brain and makes my throat so dry I can hardly choke it down—you'd think I'd remember to the minute. I turn on the lamp to read the marks on the yellow note pad. Another half hour to wait.

I rearrange the comforter, pull a second pillow over, and lean back on its chilly surface. The shaking begins, and I must do something to stop it. I draw a deep breath and hold it. If I want to get out of bed, I must wake my daughter who is in the next room. I don't like to, but I'm not supposed to be up alone. Surgery has left me weak, and the drug that addles my judgment impairs my balance, too.

When I lower my feet to the floor, blood flows suddenly into the swollen tissues and throbs hotly. I feel awake and strong enough to manage the trip alone, but I do as I'm told. My daughter trusts me to be a good patient. I give the little brass bell a slight shake, and as I shove my right foot into a slipper, she calls to me to wait.

"Put on your robe," I answer, still automatically the mother, and chide her when she appears without one. I stand on one foot within the safe space allowed by the walker. My left foot and ankle are trying now to burst out of the cast, but moving lessens the pressure a little.

"Slowly, Mom, please," she says.

Back in bed, I let her tuck the covers around me, and I watch as she breaks the big dry pill into halves and hands them to me before writing the time on the yellow pad. She kisses my forehead and feels that I am still trembling.

"Are you cold?" she asks and I say, "No, I'm fine, thanks, I've had my fix; the shakes will stop soon. You get back to bed."

Instead she turns out the light and holds me, pressing my head to her breast and gently rubbing my neck and shoulders. I want to weep.

The drug is quick to work, and with my leg elevated pain seeps away. Yet I remain awake, overwhelmed by love, grateful to all of my children for their devotion. Yet I feel guilt and regret, too, that in one ill-timed step, I have laid waste to their lives and mine. The doctor and others have told me I must allow myself to be taken care of, that I am fortunate to have such support in my family. And true as that may be, *I am the mother!*

A friend who has no child says I must remember how many nights I got up and crossed cold floors to reach a child's bed. I can think only that she does not truly comprehend what it is that mothers do. This is not payback time. I am the one who is supposed to take care, to be in charge, to be strong. Yet as I lie here moved by my daughter's love, I remember my mother. I think about all the things I might have said to her.

JANUARY 1995

Dear Mom,

It is twenty-nine years almost to the day since you died—and nearly that many since I've written. I know you don't need any excuses. There used to be so many letters, sent every week from San Francisco or Cairo or London, postcards, too, from northern lakes and national parks. You saved them all, and if I read them now I hear my voice, my good-daughter voice, telling the good news—how the kids were growing, what we were seeing and learning—all things to make you smile. You always tried to teach me to be cheerful, and like the sundial in the garden, to record only the sunny hours. "If you can't say something nice, don't say anything," you would admonish me. I practiced that with you—at least in my letters, where I could control my smart mouth and quick retorts. And I chose not to write about fears and worries or betray my inevitable moods.

After your death I often found myself composing letters to you, almost forgetting they would not be mailed or written. I'd have you with me in my dreams, too, and carry the illusion of your presence halfway through a busy morning. I think it was after Dad died that the letters and dreams stopped. The kids were older, and so was my marriage.

My life changed. It seemed to speed up, get messy and out of control—not the sort of life I'd have liked to tell you about. At times I felt relieved that you were not around for so much that was foolish and hurtful, so many things you'd have to know and worry over. You would have grieved over my mastectomy, but you'd have hidden your tears. Now, I know that you could have borne it all—would have understood about the divorce, too. And of course, you never expected the kids, or me, to be perfect! So now I could certainly tell you about this broken ankle, a small misery in the scale of things.

What it really comes down to is that I have no need to write letters, for you are with me. In dreams all of us are often together, our varied chronological ages shifting irrelevantly, and we are contemporaries. And in memory, too, you are with me whenever I put more leaves in the dining table so I can feed the whole family at once. You are here when I spoon cranberries into the cut glass dish, the footed one, and put the pickles and olives in the flat one. I feel your presence when I knot a twine trellis for the sweet peas to climb and when I pick violets and breathe in their fragrance—the only scent you ever wore.

Your pleasure in the simple acts of daily living taught me joy. Whenever I touch things that were yours or do something you did, unexpectedly you are with me, and I feel that joy. Then, too, I see you from time to time as I pass a mirror or catch my reflection in some shiny surface. When I recognize you in myself, I don't experience the regrets I hear people joke about—don't sigh for my growing old or lament my heredity. For that fleeting moment, I think that I may have grown into the sort of woman you were, if appearances don't lie.

Appearances are clues. Your smile and gentleness made everyone around you feel good, comforted by what I now recognize as an abiding serenity. That is the quality I hope to achieve. I wish for serenity as I once wished for happiness or adventure, not knowing in what small portions those are available.

My children understand some of this, too, even though we seldom talk about it. You would be proud of them, as always.

But before I close, I need to tell you something that continues to disturb me.

While you were so ill—while you were dying, I was younger than my children are now. You lay so long, so patiently, in that cool, bright room in a hospital called Mercy, and once or twice a day I came to you, bringing Dad and his terrible grief. I do know I tried to look after him as you wished me to; I tried to comfort him. But did I comfort you?

I remember rubbing your swollen feet, brushing your silver hair and tying it back with a blue silk scarf. I sat close to the high, white bed and held your hand in both of mine. But I do not remember what we talked about—except once, when I told you Dad was out in the corridor explaining me to the priest. Evidently the priest wondered, if I lived so near, why he had not seen me at mass. And you said, "Well, that's my fault—if it *is* a fault." And thus you graciously let me off the hook with God.

Mostly, I recall that you never chose to talk about your days and nights in the hospital but always wanted to hear about the world outside of your pain. I feel certain, too, that we often laughed. Each night I kissed your ivory forehead and told you I loved you and left you there alone.

And now I still wonder: did I comfort you—enough? Did I keep you awash in love as my children do me?

Treasie Lou

Connie May Fowler

Lee May, daughters Deidre and Connie May Fowler (Connie is the shorter of the two) at the Travelers Motel The boy walking along the pool's edge is David Terino, the motel owner's son. For several years, Lee and her daughters lived in an old travel trailer at the rear of the motel.

Tampa, Florida; c. mid-1960s

Connie May Fowler was born January 3, 1958, in Raleigh, North Carolina. Shortly after she was born, the family returned to their home in Florida where she has lived ever since. She is the author of three novels: *Before Women Had Wings*, which is the recipient of the 1996 Southern Book Critics Circle Award for fiction; *River of Hidden Dreams*; and *Sugar Cage*. Her essays and short fiction have appeared in *The New York Times Book Review*, *Allure*, *Southern Living*, *Story*, and *Southern Exposure*.

Lenore Monita Looney May was born January 21, 1917, in Grundy, Virginia. She died June 26, 1978, in Tampa, Florida. At various times in her life, Lee May worked as a nurse, a bookkeeper, and a Red Cross volunteer. She was the widowed mother of three.

If Only

Dear Mama,

Every day for the past seventeen years, I have engaged in an act of mournful folly. I try to will you back from the dead. I imagine that we're sitting at our supper table, quietly talking. The smoke from your cigarette swirls through the air, smudging the space between us. You do not look like a woman whose bitterness pockmarked her soul or whose cruel, steel-edged temper destroyed her children's self-esteem. No. In my daydream you are the infinitely inspiring mother who loved Tchaikovsky's symphonies and Jimi Hendrix's guitar riffs, Pablo Neruda's poetry and Hank Williams's lyrics, William Faulkner's fiction and FDR's politics. I reach for your hand and rub it across my cheek. When you were alive, my fear of you prevented me from touching you. But this, after all, is a daydream, a world where anything is possible, where you might—at any moment—lean across the table, kiss me on the forehead, and whisper, "Child, I love you."

I cannot think about your life or death without conjuring Daddy's disparate personalities. Like you, he was so full of contradictions that St. Peter himself probably threw up his hands when he arrived at the pearly gates. When I was a little girl, Daddy would lift me high into the air and tell me I was his sunshine. I remember how tenderly he held your hand in public and how desperately he seemed to depend on you. "I can't make it without you, Lee," I often heard him say. It is still difficult for me to believe that in the years prior to my birth, he broke your nose and knocked out three teeth. Your battered face, however, was a silent and constant testament to his violence.

And even though he mellowed as he grew older, your forgiveness forever ran in fits and starts. Nearly every night after supper, Deidre and I would sit in our bedroom and listen as the two of you argued. With alcohol stoking your anger, you would tell Daddy he was a no-good louse who would never amount to anything and that you rued the day you married him. "I'll try harder, Lee, I swear," he'd promise. But his pledges could not erase your insecurities or heal your memories of broken bones. Your tirade would continue, and when he'd had his fill of insults and threats, he'd get in his Chevy and flee to a bar.

But the second Daddy was out of the house, your emotional pendulum would swing in the opposite direction. In a fit of tears, you would bust into our bedroom and tell Deidre and me that you loved our father so much you couldn't live without him. "I need him," you would say. Then the three of us would pile into the station wagon and barhop, as you called it. We'd slowly drive past honky-tonk after honky-tonk, from Jacksonville Beach north to Neptune, and when we'd finally spy Daddy's car, you'd make Deidre and me go inside and retrieve him. We never really minded venturing into those smoky, juke-music-filled bars because Daddy always seemed downright tickled to see us. He'd flash us his cockeyed grin, introduce his "beautiful girls" to his pals, and then follow us out the door without a peep of protest.

I remember the night he died as if it were yesterday. We'd pulled him out of a bar on Atlantic Beach, and before getting into his car, he stared up at the heavens and said, "My God, Lee May, I love you."

Without an ounce of apparent anger, you laughed merrily, as if you were enjoying the antics of a naughty child. "Henry, let's go home," you said.

Four hours later he was dead. You were beating on his chest, screaming at him to come back, Deidre and I were huddled together in our bedroom, not speaking or crying. Deidre didn't cry much back then, perhaps because by the age of thirteen she'd witnessed so many brawls and been called so many names that hiding her emotions had become a survival technique. As for me, I was only seven years old. I think my meager years provided a measure of emotional protection. With a reporter's detachment, I watched the next few days unfold, dropping not a single tear, gobbling up detail after detail: Aunt Lil cleaned the vomit out of the tub (Daddy had thrown up so violently that his dentures hit the porcelain tub and shattered). You put on his cowboy hat and didn't take it off until the wake, which I wasn't allowed to attend. I even remember how Daddy looked in death. Before the ambulance took him away, while you were on the phone explaining to somebody through your tears that you thought he'd been stricken by a heart attack, I walked down the hallway, peeked into your bedroom, and saw him for the final time. He was so big he looked like Gulliver sprawled on that bed. His eyes were open, aimed toward heaven, and he was smiling. I guess he was glad the struggle was finally over.

Our lives were irrevocably changed. Suddenly, you were a widow with two girls to raise and no one to turn to for help. Your only grown child—the fruit of an earlier marriage—lived three states away and was preoccupied with the vagaries of trying to put himself through college. Jimmy, who had left home before I was born and who, to this day, claims that my daddy, not his, was the single most influential male figure in his life, drove down for the funeral and before returning north told Deidre and me to be good daughters and take care of you. We tried. We really did. But no amount of good behavior was going to bring Daddy back or transform you into a happy woman.

You loved and hated Daddy with even greater vigor and confusion than when he was alive. But then again, he inspired confusion and longing in each of us. We wildly loved a dead man who, you insisted, didn't deserve our devotion. But we couldn't stop ourselves. Daddy had been a man full of good intentions. After he strayed off the course you had set for him or after he committed an occasional despicable deed, he would always plead guilty, sheepishly apologize, and cry like a baby. Maybe that's what we loved about him—his vulnerability, his childlike attempts to please you, his humanness.

With Daddy's passing, we discovered that even though the dead are beyond our touch, they remain fully dimensional, fully capable of affecting our decisions and quandaries. Indeed, Daddy's absence was as painful as his presence sometimes had been. His death plunged us into biting poverty and turned us into a family of wistful dreamers who began far too many sentences with the words, "If only . . ." "If only Daddy hadn't died, we'd live in a nice house." "If only my teacher wouldn't tell me to make Mama a present for Father's Day, I wouldn't feel like such an oddball." "If only your father had believed in life insurance, we wouldn't be this broke." "If only you girls had a father, I wouldn't have to be so hard on you." It was as if Daddy had been the legs of our family, and with him gone, getting around wasn't easy. None of us felt comfortable in the world anymore. It itched and ached—that space where he used to be.

You survived him by nearly a decade and a half, but I am convinced that the liquor which ultimately killed you by turning your liver to stone was actually a symptom of a greater problem. Mama, I think you died of a broken heart. And I think the guilt that your three children have carried around with them since your death needs to be shucked, because the sad fact of the matter is, there was nothing we could have done to heal you. You wanted your husband back and we were sorry substitutes. At every turn, we reminded you of him. Especially me. "You look just like him," you would say. "I can't take it."

I am thirty-seven years old and am just beginning to understand you. As your complexities become less mysterious to me, my capacity for forgiveness deepens and my sorrow grows more profound.

Let me tell you what I've learned:

Mama, you were a woman brimming with secrets, running from madness. At your best, you were smart and witty, generous and levelheaded. But depression fueled by alcohol could, in seconds, rip apart your goodness, and you would become the bad mama, the one I was afraid of, the one who—as she helped me name the clouds—would suddenly gnarl her face, accuse me of being a liar, and slap me. On your good days, you loved liberalism, social causes, and hardcover books. On your dark days, you said charities were run by swindlers, that the haves of the world were too greedy to ever truly help the have-nots, and if I wanted to keep a full head of hair I'd better spend less time reading because books were cluttering my mind "with too many crazy ideas." You were a wife to several men—I am uncertain of how many—and a widow to one. Throughout your life you were frightened and assailable, forever stalked and made worse by a bone-snapping fear of loneliness.

I don't believe you intended for us to remember or take personally the beatings you administered by hand, fist, belt, brush, and broom. The epithets you hurled with lightning speed were not supposed to stick in our hearts as if they were thin silver daggers that snapped in two each time we tried to remove them. I do not believe it was your intention that decades after your death, I would wake from a deep sleep or—in the light of day—be rendered still and scared by the memory of these words: "You're so stupid it makes me sick. I can't believe you came from my womb. You are your father made over—evil and mean. He couldn't stand having a daughter as terrible as you. Yes, it's your fault he's dead. You killed him."

I was fourteen when Deidre got married. She and I still stumble through those strange events—how you played Cupid between her and Phil and how once they announced their engagement you lied, claiming you had cancer, pleading with her to stay home and nurse you, accusing her of betraying you. But Deidre found her backbone and refused to cave in. Her engagement prevailed, your cancer miraculously disappeared, and on her wedding day you were a gracious mother of the bride.

So for six years, until you died, I was the solitary focus of your fury. At the risk of sounding like a simpleton, I have to say I did not deserve what you wrought. I didn't cuss or smoke. I never skipped school. I tried to keep our series of rented hovels clean, but in one of your more puzzling behaviors, you would beg me to leave them dirty, and if I didn't, you'd beat me or, far worse, give me a tongue-lashing. I always made the honor roll, was editor of my school paper, held down a thirty-hour-a-week job, never had sex until I was in college, although you accused me of all manner of sexual misconduct. In retrospect, I wish I had overcome my fear of you and been a wild teenager. At least then your threats, name calling, and beatings would have made sense.

The day you died (the culprit was liver sclerosis, not cancer) I visited you in the hospital and said, "Mama, I just came from school. Dr. Solomon and Sue Gabizo said to tell you they're thinking about you and hope you get well soon."

You looked up at me and said, "Tell them to go to hell. You go to hell."

Those were the last words you spoke to me. And while I am haunted by their inherent despair and hatred, I cannot allow myself to believe in them. I have to trust that you were so near to death your dying brain played a trick on you. Maybe what you meant was, "Connie, dear, I love you."

A year ago, Jimmy, Deidre, and I asked Jimmy's father—the man we thought was your first husband—Colonel Friend, to sit down with a tape player and record his memories of your years together. You see, as time progresses, we don't think about you any less frequently than when you were alive. In fact, our hunger to gain a truer image of you grows.

The tape arrived in the mail with a note from Colonel Friend. He wrote that he had tried to make his recollections exact, had relied on his files to make sure dates and addresses were correct, and he hoped the information and his impressions would help us.

In clear, even tones, this seventy-some-year-old man explained that Daddy was not your second husband but at least your third. Colonel Friend was second or third in line. You were married twice to a man named Woods who shot you when you tried to leave him (you told me the scar that marred your breast and upper left arm was from a stabbing you suffered in a robbery). Colonel Friend had reason to believe that there was an even earlier marriage to someone whose name he did not know, but he couldn't confirm his suspicions. He spoke about your idyllic life together when he was state-side ("She was a good wife and a devoted mother. The other army wives adored her."), and how erratic and bizarre your behavior became each time he was ordered overseas ("She would leave home and wouldn't let anyone know where she was. Sometimes she would move in with strangers. When I was away, she would haul Jimmy all over the country."). He said, "Your mother was a good woman. But she couldn't stand to be alone. Loneliness made her crazy."

Mama, he spun a tale of a lovely, intelligent, hopeful woman who, in the face of loneliness, cracked. Daddy's death seems all the more tragic given the fact that, despite his back-sliding ways, he possessed the ability to make you feel wanted, loved, surrounded. Your random displays of verbal and physical abuse must have been born out of a primal fear of being forsaken. And that is the one constant of your life: your mother died when you were a small child, your father gave you away, various relatives shuffled you from household to household, a series of men tossed you aside as if you were a dirty sock, Colonel Friend's first loyalty was to the army, Daddy died in his prime—you felt forsaken by all of them. And as for your children, at some point each of us would leave the nest. That is any child's destiny. But you interpreted our inevitable march into adulthood as abandonment.

Feeling lost and anchorless, I came home from the hospital the day you died and, with single-minded vengeance, began to clean our Kennedy Boulevard skid row apartment. Spotless floors, dustless sills, sparkling linoleum—in the immediate aftermath of your death, these were my goals. I balled up your soiled bedclothes that draped the couch where you slept (another sign of husband madness: you never again slept in a bed after Daddy died) and threw them in the trash. I moved the couch away from the wall so that I could sweep behind it, and as I pulled, there rang a bright crescendo of breaking glass. All along the wall, in a rubbled heap, hidden from me for months, possibly years, were the symbolic pieces of your broken heart: empty whiskey bottles. The cheap booze had been purchased at the corner liquor store that was frequented by the bums who panhandled in our neighborhood. Later, I learned that while you were still moderately healthy, you would walk down to the corner and buy the booze yourself. But as you became sicker, you would ask various folks living in our building if they would go for you. They all told me they thought they had been doing you a favor. "I was just being neighborly. I felt sorry for her," one tenant explained. "I had no idea she was asking everybody to buy her booze."

Nor did I. To this day, I am ashamed and angry that I did not know. How very sad that, right before my eyes, you drank yourself to death.

Last summer, Deidre, Jimmy, and I ventured to the cemetery where you're buried. What a strange trio we were: we could not find you, and we each wandered in a different direction, searching. I tried to clear my mind and let my deep memory, or my intuition, guide me to that plot of earth that I hadn't visited in years. It worked—after about thirty minutes, I stumbled upon your grave. The headstone was nearly covered with sand. The only word visible was your last name. I called Deidre and Jimmy and began pushing away the sand with my foot, but suddenly an army of ants swarmed into the sunlight. Your gray headstone turned brown as the insects scurried in frenetic waves all across it. I began crying and stomping on your grave, trying to kill the ants. Jimmy and Deidre joined in my crazed jig. But the ants just kept coming. Finally, Jimmy said for us to wait there, that he was going to the store to buy some insecticide.

Deidre and I watched in sad amusement as Jimmy returned with a sack full of sundry potions. First, he emptied a bottle of ammonia across the headstone, then rubbing alcohol, then Pine Sol, and finally he sprayed the entire contents of a can of Raid. I said, "Dear God, Jimmy, if you're not careful you're going to blow her casket sky high."

"I'm killing the bastards, that's what I'm doing," he said.

With the scent of ammonia, alcohol, Pine Sol, and bug spray heavy in the air, we prayed. In an awkward, unintended fashion, we were performing a spontaneous purification rite. We weren't just cleaning your grave, we were struggling mightily to obliterate our family's sins.

Through the years, I have learned that no amount of atonement or forgiveness eases our longing for the dead. And nothing erases our desire to suspend death. If only ghosts had visitation privileges with the living, if only I could wake you from your eternal sleep, I would sit down with you, have a cup of coffee, and we would behave as if we were longtime and decent friends. No harsh words, no recriminations would pass between us— only truth. I would tell you how much I love you, how each of your children yearns for you, and how we ache at the thought of your sad life. We know you were a woman of ascending potential. That's what hurts the most—the knowledge that your good mind and gentle disposition were battered into submission by a tumultuous, fear-studded life. I would say, "Mama, may I have your recipe for chicken and dumplings? What did you do to the dough in your blackberry cobbler to make it so buttery and light? You should be proud of us, Mama. Despite immense odds, each of your children graduated from college. We're married to wonderful people whose natures are just and kind. We're accomplished in our chosen fields. You have grandchildren you never met, but I know you would love them—you would be a doting grandmama. All of your children own houses. We've never gone to jail. As grown-ups, we're closer than we ever were as kids. Yes, each of us battles with the demons of the past, but if you had raised lesser children we would have been destroyed by our collective experience. Listen to me, Mama, we love you."

Sometimes at night, before sleep comes, I close my eyes and see you as I did the last day of your life. I enter your hospital room and offer you greetings from the living. But this time, you do not stab me with an epithet. No. You pull me close. We hug and I am not afraid of you. I feel your frail heart through the sunken wall of your chest and your breath against my ear as you whisper the words that eluded us when you were alive, the words that years after your death I still long to hear: "Sweetheart, you're a good daughter."

With love and respect,

Connie

Joan Frank

Marion Lippe with her daughter Joan
Phoenix, Arizona; c. 1950

Joan Frank, born in Phoenix, Arizona, October 2, 1949, is a San Francisco writer whose short stories appear in national literary journals, and whose essays appear regularly in the *Chicago Tribune*. Her book of collected essays, *Desperate Women Need to Talk to You*, was published by Conari Press. Her short fiction appears in *The Book of Eros* published by Crown.

Marion Lippe was born in New York City in August 1918, moving to Phoenix with husband Robert Frank when he took a teaching position with Phoenix College. Joan was born in 1949; Andrea was born in 1952. Marion died in September 1961.

The Ways Things Go

I will say the word and say the word and say it. For all my years I could not say it and now I will: say it until it loses the cold tang of talking not just to the dead, but to one who died so strangely. *Momma*.

I know so little. I know a few things. Your name, Marion: shapely flow of liquid name, roundly modulated like your voice, and I still hear the melt of it. The voice has never left me. When I turned perhaps ten, your voice told me of searching out an opal pendant for my October birthday, and you mimicked the saleswoman who announced, "I have an opal." As if the saleswoman had been a signifying character in a fairy tale; a Magic Guide materializing. You said "oh-*pal*," pressing the second syllable like *objet*, making this rainbow-filtered pearl an even rarer prize—making a gift of the story; the story itself a numinous talisman.

If you were here as you were, I would bury my face in your Pond's cold cream-and-*Arpège* smelling lap. I would say I was sorry for everything; for your last image of me as a selfish smart-mouth to despair of. Could you have believed, while we lived together, that I meant no harm—not in my deepest heart, where in an eleven-year-old, inchoate dark things crash and tear into each other like angry trapped sharks. How can the woman I became answer for the girl I was, for why it came out so arrogant and cruel? Did I unthinkingly participate in a stoning?

I still curse like a man, and eat like a man. I dress simply, from odd whims. But my good sturdy curves and gentle breasts echo yours. Can a demure mother ever, if she lives long enough, accept her daughter's rough ways? When the daughter rejects the awful yellow-and-black skirt her mother chose for her at Easter—*embarrassing, mawkish, all wrong*—when the mother stalls and waffles on buying the girl her first bra, though the girl longs to look in the mirror and see the telltale white bands visible beneath crisp translucent white of an ironed blouse—how relieved I am you are not alive, relieved so often it would break your heart. I gush. I do not cook. I do not take pains. Some think it is because you left early: I suspect it would not have mattered. But people say I am handsome; womanly. And now I believe it a terrible, important, difficult charge, to guard a bristling brain inside the female form.

I keep a postcard: an old black and white photograph of the artist and iconoclast Tina Modotti. She looks like one of the young Gish sisters, but with none of their retiring innocence. At 23, Modotti sits like Rodin's *The Thinker*, chin in hand; her expression drifts off-camera in private *dolor*, weary, wry, still deeply passionate. She knows too much, demands everything— the whole conversation lucid in that beautiful old-young face.

How would you look, had you lived to now—to seventysomething. Would there be traces of me or Andrie in your delicate sagging face, or would it be happening to you—that which is happening to the mothers of my friends, mothers losing their reason and becoming as children, petulant, frail? Then losing control of their bodies, a grim tailspin unto death—my dear friends dull with exhaustion and disbelief as they go about diapering their mothers, cajoling them to eat, to speak, to remember their names, to rest, mothers who were the standards of crisp or canny or ripe and trenchant womanhood, who achieved children and households and wages and who squared off with men, brilliant or crazy or wounded or monomaniacal men. The taking of the parents of my friends has a largeness to it, like the wide scything of a crop—yet my friends and I see that even in ragged retreat, the body wants so fiercely, so fiercely, to live.

Marion: I am a writer. I have traveled. I make my way. I have begun to write the truth about the family. It is perhaps vulgar. Perhaps if my own life were told as cavalierly not long from now—say by a relative, after my death—in hot flamboyant particulars; the drunks, the affairs, the romantic effusions that alienated people—yet I will argue that, beyond a mottled, shapeless embarrassment, what can it matter? What is the worst of it—a book, an article people may cluck over? Here is something I know, seeped in over what time I have had: To honor a life, to make a life known, must surely be a hopeless project—except perhaps, fractionally, in the work of the writing.

Can you believe: Andrea had *three* fine sons, Caesarean each time—she didn't like that, but steeled herself for the feeling, as she called it, of dogs and cats walking over her stomach. The last one's father lifted him high as soon as he was wrapped, strode him around the room and up and down the fluorescent-lit corridor of Tahoe Forest Hospital, telling the nurses and passers-by, *this is my son.* And each growing-up boy looks like a piece of Daddy or me or Andrie, dark brows, long lashes, same intelligent foreheads; and you'd be amazed, that little lioness who fumed and keened when the sun went in her eyes, standing for photos on the Phoenix lawn before Daddy's Brownie camera, in her husky jeans and yanked-back brown hair, that fierce little creature grew up to be an adoring mother, your youngest tomboy daughter. She tries to give the boys everything she loved: swimming, summer, the lake; finger paints and glue-on sparkle, parades, movies, hamburgers, chocolate. They are good children, if they are wild and demanding. Would you have liked them, we wonder; would you have liked the wild boys, their mountain bikes and martial arts, their swords and capes and computer wars?

Andrie is so tired. I remember your fatigue, as we two girls raced through sprinklers and splashed and shrieked, *Momma watch Mommy are you watching.* It would seem the children flourish exactly in proportion to the adult's depletion; as if a literal tube pumps essence directly from parent into child. She is beloved to me, my tired sister. We struggle to sustain memories, because they go more gossamer each year. She remembers the day of your death differently from me. We struggle for money. I want to help her. I believe you may have only wanted to sleep. I wonder if you'd love us now.

*   *   *

Everything changed after that day of finding you. Whatever we had known was razed, and I became dozens of people, sometimes in succession; sometimes simultaneously. I'm older now than you lived to be, and I wrote once how that felt like working a phantom limb, to live beyond the boundary of one's mother's age at death. Everything is easier now in some ways, much harder in others. Certain kinds of foolishness drop away; others cling. I think about death.

—flinching in the chair like a puppet. I look out the window at the hazed afternoon, full of pale polleny sun as if someone were cleaning their powder puff by banging it out in the air. I phone to beg more time for this letter, bite my lip and twist my hair and feel sleepy, think of candy, television; house cleaning, phone calls, other things I would much rather write. Every possible evasion.

You had a powder puff, and a dark *faux*-tortoiseshell compact that snapped shut with superb, crisp finality. Soft skin and voice; later the voice screamed hoarsely at me, for sassing, which came from shame—my shame for a shabby house and mismatched plastic plates and lumpy white bread. Your voice screeched at me, and then later fury went out of you and instead you began melting away in defeat before our eyes, flesh of your face and body sliding down, light of eyes dulling, until one evening you chose to swallow some pills prescribed for my father, him six feet something, you scarcely five, scarcely a hundred pounds, and somewhere in the midst of druggy sleep your heart slowed, beat once or twice—I think of the last beat or two, weakened reflex, dogged cellular insistence on what it had always supposed it was made to do—and then it stopped. Next morning your skin was light blue, a darker blue rimming the lips, their corners sagged in a way that has never left my vision, the loss of musculature only making more emphatic an expression I had grown more and more accustomed to seeing in those last years.

I learned later. I wrote people when Daddy died, when I was twenty-four, and they wrote back they felt I was old enough to know. About his compulsive infidelities (a colleague said, "It was as if he had something to prove"), your deepening loneliness, so

few friends in the desert town, just two noisy little girls to chap-
erone, day in day out. No networks. No hotlines. No recourse.

We left town. I think sometimes of the gossip. *Did you hear
about Bob and Marion—*

I never ceased to love him, even after.

Shall I tell you about my hands.

Nothing I can do about them.

They read, for better or worse, as such a blueprint of the
soul—like light in the eyes, or timbre of the voice—but also as a
potential expression, or measure, of their owner's femininity.
Alas, my hands are meaty (Daddy), shapely (you), visibly ten-
doned and veined (you), with a fine down of interstitial hair
along the fingers (Daddy). What were called freckles are now
called age spots. They look lived in—and in spite of everything,
I've grown to like them. They are womanly; capable. The fingernails rarely last at fashionable length.

You polished yours in the early years, years before you began
to shut down. The polish matched the lipstick, blood red, gleaming red tinged with blue, not fire engine but Chinese enamel, or
dark cherry. The lipstick smelled like roses, the polish like fierce
distilled spirits. Dressed in turquoise-and-silver Mexican jewelry,
the conch belts, the jade earrings, the brilliant squaw dresses
with iridescent rickrack along the hems; full dirndl ensembles
setting off your black hair—and those reds, seen and smelled
together upon your lips and hands, took my breath away.

In the beginning there must have been some happiness.

I saw a photo of a morning-after-sleepover, you and my father
in bathrobes, mugging with another couple on someone's back-
porch, amid the just-delivered, shining-full milk bottles. Daddy
has a sweater tied over his head and a cigar jutting from his grin
at an insolent angle; he brandishes one creamy milk bottle aloft,
like quarry: your black hair spills forward over your shoulder in
a long disheveled braid, you grin into the morning sun, gracefully acceding to the fun; full of sweetness; pretty teeth gleaming
with wry irony.

I look at my hands. As a girl, I longed for them to be the girl-
kind one saw in magazine pictures, delicate pink, perfect ovals,
shellac-shine drawn in an unwavering straight line out to the
precise tips. Women on posters and in movies that some men

like very much still flaunt long hard shining nails, nails that practically curve like claws; toenails, too, flashing earrings and necklaces and gleaming lipstick, eyeshadow; the whole business tires me, tires me just to recite.

My hands now have those veins forming at the top, which yours did; also the brown spots seeming to betray one in an age so adjudging of our relationship to time—as if time were a conveyor belt, and our position on it something we had stupidly reckoned wrong—inflicting on women a harsh, automatic indictment. That is one thing I learned since you left.

I sat in the big easy chair the Christmas after you died, twelve years old, still stupid with inability to name what had happened, trying to feel as badly as I could that you could not have Christmas with us. The lights were pretty, the fire crackled from its gas jet in the rented suburban home, the others had gone away somewhere for a time, perhaps shopping for presents. I concentrated, but could not make myself cry: finally climbed out of the chair and wandered away. Someone once suggested that moments after being cut down from the hangman's noose, you only wonder then whether to go to the toilet or get a sandwich. But my dearest friend says that is not always the case—that Dostoevsky wrote, after his own false confrontation with a firing squad, straight from the realization he was alive, alive.

Please. If you could know this: It is a thing I can forgive, the need to run away.

It has always worked for me. It worked for you.

The bafflement has always been, wondering what you'd planned for us, your little girls.

I think you were too tired to plan anything anymore. I've been that tired.

My hands, Marion, have a gentleness and a symmetry, a capable tenderness that is yours. I know because I memorized yours, their smell and smoothness and strength. In the photograph I sit before the morning paper, your sure arm around me, your hand grasping the paper while firmly enclosing the blonde-feathered baby in your lap who reads along with you, game to decipher the mysterious markings. Ah God, how I have looked for you! How I have longed for even a moment's laying down of the burden, in the arms of my mother: the refuge some still enjoy. I saw a movie in which a young athlete lost his game, walked straight into his mother's arms, and wept there freely, and though she could not protect him, could not help him tame the anarchic world, and the child knew it, yet he sought solace nonetheless in that familiar bosom, familiar warmth and smell—the embrace was theirs, a momentary bulwark, and in those moments the understanding seemed almost that of lovers.

The fingers have interstitial hair, very lightly; they are a bit too dense, and that is Dad's part, when he would drum out complex jazz background riffs on his big desk made of a door. Andrie has the same hands; I see our hands in photographs and they do not change, and when I look at mine I think, *this is the thing about a mother and father,* though their living forms are dead: We can see each flowing in the very shape of our own living hands. We carry the two in our thirdness.

I left college early and joined the Peace Corps and went briefly to West Africa. I can speak and write French; I know that would please you. Daddy told his classes; I sat in on one in the very back, hot with celebrity. Daddy remarried a glamorous woman you were shy of at cocktail parties, who told me you once offered your place to her beside our father in a car. She did not have an easy time, because he drank. I don't know that he hit her, but they yelled sometimes, and toward the end, before he died, they slept in separate rooms, both too tired to go out and start over. It was something I swore then I would never do in my adult life; now I think it the mildest of arrangements. I wonder what you would say now to a world in which women begin to tell and tell, to tell everything and to ask everything. Laws are made to help women, but it's still crazy, and often I am thankful I was not born a moment sooner because I am fairly certain that a moment sooner could have buried me, as it did you: at least the evidence for this is strong—at the same time I would have given anything for the changes to have come earlier, perhaps to save you; perhaps to help you want to save yourself, though this may oversimplify, this may romanticize.

Marion Lippe, who married wavy-haired Robert Frank when you were both secretaries back East during the war (It is still *back East* and *out West*, still!): You were very small, delicately curved and full-breasted, and he massaged your feet. I remember your breasts, the cool pale pear-shaped meat of your buttocks when you dressed at the closet door—surely familiar and compliant to you as old friends. To attempt to envision the demise of that flesh is dizzying, as a child deliberately limns with her tongue the gummy crater of the lost tooth, or at night alone in bed seeks to grasp a notion of infinite universe. How could what was my mother's flesh go blue then black then burn and the ashes be dumped somewhere where ashes are not claimed? Bodies, yours and Daddy's, once sturdy and warm and freckled, pulsing quietly at wrist and throat and ankle as mine does now: mystery of the fleshly container, whose limbs travel fondly along as if they always would! When at times I dream that death approaches in one guise or other (someone threatens to kill me, or I am told I carry terminal illness), my panic is squalid, graceless, ignoble. I believe nothing anyone says about what happens after death. Yet we address the dead as if something did.

You grew up loving homemade blackberry jam on fresh-baked bread, the middy blouses you wore to school, MacDowell's "To a Wild Rose"—under the domineering Bertha, and a man named Bernard, whose scowling snapshot is all we were to know of him, except the rumor our stepmother cited, long after you died, that he too had taken his own life. Bertha Lippé frightened us, big and fleshy, with a nasal Jewish whine, emerging at once from the airplane at Sky Harbor Airport spewing gossip and complaints; you drove us stiffly home, we little girls in the backseat mute with fear, your hands tight on the wheel of the turquoise '49 Ford, your face, lovely high cheekbones and red lipsticked mouth tensed as they were in the last driver's license photo, as if before a firing squad.

I want to say this.

You were born in 1918, two years before Daddy; you died in 1961, September, Labor Day. August 10 was your birthday and so you were indeed forty-four at death, as I was told. I am forty-five as I write this, and so have ventured out beyond the limit of your endurance, onto a kind of transparent new branch of the tree. Understanding this suddenly, my eyes fill as the car emerges from the tunnel to face, from cliff height, the opening-out panorama of the city of San Francisco, where I live, a charmed kingdom on its fist of land; both bridges festooning, connective arteries across the brisk blue bay. A fat freighter scoots rapidly out to sea in that extraordinary late-afternoon light, polleny gold blanching the pastel faces of the skyline, windsurfers buzzing the choppy surface of the water from that distance like mosquitoes, the city in many ways as beautiful as it was when you so loved it. I gaze, and recall a Lombard Street hotel room at night during a family vacation, hearing my father commence sudden intense sex with you. As a young girl knowing but not knowing what was happening, what it meant with him saying roughly at the end, "That'll help you sleep." Knowing also when I heard you murmur, in wonder, "So beautiful," that this was something you had decided to believe.

I am looking for models, Marion—women who are going on with grace and keen attention. I am tired, daunted, but more than anything I can imagine I do not want anyone to have to find me blue, cold, heavy and dense and unresponsive to the shake of the upper arm, the choked cry. My tears are not for death, which of itself must surely give reprieve, but in prayer to the No-Thing a rational adult petitions in this century, not to ever, ever let it happen to someone I love, to have to find anyone that way.

I have fancied it a queer, elegant, harrowing reversal: when out from a young woman is pulled a wrinkled girl-baby whose face clearly mirrors the old woman she will grow to be—*that* is the snapshot, the cosmic identification photo—as the prune-faced baby unfolds into the vital woman who will nurse her withering elder. It's all very rhythmic, except that I have no daughter. It is not that I did not want children. It was that no man was ready at the time they were ready to come, and I knew better than to attempt it alone. It was never my wish to trick any man, and I had seen enough, and come from enough, not to bid for a future in chains.

But I have seen the photo of my own newborn face, and so I know already the countenance of my extreme old age.

About men, I cannot wish to sow divisions, nor turn away. I still imagine we must proceed with belief (even if bundled in the basement of the heart, amid the yellowed papers, cards, and tokens)—belief in a basic appeal to frankness, to an eye-to-eye stating of what is the case. I imagine, despite aridity, sorrow, despite what happened to my own mother, inflicted by my own father, that not only is it possible to make contact: it is still worthy and compelling, as we walk around in these skins, this fragile sheath of tissue and piping, to *desire* to make contact. Had you lived to see women become strong, Marion, and lauded for it, then I wonder how it might have changed you, and how it may have changed all of us, had we all been able to continue together. But knowing even what little I now know of the ways things can go, I can divine very much of how it was: for you; for my maddened lonely father; for us heedless hapless little girls. And I could no more be angry with you for any of this, for how it went, for what you had to do, than be angry with the moon and sun and tides. It was so. Even the nonbeliever invokes blessing, at the last. You were my tender mother, whom I did in fact, beneath and beyond whatever came before and after, love.

Joan

Lynn Freed

Anne Freed, mother of Lynn Freed
South Africa; c. 1932

Lynn Freed, on her wedding day
Greenwich, Connecticut; 1967

SUZANNE SZASZ

Lynn Freed was born on 18 July, 1945, in Durban, South Africa. She came to New York as a graduate student in English Literature, receiving her Ph.D. in 1972. Her essays, memoirs, and short stories have appeared in *Harper's, The New Yorker, Story, Southwest Review, The New York Times,* the *Washington Post, Newsday, Mirabella, Elle, Vogue, House Beautiful, House & Garden,* and *Vogue.* She is the recipient of fellowships and grants from the NEA, the Guggenheim, Rockefeller and Lannan Foundations. Her novels include *Home Ground, The Bungalow* and, most recently, *The Mirror* (Crown, 1997). She lives in the town of Sonoma, California, and has one daughter.

Anne Freed was born Annie Moshal on 19 January, 1908, in Durban, South Africa. She was the seventh of eight children born to Jewish Lithuanian immigrants. She attended the Maris Stella Convent in Durban, distinguishing herself at an early age both as a singer and an actress. When she left school, she went to London to attend the Royal Academy of Dramatic Art and the Royal College of Music (singing). She returned to Durban in 1933, where she founded her own speech and drama academy, produced stage plays, sang in concert, and was active in radio drama. In 1935, she met Harold Freed, just back from Cambridge University, and cast him as the lead in "Daddy Longlegs." During the sixty wild years of their marriage, they acted together both on stage and radio, or she directed and he acted. Until she lost her sight at the age of eighty-two, she worked a good ten hours a day.

Call Home

Oh, Ma!

Surely you realise that I am the victim of your own mixed metaphor?

When I was twenty-one, I phoned to ask you whether I should marry a man about whom I had my doubts.

"What doubts?" you said.

"I don't want to be stuck," I said, "and I want to travel."

"Travel!" you shouted. "For God's sake. When are you going to come to grips with your itchy feet?"

As phrases go, this one had real power. It carried both the horror of life as a bag lady and the seduction of serious intentions—a proper education, a husband, children, a house, and

145

lots of things to put in that house. As to my feet, my idea of travelling had nothing to do with walking. Nor with your hostels, backpacks, sensible shoes that could double for a night on the town. What I wanted—what I had wanted ever since I could remember—was the vague delight of being a stranger in a strange place. Someone just arrived, just about to leave, and always with somewhere to go home to.

"Marry him first," you suggested, "and *then* travel."

Clearly the home I'd grown up in—your home, our home—was wearing thin. I'd have to come up with another. But how could I know that the man who was promising me a houseboat on the Mediterranean, trips down Africa in a Land Rover, would come to embrace phrases like "discretionary income" and "fiscal responsibility?" That he himself would take on Home as a hobby, fill the house we'd bought with his creations in knotty pine and butcher block?

Every evening, every weekend, he descended like a woodchuck to his saws and sanders in the basement. With a heap of degrees in a job market run dry, I took up carpool and dinner party, factory outlet, sewing machine. Our sweet Edwardian house succumbed to bold earth tones, flokati rugs, giant pillows, Marimekko, Arabia-ware, and a daily dose of *Sesame Street*.

"You sound a little bored, darling," you said. "Why don't you come home for a holiday?"

But he objected to the very thought of my going home. Home, he said, was where he was. In America. Anyway, he wanted to go to a family camp in some mountains nearby. And so we went. We stayed in a cabin with a tentlike roof, and had our meals, kibbutz style, at long tables—some for adults, some for children. Every day, the children were organized into groups and taken away. The adults could choose their own groups. There was water polo, sailing, hiking, volleyball, pottery, macramé. I'd never been much good at Group, so I tried Sitting on Steps of Cabin with Book. After a while, though, I found it hard to breathe. However much I tried, the air wouldn't go any deeper than my shoulders. I thought it must be the dust. Dust billowed as one walked. It lodged in one's clothing, up one's nostrils, between one's teeth.

The camp doctor looked and listened. Then he let his stethoscope drop. "It has nothing to do with the dust," he said. "You're suffering from unhappiness. I suggest you go home."

Soon after we got home, you phoned. "Darling," you said, "I have an idea for you. You're always writing this and that. Why not turn your hand to writing a best seller? Writers can live anywhere in the world, you know. Anywhere they like."

But I'd just got into law school. Law school was the thing women did in the seventies. Several friends had taken it up, together with tweed suits, sensible pumps, and a multitude of high-minded causes. As a lawyer, I thought, I'd make some discretionary income of my own. I'd use it to travel indiscriminately, wherever I wanted to go.

His ideas were different. With my income as a lawyer, he pointed out, and when our child had finished college, our discretionary income would rise. And then, when we retired, we'd do nothing but travel. Travel here, travel there, life would be a festival of travel.

That's when I turned down law school and became a travel agent. Three nights a week, I went to travel school. I learned how to write an airline ticket from Kalispell to Nairobi, how to work out minimum connecting times between the airports in Milan, and where to find a walking tour of Patagonia. During the day, I wrote a novel about a woman who gave up a career in medicine to take up the piano. She took a lover. And then went off to Mexico with him. And then came back again to find that her husband had left her.

After a year, I sold my novel. I also began to travel in earnest. I went to ancient cities and modern cities, to remote tropical islands, modern tourist traps, rain forests, mountain ruins, on ocean cruises and river cruises. I stayed in hotels and palaces, beach bungalows, a converted convent fifteen thousand feet above sea level. Usually, I travelled alone. I never travelled light. I never had the right shoes.

"Darling," you said, "is it sensible to leave a husband and go waltzing off on your own all over the world? Is it wise?"

You didn't have to ask. Every time he drove me to the airport, grim at the wheel, I suffered loss of breath. I wanted to turn back, to give up, to give in.

But I went anyway, and I came back again. I wrote a novel about a woman who leaves her husband and sons to go to Africa with a lover. I wrote another about a girl who grows up in Africa and leaves to live in England. Coming back from a trip, my house always seemed smaller. It also seemed dark and cold, lonely and remote. So did my life.

You sent me a newspaper clipping, a quote by an Australian Aborigine. "A house is a good thing to have," said the Aborigine. "You can lock it up and go and live anywhere you please."*

I put the clipping on the fridge door. By the time it had browned and curled, he had left and taken his furniture with him. The house was sold and I bought another for myself. As soon as I had settled my things into the new house, I locked it up and went to live on the other side of the country. Then I came back again.

"Darling," you said, "what kind of life can you be leading, living all alone? Living out of a suitcase like a gypsy?"

This time, I laughed. After eighteen years, I had begun to understand, to accept the natural affinity between travelling and the fiction of my life. Between travel and fiction itself. Playing stranger in strange places—riding across deserts, eating crocodile in vast colonial dining rooms, sitting on verandahs where no English is spoken—gave me the perspective of other worlds from which to examine my own. Estrangement, I realised, was a necessary ingredient of my work. Over the years, I'd begun to feel more or less strange everywhere. I also felt more or less at home. Permanently displaced. Free to come and go at last.

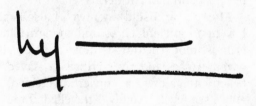

*The quotation is from *The Creative Explosion* by John E. Pfeiffer, Harper & Row, 1982, New York.

Carol Frost

**Twin sister, Suzanne; mother, Renee Kydd;
and Carol Frost—at their grandparents' home**
Westford, Massachusetts; c. 1954

Carol Frost was born in Lowell, Massachusetts, February 28, 1948. She is the author of five full-length books, including *Day of the Body* (1986) and *Chimera*, which was named runner-up for the 1990 Poet's Prize. Her other awards include a Pushcart Prize, sole honorable mention for an Elliston Award, and two NEA fellowships. She is writer-in-residence at Hartwick College and founder and director of the Catskill Poetry Workshop there; she has also taught in the Warren Wilson MFA Program for writers; at Bread Loaf Writers Conference; and at the Vermont Studio Center. A recent collection, *Pure*, was published by Northwestern University Press (TriQuarterly Books) in 1994. TriQuarterly Books published *Venus and Don Juan* in the fall of 1996.

Renee Kydd was born in Vienna, Austria, December 24, 1928, the daughter of Bertha and Rudolph Fellner, a World War I hero. Her two brothers, Edmund and Otto, were killed during World War II. She attended the University of Vienna briefly during the war and immigrated to the United States in 1947. Her favorite Austrian poet is Nicholaus Lenau, 1802–1850. She has worked in real estate, jewelry and cosmetics, and furs. She has also been a restaurant manager, a model, a dance instructor, and a health spa instructor. She has two other children besides the twins and six grandchildren. Presently she lives and works in central Florida, where she swims a mile every day.

A Secret Gladness

So they loved as love in twaine,
Had the essence but in one,
Two distincts, Division none,
Number there in love was slaine
—SHAKESPEARE

Dear Mum,

Adventuresome and sensual, you seemed unlike any of the other mothers—mothers whose daughters held less interest for me as playmates than boys. Boys played baseball and let me play the infield. Boys wore dungarees and stood on the playground swings to pump. I remember the cold chains in my hands as I stood on the wooden seat, bending backwards, and the world of trees upside down as I tried to go over the bar. I remember falling

150

and hurting my chin in the cinders, you picking me up, the white ceiling and bright light in my face as the doctor sewed seven stitches. I had a dress on that day, but many days I wore dungarees. Like the boys, until I was nine, I went shirtless because I wanted to and you let me. I can remember the wind on my bare chest afternoons as I ran in the sun as vividly as the numb pulling sensation of the thread as the doctor sewed.

The early physical world, intense and bright, I associate with you—the taste of lemon curd, the fingertips of blossoms from the bleeding heart still hanging from their stem and dropping up and down in my hand with a breeze, satin for our polka dot dresses—yours, mine, and Sue's—as it slid and bunched when we sat together on Nana's couch so Gramps could take our picture. My favorite secret recollection is of baking a potato in a fire. I must have sneaked it from the pantry or known I shouldn't be in that rubbled lot to have the delicious sense of guilt I recall I had. The potato was so black and moist and white. The fire was a thrill then, as in memory. And only last year did I find out from Friedel, my cousin, that we had made the fire together in Vienna. That she had taught me to swear in German. I must have been three.

How odd that even my secrets belonged, in a sense, to you—more to you than to Sue, though she is my twin and must have been with me in the playground, in the marshes where we skated and ran bare chested in the summer, in the bombed-out lot in Vienna. Or is it always that way for the very young—to be so in love with Mummy? Why is Sue absent from my recollections? I think it may be because though you called us "the girls" when you spoke about us, you acknowledged our separation, as if after the first division into two eggs we had ended our perfect sameness. I know I wanted to be *my* self and not half of one or even one of two, even as I longed to have a strawberry birthmark like Sue. I don't really know what you said or did to help me grow fiercely, if quietly, into my own ways. Perhaps there was nothing overt. But I felt in your eyes in sole possession of my present and future. It stands to reason that the past should be the same.

Though it may seem whimsical, I've wondered if in some way my being an identical twin and feeling both alike and very different from the girl who dressed like me until sixth grade didn't illuminate for me the central task of a writer. There can't be a direct correlation between being a twin and being a writer (there are many examples of one twin in a pair being a writer—Derek Walcott, Philip Levine), but writer and twin have things in common. A writer is one whose imagination must contend with paradox and reconciliation. Coleridge tells us that the imagination "reveals itself in the balance or reconciliation of opposite or discordant qualities," among them sameness and difference. For twins this can be a problem or magic—for them the word *twin* is double, but their natures are single. A mother cannot solve this: the paradox is the solution. So it is in poetry.

When a human paradox is badly solved, souls may be hurt; so it was with us, Mother. After so much closeness, separation followed. Did too much love cause the years when "love was slaine"? I no longer want to know. I think I can hold in my memory now a balance of joyful and sad days with Suzanne and with you. If you, and she, gave me the qualities I needed to be a poet, practicing imagination's magic and invisible power, as I believe you did, then poetry and imagination's pursuit have given me what more I needed for our pasts and our enduring love to be acknowledged. Though I write almost no poetry to or about family, with no dedications, confessing nothing, all the lines are, in some essence, for you—and Sue. I can't say fully how. Or why. It's been a secret gladness for many years.

000
XXX   Love,

Carol

Deborah Galyan

*Norma Joan Jones,
age seventeen*
Indiana; 1946

*Deborah Galyan,
age five*
Indiana; 1960

Deborah Galyan was born in 1955 in Bloomington, Indiana. In the fall of 1960, after a brief, age-inappropriate discussion of the issues, her kindergarten class voted to elect John Fitzgerald Kennedy over Richard Milhous Nixon, mostly on the basis of their photographs. In recent years, her fiction has appeared in *Best American Short Stories, 1996, The Missouri Review, The North American Review, Chicago Review,* and elsewhere; her story, "The Incredible Appearing Man," won *The Missouri Review*'s 1995 Editors' Prize in fiction. She is currently at work on a novel, and lives in Provincetown, Massachusetts, with her husband and son, Dylan, age four, who will soon go to kindergarten, too.

Norma Joan (Jones) Galyan was born on a small farm in southern Indiana in 1929. Growing up in the 1930s, she remembers bathing outdoors in a galvanized tub and the first time she saw white "store-bought" bread. She remembers hunger. She went to work in 1944, without finishing high school, and worked every day until she retired in 1990, despite debilitating arthritis. She married, had two daughters, and taught them both to read before they went to school. Somehow, she insisted that they believe in justice and in hope, even when she, herself, could not.

Boxes

Dear Mom,

I've been making boxes for you. I know you don't need anything. None of us needs another thing. We can both agree on that. But these boxes are different, you will see. I've been making boxes for you ever since a man I once knew took me to see Joseph Cornell's boxes at the Art Institute of Chicago. (He was a man I should never have been with, I know that now, but that is another story I've always meant to tell you.)

It was January. The lions guarding the Institute were bearded with ice. (He was not the sort of man who would take his kids to Disney World, he was not a *kind* man, but there I was, nevertheless, standing beside him in the flat winter light of Chicago.)

I had made my bed, and I was going to have to lie in it.

I stood for hours looking down on Cornell's constructions. I stood for hours looking down on the *white metaphysics of ephem-*

era, as Cornell described the contents of his boxes. The problem, as he saw it: How to contain the uncontainable? A mood evoked by music? *No words can ever hold.* The glance of a stranger could haunt him for years. *Young girl in red coat church quiet mood.* Could memories be recovered and preserved? *Cubes of ice in a deep blue velvet box.* The *flotsam and jetsam of childhood.* Can such things be dried and pressed? *Collage* = <u>*life*</u>, he wrote. The ethereal Luna Moth pinned under glass. Captured emotions, like elixirs in glass vials.

Ruby red = regret.

Emerald green = desire.

Another clue: Blue is always Mystery.

The laughing children in the shrubbery . . . *the moment in and out of time,* T. S. Eliot wrote. Joseph Cornell got it right away.

(The man I stood next to in the Art Institute was a painter from California. The man I stood next to was the wrong man, I know that now. At the time, I was burning for him, burning the busy orange fire of well-banked coal, burning like Joan of Arc, under my powder gray coat. Every so often he would look at me, and the fire would pop and spatter in the fat silence of the museum.)

I stood for hours looking down on Cornell's *Penny Arcade Portrait of Lauren Bacall,* 1946. I know you wouldn't recognize the *white metaphysics of ephemera* if it walked up and tried to snatch your purse. Who would? We can both agree on that. But listen: Think Lauren Bacall. Think 1946. Dad—in the army, bulldozing what was left of Germany. After a while, he is reduced to a postcard in the mail every other week—curled at the edges—a ruined fortress on the Rhine.

Me—nothing but a smudge. A smoke ring in a dream.

You—alone. Waiting for the rest of your life to happen. Waiting tables at the Book Nook in Bloomington, Indiana, a little college joint where Hoagy Carmichael came to play the terrible upright piano. Down the street after work with a four-dollar paycheck, into the Princess Theater. You (forever) disappearing into the Princess Theater, alone, waiting for the rest of your life to happen.

Joseph Cornell got it right away. Lauren Bacall in profile. *The moment in and out of time.*

How one look, one gesture, could stop time.

It was an epiphany, Mom, standing in the Art Institute, looking at Cornell's boxes next to a man who made me burn. No wedge of cynicism. No irony, at last. Just you and me and the *white metaphysics of ephemera.* I knew then, what I could give you. I knew then, how I could show you that nothing is ever lost between us, how everything you have ever given me I have saved. I've been making boxes for you. I'm not yet sure which of them are finished.

Let me show you. Look.

Box #1: "The Accident of Childhood"

Construction: simple pine box (12″ × 12″ × 2 5/16″) with symmetrical compartments, three across, three down.

In the first three compartments:
Three identical photographs of you, 1937, the better to study the face of your eighth year. A white violet of a face with Indian summer eyes. A dimestore locket at your throat, made radiant by you.

In the fourth:
Scattered biscuit crumbs and the bleak tin cup of lard, smeared on the feathers of a paper peacock. The Great Depression, smeared over your childhood.

In the fifth:
Shred of a green-and-red striped sock, pinned on a velvet background. One of a pair you desired more than anything else in the world. *More than anything else in the world.* A pair of striped socks. They charmed you like witches across the road. A few scattered kernels of corn and gravel. The forbidden road. Indiana, 1937. Dried kernels of a poor child's dream, run down by a truck.

In the sixth:
The toy truck pauses (forever) on the wooden wedge above the shattered crystal bird. Dashed on the floor—it had to be broken. Hours spent putting it back together—toothpicks tipped in glue. While I worked, I thought: You are proof things can be put back together. Glass and bone. But it is never the same after these things have been broken. The cracks are always visible. It is never the same. Either you think the cracks are beautiful, or not.

In the seventh:
A family photograph. Summer, 1938. Your place remains empty. Five brothers and sisters surround the absence of their middle sister, glued to a blue horizon. Ten black eyes glittering in their skulls, feverish with their own survival. *Flushed out like starlings in the path of the truck,* you remembered, *spilling their cries all over the road.*

In the eighth:
A blue sphere balanced on a wire. The days and months you remained suspended, in and out of life.

In the ninth:
Seen from behind a magnifying glass, in a velvet presentation box intended for a pearl, the tiny mauve egg of a hummingbird. Me. I have always feared that you had to be broken, so that I could be whole.

Box #2: "Domesticity and Comets"

Construction: blue Tupperware container (22″ × 16″ × 4 1/4″), divided into twelve compartments, lined in wax paper.

Isn't it funny, Mom?
Isn't it funny? All those little cans of *Comet*?
You wonder how I got them all in there?
All those little plastic cans of *Comet*?
How many cans of *Comet*, Mom?
The little plastic ones. The *personal Comets*, Mom.
The little plastic pink, green, blue ones.
The Comets I begged for at the grocery store,
Week after week.
The *individual Comets*, Mom. The *luxury Comets*.

If you had listened to me, every sink and tub
in our little white house would have had its own
personal, individual, luxury
Comet.

You would not listen to me, Mom.
You always bought *economy* size.
You bought it without hesitation.
You bought it with resolve.
You bought it with a sense of duty.
You would not entertain the idea.
The idea of dainty personal pastel *Comets*
for our sinks and tub.

I thought you had no imagination, Mom.
I thought you had no idea for your life.
No *theme*.

If it was what we were meant to be, Mom,
if we were meant to be the *ones,*
the ones who made the rounds,
to the grocery, to the bank,
the rounds of bread and meat,
round and round the tub and toilet,
round the sink with can after can,
if that was *it*, Mom,
if we were meant to be *The Cometeers,*
then we needed imagination.
We needed vision, at the very least,
a craving
for the kind of *luxury*
that only individual *Comets* could provide.

You wouldn't listen to me, Mom,
when I knew what we needed.
You looked at me like I was nuts.

Isn't it funny, Mom?
How this box has all those luxury *Comets* and
photographs of comets scissored out

of *Scientific American*?
It was a long time before I knew the difference
between *Comet* and comet.
A long time before I knew about
Scientific American comets,
there being no room for lazy,
nondisinfecting comets in our house.

I thought if we were who I *feared* we were . . .
I knew we needed a *theme*.
I put a few more things in this box:
Over here, the red rubber jar opener.
(Ruby red = regret)
You could never open a jar without it,
after arthritis made your hand a claw.
The legacy of your childhood accident.
The shattered crystal bird, again.
The icy blue mothballs rattling around,
slowly vaporizing.
Something about mothballs and
the icy blue smell of *Ben Gay*.
Something about the smell,
Something about the *Ben Gay* was like
the blue velvet space between stars.

No words can ever hold.
The icy blue space in your childhood
that made your hand a claw.

We needed *glamorous* aspirin, Mom. We needed *Bayer*.
A pink plastic aspirin dispenser next to the *Dixie cups*.
Fast-acting relief. *Glamorous* relief.
Relief enough to straighten your crippled hands
and force them into Playtex gloves
and do the dishes with Joy.
I thought if we were who I *feared* we were . . .
I knew we needed a *theme*.

But isn't it funny, Mom?
All those *Comets*?
How many cans of *Comet*, Mom?
I made this box for you.
I didn't want you (or me) to forget.
The *luxury* of it all.

I am (forever) looking down on Cornell's boxes and dreaming
up my own. I know you wouldn't recognize the *white metaphysics of ephemera* if it walked up and tugged your sleeve. Who
would? We can both agree on that. But Joseph Cornell was on to
something. *Collage = life,* he wrote.

Mechanic of the ineffable, somebody called him. Carter Ratcliff
I think. (No, not the man in the museum. His name was some-

thing else. He was the wrong one, I know that now. How could I, Mom? God knows. We can both agree on that. He wasn't even *kind*. He was from *California*. Whoever heard of such a thing? He liked to say cruel things that were also true, so that I did not feel justified in my offense. Another story, entirely.)

I had made my bed, and I was going to have to lie in it.

Box #3: "Lost and Found"

Construction: unfinished oak box (15" × 11" × 3 5/16") with cabinet drawers built into the bottom row for objects not meant to be visible. Compartments for visible objects lined in dandelion fluff. All visible objects are arranged left to right and chronologically, in order of original loss.

In the first compartment:
A tattered tintype of a dead baby brother, curled in his coffin like a leaf. 1934. Eyes shut tight against the white winter light.

In the second:
The cracked porcelain head of your favorite doll, dashed against a chestnut tree and broken by your brothers. One eye, open. The other, shut. Circled by rotting chestnuts, as planets circle a sun.

In the third:
A snow scene paperweight. A winter's night. A pine tree peppered with snow. Stars *like cubes of ice in a deep blue velvet box*. Like the picture you painted in a one-room school in Indiana, 1935. (The bleak tin cup of lard, again.) The teacher said you could be an artist. *Ought* to be an artist, the teacher had said, claw hands forced into your Playtex gloves, doing the dishes with Joy.

In the fourth:
A dimestore locket with a broken clasp, mother-of-pearl and a single garnet. Cheap, made radiant by you. Ripped from your neck by your husband (my father) at the apex of an argument. 1961. Containing a tiny photograph. Of him. And more.

And more in the drawers below—painted an uncertain green—*for objects not meant to be visible.*

Tattered maps of continents named for sisters and brothers who drifted away.
The lost continents of Homer and Donald, of
Bernadette, Suzanne and Constance.
Misplaced compasses.
Unremembered contours of the bodies of children
—the lost topographies of Eden.
Uncharted regions of disappointment,
some the size of Greenland.
And more.

There I was, (forever) looking down on you in the fat silence of the museum.
Confusing you with Lauren Bacall.
You—shimmering like a star, burning in the Book Nook, 1946.
Hoagy Carmichael had just left the stage.

Now you know: nothing is ever really lost between you and me. Each thing you thought you had lost blew like dandelion fluff over the meadows of your regret and sprouted inside me. Whenever I think of you and me, I think of *Comet* and comet. Ruby red = regret. The ethereal Luna Moth pinned under glass. The map of your love, heavily creased, with its smudged legends of silence. The lines of your palm and their points of correspondence. The lines of our palms running out to the icy blue space between stars, crossing at the heart of heaven. I work at you as an astronomer works at a dark mass in deep space. I study grainy photographs. I theorize your origins. I calculate the distance. Like *Scientific American*, I work at you.

I'm making boxes for you. Some of them are never finished. The work goes on. It goes very slowly. Life intrudes. A loving husband and a beautiful child. The man for whom I once wrongly burned vanished in and out of time. Few artifacts remain:

A key to a room in the *Hotel de l'Etoile*.
From California: vials of yellow dust.
A picture postcard of a Medici prince, seen through the distance of dark blue glass. Message on the back: *How to contain the uncontainable?*
Another story I've always meant.
We have made our beds.

Some of the boxes I started for you, I have ended up finishing for myself. I chart the maps, record the points of correspondence seen through the distance of dark blue glass. I build the apparatus. The work goes on. The work of love goes on until, as Cornell wrote, *all the enigmas have been canceled out.* I've been making boxes for you. I'm not yet sure which of them are finished. Another clue: Blue is always Mystery.

Love (forever),

deb

(The author wishes to acknowledge Mary Ann Caws's fine book *Joseph Cornell's Theater of the Mind: Selected Diaries, Letters and Files.* Published by Thames and Hudson, New York, 1993.)

Sonia Gernes

*Sophia Boerboom Gernes shows the family's new milk
pasteurizer to daughter Sonia, age five*
Winona, Minnesota; 1947

Sonia Gernes was born in 1942 in Winona, Minnesota, and grew up on a dairy farm nearby. She teaches Creative Writing and Women's Literature at the University of Notre Dame, and has also taught in New Zealand, London, and Western Australia. Gernes has published one novel, *The Way to St. Ives*, and three books of poetry, *The Mutes of Sleepy Eye*, *Brief Lives*, and *Women at Forty*. *A Breeze Called the Fremantle Doctor* (poem/tales) is forthcoming.

Sophia Boerboom Gernes was born in 1909 in Ghent, Minnesota, to Dutch and Belgian immigrant parents. She studied Home Economics at the University of Minnesota, worked as a 4-H agent and as a teacher at an Indian School in Pipestone County, Minnesota, and married Albert Gernes in 1932. She assumed multiple leadership roles in her rural community, but currently, at age eighty-seven, suffers from Alzheimer's disease. Sonia is the youngest of her four children.

Unnaming the Flowers

JULY 1995

Dear Mom,

I went alone to Pipestone last month. I stayed in the old hotel built of Sioux quartzite, walked to Winniwissa Falls, saw the flesh-red veins of sacred stone that lie beneath the prairie grass, and waded through volumes of archives. I even drove through the Vo-Tech campus that occupies remnants of the Indian Training School. But I couldn't find your name there, or the cottage where you lived, or replicas of the now-lost pipestone paperweights you so proudly kept in the top section of your fold-down walnut desk.

You were twenty-one when you taught at the Indian School. You were the oldest child of Dutch/Belgian immigrants, a young woman buoyant with energy, in love with a farmer from the other side of the state. You were proud of having a job in the depths of the Depression and of earning a monthly wage of $113. But you were also tentative and unsure at times, dependent on

162

your father's advice, awed by the society of the superintendent's wife and the Kiwanis Club men, and "tickled" by your own success. I know these things from a box of letters that came into my possession last summer. By the time I slipped into your life, a dozen years after Pipestone, you had become someone else.

In our rural Minnesota world, you were the most powerful person I could imagine. You knew the recipe for lye soap, how to cane chairs and make bound buttonholes, why sons and daughters (other than yours) might need some counseling, and why women should get an education (because you never knew when you'd need to fall back on it). You played the organ at church, ran the Sunday school, organized a 4-H club as soon as your oldest child turned eight, gathered the local farm wives into a *homemaker's* group (you rejected the word *housewife*), and became national chair of Rural Life in the Conference of Catholic Women. You were the neighborhood arbiter, adviser, barber, and reference desk, and I resented it—resented the fact that you could counsel, cajole, and encourage the neighbors on any sort of moral or practical dilemma, but always seemed to apply higher standards to me. At one prickly and delusional point in adolescence, I wished you'd just disappear and let me grow up by myself.

Now you *are* gone—not dead, but missing—slipped down somewhere inside a brain ruled by the erratic and inexorable progress of Alzheimer's disease. You no longer know my name; you don't know where I live or how I'm related to you. At Dad's funeral, you said, "Who is that man?" and "Did he have a family?" If you ever read this—and letters go unopened now—you will forget each sentence as you begin the next. You, the most powerful person in my life, have no power whatsoever now, and I'm having trouble dealing with that. It's why I went to Pipestone, why I am compulsively constructing a woman who was not my mother yet.

It was not easy having a paragon mother. As a child I used to watch you standing in line for confession at our little Catholic church and wondered what sins you could possibly have to tell. In an adult analytic phase, I told friends that you ended up on too small a stage, that your talents were too great for the Wilson Catholic church and Witoka Calf Show, that your frustrations made you controlling, made you a compulsive talker, made you the heroine of every tale you'd tell.

Maybe that was true, maybe not. One afternoon in my late thirties, when I had been out of your direct control for nearly twenty years, I had a moment of revelation. I was sitting in my sunroom in an old family rocking chair, trying to think through a character in one of my stories. She was a rural housewife around forty, living in the early 1950s, and trying to deal with a sense of malaise. *Had she made the right marriage? Done the right things? Did other women feel this vague, amorphous longing they couldn't name? What was wrong with her that in the middle of her life she didn't have the answers—was still unsettled, still perplexed?* The woman in my head looked like our farm neighbor Alvina, and I realized that the real Alvina too must have been a long way from understanding her life. And if Alvina, then what about you, my all-star-Catholic, reference-desk mother?

Over the years I'd seen evidence that you weren't omnipotent. Once, as a graduate student, I accompanied you to the Social Security office and was amazed to observe a timid, tentative woman, cowed by a petty bureaucrat I wanted to kick. Later, when you'd finished a history of your family (mother, father, eleven siblings and who begat whom), you asked me to see if it was "all right." One treads lightly through one's mother's prose, so I changed a few commas and said it was fine. "But I wish you'd told more stories," I said, "like the one about Grandpa having a tapeworm when he was a little boy, and the gypsies coming through and curing him with a tea made from tree bark."

"I could tell plenty of stories," you said, "but there are people who wouldn't like it one bit!" "Why not?" I pressed, and you talked about poverty, and the Depression, and the shame of it. "Remember how I said we had to move from that one house because the foundation crumbled? Well, what really happened is that they made the bricks out of local clay which wasn't brick-making quality, and the pigs and chickens were given free range, and the pigs ate the foundation of the house."

"That's a wonderful story," I said. "Put that in!" But you were adamant. Your power was not proof against all those relatives who were more powerful still.

By that time, I had bits of power myself, though it was mostly a facility with words. The secret, dreamy fantasies by which I both escaped the boredom of farm chores and created worlds you couldn't critique had turned into a habit of poetry. It was a way of claiming possession of the self, I suppose, but it had also gotten me through grad school and helped me land a job. Now I could use it to begin constructing a mother:

FAMILY HISTORY

My mother will not say "the pigs
ate out the bricks" in those years
so lean there was no turnip blood
and cold snouts sucked a clay foundation.

Old aunts scowl through her prose,
and she writes: "The house
had to be abandoned; bricks crumbled . . ."

She lists dates, years, siblings
tumbled like a wagonload of beets
(though she does not say it)
out of muffled darkness, small
disturbances in sleep. She writes
a clean and tidy record.

My mother does not say she stood
as I see her, slim girl on the plains
of too much sorrow—the crumbled house,
the hatchery gone, the father's death
rounding her mouth like a stone.

—does not say she left that graying house
while a spotted sow, her teats gone slack,
her nostrils dusty, moved toward a foundation
I see clearly now, sniffing out
the blood of a house, rooting, rooting . . .

The one area in which I always knew you had no power—the great sorrow of your life—was the death of your babies; I was the youngest only by default. When the first little girl died an hour after birth, the doctor was baffled. When the next was still-born, he knew more, but the Rh factor—the mother producing antibodies against the child's blood—had no cure in the 1940s. I remember nothing of those occasions, though I must have absorbed the sadness in the house. When I was nine, you became pregnant again, though I pretended not to notice. I'd asked earlier about the connection between big stomachs and the arrival of babies, but you put me off. I knew it was forbidden knowledge—the business about babies coming out of a "third hole" that I'd picked up on the playground, the explanation of intercourse my brother gave, citing the ever-present example of cows and bulls. When this baby too was stillborn, I joined in the grieving, but soon became aware of another consequence of this tiny death: my position as youngest child was permanent. I thought you held on to me more tightly than the others, wouldn't grant me independence, wouldn't let me grow up. In truth, most adolescents feel some of this, but behind it was another, less conscious fear: in the rural community, youngest daughters often stayed home to take care of mother, to be with her until her death.

Not until I was forty and a university professor did you give me the details of those three lost daughters. (I joked to friends that I was finally old enough to hear about something connected with sex.) The pain, as you talked, became fresh again. After our talk, I turned to poetry, as I often do, but this time I wanted not to construct, but to commemorate—to build with words my own monument to those three little deaths:

LITTLE SISTERS

This birthday I have reached the age
where my mother bore
the last of her dead daughters—
one that was whisked away
before its first clean cry
could scour the naked room, the later two
a blue that refused to brighten.

"Baby Girl, Infant Daughter of . . ."
the little markers said,
and I listened from behind the stove
in her last pregnancy,
watched her body swell and sag,
knew from the shape
of those whispered words

that something was amiss—
she was weighted already
with two small stones.

Summer mornings I called them forth—
the little sisters I had never seen—
made them faces
from the old ache
in the air above the garden,
hair like mine
from the grassy space
where root crops should have been.
I learned of blood tests, transfusions,
a factor called Rh,
my little sisters
dreaming their aquatic days
on lethal ropes, my mother
almost dead.

Now at the kitchen table
lighting candles on a cake,
I am empty-handed,
empty-wombed,
no daughters to give her
as she counts again
my miraculous birth,
fourth and forceps-born,
her last survivor in that war
of blood with family blood.

I reach for her hand and hold it,
but there are spaces here,
tender lacunae we cannot fold away.
Still somewhere the hand stitched garments
the gingham quilts, the counting game.
Still the soot-smudged corner
where I crouched beneath the stovepipe
and fingered like a rosary
the small pebbles of their names.

In your later years, before we realized that Alzheimer's was
making imperceptible but steady inroads, your need for control

seemed to become stronger again. You monopolized conversations, questioned any household technique you hadn't taught me, talked over and over again about the glory days of your pre-marriage employment. "I could have been a career woman, too," you kept saying. "I had an offer from the state office!" For me, your tone implied: *Don't think you're so smart with your fancy job!* "But I didn't want that," you'd continue, "I wanted to get married and have children." This I took to mean: *You've made the wrong choice.* My sister-in-law Pat set me straight this time: "I think she sees herself waning," she said, "I think she's just trying to say, 'I was important too.'"

We'll never know how conscious you've been of your own mental deterioration. For years you covered pretty well. Even when we pushed you into joining Dad in the nursing home, fearing you'd wander off and freeze in the Minnesota snow, you'd say, "Well, we're luckier than a lot of folks here. We've still got all our marbles."

My sister took you to the appointment at which Alzheimer's was diagnosed. She says that when the doctor pronounced the word, you said "Oh, no . . . !" but immediately seemed to forget it. On the phone, you told me the doctor ran a lot of tests but didn't tell you anything at all. The rest of us cannot forget so easily. For weeks, I was haunted by a simple test the doctor ran:

A CHAIR, A TABLE, A YELLOW BALLOON

Three things to remember,
the doctor says—a test,
a simple memory check, a warding-off
of tiny hammers that harden in the brain,
swell as knuckles do (*Does this hurt?*)
or water on the knee.

Three things, he says
as though she might forget,
and she lines them up
or almost does, but the stethoscope
is cold upon her back, and she breathes,
breathes, at his command,
the light lying down across the wall,
the table stretching to her own white bed

where fingers warmer than these
once found her skin
firm and fair and quick.

Three things? A bed, a lamp, a silky gown . . .
but she reads error in his eyes and starts again:
a yellow flower, she is sure of that,
but as she looks for confirmation
something around her breaks and lifts:
a petal, a yellow sphere,
an oval wordless as the sun.
She hears the doctor's voice,
but the afternoon is a vast white room
where something drifts,
and as he waits, she reaches,
reaches, but cannot catch the string.

Sometimes I can't catch strings myself, Mom. Sometimes I reach for a name or a word that vanishes just as I get there; I go upstairs and stand there thinking: what did I come to get? My friends laugh and say that if I'm getting Alzheimer's, they are too, but the fear is there because I have come to recognize how much I am like you, and that most of that likeness is good. You gave me a home in which parents obviously loved each other and cared deeply for us. You kept on learning new facts and skills your entire life. You gave me the optimism to try just about anything, the curiosity about other cultures that led me to three periods of teaching abroad. Along with how to gut a chicken and how to alter a dress, you taught me not to fear public speaking, to be generous with friends, to get up again when I've been knocked down. Although you were the consummate, law-abiding citizen of both country and church, there was often a subtext in which you were a young rebel—staying in school when girls had no need of high school or college, bobbing your hair when the nuns thought it was a sin. At age sixty, you had the courage to look back on your Indian School days in the light of *Bury My Heart at Wounded Knee,* and to tell me "Well, we thought we were doing good, but really we were trying to make whites out of them."

Now I am faced with the fact that the mother who could do

everything can no longer tie her shoes, or find her room, or finish a sentence, and I am powerless again. All I can do is write letters you can't really read; make visits you will forget as soon as the elevator closes. I can pray for a swift and painless death rather than an inexorable regression back through all the stages that distinguish humankind from other forms of life. I can write poems for my own consolation:

UNNAMING THE FLOWERS

My mother at the window of her room
stirs the leaves of cyclamen,
the ratty fern, as though some veiny braille
could tell her genus, species, names
that like the names of all her kin,
disperse on airborn wings,
are subject to the wind.

"That plant I had," she says, "that place
we lived . . ." And as her fingers trace
the serrate reniforms, I say the names;
delphinium, a bleeding heart,
monkshood with its poison leaves,
the woody nightshade we called bittersweet,
anemones, the bridal wreath.

But nothing clicks, no label stops
her brain's black rose from blotting out
its name, its class, its journeys through
evolutionary time to this pale room
with metal bed, call-button pull,
the quilt she finished on the farm,
the photos she's turned upside down.

"You," she says, not "Sonia,"
daughter, progeny . . .
Her hands dodder on the marble sill,
move back toward nameless meadows,
nameless brooks, the sun on mountains
newly made, a hill where nothing sees
the petals unwrap, no one stoops
to give a flower its name;

nothing is expected
to remember its fruit.

When I finish this letter, I will work on a new poem, Mom.
It's called "The Indian School," and it begins with a statement
from the first of your Pipestone letters:

I who said I would never teach . . .

But you did, Mom. You did through all these years.

Love,

Sonia

Ellen Gilchrist

Ellen Gilchrist and her mother, Aurora Louise Alford Gilchrist
Moundsville, Illinois; c. 1939 or 1940

Ellen Louise Gilchrist was born February 20, 1935, in Vicksburg, Mississippi. Married four times. Twice to the father of her children. She has three sons, and seven grandchildren. Four grandsons and three granddaughters. She has published fourteen books. Once she almost died in an airplane crash, and as the plane was falling, she said the names of the children to herself and then the names of her books. So this must be the only biographical material that is of any real importance. She has a B.A. in philosophy from Millsaps College in Jackson, Mississippi, and several honorary degrees in Letters, of which she is very proud. She lives alone in an old wood house with glass walls on the east and west and paints everything white and grayish blue. She wears blue and white except for when she is feeling wild, and then she wears yellow, or, very occasionally, dark pink. She reads and studies and writes and takes long walks and talks on the phone and rides bikes and believes in DNA.

Aurora Louise Alford Gilchrist was born February 27, 1908, in Mayersville, Mississippi. Second daughter of Stewart Floyd Alford and Nell Biggs Alford. Blue eyes and blonde hair. Five feet six inches tall. Weight 130 pounds. A dancer. Winner of many Charleston contests in the 1920s. Graduated in 1929, with a B.A., the University of Mississippi in Oxford, Mississippi, a degree in French and home economics. Elected Most Popular Girl her senior year in college. Married William Garth Gilchrist in 1931 on the porch of Hopedale Plantation in Issaquena County, Mississippi. She was wearing a blue lace dress and matching silk shoes. This dress was later lost by a friend who borrowed it for her own wedding. This was in the heart of the Depression. She is a devout Episcopalian and a charter member of Tau Chapter of Chi Omega. She is the mother of two sons and one daughter. The grandmother of sixteen children. The great-grandmother of seventeen children. The great-great grandmother of two children. She lives with her husband in Jackson, Mississippi, where she raises roses and dispenses sympathy both over the phone and in her kitchen, den and living room, which is always filled with people. She does not have an answering machine and answers the phone herself.

JUNE 4, 1995

Dearest Mother,

 I want to thank you for the beautiful blue and white cups you sent me on my sixtieth birthday. For the blue linen napkins and

173

the white placemats. I want to thank you for introducing me to blue. The cobalt blue of your beautiful English eyes. It must have been the first thing I ever saw. Smiling down at me as they have for all my sixty years. Thank you for not dying. Here I am, sixty years old and I have never had to grieve for deep or tragic loss. That's what your death would be to me. Imagine not being able to call 601-236-2262 and tell you my troubles. I tell you my troubles to take your mind off your own. I never told you that, did I? It's a secret I've been keeping for about twenty years. You are twenty-seven years older than I am and your troubles are harder than mine, so I always call up and tell you about my allergies and my back and neck and insect bites. Everyone knows there is nothing wrong with me. I pretend to be a hypochondriac in order to deliver messages to you. The message is, our bodies heal themselves. Thank you for the powerful healthy genes. Tomorrow the sun will be shining and we will be like new. I know you. Every morning you think the world is beginning all over and all will be well with the world. I think so too. Where do you think I got an idea like that?

But mostly the thing I keep forgetting to tell you is how much I love the aesthetic that you gave me. I travel a lot. I run into my distant cousins, in California and New York City and Colorado. There they are, with those blue eyes and that darling nose, wearing Chanel 19 and dressed in simple, elegant, tasteful clothes. "Your necktie rich and modest, but asserted by a simple pin." I used to think it was funny that I can't talk myself into being tacky. I used to try. I would go out and buy outlandish clothes or shoes or think of painting something red but I could never carry it off. I like blue and navy blue and black and white and yellow. The way you dressed me when I was a child.

I want rooms simple and clean and quiet, with a bowl of fresh roses or lilies on a table. Not two bowls of flowers. One bowl of flowers. I don't want to outdo anyone. I want to make things that people think are beautiful and let them look at the things I make. When I write I want to solace and amuse my readers. Sometimes I want to shock them into being solaced. I didn't learn that from you. I know I have a hit on my hands when you call me up after I have written a book and tell me, Ellen, this is filthy. If you knew how much I love it when you say that, you would never do it.

Do you know where cobalt blue comes from? Our favorite

color. It was brought to China from Turkey by the Chinese traders on the Silk Road. They discovered the cobalt tiles in the temples of Turkey and brought it back just in time for the Ming dynasty. I love those cups you gave me for my sixtieth birthday. I drink coffee out of them each morning. I put one in each bathroom in my house. I put those beautiful white placemats on the table and blue linen napkins and eat dinner in the heart of the civilization you passed on to me.

I am sorry you are growing old and have to have your knee operated on and put up with the long recovery. I'm sorry that it takes so long for cuts to heal. But I never say this to you. I call you up the minute you get back from the hospital and start telling you my problems. A girl with a mother like you should have better manners than that. A girl with a mother like you should know how to exhibit sympathy. Instead, I do it the way I have always done it when you were sick or injured. I call 601-236-2262, and, as soon as you answer, I say, "Hello, my mother. This is me."

"How are you," you immediately ask.

"Well, my allergies are better but I've had to go to the chiropractor about a hundred times this week for my neck. You should see my cherry tree. There are five million cherries on it and about a thousand birds. There are twenty different species in that tree. There are redbirds and bluebirds and blue jays by the dozens. There is a piliated woodpecker the size of a dinosaur. How are you? How's your leg?"

You know me like a book. I can't fool you. You know what I am saying, don't you? Like you know how much it pleases me when something I write shocks you. Scares and pleases me. In your presence I am not a writer. I am a hyperactive, redheaded child whom it is your duty to love and civilize.

You don't know how you have civilized me. You will never know how much you've taught me and how deep the lessons go. I think you know I love you. I know that you love me.

Don't die.

Love,

Ellen

Natalie Goldberg

*Natalie Goldberg and her mother, Sylvia Edelstein
Goldberg, at the beach*
Florida; 1995

Natalie Goldberg was born January 4, 1948, in Brooklyn, New York. She is the author of *Writing Down the Bones* (Shambhala 1986), *Wild Mind* (Bantam 1990), *Long Quiet Highway* (Bantam 1993), and a novel, *Banana Rose* (Bantam 1995). She resides in Taos, New Mexico.

Sylvia Edelstein Goldberg was born July 18, 1919, in Brooklyn, New York, and spent most of her life in that state. She was a homemaker with a short stint selling cosmetics at Macy's department store. She currently resides in Florida with her husband, Ben Goldberg.

To My Mother

It is my fear that when I join a Zen monastery far away in the foothills of Japan and I go to answer the koan—What was your original face before you were born?—the answer will simply be your face, the woman living in her parents' apartment in Brooklyn, leaning over *her* mother's mushroom and barley soup, feeling the steam on her cheeks as she blows on the thick liquid and spoons some into her mouth.

And if I become truly wise in that monastery and get to answer the koan again and rip off your face to see the original face behind that, it will be Grandma's on 91st Street, her hook nose, long earlobes swinging diamond studs bought in my grandparents' heyday when the poultry business did well. Did my grandmother wear glasses and lipstick? I ask myself. I almost can't remember, but those significant questions are what will link me up to Shakyamuni, deep in a cloister, outside Kyoto, surviving on pickles and a soupy rice eaten in silence, trying to call up all at once the smell of chicken, the sound of teeth chewing challah, the feel of Rose Edelstein's small gray hairs on the nape of her neck.

Mom, what is it I've really meant to tell you? I remember sitting on the edge of the tub as you applied makeup. I was twelve; you were forty-four and I told you about reading *Gone with the Wind.* I believed you were forever, never to tumble down the clock, never to become eighty, that our love bonded the whole

177

universe, that our world was *the* world, that your hands with the gold wedding band were the marriage of all time, threw me out into the wondrous world of that green split-level in the split-level development in Farmingdale, New York, with Grandpa's teeth in a glass on the counter at night and Grandma's enema bag swinging from a curtain hook above my head.

No Japan will carry me away from you, and no death either can possibly forget your long-distance voice and the one line that matters, "Natli, it's been so long, are you okay, how are you?"

Natalie

Susan Griffin

Back row: Left to right, *her grandfather holding
Susan Griffin, next to her mother*
Front row: *Her sister*
Los Angeles; 1945

Susan Emily Griffin was born on January 26 in 1943. She was raised variously by her mother, her maternal grandparents, her father, and an adoptive family. She had the benefit of a college education. During her first and only legal marriage, she bore one daughter and earned a master's degree in English literature. She has entered what for want of a better word might be likened to a marriage with three women in her life. She has written since the age of nine. Among her published works are *Woman and Nature* and *A Chorus of Stones*. This last book was a finalist for a Pulitzer Prize and the National Book Critics Circle Award. She has received a MacArthur Grant for Peace and International Cooperation. And her play, *Voices*, was awarded an Emmy.

Sarah Emily Colvin Williamson was born on March 12, 1914. She was married twice and bore two daughters. She worked for two brief periods in her life behind a lunch counter. As a young woman she studied interior decorating but was discouraged from this pursuit by her parents and her first husband. All her life she made things with her hands, paintings, dolls fashioned from apples, knit animals for her children and grandchild, embroidery and needlepoint. In the last two decades of her life, after the death of her husband and her parents, she experienced a flowering of her soul. She healed herself of alcoholism and worked to repair her relationships with her two children. In this same period she learned French and read widely in both French and English. She was fascinated especially with the work of Pierre Loti and the history of China. She died in August of 1992.

Ma, Ma, you were so small in that bed. We could hardly find you. The frail form lying there didn't seem like you anymore. I could feel you elsewhere, hovering, watching, as tenuously I whispered into the air, *Ma, Ma.*

These are not syllables I ordinarily spoke. I cannot remember by what name I summoned your presence as a small child. I have long since shed the memory of that cry, though here the words are, bright with passion, returning as I write to you.

It is only now, after your death, that this passion can be resurrected. And this is perhaps because when I remember your death and cry, as I still do, it is as if every thread of the long sinews of pain between us have dissolved leaving one wide body of sweetness.

I miss you. I can say this now without reservation. Yes, it has been almost two decades since we joined together in acts of contrition and forgiveness, before you entered the last months of your life. Yet time put us through another round of distance. A subtle barrier had arisen between us, and, though I did not wish for it, a slight taste of bitterness came to my mouth again when I thought of you.

Shall I list the agonies of the child once more? They are drawn like maps over both our souls. The long nights of your drunkenness, which became my own long nights of sober recollection. The acrid smell of your breath full of beer and old cigarettes. Your eyes spinning errantly, homelessly giving me an inward terror. Your voice, clever, sarcastic, sharp, severing every bond between us.

And yet, Ma Ma, this is what makes me cry now, not all those injuries but the simple syllables of a love, buried for years, which is being revealed to me even at this moment. It is that love a child bears a mother, hot and steamy as food, as intestines doing their work, dank as midwinter earth, implacable as night, irrefutable as dreams insinuating their strange reason into daylight. The love between mother and daughter, webbed together like flesh and bones, Ma Ma, a love which, I am learning now, passed between us too, that always *was* between us, even if silent and hidden in the deepest regions of ourselves, however much we chose to ignore it.

And this is what I want to put on paper now. An homage to what was never given voice between us. Though I do not blame myself for the silence. What else could she do, that shivering six-year-old sent to her grandmother's home, after so many requests for your presence, but keep silent on this subject and forget? So there was a long period of supposed indifference. The resignation. Betrayed only by a certain shyness, a kind of formality accompanying all feelings of intense love.

It is only after many years of a life that one begins to understand that every betrayal of the heart, every hidden feeling gives birth to countless consequences which one day will have to be peeled back, layer after layer, to reveal the simple logic of pain.

And we did go very far in that direction, you and I. The shouting matches we had when last I lived with you. The years when I spoke and wrote my bitterness. Both of us withdrawing. Both of us unyielding, until you made one gesture forward and then I responded and you came forward again and I again. And then, a few years before your death, that slight but growing chill between us, when we did not yet know that still another level of meaning was beginning to work its way up from the mute past.

Only now can I read the signs in myself. They came to me as marks of deprivation. I am remembering, for instance, the time I visited you with a friend, the one you liked so much, Emily, who several years afterward went to see you in the nursing home during the two weeks before we could ferry you north. On this earlier visit she noticed how formal we were together, telling me it was almost as if we were not mother and daughter. Then I felt a clenching sorrow, which had as an aftershock a heavy resentment, that you were not warmer with me. More comfortable, more casual. That we did not have between us that daily immediacy that allows one to take certain things for granted. To bicker. To call upon, each in quiet moments, a storehouse of ordinary time, domestic detail, those tiny intimacies that make for a steady, reliable closeness.

There were too few times that we tried on clothes together, that I remember you brushing my hair, that I watched you brush your hair, that we cooked meals, sat in the sun, so few days we spent in each other's company from sun up to sun down, sharing the flavors, scents, weathers, small occurrences, waxing and waning light of a day. And it seemed to me as if all the days that we did have together were punctuated, framed, infused with the drama of your drinking.

I had already expressed my rage and forgiven you for the larger acts of abandonment, the wider swaths of abuse. And I had come in that very expression back to the fact of my love for you. But it was this same love that eventually opened me up to another kind of anger, an anger over small things. That you never came to pick me up at the airport, never came to see me in the hospital. That you had not helped me to shoulder my daily terrors. Had provided no proverbial safety for me in the arena of words.

Though this last complaint was injust and now I know it. You tried to be a mother to me in this way. I was the one who would not enter this arena; I would not tell you my fears. Though the words should read *could not,* because something from the past that had as yet not eased in me made me unable to trust you in this way.

In truth you were a remarkably accepting person. Except when you were mean with drink, you encouraged me, praised my accomplishments, my character. And this all carried me, even despite the bitter reversals when you drank; I have a certain confidence, a belief in myself. I took courage from your esteem.

But of course the bitterness wormed its way into the core of my idea of myself, as if I were hiding another self, miserable and reprobate, even foul in some way. And this fit very well with the absence between us of a daily intimacy, becoming in some way an argument for abandonment, reasoning that such closeness with me would be unwise or at the very least, unsavory.

It is so difficult even now for me to write this. It brings tears to my eyes, not only because of the truth of this description and the awareness it awakens inside me but because I do not want to cause you pain. One would think, that once you had died I would be able to write entirely freely about all that transpired between us. And in truth it *is* only after your death that I can put these words on any page, whether meant for you or not. But this is not for the reasons I supposed. I thought you would *not* be listening and for this reason I would be safe. But it is instead because, at least in my inward soul, I feel you *are listening* that I can write so honestly.

And this brings me to the intimacy we have now. Is this because the feeling between us was so sweet in the months before you died? Though I was often overtired, I liked taking care of you. And though you were in pain and fading daily in your vitality, you radiated pleasure in response to the care I gave you. I could feel you open yourself up to me and I could also see that you had chosen to do this, and that this opening was a last gift. Every small event was moving. The games of Scrabble we played. The balloons you loved so much that I put in your room and tied to the foot of your bed in the hospital. Because you preferred them to flowers, at your memorial, though we had flowers for ourselves and our own grief, for you we assembled a bouquet of white balloons and let them go into the sky. The vanishing of those balloons. The vanishing of you. This gave an invisible edge of meaning to every encounter. Every evening when I left you and you would stare into my eyes, I knew you were drinking me in and saying good-bye, and I was doing the same.

But there was something else too that made even the smallest moments between us luminous. Somehow for the first time we really had each other. We belonged to each other. We were flesh and blood and more than at any other period I can recollect, living out the truth of this in a daily way.

Though I could not yet fully open myself with you. This was not yet possible. And at all our encounters I carried an ache and fear. Though you had never read it, you were so proud of the book I had just written. Yet though you asked to read it, I told you it wasn't quite finished. I lied to you. And now finally I can tell you why I kept the book from you. It was because of the harsh memories I recorded there. I wrote about the times you were drinking and mean to me as a child. And I did not want you to see this. In truth you were too ill, too weak, your hearing too poor, to be able to hear or even survive what would have been a shock (though we had already spoken of all this), to read in print what you had done when you were drinking, what you said and did (and forgot in the morning) and how the pain of that had migrated into the marrow of my life.

And I had no need to remind you again. You had already given me acknowledgment enough. But how I would have wanted to say these simple words to you that I am going to write now. *You know, Mother, those stories became the stuff of my life. And that is why when I write I cannot conceal them.*

But there is something more I would like to tell you that is the other side of this story from our lives. It gives our pain a meaning and a depth, connects us to a larger history, and even to hope for the lives of others. On the last day of your life, when I went for a walk in the canyons outside Santa Fe, I began to think about how ice carves rocks, making mountains and beauty. And staring at the cliffs made in this way, I could sense that the pain between us was part of a larger movement, even possibly a healing of a great woundedness belonging to the history of this place, the westward movement, the slaughter on this ground of those who had lived here before, a cruelty and rage which was another kind of inheritance and must migrate through so many American families. And suddenly I could see that you made this cruelty and rage visible. You revealed it. So suddenly and unpredictably an event occurred in the inner landscape of my soul that would have seemed wholly improbable to me had anyone dared to suggest its possibility. I became grateful for something that those drunken nights had given me. And aware in the most irrevocable way that the very visibility you provided also gave me an opening. A way to begin to free myself from that past.

And what is also surprising to me is that my ability to speak more honestly to you has more to do with your presence than your absence. A memory of you and the sweetness between us at the last stays with me, reminding me how birth and death have knit us together. And even more strange and marvelous, this abiding, daily quality has restored to me that underworld of warmth, of fecundity, of embrace which has been the work of mothers and children. Though I cannot of course claim to be healed of the history we share, I can feel myself entering an atmosphere of hot acceptance, a love that cradles imperfections and even transgressions, that loves the roundness of a life, as I have grown to love yours, *Ma Ma*, and you.

Susan

Jan Haag

Jan Haag and her mother, Darlene Haag
Long Beach, California; c. 1959

Jan Haag was born July 30, 1958, in Long Beach, California, and moved to northern California with her parents at the age of eight. A former journalist recently turned to fiction writing, she holds an M.A. in journalism and English from California State University, Sacramento. She covered the California Legislature for United Press International for eight years, in addition to covering stories elsewhere in the United States and in Mexico. The former editor of *Sacramento* magazine, Haag is currently department chair of journalism and also teaches creative writing at Sacramento City College. She is at work on her first novel, *Louie, Louie.*

Dorothy (Darlene) Haag, R.N., was born July 6, 1931, in Chicago, Illinois. Raised and educated in the Chicago area, she is a graduate of Wesley Memorial Hospital School of Nursing and holds a B.S.N. from Northwestern University. She married Roger Haag in 1957; they have two daughters, Jan and Donna, and two grandchildren. In addition to being a high school nurse for twenty-six years, she is a holistic nursing practitioner, using a variety of energy bodywork modalities, and is a consultant regarding nutrition and stress reduction. She is a charter member of the American Holistic Nurses Association.

Rotten Mothers

MOTHER'S DAY, 1995

Hey, Ma:

I know how occasionally you get to thinking about the days when your kids were small, how you look at Donna and think what a good job she's doing raising her kids, how part of you wishes that I'd have kids—and you think, not for the first time, "I was a rotten mother." It meant a lot to me when I first heard you say that, acknowledging mistakes of the past, admitting that you had been far from perfect. Because I remember my mother as the person with the poster behind her favorite chair in the living room that said, "Those of you who think you're perfect are annoying to those of us who are."

True, you had moments when I thought I would never understand you. You and Daddy spent more than half my childhood fighting over difficult matters, I'm sure, but what I remember is cowering in my room, covering my ears, and waiting for the storm to pass . . . and hoping it didn't hit me. Which it did, too often. Sometimes what followed the fighting was, as singer Mary Chapin Carpenter says in one of her songs about her family, a silence "you could cut with a knife." I still hate fighting; I go out of my way to avoid verbal conflicts.

When you began practicing Transcendental Meditation when I was fifteen, oh, how things changed. We thought you were weird, sitting on the sofa humming your mantra, but I have always been grateful that you started down the path you're still on—to inner peace, studying natural, holistic healing methods, working with therapeutic touch, genuinely helping people. I still like to brag, "When my mom started meditating, she stopped yelling." Now there's a testimonial for meditation . . . and one reason I also do it as a grown-up, to calm myself and the voices that threaten to burst out of my head and heart.

There were other challenges, of course. You wanted so much for me to be perfect that you unintentionally added pressure to an already Type A kid to succeed—so much so that I have spent years trying to assure myself that I really didn't *have* to whip through two careers in my first fifteen years as a grown-up, that I have as many inner successes as outer ones. I have learned to slow down, to take time to contemplate.

You also were overprotective of your clutzy older child. And while all the "be carefuls" and "are you sure you shoulds?" were probably warranted, I grew up thinking I was the most awkward person I knew. I felt, in many ways, that you viewed me as a direct reflection of you, and that my failures and embarrassments were your own, and therefore not to be tolerated. I cried too much, I was a "creative" child, and that must have been hard for you to understand—but I often found your analytical, left-brain self just as hard to reach. I remember longing for hugs but being afraid to approach you for them.

But if you were not perfect, neither is it true, Ma, that you were a rotten mother—not at all—and I've come upon three parents in the last week who reminded me again that you may not have been the most perfect mother on the planet, but you were *my* mom, and you did the best job you could. A great job, even. Donna and I are living proof of that, having turned out not half bad, if I do say so myself, and you tell us this all the time these days—which we also appreciate.

Admitting some of your faults as a parent does not make you a rotten one, by any means. I should also point out that by having deliberately chosen not to have children, I really shouldn't be criticizing those who do. But like you, I have strong opinions about these things, and you taught me well.

Example No. 1: My friend, Jeannie, whom I believe has quite lost her mind, is currently mothering not one but two foster children, both age 2. This I consider a good thing, by the way, since both of these children were born to parents on drugs. One, the boy, Sam, was living with an AIDS mother who didn't know she had the disease until her second child was born with it. Both children were taken away from her, and Sam now lives with Jeannie, who would love to adopt these two and raise her second batch of kids, since her first two turned out so well.

Anyway, Sam is supposed to be taken by his social worker for weekly visits—very closely supervised visits—with his parents, both of whom are still presumably doing drugs and who refuse to be drug tested. Sam, who has grown very attached to Jeannie, is nonetheless a gregarious kid and goes willingly with the social worker. Though he calls Jeannie "Mama," he knows the difference between her and his natural mom, and looks forward to the visits.

For seven straight weeks now, the social worker has picked up Sam on time, taken him to the appointed meeting place, and for seven straight weeks, his parents have failed to show up. Sam, even at 2, is aware of this and sobs all the way back to Jeannie. They call the parents, who promise to show up next week, but they never do. It is heartbreaking to watch this little boy cry week after week. These are rotten parents.

Example No. 2: Years ago, when I coached the synchronized swim team during my summer vacations from college, I had girls on the team who won my heart. I had others who made me crazy. One of the latter was a pretty girl named Liza, who, at age 12, was one of the best swimmers on the team. She could do magic in the water—hanging upside down, sculling madly over her head, with her legs cutting swaths through the summer night air like scissors. She swam majestically, as though competing for her life.

She also had a major attitude. Liza was the girl who wouldn't share extra bobby pins to put up a teammate's hair before a meet. She had talent, and she knew it. She had only one friend on the team. Carrie, a tiny 10-year-old, adored Liza, who pretty much ignored Carrie. "She's wonderful," Carrie would say, watching

Liza dance through the water. Liza, for her part, returned the admiration with a smirk, but little Carrie never wavered in her devotion.

I was young enough to be so annoyed by Liza's pretentiousness that I never questioned why this talented girl thought she deserved to be queen. Until I met her mother. A tall, elegant woman with an Audrey Hepburn-like crown of hair, Liza's mom swung into the pool one day to pick up her daughter from practice. I'd never seen her before. She looked around the pool for her daughter and called out sharply, "Liza!" Liza, toweling off at the opposite end of the deck, hurried to her mother who spoke sharply to the girl and with a slight push, ushered her out the gate.

"That's her mother," Carrie whispered to me. "She doesn't like Liza to swim. She says it'll ruin her for modeling."

"Is her mother a model?" I asked.

"Oh, yes," Carrie said. "She used to be famous. She says Liza will be, too. Liza only gets to swim because her dad said it was OK. Her mom kinda runs the rest of her life."

Meeting her mother later in the season, I saw in her Liza's imperious attitude, a defense against any slight the world might hand out. Her mother informed me that her daughter would no longer be swimming on my team, that she had "more important work to do."

I have no idea whether Liza went on to become the model her mother hoped for. But I suspect that her mother became a (role) model in ways she might have come to regret. A regrettable, if not a rotten, mother.

Example No. 3: I have the two best next-door neighbors anyone could ask for, Anne and Joe. They remind me a lot of Auntie Lo and Uncle Bob—good, kind, churchgoing folks, who take great pleasure in hosting little old ladies for dinner on Sundays. Joe mows my front lawn every week, insisting that it's no trouble; he's mowing his own small lawn at the same time. They look after the house when I'm gone and would rush to the rescue if I ever needed it. They are about your age and have two daughters about the ages of Donna and me.

But oh, what a difference. Anne has told me on more than one occasion that their daughters have led screwed-up lives since they were in high school. One of those daughters has a 13-year-old daughter who was repeatedly raped by her mother's boyfriend. Anne and Joe just learned about this and urged their daughter to press charges. She did so, and their granddaughter is now involved in a huge trial in Idaho, where they live.

I said to Anne one day when she was telling me about her granddaughter, "How did this happen? You've said your daughters picked men who were terrible to them. Why?" And I heard a horrifying story. In high school, the oldest daughter began dating and sleeping with boys that her parents disapproved of. Anne, trying to be a tough guy, told the daughter in no uncertain terms that unless she stopped seeing the boyfriend and lived by her parents' rules, Anne would kick her out of the house. The daughter refused, and at 15, her parents kicked her out of the house.

The same thing happened with the second daughter—rowdy, skipping school, dating bad young men—and her parents kicked her out, too, Anne told me. "I couldn't live with them," she said. "They just wouldn't listen to me."

Those girls didn't even finish high school, let alone attend college. Because they apparently had such low self-esteem, they married and were involved with a series of bad men who beat them, emotionally abused them, and took their money—not to mention the one who raped the 13-year-old daughter. Anne and Joe periodically tried to help, buying the houses that the daughters lived in after their divorces, letting the granddaughter live with them periodically, but Anne said that both girls blame their lives on their parents. "Like I helped them make such bad decisions," Anne says.

Now I believe that these daughters made horrible decisions about their lives and must take responsibility for their own actions, but I can't help thinking that some of the horrors began when their own parents gave up on them and said, "Fine. We disapprove of you—you go live somewhere else." How can you expect 15- or 16-year-olds to get their lives together if you, their parents—people who are supposed to care for them when no one else will—kick them out? How can you hope that they'll "straighten up" if they have no good influences?

These women are in their thirties now and just beginning to try to turn their lives around. They are angry with their parents. And I'm not blaming Anne and Joe for every bad thing that happened to their daughters. But when your parents give up on you at your worst moments—like those rotten teenage years—who will have faith in you?

Thank you for not giving up on Donna or me at our worst moments. You must have wanted to kick us out, too, sometimes, but you persevered and believed in us, always. You did the Great Parent thing of endless driving to band practice and synchronized swimming meets; you refereed those meets. You made us take piano lessons and march in the band, and in the end, we loved it all. You took us on Girl Scout outings and served as cookie chairman, buying endless packages of cookies (poor Daddy—that was such a sacrifice for him, eating all those cookies!). You taught us to water-ski and to sing harmony; you taught us to love old Broadway and Hollywood musicals, and I can never listen to Judy Garland sing "Somewhere Over the Rainbow" without thinking of you and getting all teary. You taught us how to drive (I know, that's where your prematurely gray hair came from) and gave us cars to use and paid for us to pursue our dreams in college. You encouraged me to write and work on student newspapers, and you helped Donna find her career as a physical therapist. You made us believe we could do anything we wanted to do, and we have done so.

That's not a rotten parent by any means. You never abandoned us (OK, temporarily leaving me behind at Johnson Pool doesn't count), disapproved of us as people (though sometimes, appropriately, of our actions), or gave up on us. You were a great parent, if not a perfect one—I don't think anyone ever is—who stuck by us, always. My friend Connie Warloe often has described herself and her husband, parents of twin boys, as "bumbling parents." I think the best ones are, and they realize their flaws but raise great kids anyway.

Best of all, you let us grow up into our own people and no longer try to "parent" us as adults, yet you still care and lend advice when we ask and offer companionship as people we love and trust. I can't think of a better gift among the many you've given us. Thank you for all of them.

I send you all the hugs I never gave you, and as we say in journalism, more TK (to come!). Happy Mother's Day!

Love,

Jan

Joan Joffe Hall

Leah M. Joffe and Joan Joffe Hall
New York City; summer, 1960

JAMES BAKER HALL

Joan Joffe Hall was born in New York on February 16, 1936. She was educated at Vassar and Stanford and is a professor of English and women's studies at the University of Connecticut. She has published two books of poetry, *The Rift Zone* and *Romance and Capitalism at the Movies;* and a collection of stories, *Summer Heat.* She is married and the mother of two sons and three stepsons.

Leah M. Joffe was born in the Bronx, New York, October 17, 1908. She died in Connecticut, September 1, 1991. She had two children, Joan and Steven. She taught in New York until retiring and, after moving to a town near her daughter, became active in senior citizen affairs and Head Start.

Loving Dogwood

Oh, Ma, our grocery closed one day while you were dead. Likewise all G. Fox department stores—out of business. David and I separated for six months last year. Matthew married halfway through law school. You'll never know. It's spring. The dogwood we planted blooms. Remember how we christened it? I never realized till then that you, city girl, loved dogwood. Last week we scattered your ashes in the pond in the woods behind our house.

So everything is normal although I've been out of town for months. Sugar Shack now serves "Bread" as bad as their doughnuts. Sis has cut her hair at your behest. We each think we're your favorite. Confronted with this once you laughed, said you'd done a good job. "Good job of what? You know Ma lies," Sis says. I say, "Would it be better if we knew?"

"I wanted to show you this." Sis hands me a letter to the Alzheimer's Disease Research Center in Durham, North Carolina. *I should like to have my body, on my demise, utilized for research or for the harvesting of organs as appropriate. I should like to donate what is left of my remains after such harvesting to your Alzheimer's Center, if such is feasible. Would that detract from your research?*

If not, could you arrange for it, or put me in contact with the proper authorities?

"Did Ma write this?" I want to know. "I feel robbed," Sis says.

I want to be cremated. I don't believe in any afterlife. I want my ashes put in my blue Chinese ceramic vase. I want the vase put on the mantelpiece over our fireplace. "So you can hear everything?" Sis says. "Just in case," I tell her.

She waves good-bye. "See ya." E, C sharp, her signature. I sit there smelling caramel. Your advice: If I eat at a place like this don't complain. Tinny reggae whines in the loudspeakers. Already my left index fingernail is twisting sideways like yours. It disgusts me. Yesterday I had three more keratoses burned off my skin. Oh, Ma, I feel my face turning into a waffle. Pour syrup. Lick me clean.

A mother and daughter quarrel. They look daggers at each other. The daughter: herself a parent, in her thirties, living at home. Still attached. Their quarrel squawks its black notes around the kitchen. One of them will kill the other. But which one? Or maybe both will be killed. They quarrel about putting away silverware, better jobs, Freud, fried food that spatters the stove, child discipline, who has grieved more for the father/husband, how to hang toilet paper, which one will prevail.

When a child is born the mother thinks: Forgive me, I have given birth to something that will die. A mother and daughter are Siamese twins and only when they separate can each develop. Even afterward, the daughter continues to know what the mother feels; she has to.

I am middle-aged, return home. But home keeps shifting, being revised. Why does she alter the house whenever I leave? I want my mahogany four-poster bed back, my collection of actors' faces on Dixie cup lids, my father. I use the old half-bath on the landing, where the hexagonal tiles blur in and out of focus in the distance, like computer-generated 3-D images. Then I discover she's installed a new bathroom right near her third-floor bedroom. Smell of camphor. Towels for me in the bath cupboard stiff from underrinsed soap and outdoor drying. My bed in the spare room a daybed with hard plaid pillows.

In the morning I sneak downstairs. I know what's down there, the carnage. One body, two bodies, hardly any difference. Will their faces be intact after the quarrel? Will clothing be awry? What exposed? I expect Ma in the dining room, Sis in the downstairs bedroom. I don't want to look at them, grab a glass of juice from the refrigerator, no time to squeeze fresh, turn back to the stairs.

On the second-floor landing I pass a doorway, the last bedroom. A girl still pudgy in childhood, still baby-toothed, stands facing the wall. Dark braids ladder her back: my niece. The child's been down there, surveyed the grisly scene, thinks it's her fault. If she turns away nothing will happen. I can't reassure her. I abandon her stuck in the corner and back away to the stairs.

On the third floor I glimpse my mother's figure in her bed, not sprawled under the dining table. She cannot be alive. The camphor smell keeps pests away. I walk into the room anyhow. Is that an eyelid flickering? I turn to leave, don't want to face this. Fasten those eyes shut. Drink the juice, go about your day.

But have I missed my chance? Hours pass and prod the guilt. Later I return. As I stand there, dust motes shape the sunlight and shadows lengthen across blue Wilton carpet. I ask myself how I will feel if she's dead. I take her hand, smooth and cool, like the jade she gave me. Her eyes flicker.

"What is an eighty-year-old woman doing asleep in the afternoon without even TV to zonk her out?" she says. "So it didn't happen?" I ask her. Our hands hold tight. "Let's eat something," she says; "I dreamed I went to McDonald's but the tables were full of class warfare."

People come and go: my younger sister, my niece flit shadowy in and out. Sis pivots the bedroom mirror back around; a family portrait it reveals us all. "Is this the way into Grandma's room?" the child asks; "is this the door?" Tartly I say, "It's not a door, it's an optical illusion, walk through it." And she does, smiling.

The doctor arrives with his black bag to certify Ma's alive. I worry about ID cards, driver's license, health insurance numbers: do I still have them or have I already cleaned up? Can I prove who she is? Her eyes are green. But I've donated her clothes to the Salvation Army, even the wool challis we bought in California and which I could wear, or Sis.

"I saved some of your china." I am eager to make up. "The red plastic soap dish from your bathroom, the vegetable brush." I say my sister took the pots. Apologies tumble out of my mouth. "I see," she observes, "you're still stuck on family."

The next morning she comes downstairs. "I started your Volvo," I tell her, "the battery wasn't dead after all."

Practicing music, I used to try a measure over and over until I could play it right. But often I just had to go on, imperfect.

I play this game with my niece: what does she have in her life that I didn't at her age? A CD player, a computer, a VCR. "A microwave," she guesses. Alzheimer's, I don't say, nor AIDS. An answering machine, an area code. "Really?" Velcro. She echoes the word slowly: "Vell-crow."

Last year for Christmas cards David and I mailed photos of ourselves around a big basket inside which was printed "Empty Nest." The text on the reverse made light of how far away our children have flown. A self-pitying comic note. I want them back in all their bedrooms and you in the next town.

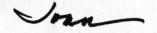

Phebe Hanson

Phebe Dale (Hanson), age three, and her mother,
Hildur Linnea Erikson Dale
Minnesota; summer, 1931

Phebe Dale Hanson was born on March 9, 1928, and grew up in Sacred Heart, Minnesota. She became a high school English teacher, married and had three children. She began to write poetry in her late forties and has published one book of poems, *Sacred Hearts* (Milkweed Editions). After thirty years of teaching high school and college, she retired to hang out with her five grandchildren and write more poems.

Hildur Linnea Erikson Dale was born in Stockholm, Sweden, on November 24, 1904, and came to Duluth, Minnesota, with her parents, George and Wilhelmina Erikson, and brother, Harry. After graduation from high school, she worked a few years as a secretary, then married my father, a Lutheran minister, had five children (one died in infancy), and died in 1936 of heart disease caused by rheumatic fever.

TRINITY LUTHERAN CEMETERY, SACRED HEART, MINNESOTA
JUNE 12, 1995

Dear Mother:

Here I am, sitting on the grass in front of your headstone in this little cemetery on the edge of town, next to a field of soybeans. The cottonwood tree in the corner gives off soft soughing sounds as the prairie wind you know so well blows through it. The peony bush Daddy planted after we buried you on August 24, 1936, has long been gone, dug out after the cemetery committee, to make maintenance easier, declared all living plants and flowers must be removed. Now only a few bright plastic flowers, left over from Memorial Day, decorate the graves.

I trace my fingers over your name, Hildur Linnea, and the Bible passage engraved in the polished granite: "Thy grace is sufficient for me." Today after fifty-nine years of missing you, of feeling bereft every day of my life, I want to think about what it was like for you, thirty-one years old, mother of four children, including a baby only six months old (and one buried three years before you died, now sleeping beside you), to have to say goodbye to us all. You never got out of bed after Milton was born; your heart, damaged in adolescence by rheumatic fever, gradually gave out, and you slipped away in the August heat while I lay on the davenport and asked God not to let you die.

I remember how I stood in this cemetery with my brother, David, and sister, JoAnne, and Daddy, who was holding the baby, and watched men throw dirt on your coffin, then lower it straight into that deep hole. I felt so old, as if I would never again go out in my backyard and make mud pies with Patty or make paper dolls from ladies in their underwear cut from the Sears catalog. Never again would Lois Ann and I color all those pretty dresses. Never again would I feel like racing out the back screen door and into the pergola house Daddy made for us by the goldfish pond, where Lorene and I used to sit through the long summer days and read *Dandelion Cottage* and *The Five Little Peppers and How They Grew.*

Here in my journal is the picture printed with your obituary, and I stare at it, as I have so many times before, into those eyes, which seem to be gazing far beyond me. Sometimes I think you already knew that soon you would go deep into that other country. On your lips, a small, tender smile, almost as if you were looking forward to what lay ahead. You loved your Jesus and used to tell me how my baby brother had gone "home to be with Jesus, where there's no more pain or sadness." The day you died, after the doctor had told my father it was over, you suddenly sat upright in bed and held out your arms to him. "Oh, David, I see Jesus and how I wish you could see him. He's shining with light and he's beckoning me to come home. And I see our baby, too, our little John Phillip. I'll get to hold him again."

Yet, I know you loved this earth, too, and all the things of your world. Even the dress you're wearing in this picture—I remember it so well, the softness of the silk crepe de chine, the delicate pleats, the silk cord I used to love to pull open so I could practice tying a bow. And you always let me, as I sat nestled in your lap at Ladies Aid, never scolded me, even the day I crawled out of your arms at Mrs. Skardal's house and crept across the cool linoleum floor to the black suede shoes Mrs. Lerude was wearing because I wanted so badly to stroke them, to rub my hands across their dark softness.

You loved to laugh and act silly. Here you are with six of your girlfriends in black one-piece bathing suits, on the sandy beach of Park Point, that narrow strip of land that juts out from Duluth into Lake Superior. You're all making faces for the camera and striking ridiculous poses. And there's one of you in a fancy dress, long black stockings, and elaborate cloche, swinging a baseball bat! All the pictures you carefully attached in the pages of albums with little black photo corners, then wrote captions with white ink in your delicate slender handwriting.

Even after you married Daddy, who thought being a minister meant it was important to comport oneself with dignity and a serious demeanor, especially in public, you weren't above occasional frivolity. Years after you'd died and I was a mother myself, I ran into two old women who'd baby-sat for me. The stories they had to tell about you! "Oh, how your mother loved to laugh! She was always telling funny stories on herself. Once she was walking downtown to buy chipped beef and milk for supper and had discovered some peanuts in her dress pocket. Well, seems she decided to toss one in the air and try to catch it in her mouth. It was so much fun she kept on doing it, until she realized one of your dad's parishioners was walking by on the other side of the street. I guess he just stared at her with amazement."

And then there were the backyard theatricals. You'd plan them with Delores, who lived next door and was always sickly. You thought she needed cheering up, and you certainly made her laugh. (Later they found out she had tuberculosis, and she had to spend years in a sanitorium.) Remember how you'd get all the neighbor children to learn little recitations and put on skits which you wrote on lined notebook paper? I still have them. You loved to make costumes and decorate that makeshift picnic table stage with flowers from our garden. My father mildly disapproved, thinking it smacked a bit too much of worldly entertainment, but he enjoyed hearing me recite the very first poem I ever memorized: "Roses on my shoulders, slippers on my feet, I am Daddy's little darling, don't you think I'm sweet?"

Daddy disapproved of other things, too, like that hat you bought on a shopping trip to Minneapolis with the Erickson girls, the ones who used to baby-sit me. They told me how beautiful it looked on you, with its long sweep of a feather curving around your face. He thought it would call too much attention to you, be inappropriate for a minister's wife. But you wore it anyhow, refused to remove the feather. I wish I had that hat. I look for one like it every time I go into antique shops, but so far have failed to find anything that reminds me of you.

And the dress you wore in your confirmation picture. You still had it stored away in our attic, carefully wrapped in tissue in an elegant box from The Glass Block, Duluth's finest department store. When Daddy said we couldn't afford to buy me a new dress for the Christmas program, you cut right into that beautiful white dimity and made me a lovely lace-trimmed and smocked dress. I even wore a bow in my side part like the one you wore in back of your hair on your confirmation day. And you put up my hair in rags the night before so I could have curls like Shirley Temple's. We never got to see her movies, because Daddy wouldn't let us, but my friends had dolls that looked just like her.

One of the few pictures I have of you and me together was taken the summer of 1931, in the backyard of your parents' home in Duluth. You're pregnant with my brother David, and your ankles are so swollen, your flesh barely contained in your shoes. My heart aches for the pain you must be in, as you so often were in those years the inflammatory rheumatism was acting up, getting ready to destroy your heart. But I am blissfully unaware of your sorrow, leaning happily into your body, still your darling and doted-upon only child. "God must have known how much I wanted you," you wrote in my baby book.

A few summers ago when I drove through Duluth on my way to the North Shore, I stopped at McDonald's for lunch. At the next table sat four white-haired women, who were at least in their eighties. One of them had her long hair combed back smoothly from her brow and twisted into a large bun, the way you used to wear your hair. They were relishing their Big Macs and dipping their fries in catchup and laughing and talking with the excitement of young girls. I wanted to lean over and ask them if they knew you, if maybe they'd been in your class at Central High. "She'd only be eighty-nine," I wanted to say, "and still in love with life, the way you all are."

Phebe

Joy Harjo

Brother Allen, mother Wynema Jewell Pickett, and Joy Harjo
Oklahoma; c. 1953

Joy Harjo was born May 9, 1951, in Tulsa, Oklahoma. She has published several books of poetry, including *She Had Some Horses, In Mad Love and War,* and *The Woman Who Fell from the Sky,* in addition to a recent CD with her band Poetic Justice. Forthcoming are a memoir, *A Love Supreme,* and an anthology, *Reinventing the Enemy's Language,* both from W. W. Norton. She lives in Albuquerque, New Mexico.

Wynema Jewell Pickett was born December 8, 1931, in Decatur, Arkansas—at home. She spent most of her life in Tulsa, where she worked as a chef and a waitress and owned a bar north of town. She now lives in Claremore, Oklahoma.

The Immensity of Your Gift

Dear Mom,

When I was four I never wanted to let you go. I remember those muggy early evenings in the late summer light. They mark the happier times in my early childhood. The radio played often (you preferred heartbreak crooners like Nat King Cole) as you cleaned or sewed or otherwise attempted to make your home perfection. Our small frame house, duplicated in rows after the war, was your heaven. (You had grown up barely getting by near the Oklahoma state line.) Once you and your family were forced to live in an abandoned two-story house because you had no place else to live and winter was coming on. It was haunted, and no one could live with the ghosts, who began their perpetual party every night upstairs. They clinked their mugs of beer, danced to the sounds of the player piano (that was no longer there), and roused themselves into a terrible fight in the early hours of the morning. The family, who did not go into the territory of the ghosts upstairs, huddled in one room downstairs to keep warm in the huge, drafty house. They would hear the fight, gunshots, and then the sound of a body being dragged downstairs. This went on every night, but one never gets used to the rituals of ghosts.

Early evenings last for eternity, and often attract ghosts and spirits who are lonely for humans. They usually appear at dusk, and settle in on the music the world is compelled to make during that hour.

In those years of early childhood, the earth turned solid and swift. The earth's song combined with the chorus of cicadas in elm trees, and the crickets, children's shouts and cries, the laughter and fights of their parents, the occasional vehicle against the ticking of the moon. You added your voice to the song the world was making together. Most often you sang a tune written by a lover yearning for his German girlfriend, or something from Patsy Cline, who was the voice of the young woman bereft of her most perfect love. You sang for the love of adding your voice to the concatenation of voices rising from the wet, thick air, flavored by the spirits joining us there.

I wondered where your voice came from. I had never heard your mother or your father sing. Perhaps you were born of a need to sing, in a place whose singers had forgotten the songs. There was a family myth of a singer from your mother's people who was gifted and touched many people with her songs. She would travel through the countryside with her voice. When she sang people were miraculously healed. The crippled would walk. The deaf would begin to hear again. All terrible sadnesses would flow from the body like sweet springs through rocks. The people would cry and laugh together. Ghosts would be released from their burdens and fly toward the sun. I remember how your singing could change the light in the room, could make us smile after you had been crying from yet another heartbreak from your husband, my father.

There are giant emotional waves that sweep through cities, the countryside, nations, through periods of time, and take us along with them. We were in the wave of the early 1950s when everyone had been promised a piece of the American dream pie, a pie made from the lands and resources stolen from my father's people and your mother's people, as well as from other colonized lands far from our country. It became easier to forget as televisions became the altars in our homes.

Crucial to that dream was the perfect house, the nuclear family of husband, wife, and two or more children who fit the ads of the appliance makers and other marketers. You and my father had much to forget in the struggle to construct this illusion from your families and tribal histories. For you this dream shimmered in the distance from the desert of poverty. If you could attain this then you would have self-worth, a value no one could dispute. You would no longer be the extra mouth to feed at the table, dependent on a mother who didn't love you. The other children couldn't make fun of you anymore as you carried your lard and water-and-flour biscuit lunch to school in the same dress you always wore.

I can still see you walking away from a ragged house filled with children and little else, with your best friend, Elvira Guerrero. Your father disapproved of your friendship because she was Mexican. You were supposed to move away from your Cherokee mother's brown people, toward the whiteness of the American dream. You hitchhiked into Tulsa to work as a cook and waitress at the White Knight. You carried an utter need for dignity in that body from which I would be the first born.

I was born of your tempestuous relationship with my father, a Muscogee Creek man who knew how to shine on the dance floor, his hair the color of petroleum. He had been born in a twenty-one-room house, his mother's inheritance from the oil boom that made many Creeks richer, and as many poorer, as the oil rich land was stolen, the inheritors destroyed for their riches. This was the history of Tulsa, a town that sprang up around the oil pool, the town in which you met, determined to make the best of yourselves. You married very young and in love. You were faithful to that love. My father could not be.

In that dawn of childhood you were the perfect demigod. You worked hard to make sure my brother Allen and I were cared for. I can still taste the gingerbread men we would cut out on the red Formica table, and the fried pies made of peaches and apples. I remember leaning on your knee, as you sewed matching outfits with a plump animal pattern for Allen and me. You were happy then, too. You wrote songs and sang them. You were beautiful with your dark auburn hair pulled into current styles, your body energetic with hope. I was in love with you in the way that children are focused on that which utterly pleases them. Nothing smelled better than White Shoulders mixed with the leather of my father's jacket you often wore, as you carried me feigning sleep after parties with your friends.

You had a home with no apparent ghosts. It was too new to have ghosts or the layers of history and myth that follow any family or tribe that stays in the same place. Everyone in that town had moved there in the last fifty years with heightened hopes, dreams, and fears. Most of them were European settlers. Many of them African. Few were of the original tribes who occupied the area since the beginning of time. Some were our tribes who had been brought here against our will. Together we were memory, and memory is persistent, fueled by the great vortex whirling from the heat of the earth burning from the star in the center. Spirits travel the vortex at high frequency, bringing gifts and resonance along the bloodlines. Ghosts are the burdened ones and are fueled by gravity. We were surrounded by spirits, but more often than we knew it, ghosts.

Several nights during those years my spirit stood free of my sleeping body. I would marvel at the freedom of spirit—different from the emotional density of ghosts tied by tragedy or other unfinished business—and travel through the house protecting us. I would stop last in your bedroom and look closely at you and my father as you slept next to each other. I could see the flicker of your love, and how that love would be failed many times by my father's inability to love himself, and how your deep need to fulfill your dream at any cost would nearly destroy you, and us. I would then fly through the neighborhood, over the city built on tribal lands, could see through time to what was here, before returning to the worlds that were more familiar before birth. The journey would take me from remembering everything back to forgetfulness. The gleam of my spirit's umbilical cord kept me tied to the house of my body, in that house made of promises, tied to you.

Maybe I was preparing for our departure into the abyss, a journey that would take us through the destruction of the dream in that house, from the loss of our father to perfumed strangers and alcohol, into the house of a monster who would keep us pressed against disaster, whose relatives manufactured the dream of owning the land and the people on it. He was the ghost haunting all of us through our childhood. There was no music, no dancing or singing in his house. The ghost would keep you in slavery for thirty-two years until he died in a house made of your money and dreams.

Through this nightmare I could no longer reach you. I had gone from being the beloved and cared-for child in a house of certainty to being the silent witness of a terrible destruction that you could not look at, pretended wasn't there—to endure. Perhaps several pages of this letter should be empty, nothing written on them to express this place in which we had lost our souls, become as ghosts in homes owned by this man but paid for by you—this man who was the epitome of the American dream: white, believed your family could be civilized by him, worked full-time for American Airlines, was a member of the Elks Club, who forced you to play Russian roulette with a loaded gun, and otherwise threatened you and us.

In this space we had no voice. I never heard you singing anymore. No one sang. I lost you. And myself. And several years of knowing you. And being mothered by you. I still feel like I cannot find you when I see you clinging to a false dream in which you have lost your ability to see, you who were gifted at birth with the ability to see beyond the ordinary confines of earth.

So this is a cry. Of sometimes being so angry, I am whirling and fierce as flames kindling the center of the earth. Of being so grief stricken at the loss of us, of our lands, our songs, that I am a ghost of forgetfulness.

I am trying to forgive, to find a path of meaning through the abyss. It has taken years. Yet through these years, those songs always return, songs of terror and beauty from which we must continue to make songs to renew our children and grandchildren.

Then the ghosts will sleep. Then the spirits of renewal will join us.

I want to tell you that you are always a part of me, as is this shared history of shame, the tale of rising up through the ghosts of ashes. We have to claim it so we won't be destroyed by it.

I want to hear you sing again, I want you to love yourself without the approval of any false dreams.

It is early evening as I write this in a place not far from Oklahoma, where you are living. I am aware of the spirits who bless this house, who tend the plants. They remind me that what we poor humans are made of is closer to the consistency of songs.

And I think of those ghosts in that poor house from so many

years ago and wonder if they're still caught in the need to repeat failure because it so horrifies them.

The particles of late sun that have spent the day gathering stories from one side of the hemisphere to another blink with wisdom. I realize how deeply our destinies are tied. I realize the immensity of your gift to me.

Love,

JUNE 1995
ALBUQUERQUE, NEW MEXICO

Mary Hebert

Marie E. Lagana,
age twenty-three,
42nd Street
New York City; 1933

Mary Yorizzo,
age four
Bronx River Parkway;
Mother's Day, 1954

Mary Yorizzo Hebert was born July 18, 1950, in Bronxville, New York. She is the author of *Horatio Rides the Wind*, published by Templar PLC. As one of sixty U.S. writers selected for WritersCorps 1994/95, she conducted weekly writing workshops for children in the northeast Bronx. She is the editor of the WritersCorps anthology *Not Black and White: Inside Words from the Bronx WritersCorps* (Plain View Press, 1996). She lives in New York City.

Marie Lagana Yorizzo was born July 14, 1910, in Scarsdale, New York. She worked as a seamstress in New York's garment district until her marriage to Joseph Yorizzo in 1935. Mother of five girls, she died in Montrose, New York, in 1964. Among her girlhood possessions were medals for tennis and running.

Something Ordinary

After 30 years, Mom—

The age you were working in the garment district
crossing under the park avenue bridge
at grand central in your red gabardine, was
the age I sat writing poetry on sunset road
in thin jeans taking the train to college
in the bronx. *I wish I had danced.*

Despite the dancer's body you gave me
I never danced, was a cheerleader *don't laugh*
all-round girl chairman of school spirit at 16
but shy like you easily scarred by opinion
still remember how you call me miser when I am
all of 6 and not wanting to empty my piggy
bank for some forgotten cause, know
there must be something that is mine and hold on
to my virginity until almost 20 as hungry as I was
for love didn't understand men's directness,
back-to-the-party quickness. How many lovers
it's taken since to fill the emptiness that hit

me like a brick wall when I turned that
red velvet corner of womanhood and found you
gone, keeping your date with death.
I wish I had danced.

How you would hate
most of my life choices,
greenwich village solitude
phantom husband now remarried to have his
first child after 12 years of our dances with ghosts.
How of all you sewed on your necchi I remember
only blue and green plaid bib white
collar; how all I have from my tuckahoe
childhood are my bronze baby
shoes the name mary on a blue stone
statue of the virgin making me think
I am protected always by the goddess
she became after I wiped away the
cobwebs of catholicism. Some nights
I would hug those stiff bronze shoes
believing this was your rosetta stone
to me that I must decipher, your happiness
at birthing me your last witness
to innocence o innocence
left us early as I drink your sadness in
the wallace street kitchen, catching
your finger in that monster with wringers
in the cold water flat,
flattening your joy for 19 years
I can only imagine
lived in you, that undated photo.

I wish I had danced in that childhood
left eagerly for drawings
and early poems, limericks about dogs
and dust that gave way to darker ones
voicing the terror of being left
on that moonless road to womanhood
in that eclipse of your life.

After thirty years on the road of my own
signposts, I want to say something ordinary

to you like, "I bought you a blue sweater"
not, "Tell me about the sadness," but
something ordinary like, "Did you get my card?"
Not, "Grief sits still in my heart between
the petals of unborn child and mother."
Before I can say something
extraordinary to you, like your death
gave me wings that are flying
me higher than you ever imagined.

And for you, the bird who tore
off her wings so I could fly, I wish
I had danced, danced on the grave
of my shyness, pulled on the tiny
black leotard on main street, danced
away the legacy of sadness that howls
in the shafts of our mediterranean bones.

Until all I have left to say, if I could see
your extraordinary face just once
with my adult eyes, is a whisper
as ordinary as, *good-bye.*

Love,

Mary

Kathryn Hohlwein

Helen Joyce Yeoman Jerrell and her daughter,
Kathryn Joyce Jerrell Hohlwein
Bryce Canyon, Utah; 1970

Kathryn Joyce Hohlwein was born May 18, 1930, in Salt Lake City, Utah. She lived in the same house and knew the same friends from kindergarten to university graduation. She received an M.A. degree from the Bread Loaf School of English and went on scholarships to France and later Spain, where she met artist Hans-Jurgen Hohlwein. They later married in Beirut, Lebanon, and did their first teaching there. After a year writing and painting in the Scottish Highlands, they began teaching at universities in the American Midwest. In 1966, they moved to California State University, Sacramento, where Hans taught printmaking and drawing and Kathryn taught, and continues to teach—poetry, creative writing, humanities, and a Homer seminar. They had three children, Reinhard, Andrea, and Laura and now have a granddaughter, Emily. They divorced, and Hans died in 1977. Her books include, (with Patricia Frazier Lamb) *Touchstones: Letters Between Two Women, 1953–1964* (Harper, 1983) and *In the Middle Kingdom* (*Neue Frau* series, Rowöhlt, Hamburg, 1987). Poems and scholarly articles have appeared in numerous journals. For twelve years, she was the poetry and art editor for the quarterly, *Studia Mystica*.

Helen Joyce Yeoman Jerrell was born January 24, 1898, in Rensselaer, Indiana, and died in Salt Lake City, Utah, on November 1, 1976. She grew up on a big wheat and dairy farm with her three brothers and three sisters. When she turned eight, her birthday present was a piano, and music was central to her work and her life and to the family's life. She married Warner Phillips Jerrell, a fellow student in Kingman's High School, and they moved to Salt Lake where they lived out their lives. They had two children, Robert Emerson and Kathryn Joyce. They were Unitarians, political liberals, and they loved each other.

And Yet You Will Weep and Know Why

Dear Mother—

The journey here was a small labor, much milder than the one that brought you alive into the green and windy prairie lands of Rensselaer, Indiana, in 1898. The century was about to end then, as the century and the millennium are about to end now, in 1995. I have traveled to find you again, you who are never lost to me. I am looking out at the old bandstand on the Courthouse grounds, wondering if your mother ever dandled you here, her black-haired, curly-headed daughter, her Helen, and I know I *want* to imagine you here. I know I am conjuring all this out of the wavering wheat fields, but every mother lifts her pretty baby in the air, doesn't she?

I have just been to a reunion of Yeomans, your people in Kingman, Kansas—almost the mathematical center of the United States. A small town, a beat in the heartland. The sweetness of the encounters and the strangeness of the branchings and divergences have made me ponder many of your dearest qualities as well as how far you traveled when you left.

Normally, I think of myself as the child who went off, who encountered, then married, other ways and other reasons for doing things differently. But you and my father, our Warner, were exiles, too, harboring and passing on to me the virtues of the farm community you left. You never scorned them, as I have never scorned your "free-thinking" rebelliousness from the mid-American Bible Belt. If we are wise, we enlarge our minds and hearts rather than discard that which gave us our first base of understanding. So long as it was grounded in love, as yours was, as mine was.

I was born a Sunday child, and folk rhythms had it that I was to be "bonny and blithe and good and gay." And certainly those were the wishes you held for me. You did all in your power to make me "bonny," stitching and pleating perfect dresses for me that turned me into "a little confection," as one of your friends described the child I was. And, as all sane parents everywhere, you wanted me to be "blithe," and I was. The only problem was that, blissful as life seemed to be and wildly as I played, I early on suffered nostalgia in reverse. That is, I was by temperament melancholy as well as blithe. I always have known the oppressions of time, or, at least, I sensed them early. Agnostic as you raised me to be, I nonetheless felt the gates of Eden closing, and I knew that we would mostly forget that such a loss could happen, and had happened, and always would happen. The ache that resulted from the long apprenticeship in this acknowledgment has left me permanently hungry. And filled with "the tears of things."

Since you did not take your morality from the Bible, your

sense of wanting me to be *good* was homegrown. You wanted me to be *wholesome*. Ah! To be good *and* happy *and* good *and* gay. Darling Mother—if "I've always meant to tell you" something, it was of my suspicion that one could never be good enough, good enough to sustain our intuitions of happiness.

To be sure, on an adolescent level—there were all kinds of secrets. How could I grow up a passionate Unitarian child in Mormon Salt Lake City without having secrets? Secrets of wanting to be Mormon, secrets of why I was glad I was not. They mostly revolved around sex, and certainly I had no desire to tell you of all that and make you suffer, though now I can—of steamy encounters in your car, of hours-long deep kisses right beneath the dining room window, of erections suspected, hoped for, felt. No, never since my only unjust punishment, at five, for playing freely with my neighborhood friend, Teddy, have I longed to tell you of my sex life, or more suspect yet, of my erotic life. What joys, what miseries and misreadings, what fears—they have been my own, not meant for others, for mothers.

But I always meant to tell you something strange about my affirmations, my pagan beliefs, my sense that the gods are in all things and how, in spite of that immanence, we weep. My students, at least the natively pessimistic ones or the ones who savor the bittersweet, have insight into my take on life that perhaps you never did.

(Outside, the summer wind is whipping branches into the bandstand. I wish I could hear the music, played on Wednesday nights, floating across the Iroquois River. I wish I could live forever.)

Today I went to the oldest cemetery in your birth town. There were many tombstones for Yeomans, many small ones ("Beloved child of") with only one date, the single day the baby lived and died. There were names that had the distant ring of gossip or lost tales, friends or uncles, or friends of uncles. And one that brought tears—a tilted, sinking stone with little visible writing left. All it said was "Sacred to the memory of . . ." and the rest was blurred. The specifics, the name, the person, the person-hood—vanished. There was no marker for Chief Wapakanotta.

We *are* like generations of leaves.

I have taught Homer for many years and I never weary of him.

His *Iliad* is brutal, heartbreaking, magnificent and exact—"the most just and impartial of all human inventions," to quote Hobbes.

I see I am writing of myself—more than I am of you. It's because I want you to see me, as I see myself. I want the secret of my melancholy love of life not to divide us. Pasternak wrote that poets "are people who meditate upon death and thereby create new life." Even though it is hard to understand (for one who loved gaiety, who laughed easily and loved to dance), it is what you most need to know about me.

Whenever I divide bulbs, or tap upon melons, whenever (so rarely now) I see clothes flapping on a line, whenever I watch an accompanist, and listen, or note the light now changing, I think of you or feel your life in mine. I can barely look at fabrics, for I remember them all—pongee, seersucker, taffeta, percale, linen, corduroy, fine wool, gabardine, and I see my ankle socks fractionally turning on the living room carpet. I feel myself turning as your dear hands move, one pin at a time.

This little midwestern bandstand is all awash in shadow.

It has taken me all my life but now I know that, just as you had hoped, I *am* wholesome and I am happy.

Your loving daughter,

Joyce

Nicole Hollander

*Shirley and Henry Garrison with their daughter,
Nicole—in Aunt Belle's living room*
Chicago, Illinois; c. 1944

Nicole Hollander was born in Chicago, Illinois, on April 25, 1939. She is a syndicated cartoonist and author of the comic strip *Sylvia*. Her latest book is a collection of essays and cartoons and is called *Female Problems: An Unhelpful Guide*.

Shirley Garrison, Nicole's mother, was born in Maywood, Illinois, on October 16, 1918. She was director of admitting for a suburban hospital and a great drawer of women in profile. She died in June 1994.

SYLVIA ON SUNDAY   by Nicole Hollander

220

Ann Hood

**Gloria Hood and her daughter, Ann,
in front of the family home**
West Warwick, Rhode Island; 1963

Ann Hood was born in 1956 in West Warwick, Rhode Island, and grew up in the house her mother and her grandmother were born in. She is the author of six novels, including *Somewhere Off the Coast of Maine, Places to Stay the Night,* and her most recent, *The Properties of Water.* She is a contributing editor for *Parenting* magazine. In 1993 she moved back to Rhode Island after living in other places for fifteen years. She lives in Providence with her husband, Lorne Adrain, and their son, Sam.

Gloria Hood was born in 1931 in West Warwick, Rhode Island. She is a tax auditor for the Internal Revenue Service. She lives in the house that her grandparents bought when they arrived from Italy in the early 1900s.

At My Table

Dear Mom,

Probably the last thing you expect me to write about is a kitchen table. Not just any kitchen table, but the green and brown enamel-topped one that sat in your grandmother's kitchen, and then your mother's kitchen, and your own kitchen (until modern life seeped into our house and you went to Ethan Allen for a new Colonial dining room set). For the last twenty-five years, that table has been in the garage with a green plastic drop cloth on top and dust gathering in its curves and grooves. And now, even though it is missing one of the matching chairs—broken? misplaced? no one can even remember—it is sitting in my kitchen. At last.

I have dreamed of taking that table home with me for most of my adult life. I remember when I was young and I'd sit at it to eat my breakfast in front of the coal stove that heated our house until modernity took that too and brought us a furnace and sleek baseboards that required dusting once a week. I remember opening the drawer on the side—that's lost too now!—and removing the silverware for dinner. I remember my great-grandmother, and my grandmother Mama Rose, and her generation—Naneen and Auntie Etta—and then you and your sisters, and all of my cousins, and me, all of us sitting there at that table.

Why do you want that old thing? you asked me as I hauled it out of the garage and then set about dusting it off.

It is appropriate that I'm writing this amid unpacked boxes and unhung pictures, sitting in the house I always dreamed I would live in someday. Remember, when I was seven, how I used to love the TV show *Please Don't Eat the Daisies*? I loved that the mother in it was a writer. And I loved that old house they lived in—filled with secret doors and extra staircases and a big kitchen. Even when I imagined a child's version of that life.

So here I am, on the third floor of a restored Victorian house, looking for a way to tell you what brought me here. Trying to let you know that it is all the things you gave me that led me to this place. Struggling to explain about why I wanted—*needed*, really—that old table of ours.

I know what you were thinking when you came to this house last week for the first time: *Why does she want to live in such an old place?* You imagine me in a sparkling new split-ranch somewhere, with a circular driveway and wall-to-wall carpeting, when what I love is this: the old wooden floors in need of polishing, the creaky stairs, the cracked paint on the walls. What I love is a house with a history, a story to be told.

You think that points to how different we are, don't you? But, Mom, instead it points to how much we are alike. One of the best things you gave me was a home. And not just any home, but a home filled with stories. When I think of my childhood, it is noisy and busy and rich with people. It was your grandmother—my great-grandmother—who moved to that house in West Warwick, Rhode Island, from Naples. And she stayed there until she died, right up in the bedroom you and Daddy still sleep in. I remember when she died; it was winter, it was cold, and I was in the first grade. You kept me home from school the day of the funeral so I wouldn't see everyone crying when they left Sacred Heart church, right across the street from my school.

A lot of people died in that house, and I believe their ghosts walk around there still. It sounds crazy, I know, but another thing you gave me was my Italian blood. When someone looks at my blond hair and green eyes and shrieks, *There's no way you can be Italian!* I have to laugh. My great-grandmother had blue eyes and fair hair; your mother, Mama Rose, was a green-eyed redhead. Those women, and all the aunts and great-aunts who visited us, convinced me that there are ghosts. They would sit around the kitchen table—the very table I just took from your garage and polished for three hours and put in *my* kitchen here—and tell stories. Stories about ghosts and babies born with fish gills and teenagers who could light candles without any flames, just by sheer will. You had your own stories to tell—the woman who lived up the street and was a witch. She did magic with candles and told you that Dad was the man who loved you, the man you should marry.

So why shouldn't I believe that all the people who died in that house—both of my great-grandparents and both of my grandparents—are still there? Every toddler who has played in our living room points to the same corner and claims to see a red-haired woman standing there. Now even my own son is doing it! Sam is convinced someone's there, and so am I.

But for all the people who died there—dramatically, after falling down the cellar steps; or quietly, like Mama Rose, who made a gallon of spaghetti sauce, then sat down at the table and died—there were also plenty who were born there. All ten of you Masciarotte kids. I grew up saying all of your names like a mantra: *Joe Connie Emma Angie Brownie Rosie Chuckie Ann Gloria June.* I listened when you told me stories about the house then, how six of you girls slept in one room, three to a bed, and the three boys slept in another room, and Auntie Junie, the youngest, slept on a sofa in the kitchen. That green sofa stayed there until I was eight years old. I remember Mama Rose sleeping on it, crying, after Uncle Brownie died, too young and too suddenly.

At one time, seventeen people lived in that house. Bachelor uncles and a crippled aunt and all of you kids and your parents and their parents. Those people stayed there until they got married or until they died, so that I grew up with most of them. I remember Christmases and Thanksgivings and Easters when my generation had to sit at small tables to make room for everybody and still there were adults in the living room and on the floor. Mama Rose, all four foot eleven of her, would climb onto the kitchen table every Easter, stand right there among the frittata and homemade bread and cheese and rice pastere, and sprinkle holy water on all of us, saying a prayer in Italian.

You gave me a typical 1960s American childhood: we rode around in a Chevy station wagon, I had a Beatles lunch box, I took tap dancing lessons. We went on vacations to Niagara Falls and Amish country and New York City. I wore poor boy shirts, bell bottoms, hip hugger jeans. We gobbled up TV—*Dick Van Dyke* and *Peyton Place* and *The Ed Sullivan Show*. You cooked Swedish meatballs, lemon meringue pie, cheeseburgers. We had an avocado green fondue pot, an electric toothbrush, an ice crusher. I sang along with the Supremes and the Monkees and Simon and Garfunkel. I wanted to marry Paul McCartney.

But it is the Italian part that most shaped me.

The food I remember comes from those meals for two or three dozen people that Mama Rose and you would cook. For a time, the house couldn't even hold all those people, and your father built a little one-room place that simply held a kitchen and an extra table and chairs—the Shack. Those meals in the Shack are the ones I remember most—warm summer nights, moths clinging to the screens, people talking too loud, the crush of bodies in there. Mama Rose never stopped cooking for less than twenty. That is how I cook, as if I'm expecting more people to arrive.

Sometimes you talk about selling that house, where so many Masciarottes were born, where they made a home a hundred years ago. You talk about buying a condo. Less to clean, you say. No steps to climb. But you stay there because of its history. You stay because of the stories that house can tell.

I read once that Truman Capote did not come from a family that read much; but he came from a family that told stories. This is like our family. I grew up listening to fantastic tales, stories about the old country, stories about saints performing miracles, stories about secret prayers and potions that could cure sciatica, make a man love you, take away the evil eye. Mama Rose and you and your sisters sat around the kitchen table, into the night, drinking coffee and telling stories. You see, Mom, that is what I do now: I tell stories. It is because of that house, our shared history, that I found a voice in that kitchen.

What do you need such a big house for? you asked me when I took you on the tour here, leading you up back stairways, showing off the bookcase that opens to reveal a hidden door.

I couldn't answer you then. The answer was too large. But I can tell you now.

I need this house so I can fill it the way you taught me. I want to have Thanksgiving here for two dozen people. I want children to remember all the food, the air warm with people, the crush of bodies. I want to fill it until there is no more room and people have to sit on the floor. I took our old kitchen table and put it in my kitchen so that at night we will sit around it—you and me and aunts and cousins. We will sit there into the night. We will drink coffee. We will tell stories. And my children will be there, listening.

That is what you gave me; it is what I want to give them. A table to sit at, dozens of arms to hold them, a history in progress, stories to hear, and a voice to tell those stories in someday.

Love, Ann

Pam Houston

Louise Hoff,
mother of
Pam Houston
New York City;
c. 1944

Pam Houston
Trenton, New Jersey;
c. 1966

Pam Houston was born in Trenton, New Jersey, on January 9, 1962. Her collection of short stories, *Cowboys Are My Weakness* (W. W. Norton), was the winner of the 1993 Western States Book Award and has been translated into seven languages. She has published fiction in *Mirabella, Mademoiselle, The Mississippi Review,* and *Best American Short Stories;* and nonfiction in *The New York Times, Outside, Food and Wine, Vogue,* and *Travel and Leisure.* She is a contributing editor at *Elle* and *Ski* magazines. Houston is a licensed river guide and a horsewoman. She is currently finishing another book of fiction, a collection of essays, and a screenplay, and has recently edited a collection of fiction, nonfiction, and poetry for Ecco Press called *Women on Hunting.* She lives in Colorado at 9,000 feet above sea level near the headwaters of the Rio Grande.

Louise Hoff was born in Spiceland, Indiana, on October 11, 1922. She ran away from Spiceland to Broadway shortly after making a bet with her grandfather that he'd have to give her fifty dollars if she managed to get straight C's in the eighth grade. She became a singing, dancing comedienne, and worked her whole life as an actress. From opening Frank Sinatra's show in Las Vegas to going overseas with Bob Hope's WWII USO. She worked on and off Broadway, and in soap operas and television commercials.

Your Old Torch Songs

Dear Mom,

I had a dream, three nights ago, that you were dying again. Only this time I was there and knew it was happening. You were lying in bed, and it wasn't sudden, like before. It was something slow and tractable like cancer or AIDS, and now this was the end of it, and I was going to get to be by your side. It was clear to me what I had to do. Even inside the dream, I knew that you were already dead, and that this reenactment had been designed especially for me, so that I could lie beside you those last hours, and hold on to you while you slipped away.

After dreams like that I wonder if and how often *you* can see *me.* If you know I almost never wear the clothes, anymore, that you bought me. If you know how well Father and I get along these days, if it makes you angry that everything changed between us when you died. And can you see, when I get up in front of people, how much I learned from watching you on stage and on camera? *Did you get to see your mother act,* they ask me, and I give 'em your line, *every single day of my life.*

There's a bar down the street here called the Alley that's got a piano and a microphone, and I know you won't believe this but I go in there some nights and sing your old torch songs. "Moon River" is my favorite, and "It Wouldn't Be in Springtime." Rod Dibble, the piano player who's been there thirty-nine years and knows everything, says he's never even heard of "I Said to Love."

I told him somebody famous wrote it for you, though I couldn't remember who. I remembered the song, though, every verse and your voice singing it like an angel, your hands always tentative, always shaky on the piano keys.

> I said to love when I was seventeen,
> "Come back again when I am not so green,"
> I said to love when I was twenty-one,
> "Come back again, I'm having too much fun."

It started on the two-year anniversary of your death. I didn't even know what day it was, but I went into that cool dark bar with the lingerie hanging, almost sweetly, from two fake windows painted on the ceiling, and it was like you were all of a sudden inside me, your voice, not mine, singing out and not even shy.

For a while I believed that you were up in Heaven, or wherever, pulling the strings of my life like a puppeteer. That maybe for amusement, God gives everybody up there the right to effect one person's life on earth on a monthly basis. Like the time I met the Italian architect in Bolivia, and I started to tell him about *your* Italian and he said *he* was from Palermo, too. And if it was you who were responsible for the whole married man thing last year, you went a little overboard. You probably wanted to see if I'd weather it better than you did. And I did, by a lot.

I don't tell many people this but I secretly gave you credit for Nixon's stroke. Not his death, of course, that was somebody else's mother. I knew it would have pleased you the most to have him alive, and just not able to speak. I found out in your obituary that you were blacklisted in the 1950s with a lot of your friends, just one of the six hundred million things we never got to talk about. Maybe you've gotten reinterested in politics from your new position of power. Since Nixon died, anyway, I seem to have been off the hook.

I'm not sure how much you would like me these days. I say when I'm angry now, and I cry a lot on airplanes, and I go to the grocery store in sweatpants and I almost never wear my contact lenses anymore. I don't fake it with authority figures, I don't keep my mouth shut even when I know better, and just this week, for the first time in several, I started to lose all my hope again.

And you know that story you always told about the time in the house on State Street when you and Father were drunk and screaming mad and Aunt Martha stole me from you guys and wouldn't give me back for three whole weeks and even then after a whole slew of promises? Well I just realized it wasn't funny. And I wish you had found a different way to say it besides "everything was perfect between your father and me until you came along."

The next part of the song, the bridge, I think they call it, was your favorite, the place, you said, where you really got to show off your voice.

> But the summer turned to winter,
> And the leaves came tumbling from the bow,
> And my simple heart grew wiser.
> It's so much wiser now.

And I guess I'm finally getting to the point of this letter, which is that at the moment there seems to be a man who can bear me.

I'm in Kansas now, of all places, in his house near the railroad tracks where the trains rattle past, sometimes as many as ten an hour, and there's no conclusion I can come to except that he loves me a lot. He can't say the words, of course, but he's converted the back of his truck into a doghouse and carpeted the window ledges so the dogs can lean over the edge without getting calluses on their elbows. He made the platform right at window height so Hailey can lie down and look out at the same time, and if that's not love I don't know what to call it. He even made a ramp that hinges down from the tailgate with a no-slip surface because he thought they were embarrassed, old as they are, having to be lifted into the back of the truck.

Maybe more to the point is that he lets *me* love *him,* which seems to be what I need more than anything. He doesn't love himself much, is the problem. Drinks a fifth and a half of tequila a day.

I know what you're thinking. And yes, I did put the no alcoholics rule into effect at your funeral, and sticking to it these years has got me, in this order: a stalker, a lawsuit, a compulsive liar, and a sex addict who might be gay. With that kind of record I'm tempted to agree with Aunt Martha's wisdom: *There's something to be said for the devil, you know.* And it's funny how all my skills came back so quickly. Just tonight I willed away a bartender three times using only my eyes.

I've always chosen radical mirrors, and eastern Kansas in August is about as radical as it gets. There are wife beaters and babies in the bar and the dogs are black with fleas and the river smells so bad even Hailey won't get in it. Kansans think California is the place bums go to eat shrimp cocktail on welfare, everybody walking around brimming with defensiveness and that relentless midwestern pride. Everybody's got coffee mugs with sunflowers painted on them, and the streets are clean and even, the kids blonde, wholesome and happy-looking until you look close enough to see the set in their jaw. The Union Pacifics roar past at all hours of the morning, screaming like deep throated madwomen, and twice since I've been here there's been a car that didn't get out of the way. I went to get my hair cut and a perfect stranger told me that her neighbor killed her cat with a sickle and left it in two pieces on her porch. In late summer Lawrence, Kansas, is an act of violence waiting to happen, everybody edgy with the heat and looking for something to hit.

I started crying myself yesterday, said it was just the humidity and the temperature—109 in the shade—but this morning the tears wouldn't stop and I can say out loud the truth I must have come here for: this time, as usual, the darkness is inside me.

I'd like to tell you how it feels when he gets so drunk he doesn't hear the things I'm saying. I'd like to lay out for you my decision process concerning when to tell him what: these are the things I want him to remember, these are the throwaway things it's okay if he forgets, if I say this now it might make him want to start drinking, if I say this other thing it might, for tonight at least, make him want to stop.

Did I tell you that his liver's in failure? Ketones, I think they're called, pure poison trying to get out through the soft skin in his mouth.

I told him I'd watch him die if that's what he required, and I will, as I watched you do the same all my life.

I know none of this is your fault, but I have to tell you today that it feels like it. I'm like the "before" example in an outdated psychology textbook, believing I can save all of you with the holy fervor of my love.

For the first year my hand went to the phone to call you every morning. Now it's just my guts that make the leap while my body sits still.

Your voice comes to me in the night sometimes, strong, clear and beautiful and always in the final verse of *I Said to Love*.

I had a dream last night that you were driving Byron's old chevy pickup. I guess it won't surprise anyone when I say you were stalled out on the tracks. And yes, I guess I'm still angry that you didn't want to stay here on earth any longer. And yes, I still miss you every single day. And yes, I wish we'd known how to love each other better. I'm trying to learn that these days. A train rattles the house even now as I write these lines.

Pam

Laura Kasischke

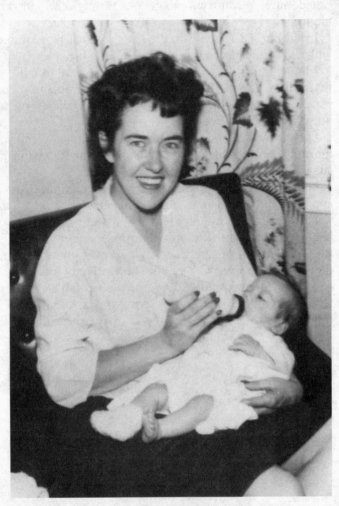

Suzanne Sullivan Kasischke with daughter Laura
Grand Rapids, Michigan; c. 1961–1962

Laura Kasischke was born December 5, 1961, in Lake Charles, Louisiana. She spent her childhood in Grand Rapids, Michigan, and now lives in Chelsea, Michigan. She has published two collections of poetry, *Wild Brides* and *Housekeeping in a Dream*. Her novel, *Suspicious River*, was published in 1996.

Suzanne Sullivan Kasischke was born in Grand Rapids, Michigan, on September 12, 1932, and spent most of her life in Grand Rapids. She was interested in theater and music. She died of breast cancer twelve years ago. Laura was her only child.

White Moths

Mother,

There are display cakes at the bakery—layer upon chaste, white layer—growing stale behind the baker's plate glass case. Who knows for whom they were originally baked, but now they'll never be tasted. Now, these are just the hopeful possibilities of cake. Or the memories of cake. One has a stiff bride and groom waiting patiently for something on its top tier, something that won't be coming. It's June, and those two look stunned in a spotlight of sun and dust, wading knee-deep through fake snow, staring straight ahead with their primitive, painted faces and nothing to say to each other. Maybe an avalanche is on the way. See how this cake is tipped a bit to the West—toward Wyoming or Las Vegas?

Mother, we've been separated now forever, and the silence between us is this bakery case. On my side, it's glare—a pure, shining plane, impenetrable as the sky. On your side, I imagine the muffled, aquarium-quiet of death, the sweet suffocation of bridal white on display, the standstill of beautiful, inedible cake.

Sometimes, I imagine all the things you might ask me to describe: images from your lost earth. Perhaps I would send them down to you on small, scrawled scraps of paper. Maybe you could snatch them out of my hand with your skeletal one— jeweled, now, with green-eyed flies or petrified honeybees.

235

Maybe those scraps of paper would burst into brief, contained flames over your grave when you touched them—like ignited white moths—but in the meantime you might see what I've seen. *Fat man on the elevator today, cradling a small, white cat. Delicate pink sweaters at the mall, too beautiful to buy. Twilight, spoon-shaped sterling. Or, morning, the sky white with haze—a weak sun in the middle like a cool, fried egg.*

It was as though, when you died, the house with all its humble objects got tipped onto its side. There we were, my father and I, with all your things and our things suspended above us for a long, long time—neither falling nor flying. We didn't say much about grief. Dad was still a mailman then, used to walking into the wind with his head down. Just past twenty, I was a stupid, selfish girl, and it would be years before your gravity got me: all that stuff crashing at last—apples, china cups, the floral sofa and the vodka bottles—into my bed one night. *How long have I been sleeping?* I'd wonder while the white stars of the fuse box snapped, the red sparks, the blue volts, the asbestos graying my hair. I was a grown woman by then with a permanent, flashing glass of poison in my hand like a fiery, doused diamond.

Well, grief gets you, as everyone knows. Or, it gets everything and everyone in your path. There are road hogs in minivans who scare the old men in their rusty Fords to the highway's shoulder. There are teenage boys who steal their grandmother's Social Security checks, and people who dump dogs they no longer want way out in the country.

And there are those dogs, who thought they were loved, wandering the dirt roads in sentimental circles looking for the suburb—hungry and dumb, stupidly confused.

It's June. In fields around our farmhouse, there are brides and cool-green heads of lettuce pushing up out of the dirt. The wind is brilliant confetti. The sky is blue and acute. Perhaps there is a wild-haired god up there who trains these simple, yellow butterflies to dance from bloom to bloom with whips and chains, the way He teaches us to love.

Mother, I mean, although you taught me all about death, slapping your white wings against the hospital glass, so ferocious with morphine that night we had to hold you down while you died;

although I knew it was the end of the world by the terrified look in your eyes—and no nice tunnels of light, no bright bridge to a valley of forgotten aunts and uncles waiting for you with champagne, finger sandwiches; although I knew, thanks to you, for a long time what a fragile glass ornament survival is, I decided not to live this life.

My best days are past, says the Saffron the afternoon it blooms.

And, as I drove recklessly through my twenties, there were many nights the 7-Eleven looked as if it were sailing toward me, a ship of fluorescent lights, across the parking lot's dark tar. A ghost ship. A tunnel of light. A brilliant instrument of liquor bottles. A summer party or a wedding. I thought, my dead mother might be waiting for me in there.

Many years later I would read something about stir-crazy sailors who saw sea cows in the waves and believed they'd seen mermaids sunning themselves on the rocks. I'd think to myself *but wouldn't those mermaids, being sea cows, have looked hairless, bloated, bestial, with only small wet holes for eyes?*

Of course not.

For better or worse? the priest asked.

Of course, I thought, without imagination.

But now I know. *Better,* it is a feather, all fluff and spine, or an iridescent bubble.

Worse, it will always be pedaling after you on its hot, red bike if you allow it to.

It's August 1982. The television buzzes before us—halo, glory, nimbus, aura—its pictures flashing faster than our eyes can separate them. Hence, this illusion of movement. Flare, kinetics—images divided by millimeters. Seconds split into frames. Cool, white electric moths projected against our window shades.

How can we not know?

Outside, it's deep, blue, cricket summer—nearly night. But in here, the TV preacher—himself a folded, brittle cricket in his black, expensive suit—stares straight into us. As I've said, it's summer—evening bleeding down, deep blue summer. Crickets whir in the suburban dark like flying saucers. *Mother,* you are wearing a silvery gown. Pure sheen. Outer space. Your pale skin under it glows in the dry, fizzing TV mist.

The preacher looks at us. He says, *Someone watching tonight suffers with cancer. God says to you, Woman, you are healed.*

You touch the skin above your heart with your fingertips then. A featherless dove under your left breast. The one with the lump.

After that, you die fast. And long after you die, that preacher still writes to thank you for the money you sent and to beg you for more. I let his letters gather stardust, lunar ash, on my dresser for a year before I take them to the trash.

It's possible to cling to grief simply because you refuse it.

For instance, this winter a mule in the remote Albanian village of Vilan was reported to be pregnant.

Though mules are sterile.

Though nothing like this had ever happened in Vilan before.

Then, the mule miscarried. The veterinarian said, "Something covered with what looked like white plastic fell to the ground."

It looked like a fetal lamb. Three pounds. With a small, white head and legs.

"It scared everyone present, so we threw it to the dogs."

The dogs tore that birth to pieces.

But now the mule itself is an evil omen. It can't be killed, and it can't be kept, and it won't die.

Only a year after you die, I marry a man I've decided not to love. I sleep beside him every night under steel wool winter sky. In summer, night birds shred the one moon in the sky, dragging black crepe paper across the face of that blank bride. I feel nothing. Even when he makes me laugh and smile, I see myself miniaturized, twice, in his eyes, as if I am driving away from him in a small, fast car, saying to love, *You can't catch me again.*

Last winter, a sister and brother stood on the rocky Mendocino coastline to scatter the ashes of their mother into the sea. One huge wave swept them together off the rocks and into the water, where they struggled for twenty minutes in waves that smashed them into the cliffs then pulled them away from the shore, tearing off their clothes, bloodying the ocean. The world's greediest, most powerful mother. It must have been like being born.

Her son crawled to safety.

But she got her daughter back.

Mothers always get their daughters back.

Mother, who died young and soaked with sweat in my arms, I know you know what I mean. You didn't want to die. For years you came to me in dreams, always angry, saying, *Don't forget, Girl, your life is mine.*

After you die you are everywhere. Reflections of yourself. A handful of dropped pebbles on the roof. The phone ringing and just the underwater sound of stopped time on the line. A pillar of violet water passes through the hallway and leaves through the closed back door. A storm on a June night, and in the morning, the wrecked splendor of apple blossoms like skinned chickens on the hoods of cars. In the afternoon, a sleek crow settles on a power line, then flies up into the blue—a ring of black in the air behind her, a trail of smaller, more intense birds, snapping their little wings furiously, looking tossed as a handful of feathers into the breeze—the breeze, which blows them backward as they fly, as they try foolishly to imitate her real grace.

You were that elegant crow of a mother. Smooth black hair. Pearls. Trunks of party dresses and stale carnations in the attic. For hours, you'd sit with me in the backyard and braid daisy chains, your fingers sticky with the bitter humidity of those green stems. But when you were done, you were done. Sometimes suicidal, sometimes bored, or drunk, you'd lock your bedroom door against my fist. *I want to die,* I heard you scream a million times before you did.

The day I quit drinking, I pass you on the street. You are wearing your camel's hair coat, and you are my young mother again. It's raining, and you have a black umbrella down over your face. But I know your gait. I recognize your shoes—those heels, in any weather. Still, I don't want to startle you. I let you walk by, just brushing my shoulder. *Don't worry—I wasn't crying, Mother. That was rain on my face.*

Ten years to the day of your death, I leave my husband. I move to the desert where every afternoon is a slide show—square, blank slides projected onto a screen too wide and white for my eye. That sky won't embrace me or learn my name, though I spend hours watching it for signs. At night, I dream about Michigan—so much black dirt squirming with sticky life. Insect ova. The twisted roots of my youth. Willows tapping their old-woman fingers through the graveyard in search of water, splitting stones. I dream about the big, androgynous angel in the cemetery where you're buried. With those concrete wings, it could never fly. Still, something calls to me incessantly from the ground there, and I haven't even unpacked before I'm back.

The desert is indifferent.

A roomy, rainless, ungrudging mother. Not like you.

I'll still be here, it says. *I'll always be here.*

Some early summer days in Michigan, there are limp, gray sheets of pale rain, shower curtains of it hanging like faded wig hair or a silver, mildewed nightgown left forgotten on a line.

That hasn't changed.

Though, this early summer, everything has changed. I am at peace, pregnant, and in love.

But it's hard to allow for this peace. *Mother.* It's hard not to smash this to ruins, too. Remember, I loved you. I still do. There are times I'm afraid I'll be bewitched by this, afraid I'll be stunned one morning by the new sun coming up: A woman under a dumb spell, frozen in a sentimental pose—a dead tree weeping sap, a homely puppy with hummingbirds and bullets buzzing around its head. I'm afraid I'll get caught happy, the joke on me, with the black phone ringing in the middle of the night, or the good-bye note folded on my pillow in the morning like a small, snagged kite.

Still, at night I curl into this new man's back with my heart full. A soggy nest in my chest. Or, a soft and bloody nest. And a stranger's tiny hand flutters in my guts.

A dove-pulse in the pulsing dark.

I put my own hand over its gentle wave and think, *I promise you, a feast. There will be honeybees. Killer bees. A net of silver fish and slivered glass like bright words at your feet.* I tap the warm layer of flesh that separates us for now—that great sky river—and I feel pale, dopey with hope.

Often, I think of you.

I think, *Mother,* here I am stepping into the future again without you—out of a wide-open window, into empty space.

Laura

Susan Kelly-DeWitt

Elaine DeSouza Sykora and Susan Kelly-DeWitt
Kalihi Valley, Oahu, Hawaii; 1950

Susan Kelly-DeWitt was born in San Francisco in 1947. Her poetry has appeared in numerous journals, including *Poetry, Nimrod, Yankee, New Letters,* and *Prairie Schooner,* and anthologized in *Highway 99: A Literary Journey through the Central Valley* (Heyday Books, 1996) and *Claiming the Spirit Within* (Beacon Press, 1996). Her awards include the Wallace Stegner Fellowship for Poetry from Stanford University, the Bazzanella Literary Award, several Pushcart nominations, and a recent award from *Artist/Writer* magazine. For several years she was the artistic director of the Women's Wisdom Project, an Arts Program for Disadvantaged Women. She has taught poetry and literature in the Sacramento area at several colleges and universities and, most recently, poetry classes for inmates at Folsom Prison. Her first book of poems, *The Woman Living Inside Me,* is currently seeking a publisher. She lives with her husband and two children in Sacramento; her mother also lives with the family.

Elaine DeSouza Sykora was born in 1919 and raised "in the Hawaiian Islands, in the beautiful Pacific, in the village of Kaumana, on the slopes of majestic Mauna Kea. My education ended on graduation from high school; the Depression caused the loss of our financial security, so much so that while attending parochial school I did ironing for the nuns twice a week. We never did recover financially; however, we made the transition from having to not-having gracefully. My mother's wisdom taught us how. Many years have passed since then. I have two wonderful children and four grandchildren who have made up for all of my lost dreams."

To My Mother on Her
Seventy-Sixth Birthday
August 12, 1995

the hard green fingers
of the trumpet vine beckon
evening approaches

the fountain at dusk
swallows its own music—sad
notes in dying light

a night wind walks by
whoosh . . . dark eyes, an old gray head
enter the forest

1.

there was a secret
book in your heart, it was a
book of poetry

written by you if
you'd had a different life
with a grass linen

cover and embossed
letters like bamboo, it was
autographed by you

> *out of the mother*
> *out of the hull of the ship-*
> *wrecked being I come*

2.

Who made the world? I
asked you once years before you
could hear, as the dust

of stars gathered me
from the void's farthest edges
a drift of unborn

far out on the string
of your being I floated
I waved like a pale

handkerchief, *hello . . .*
when the sea wind pounded waves
on Kona's lava

ledges, when it churned
greenish white along the black
sand beaches where you

collected sea snails
and played your childhood games, I
felt how you carried

me in your pockets
like an unwritten letter
I circled above

you like a hundred
wild white birds, calling, calling
white feathers of me

3.

falling around you
softly as a breath of snow
you looked up beyond

and through me as if
straining for a glimpse though I
was less than a mist

almost as if you
heard me after all, my unborn voices which were

not yet one voice, one
sad song woven from yours, voice
spun from silence—all

the years you sat still
at your school desk, not speaking
unless spoken to

I was braided like
ribbon into the tamed gloss
of your onyx hair

whenever you dipped
your fountain pen in peacock
blue ink, droplets of

my uncreated
being oozed from the pen—I
was almost a word

4.

out of the mother
out of the hull of the ship-
wrecked being I come

with ash in my hair
with ash in my mouth but still
singing hymns, praises

oh sky oh sea oh
clear blue air, singing hymns and
praises to silent

mothers whose bones burn
clean, whose flesh turns into air
whose words were never

spoken, whose poems
were never known never sung
oh there are thousands

of such women, such
lovely women with poems
locked tight in their hearts

words chained to their lips
struggled words, strangled tales, joys
even joys untold

5.

the hard green fingers
of the trumpet vine beckon
evening approaches

6.

your quiet mother
her composed sadness in its
ivory dress, lace

of bones, and her own
mother, immigrant soul—who
went blind from stitching

other people's clothes
the one who came round Cape Horn
on *The High Flyer*

a four-month journey
who gave birth in steerage, fed
the baby crumbs (told

how even the crew
learned to starve) who blessed the ground
when she walked on it

again, are present
in me—the blessing, the rough
passage of their words

that needle *silence*
needle of history, sharp
family blood drops

7.

the fountain at dusk
swallows its own music—sad
notes in dying light

8.

every created
being needs some forgiveness
the grave won't forgive

it's up to us—there
were things you didn't do right
the mistakes you made

just living is hard
enough, who knows how to keep
a girl's perfect heart

all I know is I
was growing like a woods in
the unformed dark of

your hope, the bad dreams
yet to come, the marriage to
my father who loved

and tormented us
the deaths of your beloved
mother and father

and still I'm growing
toward something though I know
not what, beloved

9.

a night wind walks by
whoosh . . . dark eyes, an old gray head
enter the forest

Susan

Barbara Kingsolver

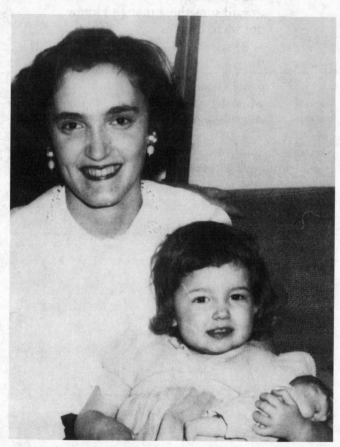

Virginia Henry Kingsolver with eighteen-month-old
Barbara Kingsolver
Carlisle, Kentucky; 1956

Barbara Kingsolver was born in Maryland in 1955 and grew up in rural Kentucky. She studied biology, lived for a time in Europe, and worked at many trades before becoming a full-time writer. Her seven books include an essay collection, *High Tide in Tucson,* and the novels *Pigs in Heaven, Animal Dreams,* and *The Bean Trees.* She lives in Tucson with her husband and two daughters.

Virginia Lee Henry Kingsolver was born in Lexington, Kentucky, in 1929. She raised three children and helped her husband establish his practice as a rural physician in Nicholas County, Kentucky, where they have lived for most of their married life. She is an active community organizer, excellent gardener, and avid birdwatcher.

Dear Mom,

I imagine you putting on your glasses to read this letter. Asking yourself, *Oh, Lord, what now?* You tilt your head back and hold the page away from you; your left hand lies flat on your chest, protecting your heart. A long, typed letter from me has generally meant trouble. The happy, uncomplicated things I could always toss you easily over the phone: I love you, where in the world is my birth certificate, what do you put in your zucchini casserole, happy birthday, this is our new phone number, we're going to have a baby in March, my plane comes in at seven, I will see you then, I love you.

The hard things went into letters. I started sending them from college, once or twice a year. They were the kind of self-absorbed epistles that usually begin as diary entries, and should probably stay there. When I was in high school, they did. But at nineteen I began to tear them out and actually mail them to you. I had to let you know I had escaped. I had friends, lovers, poetry, freedom. I had opinions about abortion, Vietnam, the Problem that Has No Name. I was reading Karl Marx and Betty Friedan. I'd escaped a miserable adolescence in which I wavered desperately between know-it-all teenager and self-effacing child. Finally I was ready to leave behind the half of me who knew nothing;

unfortunately that left us all with the half who knew too much. She took no prisoners. "I am campaigning for abortion rights in this backward state," I wrote, detailing for you my political work and eventually getting around to the real point, which was to fill you in on the great freedom women could experience if they threw off the bondage of housewifely servitude.

You cried a lot in those years, I remember. We didn't exactly fight. Whenever we were together you kept telling me you loved me. And behaving as if you wished I were someone else entirely. I did the same—minus the part about telling you I loved you. On visits home to Kentucky I wore Army Surplus boots and a five-dollar haircut from a barbershop. You left the Bridal Announcements section of the newspaper on my bed, saying you thought I might like to look at the girls' hairstyles. I gave you lectures on Capitalist exploitation of the Third World and the devaluation of women's labor while you baked chicken and mashed the potatoes; I never offered to wash the dishes. You cut out a newspaper photo of me on a stage, passionately addressing a huge crowd, and you pasted it in your scrapbook—minus the caption explaining it was an antiwar demonstration. I paced your house like a bored zoo bear, drank lots of coffee, pulled my inch-long hair, and tried to be shocking. I made sideways remarks about how you and Dad were attached at the hip, how you wouldn't even eat lunch without him, how I couldn't imagine being anybody's wife. You hummed a tuneless tune as you washed the dishes. This is how we got through whole weekends without saying what we could never say to each other:

How can you hurt me so, by turning out so different from me?

Who says I have to be just like you? What does that have to do with love?

It has everything to do with love. I'm your mother. Who else should you be just like?

How can you claim to love me when you won't even see who I am? How can we ever be close if you keep the photo and throw away the caption?

Why are you always so angry?

After every visit I returned to school feeling restless and lonely. Overmothered and motherless, both at once. In my cramped college apartment that felt like the world compared to my frilly-curtained bedroom at your house, I would sit down with my fountain pen and begin once again to explain myself to you. Argue that my way of looking at things was right, if you could only see. In my heart I believed these letters would change you somehow and make us friends. But they only bought me a few quick gulps of air. They paced out the length and breadth of the distance between us.

I lived past college and so did my hair, and slowly I learned the womanly art of turning down the volume. But I still missed you, and from the underside of my torment those awful letters grew like dark mushrooms. I kept trying, year after year. I am trying still. But this time will be different: Let your breath out. I won't hurt you. The distance between you and me is a thing we measure in miles now, and years. Lately that distance seems beside the point.

I want to tell you what I remember.

I am three years old. You have left me with your mother while you and Daddy took a trip. Grandmama feeds me cherries and shows me the secret of her hair when the everyday white coil drops in a silvery waterfall to the backs of her knees. Grandmama's house smells like polished wooden stairs and soap and Grand-dad's onions and ice cream, and I would love to stay there always but I miss you terribly. So terribly. On the day of your return I am standing in the driveway waiting when the station wagon comes. You jump out of your side *my mother!* in a lipstick smile and red earrings, pushing back your dark hair from the shoulder of your white shell blouse, turning so your red skirt swirls like a rose with the perfect promise of you emerging from the center. You are so beautiful. You raise one hand in a tranquil wave and move so slowly up the driveway your body seems to be under water. I understand with a shock that you are extremely happy. I am miserable and alone waiting on Grandmama's driveway and you were at the beach with Daddy and you're *happy.* Happy without me.

I am sitting on your lap and you are crying. *Thank you honey, thank you so much,* you say over and over, rocking back and forth as you hold me in the straight-backed kitchen chair. I've brought you flowers—the sweet peas you must have spent all spring trying to grow, training them up the trellis in the yard. You had nothing to work with but weeks of gray rain and the patience of a young wife at home with pots and pans and small children trying to create just one beautiful thing, something to take you outside our little white clapboard house on East Main. I never noticed until all at once they burst through the trellis in a pink red purple dazzle. A finger painting of colors humming against the blue air: I could think of nothing but to bring it to you. I climbed up the wooden trellis and picked the flowers. Every one. They are gone already, all your efforts, wilting as you hold me close in the potato-smelling kitchen and your tears are damp in my own hair but you never say a single word but *thank you*.

Grandmama is dead. She was alive, so thin Grand-dad bought her a tiny dark blue dress and called her his Fashion Model and then they all went to the hospital and came home without her. Where is the dark blue dress now, I find myself wondering, until it comes to me that they probably buried her in it. It's under the ground with her. There are so many things I don't want to think about, I hate going to bed at night.

It's too hot to sleep. My long hair wraps around me like tentacles. My brother and sister and I have made up our cots on the porch where it's supposed to be cooler. They are sunk deep in unworried sleep on either side of me, but I am under the dark cemetery ground with Grandmama. I am up in the stars, desolate, searching out the end of the universe and time. I am trying to imagine how long forever is, because that is how long I will be dead some day. It seems impossible to bear, to spend that much time being nothing, thinking of nothing. I have spent so many nights like this, fearing sleep. Hating wakefulness.

I get up, barefoot and insubstantial in my nightgown, and creep to your room. The door is open and I find you're awake too, sitting up on the edge of the bed. I can only see the white outline of your nightgown and your eyes. You are like a ghost.

Mama, I don't want to die.

You don't have to worry about that for a long, long time.

I know. But I'm thinking about it now.

I step toward you from the doorway and you fold me into your arms. You are real, my mother in scent and substance and I still fit perfectly on your lap when I am afraid.

You don't know what heaven is like. It might be full of beautiful flowers.

When I close my eyes I discover it's there, an endless field of flowers. Columbines, blue asters, daisies, sweet peas, zinnias. One single flower bed stretching out for miles in every direction. I am small enough to watch the butterflies come. I know them from the pasture behind our house, butterflies you taught me to love and name: monarchs, Dianas, tiger swallowtails. I follow their lazy zigzag as they visit every flower, as many flowers as there are stars in the universe. We stay there in the dark for a long time, you and I, both of us with our eyes closed watching the butterflies drift so slowly, filling up as much time as forever.

I will keep that field of flowers. It doesn't matter that I will not always believe in heaven. I will suffer losses of faith, of love and confidence, I will have some bitter years and always when I hurt and can't sleep I will close my eyes and wait for our butterflies.

Just one thing, I am demanding of you. It's the middle of summer, humid beyond all reason, and I am thirteen: a tempest of skinned knees and menarche. You are trying to teach me how to do laundry, showing me how to put the blueing in with the sheets. The swampy Monday afternoon smell of sheets drowning under the filmy, shifting water fills me with pure despair. I want no part of that smell. No future in white sheets and blueing. *Name one good thing about being a woman,* I say to you.

There are lots of good things. . . . Your voice trails off with the thin blue stream that trickles into the washer's indifferent maw.

In a rare flush of adrenaline or confidence I hold on, daring you. *Okay then. If that's true, just name me one.*

You hesitated. I remember that. I saw a hairline crack in your claim of a homemaker's perfect contentment. Finally you said, *The love of a man. That's one thing. Being taken care of and loved by a man.*

And because you'd hesitated I knew I didn't have to believe it.

At fifteen I rage at you in my diary without courage or any real intention of actually revealing myself to you. *Why oh why do you want to ruin my life? Why can't you believe I know how to make my own decisions? Why do you treat me like a child? No makeup or nail polish allowed in this house, you seem to think I am either a baby or a nun, but you don't know half as much as I do about the real world. You think if I forget to close the curtains when I get undressed the neighbor boy will rape me. You think all boys are evil. You tell me a girl's job in life is to keep them under control. Mainly by staying away from them, I suppose. You think if I go to Flemingsburg with my girlfriends I'll get kidnapped. You think if I'm in the same room with a boy and a can of beer, I'll instantly become a pregnant alcoholic.*

Halfway through the page I crumble suddenly and write in a meeker hand: *I have to learn to keep my big mouth shut and not talk back or fight with Mom. I love her so much.* I am a young woman sliced in two, half of me claiming to know everything and the other half just as sure I could never know anything at all. I am too awkward and tall, too quiet behind my drape of waist-length hair, a girl unnoticed by boys and for that matter unnoticed by girls, the straight-A school mouse who can't pass for dumb and pretty in a smalltown, marry-young market that values—as far as I can see—no other type.

I understand this to be all your fault. You made me, and I was born a girl. You trained me to be a woman, and regarding that condition I fail to see one good thing.

The wood-smoke scent in the air puts me in mind of raked leaves, corduroy jumpers and new saddle shoes, our family's annual trip to Browning's orchard for apples and cider. A back-to-school nostalgia too childish for me now and yet here I am, thrilled to my fingertips, starting college. You and Dad have driven three hundred miles with our VW bus packed like a tackle box with my important, ridiculous stuff, and now have patiently unloaded it without questioning my judgment on a single cherished object—the plants, the turtle shell collection, the glass demijohn, the huge striped pillow, the thousands of books. You're sitting on my new bed while Dad carries in the last box. To you this bed must look sadly institutional compared with my beautiful four-poster at home, lovingly lathed for us from red cherry wood by your father before he died. To me the metal bed frame looks just fine. Nothing fussy, it will do. I am arranging my cacti in the windowsill while you tell me how proud you are of the scholarship I won, how you know I'll do well here, how I should call if I need anything.

I won't need anything, I tell you.

I have a peculiar photographic awareness of this room as if I'm not really in it but watching us both from the doorway. I understand that we are using up the very last minutes of something neither of us can call, outright, my childhood. I can't wait for you to leave. And then you do. I stand watching through my yellow-curtained window and the rust-tipped boughs of a maple outside as you and Dad climb into the VW and drive away without looking back. And because no one can see me I wipe my slippery face with the back of my hand. My nose runs and I choke on tears, so many I'm afraid I will drown. I can't smell leaves or apples or wood smoke. I feel more alone than I've ever felt in my life.

At the Greencastle Drive-in on a double date this is really me, half of the couple in the backseat. We have the window open an inch to accommodate the crackling metal speaker, and the heater is on full blast. Outside our island of steamy heat, frost is climbing the metal poles and whitening the upright bones of the surrounding cornfields; it's nearly Thanksgiving, surely the end of drive-in season as we know it. Tomorrow I have a midterm exam. Surprisingly, I don't care. I feel heady and reckless. Truth be told I will probably ace the exam, but even if I don't, I'll live. Finally I have a genuine social life and the long-anticipated privilege of giving in to peer pressure: I threw *Heart of Darkness* over my shoulder at the first bark of temptation and went out on a date.

The movie is *Cabaret*. Sally Bowles with her weird haircut and huge, sad eyes is singing her heart out about being abandoned by her mother.

With a physical shock I wake up to what's been tugging at my nape all day, November 20: it's your birthday! I have *never* forgotten your birthday, not since I was old enough to push a crayon around in the shape of a heart on a folded piece of construction paper. How can it be that I didn't even think to send a card? I sit bolt upright and open my mouth, preparing to announce I have to go home immediately and call my mother. My friend and her boyfriend in the front seat are deeply involved in each other. I imagine them staring at me, hostile under rumpled hair, and begin to shrink into my former skin, the miserable high-school mouse. I despise her. The happiness of my new grownup life is so precarious, I must be careful not to wreck it like a ship. I sigh, settle back and close my mouth.

* * *

I am nineteen, a woman's body curled like a fetus. Curled in a knot on my bed so small I hope I might disappear. I do not want to be alive.

I've been raped.

I know his name, his address, in fact I will probably have to see him again on campus. But I have nothing to report. Not to the police, not to you. The telephone rings and I can't pick it up because it might be you. My mother. All you ever told me from the beginning has come home to this knot of nothingness on my bed, this thing I used to call me. It was my job to prevent what happened. Two nights ago I talked to him at a bar. He bought me a drink and told my friends he thought I was cute. *That girl with the long hair—what's her name?* Tonight when he came to my door I was happy, for ten full seconds. Then. My head against something, a wall, suffocation, hard pushing and flat on my back and screaming for air. Fighting an animal twice my size. My job was to stop him and I failed. How can I tell you that? *You met him in a bar. You see?*

From this vantage point, a dot of nothingness in the center of my bed, I understand the vast ocean of work it is to be a woman among men, that universe of effort, futile, whispers against stones, oh God I don't want it. My bones are weak. I am trapped in a room with no flowers, no light, a ceiling of lead so low I can never straighten up. If it's all the way you say it is, I don't want to live in this world.

I will only be able to get up from this bed if I can get up angry. Can you understand there is no other way? I have to be someone else. Not you, and not even me. Tomorrow or some day soon I will braid my long hair for the last time, go to my friend's house with a pair of sharp scissors and tell her to cut it off. All of it. Tomorrow or some day soon I will feel that blade at my nape and the weight will fall.

Summer light, Beaurieux, France. At twenty-three I'm living in an enormous, centuries-old stone farmhouse with a dozen friends, garrulous French socialists and British expatriates, all of us at some loose coupling in our lives between school and adulthood. We find a daily, happy solace in each other and the scarlet poppies that keep blooming in the sugar beet fields. We go out together to work in the mornings, come home evenings to drink red table wine and make ratatouille in the cavernous kitchen. This afternoon, a Saturday, a gaggle of us have driven into town to hang out at the village's only electrified establishment, a tiny cafe. We are entrenched in a happy, pointless argument about Camus when the man wiping the counter, who has never read Camus, answers the phone and yells: *"Mademoiselle Kingsolver? C'est quelque'un des Etats Unis!"*

My heart thumps to a complete and utter stop. Nobody from the United States could possibly know where I am. I haven't written my parents for many months, since before I moved to France. I rise and sleepwalk to the telephone knowing absolutely that it will be you, *my mother,* and it is. I still have no idea how you found me. I can hardly remember the conversation. I must have told you I was alive and well, still had all my arms and legs, what else was there to say? You told me my brother was getting married and I ought to come home for the wedding.

Ma mere! I announce to my friends with a bewildered shrug when I return to the table. I tell them you probably called out the French Foreign Legion to find me. Everybody laughs and declares that mothers are all alike. That they love you too much, they are a cross to bear, they all ought to get their own things to do and leave us alone. We pay for our coffee and amble toward somebody's car but I decide on impulse that I'll walk back to the farm. I move slowly, reliving in my mind the ringing telephone, the call that was for me. For me here in France, a tiny town, the only cafe, a speck of dust on the globe. Already it seems impossible to me that this really happened. The roadside ditch is brilliant with poppies and as I walk along I am hugging myself so hard I can barely breathe.

I'm weeding the garden. You admired my garden a lot when you came to visit me here in Tucson, in this small brick house of my own. We fought, of course. You didn't care for my involvement with Central American refugees or understand my anger toward the government, no matter how I explained to you the issues of immigration law and human rights. You cared even less for the fact that I was living in this little brick house with a man, unmarried. But you did admire my vegetable garden, and the four o'clocks in front, you said, were beautiful. The flowers were our common ground. They attract hummingbirds, you told me, and we both liked that.

But on this particular day I am alone, weeding the garden, when a stranger comes to the door. He doesn't look well and says he needs a glass of water so I go to the kitchen. When I turn around from the sink there he is with a knife shoved right up against my belly.

Don't scream or I'll kill you.

But I do scream. Scream, bite, kick, shove my knee into his stomach. I don't know what will happen next but this much I know: *It's not my fault! You were halfway right and halfway oh so terribly wrong, men may do vile things but this is not my work, my job is to choose my own path and my right is to walk it without this knife in my belly oh God! this evil. You may not agree but you've held on to me this long so I must be someone worth saving against the odds. If I could only tell you this I know you would say yes, oh yes you are right.* So this time I scream. I scream for all I'm worth.

I'm somewhere between thirty and a hundred and I've written a book. My first novel, but to me it seems more like the longest letter to you I've ever written. Finally after a thousand tries I've explained everything I believe in just exactly the way I always wanted to: refugees and human rights and the laws that are wrong, the terrible things men can do, the Problem that Has No Name, racism, poetry, freedom, Sisterhood is Powerful. All that, and still some publisher has decided it makes for a good read.

But that doesn't matter right now because you are on my front porch glider turning the pages one at a time and it's only a stack of paper. The longest typed letter ever, a fistful of sweet peas, a pathetically hopeful pile of crayoned hearts. I'm supposed to be cooking dinner but I keep looking out the window, trying to see what page you're on now and divine your opinion from the back of your head. All I can see is that you're still reading and your hair is gray. In another few minutes mine will be too. My heart is pounding. I boil water and peel the potatoes but forget to put them in the pot. I salt the water twice. Finally you come in with tears in your eyes.

Barb, honey, it's beautiful. So good.

You fold me into your arms and I can't believe it. I still fit. Or, I fit once again.

*   *   *

I'm thirty-two, with my own daughter in my arms. I've sent you a picture of her, perfect and gorgeous in her bassinet. Her tiny hand is making a delicate circle, index finger to thumb, pinkie extended as if she's holding a teacup. How could my ferocious will create such a delicate, feminine child? *This one is all girl,* I write on the back, my daughter's first caption. You send back a photo of me at the same age, eight weeks, in my bassinet. I can't believe it. I am making a delicate circle with my hand, index finger to thumb, pinkie extended.

We've flown back to Kentucky for Christmas. I'm thirty-five but weirdly transported backward. In all the years I've been away from my hometown, Main Street is perfectly unchanged. The commercial district is set off by a stoplight on either end of a single block: hardware store, men's clothing, five-and-dime, drugstore, the county jail. An American flag made of red, white and blue lightbulbs (some of them burnt out) blinks to life on the courthouse's peeling silver dome at dusk. How did I ever live here?

I've come into town on a few errands, and to tell the truth it's a relief to take a few hours' respite from a house overstuffed with Christmas decorations, sugary fruitcakes, a kitchen stifling from an overworked oven, a mother's bosomy hugs at every turn. How did I ever live *there?* My own life is so different. So pared down. I stop in at Hopkin's Drug to get something for the cough my daughter has picked up while traveling. At three she hasn't been sick many times in her life so I'm worried, but only a little. In my tweed winter coat and shiny shoulder-length bob I feel competent and slightly rushed, as usual. A woman of my age.

An elderly woman I don't recognize lays a spotted paw across my wrist as I'm about to leave the drugstore. She eyes me through thick glasses, her eyes swimming up and down like dark, hungry fish. *You must be Virginia Kingsolver's daughter,* she says. *You look exactly like her.*

My nine-year-old comes home from a summer slumber party with painted nails and I mean *painted.* Day-Glo green on her fingers, purple on her toes. We drive directly to the drugstore for nail polish remover.

Mom, please! All the girls my age are doing this.

How can every nine-year-old on the planet possibly be painting her toenails purple?

I don't know. They just are.

School starts in a week. Do you want your teacher to know you all year as the girl with the green fingernails?

Yes. But I guess you don't.

Do you really?

She looks down at her nails and states: *Yes.* With her porcelain skin and long, dark lashes she is a Raphael cherub. Her perfect mouth longs to pout, but she resists, holds her back straight. A worthy vessel for her own opinions. In spite of myself, I admire her.

Okay, we'll compromise. The green comes off, for now. But you can keep the purple toenails.

At forty I'm expecting my second child. I've happily waited a lifetime for this gift, but now it is past due and I am impatient. I conceived in September and now it's July. I have dragged this child in my belly through some portion of every month but August. In the summer's awful heat I am a beached whale, a house full of water, a universe with ankles. It seems entirely possible to me that the calendar will close and I will somehow be bound fairy tale-wise to a permanent state of pregnancy.

During these months you and I have talked more often than ever before. Through our long phone conversations I've learned so many things: that with each one of us you fought for natural childbirth, a rebel against patronizing doctors who routinely knocked women out with drugs. In the fifties, formula was modern and breast-feeding was crude and old-fashioned, but you risked the contempt of your peers, went right ahead and did what you knew was best for your babies.

I've also learned that ten-month pregnancies run in our family.

When I was two weeks overdue with Ann I made your father drive over every bumpy road in the county.

Did it work?

No. With you, we were in Maryland. We went to see the cherry blossoms in April, and Wendell said, "What if you go into labor while we're hours away from home?" I told him, "I'll sing halle-lujah."

A week past my due date you are calling every day. My husband answers the phone, holds it up and mouths: "Your mother again." He thinks you are badgering me. You aren't. I am a woman lost in the weary sea of waiting and you are the only one who really knows where I am. Somewhere I'm sure I have my own things to do and a hundred opinions you would not want to paste in the family album but at the same time you and I are sisters and daughters and mothers and your voice is keeping me afloat. I grab the phone.

She is born at last. A second daughter. I cry on the phone, I'm so happy and relieved to have good news for you finally. I promise you pictures right away. You will tell me she looks just like I did. I think the baby looks like my husband, but I will believe you anyway.

Later when it's quiet I nurse our baby, admiring her perfect hands. My husband is in a chair across the room, and I'm startled to look up and see he is staring at us with tears in his eyes. I've seen him cry only once before.

What's wrong?

Nothing. I'm just so happy.

I love him inordinately. I could not bear to be anyone but his wife, just now. I could not bear to be anyone but the mother of my two daughters.

I was three years old, standing in the driveway waiting for the car to bring you back from Florida. You arrived glowing with happiness. *Because of me.* At the time I felt stung, thinking you could carry on your life of bright red lipstick smiles outside of my presence, but I know now I was wrong. You looked so happy *because of me.* You hadn't seen me for more than a week. You hadn't nursed me for years and yet your breasts tingled before you even opened the car door. You felt the soles of your feet make contact with the ground and your arms opened up as you walked surefooted once again into the life you knew as my mother.

I know exactly how you felt. We are one, life and limb, I am your happiness. It's a cross I am willing to bear.

Love,

Barbara

Clysta Kinstler

Clysta Kinstler (age four) and her mother, Ethel Henry
Holbrook, Nebraska; 1935

Clysta Kinstler was born September 20, 1931, in Sioux City, Iowa. She holds an M.A. in philosophy from the University of California, Davis, and taught philosophy and women's studies at American River College in Sacramento, California, from 1975 to 1990. She is the author of a novel, *The Moon Under Her Feet* (Harper Collins, 1988), and is currently at work on *A Sacred Place*, a memoir. The mother of 7 children and grandmother to 21, she lives with her husband, John, in Loomis, California.

Ethel Loretta Long Henry was born August 10, 1910, in Glasgow, Montana. She moved to Sioux City as a young woman and married Thomas Henry in 1930. Besides Clysta, she has 6 other living children. She lives in McCook, Nebraska.

Alone in Heaven

My dearest Mother:

"I am pretty good," you write me from Nebraska. Your spidery words run off the page and I know you can't see what you write, nor read any longer the big-print letters I send you—less often now, because I know Claudia, or someone, will have to read them to you. Better to call. You sound so surprisingly like yourself—pleased to hear my voice. Not much news, every day pretty much the same since you are alone, since Daddy died, and we are all, all of us kids, scattered.

Us "kids" except for Linda are past fifty now. We talk, when we call each other, about how you're doing in your New Place, the tiny sixth-floor room with the sunny window and the elevator just outside your door that takes you to the communal dining room. We worry that you get too much to eat, and not enough exercise. We think you need new things to wear in a larger size. We wish you could have the operation to remove the cataract on your eye, but the doctor says the risk is too great since the other is blind. Still, you look at me in the way I always remember.

I am your firstborn, and I remember, Mother, when there were less than a hundred pounds of you; how you would toss your bobbed-off hair, black and shiny as a crow's wing, and cock your head to one side like a bright, inquisitive bird. You looked straight at me when you spoke, your eyes deep blue as the sea I had never seen but was seeing; marigold sunbursts lit their centers.

I was four in Sioux City when my brother was born; I didn't know that we had adopted him or that you had lost three babies in three years. The doctor said you would never bear again. You let me name him, or let me think I did: "Donnie Dan."

We moved to the little farm in Nebraska, near where Daddy had been born. "Godforsaken country," you called it. But you planted and hoed and canned; we had enough to eat and so did you: the apple cheeks you had hated as a girl came back. You could remember looking down and seeing your red cheeks, and people loved to tease you about them, delighting in your blushes.

You never instructed me except by example. Do you remember when we read Superman comics together? And Wonder Woman? I carried home everything I learned in school. When I brought you poems, you already knew them. We would recite them together: "The Liberty Bell." "O Captain, My Captain." "The Highwayman." You must have read everything there'd been to read in that little one-room Montana schoolhouse! You were so modest—you had finished only those eight grades.

I was never shy about instructing *you,* and you always listened. Didn't you mind that I was arrogant? "See no evil, hear no evil, speak no evil." Was that what you learned in eight years?

I never imagined when you recited poems to us while you worked or listened to our long, drawn-out fantasies, that you were almost always pregnant. Sometimes you fainted mornings, then got up again and made our breakfast. We dressed around the front-room stove while you sang off-key in the cold kitchen, swinging forward and back on the pump handle of the gasoline pressure range that only you could tease into proper flame: a ring of fiercely alive, spearmint worms, marching in a halo of blue.

The doctor in Sioux City had been wrong. First came Claudia, so tiny she barely lived; then Kay, a stronger, bigger baby; then strapping Joy; and little brother Tim. By that time I was not so innocent, and Daddy awakened me to help. Doc Pattin handed me my newborn baby brother, slippery wet, to bathe and dress.

Oh, Mamma. I was thirteen! You could have told me so much, so much I needed to know, but you would not. "Are you still soiling your panties?" you managed, flushed dark with your own discomfort when I had been hiding them deep in the wash basket for months. "Look here." You showed me the blue box, hidden far back in your closet where no one would see such shamefulness.

Four years later, one word—"Oh."—a shimmer of tears and no reproach for your pregnant valedictorian. You glowed at my graduation and wept at my address. You accepted my boy-husband with the grace of a queen conferring knighthood. But you knew my heart was broken. We mourned my wasted scholarships without words. "It will be all right," you said.

You came to be with me when my babies were born, one at a time, until there were seven. When I told you we were leaving their alcoholic father, you said, "It will be all right," and I knew I could go home to you with all of them if need be. But it was all right. You were proud when I started college and kept on going, and when you and Daddy came to California for my second marriage, my *real* wedding.

During all my years of study, and later teaching and writing, I have ached to bring home to you, Mother, the wonderful things I was learning, to tell you about Kant and Sartre and Heidegger and Mary Daly and Buddhism. But you were no longer listening; by then, the kind people who gave you a ride to their church had shown you "the only way" to salvation.

Mother, listen. You were my living example of natural goodness, my refutation of the Fall. From you I learned to trust my feelings and go with them, to follow a whim without apology . . . you were my model. The things you lived but did not say are my treasure.

How did you turn away, Mother, from what you were? From what I strove to be? The book of my life lies unread by you, invalid without your seal. The Serpent was not evil, Mother. And the fruit of the Tree is good. Come back! Come back to our Garden!

I remember you, Mother—I will always remember you—before judgment shadowed the bright certainty of your glance with visions of sin and damnation; taught you to fear that my free-thinking ways might tempt the others and leave you alone in Heaven.

Last June, we sat together and I filed your tough, hard fingernails, wishing I had inherited them along with a little of your silence. Mamma. How could I not forgive you? You, who forgive everything. You, who never reproach me for not finding more ways to spend time with you. (California is so far from Nebraska.) Your half-blindness does not see my sins. Kaye says you are like a little child, and I think of long ago. We were children *together*, my mother; we saw and heard and spoke no evil. So let it be.

Your loving daughter,

Carolyn Kizer

Carolyn Kizer was born in Spokane, Washington, in 1925. She is the author of numerous collections of poetry including *YIN*, which won the 1985 Pulitzer Prize, and *The Nearness of You*, winner of the 1987 Theodore Roethke Prize. In addition, she has written *Mermaids in the Basement: Poems for Women*, and *Proses: Essays on Poets and Poetry*, and published several anthologies and translations. She recently wrote a cantata, *The War in the West*, with music by Owen Burdick, to commemorate the end of World War II; its first performance was held on May 8, 1995, at the Rheims Cathedral, Rheims.

Mabel Ashley Kizer was born in Ouray, Colorado, on September 29, 1880, the eldest of five children and the only girl. She graduated from the University of Colorado and got her Ph.D. in biology from Stanford. Then she headed the biology department at Mills, and later at San Francisco State. Later she assisted Anna Louise Strong at the *Union Record* in Seattle and worked for the I.W.W. (International Workers of the World). Still later she worked for the government (!), investigating the condition of women and children in the lumber and mining camps of the Northwest, when she met my father, a Spokane lawyer and married him, after a brief courtship, in her early forties. She never worked again, outside of the home.

Dear Mother,

Today is September 29, your birthday, and also the anniversary of the day on which you died, at age seventy-five, consistent with your sense of symmetry and style. A week before you died, we were sharing a room in the venerable old Empress Hotel in Victoria, British Columbia. As I recall, we'd just had the hotel's high tea, another reflection of colonial nostalgia for the mother country: scones, very thin watercress and cucumber sandwiches, topped off with heavily caloric cream-filled goodies, as the refined ladies in the string quartet sawed away at poor Mozart.

I was lying across the bed reading a novel of Forster's—*Abinger Harvest* I think it was, not one of the more famous books—and replying absently to your occasional remarks.

"I bore you, don't I?" I was stunned to hear you say. Of course

I denied this with vigor, not the least because it was absolutely untrue. I'd often heard my father say, "Mabel (for that was your unfortunate and totally inappropriate name), there are times when you've nearly driven me mad, but you've never bored me." Ditto, Dad. You were a famous raconteuse, mistress of the snappy comeback and the spontaneous one-liner. You dominated the dinner table, no matter how many people were present. This was sometimes resented by men who were as socially aggressive as you, but they were quickly mollified by your superb cooking.

Even when I was a young child, even when we were alone together, you never ceased to entertain me. I saw the sluggish, overworked mothers of my friends, whose parental role seemed to consist of barked-out prohibitions and peremptory orders, and had sense enough to thank my stars you weren't like that. Of course, you were a mild manic-depressive, a quality I have inherited. But the dark side was confined to the dark hours when, sleeplessly, you paced the floor and worried about everything imaginable. When I describe myself to friends, they invariably remark, "But I never see you depressed!" to which I reply that I'm manic in public and depressed when I'm alone. You, too, though your example has trained me not to brood on what might happen but only on the disasters of the past.

At any rate, those conversations of ours, going back to approximately the age of two in my case and forty-seven in yours, have never stopped, not in the forty years since your death, awake in silence or vocal in dreams. I suppose a thousand times a year the thought flashes, "I must tell Mother this. She'll be so amused/ indignant/horrified." And then, too quickly, I realize that you're not there. Or at least not here. I can't quite relinquish the hope that you hear me; that you know the poems I've written since your death (the first and some think the best: "The Great Blue Heron," written just after your dying), that I've achieved some measure of the literary success that you so fiercely desired for me. Otherwise I wouldn't be writing this, would I?—this paper valentine flung into the void, the kisses I can only press into my pillow, the words that you, more than anyone, taught me to love.

Carolyn

Maxine Kumin

Maxine Kumin and her mother, Bella Simon Winokur
Warner, New Hampshire; c. 1976 or 1977

Maxine Kumin was born in Philadelphia, Pennsylvania, in 1925. Her work is published widely and appears in numerous journals and anthologies. Books include *Up Country,* which won the Pulitzer Prize in 1973, *Our Ground Time Here Will Be Brief,* 1982, *Nurture,* 1989, and *Looking for Luck,* which won The Poets' Prize in 1993. Her newest collection, *Connecting the Dots,* was published in 1996 by W. W. Norton. *Selected Poems 1960–1990* is due in 1997. Kumin was recently elected a Chancellor of the Academy of American Poets and won the Aiken Taylor Poetry Prize in 1995. She and her husband live on a farm in New Hampshire where they raise horses. They have three grown children.

Bella Simon was born in Radford, Virginia, in 1895, was the sixth child of twelve siblings. "Her father, Abram Simon, ran the general store in Radford; my mother proudly boasted that his name was carved in stone over the lintel. Old photographs corroborate this fact. The Simon family were the only Jews in Radford. They packed up and traveled 40 miles to Roanoke for the High Holidays in order to go to synagogue. My mother, however, played the organ every Sunday in the Methodist church as well as at weddings and funerals held there. At 18, she was sent north to Philadelphia to live with relatives and to seek a husband. She and my father, Peter Winokur, eloped later that same year. Although my mother had considerable musical talent, like most women of her generation she did not cultivate it after marriage. She gave birth to three sons and a daughter."

A Crown of Sonnets

in memory of my mother

"Dear Muzz," I wrote the summer I was ten,
from a seedy nature camp in the Poconos
with cows and calves, huge geese, some half-wild ponies
—heaven for the heedless savage I was then—
"I have to do this letter to get breakfast.
Kiss Kerry for me. I milked a cow named Clover."
(Kerry, my dog, already dead, run over
the week I left.) Muzz from the bosomy British
matron in charge of spunky orphans who reclaim
the family's fortunes in a book I adored.

270

My older brothers called you Dolly, cleared
as almost-adults to use your cute nickname.
"Dear Muzz, with love" however smudged and brief
from your animal, sole daughter in your life.

Your animal, sole daughter in your life,
I mourned my dog, the slaughter of Clover's calf.
You were born Bella, number six of twelve.
The butter was spread too thin, childhood too brief
shared with Eva, Sara, Lena, Esther, Saul,
Meyer, Nathan, Oscar, Dan, Jay, Joe.
The younger ones mewed to be held by you.
The older ones, above your crib, said "doll."
You made me your confessor. At eighteen
you eloped, two virgins fleeing Baltimore,
buttoned in one berth by a Pullman porter
who jollied your tears at breakfast next morning
before the train pulled into Buffalo.
Your face announced Just Married, you blushed so.

Just married, one day pregnant, you blushed so
pink Niagara's fabled sunset paled.
"Papa will kill me when he hears," you quailed
but the first grandchild, a boy, softened the blow.
You told me how your mother had slapped your face
the day your first blood caked along your thighs,
then sent you to your sisters for advice.
Luckier, I was given *Marjorie May's*
Twelfth Birthday, a vague tract marketed by Kotex,
so vague it led me to believe you bled
that one year only, and left unplumbed, unsaid
the simple diagrammatics about sex.
When was it that I buried Muzz, began
to call you by the name that blazoned Woman?

I came to call you Dolly. The Other Woman,
the one I couldn't be. I was cross-eyed,
clumsy, solitary, breasts undersized.
Made wrong. An orthodontist's dream. A bookworm.
That winter a houseguest, his wife gone shopping,
pinned me in my bedroom by the mirror

and as we both watched, took out to my horror
a great stiff turkey neck, a hairless thing
he wanted to give me. How could I tell you this,
how he pressed against me, put it in my hand,
groped my nipples, said, "Someday you'll understand"?
How tell you, who couldn't pronounce vagina, penis?
This isn't recovered memory. I never forgot it.
I came to call you Dolly. That's when it started.

At 14, I called you Dolly. The war had started,
absorbing my brothers, one by one. The firstborn fought in Rommel's Africa, then crossed
to the Italian Boot. Your cocktail parties
grew shriller that year, the air more fiercely mortal
as the second son went off to ferry bombers
over the Burma Hump. Your hair, by summer,
began to thin, then fell out, purgatorial.
The youngest, apple of your eye, was shot
down in the Pacific, plucked from his atoll
and survived with a pair of shattered ankles.
You had to wear a wig. I dared to gloat.
The rage of adolescence bit me deep.
I loathed your laugh, your scarves, your costly makeup.

Your laugh, your scarves, the gloss of your makeup,
shallow and vain. I wore your lips, your hair,
even the lift of my eyebrows was yours
but nothing of you could please me, bitten so deep
by the fox of scorn. Like you, I married young
but chose animals, wood heat, hard hours
instead of your Sheffield silver, freshcut flowers,
your life of privilege and porcelain.
And then came children, the rigorous bond of blood.
Little by little our lives pulled up, pulled even.
A sprinkle here and there of approbation:
we both agreed that what I'd birthed was good.
How did I come to soften? How did you?
Goggy is what my little ones called you.

Goggy, they called you, basking in the sun
of your attention. You admired their ballet;

their French; their algebra; their Bach and Debussy.
The day the White House rang you answered, stunned
—the Carters' party for a hundred bards.
We shopped together for the dress I'd wear.
Our rancors melted as ocean eases stone.
The last year of your life, the names you thought of:
Rogue, Doc, Tudor, Daisy, Garth,
the horses of your lost Virginia youth.
You said them, standing in my barn, for love.
Dying, you scratched this fragment for me, a prize:
"Darling . . . your visit . . . even . . . so brief . . . Muzz."

Max

Anne D. LeClaire

Louise E. Dickinson
Melrose, Massachusetts;
c. 1932

Anne D. LeClaire
Monson,
Massachusetts;
c. 1948

Anne D. LeClaire was born in Ware, Massachusetts, in 1942, and educated at the MacDuffie School in Springfield, Massachusetts, and at Miami University in Oxford, Ohio. The mother of two children, she is married to Hillary LeClaire and lives on Cape Cod. A news reporter and op-ed columnist before turning to fiction, she is the author of four novels, the most recent of which are *Grace Point* (1992) and *Sideshow* (1994).

Louise E. Dickinson was born in Chelsea, Massachusetts, in 1915. A classically trained pianist, she was educated at the New England Conservatory and Perry Normal School. She was a teacher for thirty years. The mother of three daughters, she has nine grandchildren and eight great-grandchildren. She is now retired and lives on Cape Cod.

Out of Silence

Dear Mom,

You taught me to be silent.

And so the idea of writing anything about you—about us—immobilizes me. I encounter a writer's block stonier, blacker than any I have ever known. What words, I wonder, could I write to you that could fill me with such terror and so numb my mind?

Reason evaporates.

You taught me to be silent.

Days pass. Twice, I approach the computer, stumble into beginnings. Needing to be authentic, I struggle with truth, not pretty, but real. I write of anger. Of shame, confusion, and guilt. Of the regret and sorrow that permeates my relationship with you. I write of the misunderstandings and judgments that long clouded my perception of you. I write of growing older, raising a family, working through disappointments, all of which brought me closer to understanding you. But I cannot finish. I turn off the machine. Nothing is saved in the file.

Another effort. This time I write of love, of my admiration for you, of my fierce gratitude and pride. I write of your formidable courage and strength, your beauty, your music, your sense of adventure. I write of healing and forgiveness. Again I stop. Even to record love feels forbidden. So anxious I feel ill, I erase everything from the screen.

Both of these attempts are true—or a melding of them—but another truth is stronger.

You taught me to be silent.

This was a lesson of my childhood and I am stunned to discover that even now, at a remove of many years, it still holds power, still rises from my gut, bringing fear. I thought I was finished with that, with having to push through.

"We're not like some of those families, like Italians," you said years ago, "families who scream horrible things at each other, things no one can ever forgive or forget." Obediently, I learned to curb my words lest they be unforgettable. Unforgivable.

By your example, the scholarship of your silence, I learned it was not safe to speak. Early I discovered, as you did before me, that to give voice to emotions, to tell the story of our family, was taboo, a lesson perpetuated by more than one generation of womanhood. Was this impulse born of a desire to protect and shield? Or a belief that there was safety in being invisible?

Gradually, year after year, pressing against the prohibited, I found my way out, encountered courage, discovered my voice. What did not feel safe to say aloud, I spilled onto paper.

The constraint—we must not give voice to love, to hate, to anger, to history—all this gave me something to push against and that's how we get born.

Out of pain comes life. And love. And passion.

You taught me to be silent. I learned to write.

Love,

Anne

Suzanne Lipsett

Elynore Lipsett
Los Angeles, California;
c. 1946–1947

**Suzanne Lipsett,
age four**
Los Angeles,
California; c. 1947

Suzanne Lipsett was born September 29, 1943, in Buffalo, New York, and grew up in Los Angeles, California. "I have always made my living by my pen as writer, as a 'book midwife,' and in collaborative partnerships with experts. In this latter capacity, I write the books, and my name appears on the covers—no more ghosting for me! Of my own published books, three are novels—*Coming Back Up, Out of Danger,* and *Remember Me.* My most recent release is a nonfiction book of linked essays, *Surviving a Writer's Life.* I am writer, editor, mother, wife, sister, stepdaughter, friend—in a constantly shifting order. I live in the country with my husband, Tom Rider, and my two sons, Sam and Evan." [Suzanne Lipsett died, in September 1996.]

Elynore Finkelstein Lipsett, born circa 1915, died in childbirth at the age of approximately thirty-three; the baby died, too. "I was four and a half. She was sixteen years younger than I am now. No other biographical information is known. Relatives have told me that Elynore—known within the family, I think, as Lynn—was 'full of life,' 'lots of fun,' 'a wonderful woman.' But as to what her interests and passions were, what she did all day (did she work? did she aspire to art? did she, like me, hate housework?), what made her laugh and cry, I know nothing. At age thirty-five I received a package of photographs of my mother, a treasure trove of tiny hints suggesting a vibrant personality long gone. What would the full arc of life have allowed her to become? I wish I knew."

To Elynore

Oh, Mother, you strange little phantom,
You person who slipped through a crack,
Did you know when you went
What a shadow you lent
To the life of a poor working hack?

It's been, Where is my mother, oh, Daddy?
And, Who's gonna take care of me?
And, Who's gonna show
From my head to my toe
Just what kind of woman I'll be?

It was, Oh, woe is me as a teener,
It was, Oh, woe is he (that's my dad),

It was, Oh, woe is she,
Who dies *at* thirty-three
Leaving *us* all astonished and sad.

And then, oh my God, came the family
That followed the whole tragedy:
A wife, girl, and boy,
In a house like a toy,
And a sullen Miss Muffet—'twas me.

The odd bit was having not one thing
That you might have touched or possessed.
A mom of the mind,
Unconcrete, ill-defined,
Who floated away, unaccessed.

So I read like a compulsive eater.
I wrote like a bookish van Gogh.
From my earliest days,
In just all kinds of ways,
Words were the things I could know.

I was crazy, I guess, as a hoot owl.
I suppose I was hard to endure.
I was up and then down,
First Camille, then a clown,
Who *was* I? I never was sure.

That's the thing about having a mother.
She's a model, I guess, for a while.
Then she serves as a way
To bounce backward and say
That's not who I am, not *my* style.

Which is why I could never get started
In finding out who I could be.
So I thissed and I that
And I fussed and I frat,
And I felt myself all out to sea.

Quite late, though, I had me a baby.
I had me another one, too.
And the fabulous thing:

What those small boys did bring
Was a di-rect connection to you.

Under words, under pictures and memories,
Under everything that there could be,
Lay a link to the skin
In which you had been,
Lay the touch of your hands holding me.

I could *feel* you had been a great mother,
Full of comfort and maternal joys.
I could *feel* how to hold
And to wrap from the cold
Those sweet beating hearts, my two boys.

Now, *this* was an unlooked-for pleasure.
Now, this was a source of deep calm.
To discover within
That you lived in my skin.
All along I had housed my own mom.

And without all the horrible baggage
That daughters seem always to bear:
Not "Dress well" and "Clean right"
And "Act canny, not bright,"
And "Care for your body and hair."

Instead, I sensed deep, silent loving,
And feelings of safety and calm,
The words in my mind
Were words of *my* kind,
Not the critical voice of my mom.

Now, I tell you, there's something to say here.
It's not that I'm happy you died.
It's not that I'm glad
That you left me and Dad.
It's not that I loved the whole ride.

But I learned something from this dark lesson
That showed me why people are strong:
That way down below
Is where love seems to go
And to think that it fades there is wrong.

It's the oldest soft floor of the forest,
The roots of the searchingest tree.
It's the ivory bones;
It's the riverbed's stones.
It's the gift of your being in me.

And the final result of that loving,
That presence of you that I sought,
Is the work that I love
Nearly all things above,
The books that I've rendered from thought.

So I find, after all, I must thank you.
You have been there on that deepest shelf.
You've been one I could use,
You've been my only muse—
And I thought I had done it myself!

Still, I'd love to have one moving picture,
Or one little view of your face
That shows that you think
With a smile or a wink
That you're really a wicked disgrace.

Because deepest of deep in my being
Is the ongoing love of a laugh,
Is the hope of a fine
Economical line
Slipped into a bland paragraph.

What I'd give to discover you're funny,
To learn that you're wicked indeed,
To hear you deliver
With nary a quiver,
One-liners as sharp as a reed.

To hoot and to howl with my mother!
To clutch at my belly and scream!
To gasp and to cry
With wild laughter and wry
Comments—oh, what a great dream!

But I already laugh with my girlfriends.
I do it with Tom, my dear man.

In hysterical rants,
I have wet my own pants,
At a line he's delivered deadpan.

Is that, too, a gift from my mother?
Is that something else you gave me?
Did you say something wry
As you started to die
And floated away out to sea?

Why not? I'll consider it given.
A bright, crackling gift from the past.
And I'll picture you
Tipping back on your shoe
And having an absolute blast.

The sunlight will glint off your front teeth.
A hoot will escape from your lips.
You'll reach out to me,
Squeeze my arm helplessly,
And snort in hysterical blips.

Yes, that's how I'll picture you, Mother.
Just laughing your ass off out there.
A joke on your tongue
Will be keeping you young,
Sustaining your beauty and flair.

So each time a snicker assails me,
And each time I tremble with mirth,
I'll thank you, my mom,
Not just for love or calm,
But for adding the laughter at birth.

I'm sailing myself out to sea now.
I'm having to flirt with my death.
I'm having to see
How much time's left to me
And how to hang on to my breath.

Maybe I'll see you hereafter,
And sooner than might seem quite right.
So think up a fine

And a fabulous line
To welcome me into the night.

Meanwhile, I'll work on my own lines
To leave to my family and friends.
May they laugh, too, with me,
Wherever I'll be.
And here's the best joke: no one ends.

Suzanne

Margot Livesey

Eva and Margot Livesey outside Bell's Cottage
Perth, Scotland; 1954

Margot Livesey was born in Perth, Scotland, in 1953. She grew up there and now lives in Boston and London. She is the author of a collection of stories, *Learning by Heart,* and two novels, *Homework,* and most recently, *Criminals.*

Eva McEwen was born in Scotland in 1920. She grew up there and became a nurse during the Second World War. She married John Kenneth Livesey in 1952 and died in 1956.

Writing Eva

For as long as I can remember I have known you were dead. A misty studio portrait of you, wearing a cardigan and pearls, hung over my bed in Bell's Cottage and later, at Morrison's Academy for Girls, I would tell new acquaintances, proudly, about you. I did not have nice clothes, or a new bicycle, or a piano, or a pony, but I had a dead mother. I grew up knowing little about you besides your name, Eva, and having almost no curiosity. Then a few years ago I stumbled upon an absolutely startling fact: you were not merely dead—you had once been alive.

The first part of this story, my birth, your death, took place in Glenalmond, at a boys' public school, on the edge of the Scottish Highlands. The second part took place in the States, where now-adays I mostly write and teach. What changed? I reached a certain age, the age at which you died, thirty-six. My friends had babies. I saw the love they lavished on these small, sweet-smelling, dark-eyed people and understood that just because I don't remember you doesn't mean you didn't exist. We spent over seven hundred days together, you died when I was two and a half, and in your company I learned to walk, to talk, to recognize birds and animals and trees.

Around the time of these revelations I paid a visit to my god-mother, a wonderfully upright woman in her eighties who lives in a small village in Lancashire. We were talking about her garden, the roses were not doing well, when out of the blue she remarked, "You sound just like Eva. She was always saying 'right' like that." A feathery feeling passed over me. I was using the word not for directions or politics but as you had done: a sign of attention.

Now I was curious, but you remained elusive. In spite of my yearning, it seemed impossible to gather more than a small handful of details. You had brown hair and blue eyes one person told me; a birthmark on your thigh said another; your gait was slightly uneven; you apologized to the wireless before switching it off; you were a terrible cook and, several people mentioned, you were fey.

When you were the nurse at the school where my father taught, visitors to the infirmary would hear the furniture banging around—a chair would be on the floor, a lamp on the other side of the room. These kinds of disturbances are often associated with teenage girls, a manifestation of buried anger, but you, far from a teenager, would respond with amusement or, occasionally, mild irritation. "Oh them," you would shrug. "Again." And go to pick up the overturned chair.

My guardian, Roger, not a fanciful man, told the following story. He had come to the infirmary to use your telephone. (Phones were still scarce in rural Scotland after the war.) You chatted with him for a few minutes, about the rain, a boy who was poorly, then you left him to make his call. While he was on the phone, he saw a door open and a woman wearing a raincoat come in. She nodded to him, walked across the room, left by the door on the opposite side. Roger finished his call. When you returned, he asked about your visitor.

"What visitor?" you said.

He described what had happened. "Go and try that door," you said. A few minutes ago he had seen the woman open and close the door. Now he found it nailed shut, sealed by the school carpenter the previous winter. You evaded further questions, perhaps the phone rang or one of your patients needed something, but Roger was convinced the woman was no stranger to you.

It was this story, combined with the scarcity of other kinds of information, that propelled me into trying to write a novel about you. Fiction seemed the only way to make sense of so few facts. So I wrote *Eva Moves the Furniture* about a woman, you, who is accompanied by two supernatural companions, a woman in a raincoat and a girl. While they often help her, they also passionately oppose any human intimacy that might lead her to betray them. As with many gifts, their price is loneliness.

When I tell people about the novel they sometimes ask if I have inherited your sixth sense. I haven't, as far as I know, but your death did give me dual citizenship in two countries where I suspect you too resided: the country of the imagination and the country of loneliness. My life in the former, which seems to me a great gift, has helped to keep me resident in the latter. After years of working in restaurants and supermarkets I still feel blessed to do something in which I am so endlessly interested as writing, but the solitary condition of such pleasure has led to loneliness, more than I thought possible.

I hoped, and I blush to admit this, that our novel would give new life to both of us—me as a writer, you beyond your scant thirty-six years—but so far the novel itself is not yet alive. I have poured into those pages time, energy, love, intelligence; I have waylaid friends and strangers to read them; I have spent thousands of dollars copying them and mailing them, to no avail. Such fruitless endeavor has bent my old life into a new and bitter shape. But you never asked to be written about, did you?

The novel sits in a box, several boxes, in my study, and I have turned my attention elsewhere. I wrote a new novel, *Criminals,* in one greedy swoop, trying to avoid the errors I had made on your behalf: I invented ruthlessly, I omitted ghosts. The friends and strangers to whom I sent this manuscript like it, and *Criminals* has left my study for the wider world. If there are books in the afterlife perhaps you too will like it.

And *Eva Moves the Furniture* did give you life in one way. Before I began the novel I would have answered the question of whether I loved you with an empty yes. The sadness of your early death was something I experienced only intellectually. But as I wrote the final chapter tears ran down my face—I understood you had loved me and left me and died in pain. Writing about you, however ineptly, I discovered a depth of feeling for you which I had previously lacked. Finally we had a relationship.

Sometimes nowadays when I am playing with the babies of my friends I hear myself speculating: perhaps he'll be a conductor, perhaps she'll be a mathematician. I used to wonder whether you ever uttered such prophecies over me and, if so, what professions you chose—a nurse like you? a teacher like my father? I doubt if you knew there were such people as writers. This summer I was on the train from London to Edinburgh, and as we came into Newcastle, the city where you died, I suddenly knew what profession you chose for me: happiness. And with that insight came another. I am so far gone in motherlessness that I cannot imagine having a mother, but that doesn't stop me missing you, all the time.

Margot

Mary Mackey

Mary Mackey with her mother, Jean Mackey
Arlington, Texas; 1947

Mary Mackey was born January 21, 1945, in Indianapolis, Indiana. She graduated from Radcliffe College in 1966 and received her Ph.D. from the University of Michigan in 1970. She is the author of four collections of poetry and eight novels including the first two volumes of *The Earthsong Trilogy* (*The Year the Horses Came* and *The Horses at the Gate*, both published by HarperSanFrancisco). From 1989 to 1992 she served as chair of the West Coast Branch of PEN American Center. At present she is working on *The Fires of Spring*, the third novel of the trilogy.

Jean Mackey was born December 17, 1918, in Evansville, Indiana. She graduated from Evansville College in 1941 with a B.A. in science. Besides raising three children, she has worked as a chemist, served as the president of the Grandview PTA, sat on the Washington Township school board, and is one of the founders of both Crossroads Guild (which serves disabled children) and the Indiana Museum of Art Rental Gallery. She lives in Indianapolis, Indiana, with her husband, John Mackey, a physician.

The Bird and the Rose

Dear Mother,

I have a confession to make: when I was a little girl, about four or five years old, I would wait quietly at the top of the stairs until I heard you chopping onions, taking pots and pans out of the kitchen cabinet, talking on the phone, or cooing to the baby as you bathed him. Then I would slip off my shoes and creep barefoot into your room, crouch down, and open the bottom drawer of your dresser.

As soon as I managed to edge it open, a peculiar, delightful scent would waft out, and I would close my eyes and take deep breaths. It was your scent: a mix of Chanel No.5 and face powder and sandalwood, and something else, sweet, elusive and voluptuous like your hair freshly washed or your bedtime kiss.

Plunging my hands into the drawer, I would touch the things you had forbidden me to touch. I would run your silk scarves between my fingers; lightly caress your supple arm-length white kid gloves; open a small black box and draw out a cool strand of baroque pearls so pale that they looked like smoke and breath.

In the darkness of your bedroom, in the bottom drawer of that walnut dresser you had refinished with your own hands, all the colors were muted. The reds of your scarves were rust reds, the blues somber, the yellows dim and slightly fragile. Your stockings, neatly boxed and stacked, were as thin as cobwebs, and when I held them up and made them dance, I could see rainbows in them.

You kept many treasures in that drawer—cameos, jet earrings, a gold watch you told me once belonged to my great-grandmother—but the thing I liked best was an ivory pendant about two inches long and one inch wide, delicately carved and fretted like a net. In the center of the pendant, a bird stood on a branch with its head thrust back, singing happily. Above it, the tree blossomed into a pink rose.

I would take out the pendant and touch it against my cheek to feel its gloss. Sometimes I would even lick the pink rose with the tip of my tongue because it looked like the sugar roses you always put on my birthday cakes. The ivory had no taste, of course, but I imagined that I could feel the bird move uneasily as the great child-giant's lips closed above it. Whenever I touched that pendant or made it swing from its black silk cord, I felt happy and powerful and safe, like a traveler who has gone off to some strange, exotic land only to find that all her friends have come with her.

But then, one day, when I was twirling the pendant back and forth, I heard your step on the stairs, and in my panic to get it back in the box and get the drawer shut before you walked in on me, I knocked the bird and its tree against the leg of the dresser, and to my horror it snapped in half. Jamming the broken bits back into the dark cavity of the drawer, I slammed it shut, and crawled under your bed, and sat there watching your feet as I waited for you to discover my crime.

But you discovered nothing, only went to your top drawer to get something—a hair pin perhaps or a handkerchief. When you left again, clicking out of the room in your high heels, I scrambled back to the dresser to try to repair the damage. Since I was only a child, I did not know that time could not be reversed, so at first I simply sat there, holding both halves of the pendant in place, waiting for them to grow back together.

When that failed to happen, I became desperate. If you found out I had been in your drawer and broken one of your prettiest things, you would be angry with me and think I was a bad girl. You might cry the way you cried when Johnny broke your antique fruit dish, or get angry the way you did when I ate a whole bottle of baby aspirin. You might even love me less, and I could never bear that, never. I wanted you to love me—no, I wanted more than that: I wanted to be like you, just like you, wanted to wear those scarves and that scent, to hang that pendant around my neck, to put on those stockings and pearls, to dress myself in silk dresses the way you did, to set a small hat of pheasant feathers on my head, and put your favorite shade of lipstick on my lips.

You were all beauty to me, Mother. You were everything female, everything woman. I loved you so much that I wanted to grow up to be exactly like you; and the thought that I had done something bad, something secret, something sneaking and clumsy choked me with guilt and grief, because I knew you would have never done such a thing when you were a little girl, and that if you discovered these two bits of ivory, this bird snapped in half, you would know that I was not the daughter you loved, but another, worse daughter for whom there was no hope.

I sat for a long time in that dark bedroom, trying to think of how I could mend that pendant, and finally I saw how it could be done. Walking over to Daddy's desk, I took hold of the old straight-backed chair he always sat in and carried it back to the dresser.

Making sure it was secure, I climbed up on the seat and stood for a moment surveying your cut glass jars, your bottles of perfume, your hairbrush and comb. I saw my own guilty face in the mirror, round and big-eyed, my hair as straight as a broom, everything distorted by the antique glass. There, right in front of me as I had hoped, was a bottle of clear nail polish.

I had to open that bottle with my teeth, but when I had it open and I was back down at floor level carefully dabbing the point of the brush along the edges of the break, I was filled with a sense of relief and triumph so great that it was all I could do to keep from slopping still more polish onto the bird and the rose.

The polish formed a small, clear line on either side of the fracture, thin as a bit of fingernail, virtually invisible. I took a deep breath, touched the two pieces together and held them, blowing on them and praying that they would stick. At first they kept falling apart, but gradually I began to understand that I had to hold the entire pendant level in the palm of my hand as I pressed.

The room grew darker and the shadow of your closet door crept across the floor. Before it reached my bare feet, the polish turned to glue, and the bird rejoined the tree, and the rectangular net was rewoven. There was only one problem left: a little bit of excess polish that had oozed up through the ivory. Afraid to touch cloth or paper to it, I licked it off. It was sticky and bitter, but I went on, licking like a cat until there was no trace of the clear polish left.

I felt exalted, redeemed, saved. No one could see that the pendant was broken now, not even you. The crack between the two pieces was smaller than a single hair.

This is my confession. I have never told you this story before, but you still have that pendant, Mother, and if you look at it very closely, you will see the bird and the tree and the rose, and the transparent line that runs between them proving how much I have always loved you.

Mary

Njoki McElroy

Marion Washington Hampton
Galveston, Texas;
c. 1918

Njoki McElroy
Dallas, Texas; c. 1941

Njoki McElroy was born February 12 in Sherman, Texas. She grew up in Dallas and New Orleans, and spent most of her adult life in the Chicago area. After frequent sojourns to Africa, the Caribbean, South America, and Europe, Njoki describes herself as a "Woman of the World." She divides her time as professor of Performance of Black Literature and Folklore between Northwestern University, Evanston, and Southern Methodist University, Dallas. Five of her plays have been produced, and she has recently returned from a book signing/performance tour, performing personal narratives from her book, *Black Journey: A Black History Review.* She credits her late entry into writing to a 1989 residency fellowship at the Ragdale Foundation. Now she is working on a memoir, which offers unusual insights into black middle-class life from Reconstruction to the 1950s. She is the mother of six children.

Marion Washington Hampton was born in 1902 in Sherman, Texas. After receiving cosmetology training in 1923, she began work as a cosmetologist specializing in manicures, facials, and massages at the Neiman-Marcus store in Dallas. She was the first Black female hired at Neiman-Marcus in a nondomestic capacity. After her marriage, she became a full-time wife and mother who gave 200 percent of her love and care. A keen observer of human behavior, a prolific letter writer, and an outstanding storyteller, she was indeed a generational person, leaving important oral and written legacies for future generations.

Looking Back in Wonder

Dearest Mother:

After all the years of correspondence by mail, phone, and face-to-face, it does seem unbelievable that I never thanked you for so zealously protecting my childhood. Nor did I ever tell you how my childhood experiences prepared me for an absolutely magical coming of age period in New Orleans.

I heard Jesse say recently: "Our children now go from Pablum to the Pill." It is sad, Mother, that so many children are missing what I had—time for a cherished, nurtured and protected childhood. It is the most valuable gift a parent can give a child. It was just days before your transition (at age eighty-five) when I began to really appreciate what your gift had meant to me.

We had taken our evening walk and returned home. It was the time when you shared your fascinating stories of the past with me. Our days were dwindling down, but we didn't know how few there were. I thought, however, that you had unlocked all the locks to the secret rooms of your life. You know what Grandmother always said about you: "Sister sure loves to talk—runs her mouth so much that it is impossible for her to keep a secret." Of all the stories you had told, you had never told me what you said that night: when you were a little girl, Grandmother (your mother, the wisest—most elegant—love of our lives) had left you one evening with her neighbor/friend's husband while the two women went to visit the sick. The husband sexually abused you and stole your young childhood.

As I listened to you I felt as though my insides were crunched. I wanted answers but I couldn't ask the questions. Oh, Mother! If only I had known; perhaps I would not have been so resentful of your frequent migraines, depression and other nervous manifestations, and what I felt (as a child) was your smothering overprotectiveness. All of which were consequences of your horrifying experience.

I was your only "Baby" aka "Sweet Baby." So you concentrated heavily—heaping affection, praise and attention on me (as well as your fears and anxieties). I was rarely out of your sight except for summer holidays, when I went sixty-nine miles away to my grandparents. I never had a bike because you were afraid I would get hurt. Since skates were less dangerous, I learned to enjoy skating. As I grew big enough to run with Daddy, he took me on all kinds of adventures. We went fishing, hiking, climbing cliffs and crossing elevated railroad trestles. Daddy always warned me: "Don't tell your mother or she will never let you come with me again."

In addition to the ordinary problems of mothering, you had the heavy burden of keeping me whole in a pre-civil rights Dallas. It was a time of rigid segregation, Jim Crow laws, and mean-spirited whites. You prayed every morning (as I traveled across Dallas to all-Black schools) that I would return "safe and sound." I could not attend the schools within walking distance because those were for whites. Due to the quality time you spent with me during my preschool years, I entered first grade ahead of most of my peers. I was double-promoted out of elementary school and entered high school at age twelve. The first two years, I attended Booker T. Washington High, the only secondary school for Blacks at the time. I was part of a double-shift schedule where I attended classes from noon to 5 P.M. Our textbooks and equipment were discards from the white schools. Fortunately, we had dedicated teachers who took special interest in making us know that while our educational facilities were unequal to whites, we were certainly equal as human beings and we could succeed in spite of all obstacles.

During the last semester of my second year, I had to be reminded that you were still serious about protecting my childhood. One Friday evening, a few weeks before Easter, I didn't come home as usual. Without getting permission or letting you know where I was, I attended an afterschool sock hop held from 5 to 7 P.M. I never considered how alarmed you would be, not knowing if something awful had happened to me. I strolled in nonchalantly after eight; I saw the terror etched in your face, the white migraine headband around your head. I heard you cry: "Lord have mercy, Jesus. Where have you been? Thirteen years old and out on the streets at night by yourself—and you know how ornery these white folks are." I guess that you and Daddy had to take time to agree on the punishment. The next day I was told that I would not get my usual new head-to-toe wardrobe for Easter. If you wanted to get my everlasting obedience to rules, you got it. A new wardrobe for Easter was absolutely de rigueur, an established tradition. I kept thinking until Easter morning that perhaps you would relent. It was the most devastating thing that had happened to me in my thirteen years.

When I graduated from high school at sixteen, I wanted to go as far away from my protected nest as possible. Xavier University (New Orleans), the only Catholic university founded for coloreds in the United States, was the answer to my prayers. In 1941, Xavier had no dormitories on campus. Students lived in homes approved by the nuns. I know it must have been absolutely terrifying for you to let me go from under your protected wings to the most tempting, sensuously fascinating city in the world. But you knew, regardless of your fears and anxieties, that separation from you at some point was inevitable. The prepara-

tion for my separation had been accomplished between my infancy and adolescence. Because I felt confident and sure of
myself, I arrived on campus with a strong resolve to get my degree, and nothing would deter me from making you, Daddy,
friends and relatives proud of me. But I also had an intense curiosity about the life and culture of New Orleans.

I just had to see the Orleans Ballroom, where mulatto mothers
traded their quadroon daughters to rich white men. So my friend
Girigori and I went down to the Vieux Carre (French Quarter).
The streets were narrow and shadowy. There was the smell of
heavy mingled odors—chicory coffee, jasmine, the river, sea
food, syrup for the praline makers. The buildings were flush to
the sidewalks and painted in pastels like peach, pale green, faded
rose. Intricate iron lacework balconies extended over the sidewalks. Girigori said the slaves had done all of the ironwork. The
sound of human voices mingled with foghorns from the river
and Dixieland and Spasm Bands of young Black boys playing
music in the street. Since the sidewalk was so narrow, Girigori
walked behind me. All of a sudden I heard a commotion, and
when I looked back, a group of prostitutes were trying to pull
Girigori into the brothel! We found the former Orleans Ballroom
almost in the backyard of the St. Louis Cathedral and in, of all
places, the convent and school of an order of Black nuns. There
was very little demarcation between decadence and religion in
New Orleans.

We slipped inside the Orleans Street entrance and climbed the
winding stairs to the Ballroom, which the nuns used as an assem-
bly hall. The room was long and narrow with high ceilings.
Glimmering crystal chandeliers hung from the ceiling and a high
mural dimmed with age lined the walls.

For a long time I wondered which ones of my Creole classmates were descendants of those scandalous liaisons, but you
had taught me well: my dark skin was not a problem—those
who thought so had a serious problem! The mixing of the races
in New Orleans had probably created the most color-struck city
in the United States. I was not quite prepared to see the peculiar
caste system with its maddening concentration on color, features
and hair. The fact that I had grown up loved, cherished and made
to feel special and precious gave me the self-confidence I needed
to walk through all that madness relatively unscathed.

The students who were pale-skin Creoles and could pass for white were called Passé Blancs. There were in-between and wannabee Passé Blancs who on occasion also passed. Off campus, the Passé Blancs often invaded the white world and defied Jim Crow laws and segregated policies. Many were arrogant and angry because they thought they had much going for them and yet had to contend with so many indignities.

Taxi cabs were not for hire to people of color. If a Passé Blanc was with us, one would hail the cab and before the driver could say "Jim Crow" we would all climb in. We moved the hated signs on the trolleys that designated FOR COLORED. Sometimes we moved the signs all the way to the front FOR WHITE section or just tossed the signs out the window. At the theatres we sat in the balcony while our Passé Blancs joined the whites on the main floor.

Yet I must tell you, Mother, that the enforcement of racial segregation in New Orleans was certainly less oppressive than what I had experienced in Dallas. I think whites were often confused as to who was who—quadroon, octoroon, mulatto, gens de couleur? Perhaps the fact that New Orleans was known as Fun City, the Big Easy, Sin City, created a mood of laissez faire and live and let live. There were some Creole students who had moved beyond the color, features and hair madness. They realized that the energy expended on isolating themselves along those lines was futile, since, regardless of hue, we were all considered by white society to constitute the lower inferior caste.

Living with different families during my sojourn in New Orleans afforded me the opportunity to view situations in more cosmopolitan terms. My first encounter with lesbianism, for example, occurred during my senior year. You remember, Mother, that when the Tillmans (my favorite house parents) moved back to Chicago, Mama T. moved her daughter Vivian and me in with one of her bridge club members, Coach. We did not know that Coach and her companion were lesbians until after we had moved into their home. The terms lesbian, gay, homosexual, had not yet entered my vocabulary. In 1944 people's sexual preferences were very private. It was even considered inappropriate to discuss such matters. Coach and her companion appeared committed, devoted, and affectionate to each other. Vivian, who was more cosmopolitan than the rest of us, told us we had nothing to worry about because Coach had her lady. But to be on the safe side, we never allowed ourselves to be alone with Coach.

The couple played the same stereotypical roles that heterosexual couples play. Since Coach was the dominant partner, she was treated like a king by her subservient partner. Coach reigned at the head of the table and was served first with the best of what was available. She was protected and pampered; the operation of the house revolved around her. Vivian and I had quite an adjustment to make because Mama T.'s home had been informal, lively. Our friends had always been welcomed and the ambiance had been celebratory. Coach resented our male friends and discouraged us from dating. Conflicts with Coach could be very unpleasant, so we bided her rules, and in the middle of the year we found us another home. I think the experience of living in Coach's home enlarged my understanding of human behavior in a way that I could not have found in books. I saw Coach and her companion not just as labels, lesbians/gay, but as individuals who happened to prefer each other. It added to my ability to develop an open mind and to be as nonjudgmental as possible.

I must tell you, Mother, that the real test of my resolve and determination to graduate and make you proud of me came when Sidney B. Jett entered my life. I met him during my sophomore year when I was living with the Tillman family. Sidney was not a student, but I was introduced to him by one of my male friends who described Sidney as an expansive bon vivant. Which meant that Sidney took the guys to places they could not afford. Our first date was the Homecoming festivities. Early in the day he sent me a lovely corsage and a box of chocolates. That was the beginning of many lovely surprises and gestures from him.

Sidney picked me up in a big shiny new car. After the dance that night, he drove the car onto the ferry and we went to a nightclub across the river in Algiers (famous for gris-gris, hoodoo, love potions and such). It was the beginning of an exciting and magical time for me. I was just seventeen and in my wildest dreams I could never have imagined such a Cinderella-like lifestyle. I often thought: wow! What would my little mother say if she saw this?

Sidney was not by any definition drylongso (ordinary). Lively/funny/charming sometime outrageous, Sidney was like a one-

man Mardi Gras. As outgoing as he was, however, he never really
shared that much about himself. The only personal thing I remember was he said he was from Flint, Michigan. He apparently
had been exposed to the rich because he had great style and
the mannerisms of those who were well-heeled. My house mates
marveled at my cool manner and discipline with Sidney. There
were times when my studies demanded my attention and I was
unavailable to run with Sidney. On those occasions he took my
house mates out on the town, and they, of course, thought he
was the absolute greatest.

Some of Sidney's humor derived from his ability to size up a
person and give him/her a clever nickname. He called me Texie,
Tessie or Tessie Mae, knowing that my feathers would be ruffled.
We went to all kinds of spectator events, but the ones that fascinated Sidney the most were the dance marathons. From the start
of the marathon, the floor was crowded with contestants. Gradually couples dropped out or were disqualified for breaking the
rules. After many days and sometimes weeks of nonstop dancing,
bedraggled finalists who resembled zombies leaned on each
other and dragged themselves around the dance floor. Sidney
made up names and cheered them on.

Into the second year of our relationship, Sidney exhibited a
problem that I found troublesome. One night he took a group of
us to see Duke Ellington's band. As usual he bought drinks for
everyone within reach. He loved waving his money around and
being the life of the party. Before the event ended, however, Sidney was drunk-drunk; you know, drunk as a Cootie. One of the
guys in our party took me home. Sometime later at a similar
event, the episode was repeated. That time I took the keys, left
Sidney slumped over the table, and drove myself home. After
each episode, Sidney brought special gifts and offered a plea: "Oh
Texie, my little Texie. I'm so sorry and I swear it won't happen
again. Come on now, Texie Mae, don't be mad at Sidney."

No one I talked to about Sidney (including Sidney) thought
he had a problem. Everyone said I was overacting—that Sidney
was such a great catch for me, such a sweet guy. I had to listen
to the little old folk-voice inside me: "Don't let your heart start
what your head can't stand." I knew Sidney had a problem that
was not going to be part of my future. So I began to see less of
him. I even began working in a photographer's studio so I was

less available. Now after graduation, when he visited me in Dallas, I could tell that he charmed you and Daddy. He was subdued and a perfect gentleman. We never discussed his drinking problem; after a few days he vanished from my life forever.

In looking back over my roller-coaster relationship with Sidney, I realize that my cool manner and discipline with him was due in great part to two of your axioms:

1. Don't ever run after boys.
2. Keep your pants up and your skirt down.

Without further explanation on your part, I translated number one to mean: Make sure males care more for you than you care for them—or at least make it appear so. Number two axiom simply meant: No sex was safe sex. The axioms, stories, proverbs, that you shared with me during my childhood were not forgotten in New Orleans. I regret that the painful story of your violation was revealed to me so late; now, looking back in wonder at the strength you gave me, I know what you gave me was more than just a wise mother's warning. But like protective devices, your words had helped me maintain my wholeness and gave me strength and power to do the right thing in spite of my temptations.

You did a fantastic job in preparing me for eventual separation from you—preparation that I needed in order to deal with race, color consciousness, relationships and the world. I thank you Dearest Mother, Times Twenty and more, for putting the strength in my wings and then having the confidence to give me the freedom to test those wings.

I Love you,
Njoki

Sandra McPherson

*Sandra McPherson (standing) with her daughter, Phoebe
Carlile, and her mother, Frances McPherson*
Davis, California; 1995

Sandra McPherson was born August 2, 1943, in San Jose, California. She is the author of eight full-size collections of poetry as well as four chapbooks and three fine-press editions/constructions of single poems. Her books include *The Spaces Between Birds: Mother/Daughter Poems, 1967–1995* (Wesleyan, 1996), *Edge Effect: Trails and Portrayals* (Wesleyan, 1996), *The God of Indeterminacy* (Illinois, 1993), *Streamers* (Ecco Press, 1988), and *The Year of Our Birth* (Ecco, 1978), which was nominated for a National Book Award. She is professor of English at the University of California, Davis. Honors include two Ingram Merrill Foundation grants, three NEA fellowships, and a Guggenheim fellowship. She was recently featured in a segment of *The Language of Life* with Bill Moyers. She has one daughter, Phoebe, and is married to the poet Walter Pavlich.

Frances Gibson McPherson was born September 11, 1916, in San Jose, California. Her early years were spent in Lone Pine, California, until the death of her father, a farmer, in the influenza epidemic, when she was three. She returned to San Jose, where her mother secured a teaching job, and lived with her mother, her aunt, and her grandmother. As a girl, she especially liked to sing for people and to climb trees. She graduated from San Jose State College with a degree in elementary education and married Walter McPherson, whom she had known from childhood. They adopted Sandra at birth and seven years later had a son of their own. She has been a homemaker and a churchwoman all her adult life.

To My Mother

1   Night, the blackness of the telephone,
    you on the hook
    hold down all other voices . . .

    Mother, I say, Mother why don't you write the story of your
      life?

    —*Oh, if everyone did that*—

2   Though children are raised from breasts, those halves
    as clean as cereal bowls,

those bowls are modestly put away
when not in use,
a pear or peach
painted in the center depth of each.

3   Mother sat on the beach and out of her knitting bag
grew a red sweater.
Sand knitted into the purl,
sand for eggs and long-distance calls,
sand such as wore down the teeth of ancestors who ate dried
    fish.
And she gave it to her granddaughter.
Secretly a moth gave it also
to her newest born.

4   One's history should be blank
to show you didn't use yourself
for selfish ends.

Once you held your baby by a palm tree.
Your hands itched in the humidity.
You smile toward the camera, but the truth

is you are gazing out to sea.

Love,

Sandy

Joanne Meschery

Joanne Meschery (left) with twin sister, Janice, in the lap of their mother, Mary Pritchard
DeLeon, Texas; autumn, 1941

Joanne Meschery was born in Gorman, Texas, on July 8, 1941. She has published short stories and three novels: *In a High Place, A Gentleman's Guide to the Frontier* (a PEN/Faulkner Award finalist), and *Home and Away.* She is also the author of a book of nonfiction, *Truckee*. Joanne is the mother of three children. She and her husband live in the Sierra Mountains in Northern California.

Mary Wahl Pritchard was born August 17, 1920. She grew up in Forth Worth, Texas, where her father—a fellow known to his friends and family as "Pretty Bill"—managed an oil and gas well supply company. Her mother, Edna, was an accomplished musician and church organist. Mary married in 1940, bore five children, and spent most of her adult life in the West. She died on November 5, 1985.

"For we think back through our mothers
if we are women . . ."
—Virginia Woolf

TRUCKEE, CALIFORNIA
MAY 14, 1995

Dearest Mom,

I have been reading some of your old letters. ("Never start a letter with 'I,'" you announce in one you wrote on August 27, 1939.) You'd just turned nineteen, at home in Fort Worth, home from Texas State College for Women. In six months you'd quit school to marry Joe, the man for whom you broke the "I" rule. "I love you," your letter begins—even then, your "I" outward bound, forever casting in the direction of someone else.

Mama: Didn't anybody ever tell you that a person could get lost, always looking the other way?

Years after you wrote that letter, you came to me in a dream. It hadn't been long since your death. You sat at the kitchen table. Somehow I think you must remember this. I hadn't heard you walk in, but I knew it was you—downstairs in a house you'd never seen in your life, a house three thousand miles from where you might've expected to find me. In my dream, I lay in bed a moment, listening, telling myself I needed to get up, go down the chilly wooden stairs, because you were waiting. So in my dream, I woke myself up, pulled on wool socks and draped a blanket over my flannel nightgown. I don't think you realized how cold it was in the middle of the night in that old shake-shingled house. Nevertheless, I noticed you'd taken precautions. You sat at the maple table dressed in a blue hospital gown and booties, your hair tucked under a blue cotton cap. A white surgical mask covered your mouth, as if something here could be contagious and you might catch it, even after death. Life could still kill you.

You nodded as I slid into a chair. "Sing 'Mockingbird Hill,' " you said to me.

In January of 1938 you graduated from high school magna cum laude. "Mr. Buster, school board members, Superintendent Green, teachers, fellow students, and friends," your commencement speech began. "You have just heard about the American Legion's Peace Plan. Tonight, I come before you to humbly offer my ideas on forging an adequate system of defense. First we should all remember that the lesson of war is to lessen war . . ."

You were seventeen, although some time before—you never knew exactly when—your mother had lopped two years off your age so she herself would appear younger.

For graduation, Lillian Bryant gave you an autograph book. The Bible verse taped on the cover of the book reads: "Ask, and it shall be given to you; seek, and ye shall find . . ." Inside, an inscription from Gordon King says, "Dear Mary, Be careful who you meat. They may say you are awful sweet, But that's not all there after." Your younger sister—who you always believed to be infinitely more beautiful, with the shining golden curls and exquisite name Antoinette—your sister writes in a childish scrawl: "remember when I eat your birthday party and set in your cake." . . . "Dear Mary, Here's to a smart kid who can be anything she wants. But I wish you'd be mine doggonnit. Your friend, Mack." . . . "Dear Mary, When you get married and live on a hill, Send me a piece of your wedding cake by the whippoor-will . . ."

Dear Mama: You got married too young.

Two years, she took from your age. But it might just as well have been a decade. Were you eighteen or twenty when we came along? "Came along," you told us, as if we'd simply ambled through your open hospital door. Twins—what a shock on a sticky hot Texas day. Can it be that I actually recall your astonishment at the sight of the two of us, your blue eyes springing utterly wide. Or is it only that I saw that same expression cross your face so often in all the following years.

It seems everything caught you by surprise—too much happening, too fast. Five children you had, just like that. And never enough money, not enough time. I think now that you were always way too young, never able to catch up to your actual years or yourself—the "I" that was you forever vanishing on the horizon before you could get there.

Above the surgical mask, your eyes are so bright blue. You reach toward me across the kitchen table. But I mustn't touch you, because of the sterile hospital gown. I don't want you to be contaminated.

"Sing 'A Kiss to Build a Dream On,'" you say to me.

"Dearest Joe," you wrote while on a visit to Texas when Jan and I were a year old, "this morning I mailed you a mean letter, so now I'm retracting. Darling, I don't know what gets into me. I guess I keep you up in the air most of the time. But your letter makes me so proud of you and the calling God has given you. You'll probably have so many in church by the time I get back that I won't feel at home. I've felt so darned out of place for so long. But honey, I love you to death. Please don't be mad at me. I think I might be looking a little better. Have lost a few pounds. I do enjoy being here. Everything is *fun!* But I'm getting so worried over the war. Daddy thinks it will last five years, at least, and everyone will have to go. How about my coming home and having another baby? Maybe two . . ."

In a pinch you borrowed from your parents, trying to make ends meet. You took whatever odd job you could. A yellowed newspaper clipping from the *Taunton Daily Gazette* carries the headline: GAL FROM TEXAS COVERS ALL NEWS DOWN MYRICKS WAY.

Come Christmas, Mrs. Pritchard will complete her first year as a Gazette correspondent. Wife of the minister of the Myricks and Dighton Methodist churches, Rev. Joseph Pritchard, she enjoys bringing information to the peo-

ple of her community, especially of the churches to which her husband minis-
ters. Mr. Pritchard is also studying at the Boston University School of
Theology from which he will be graduated in January.

War never called him away; his life was never threatened. Instead, you were the one who seemed in danger. We understood
how precarious—there were three of us children by then. Some
days, with him away at school, breakfast dishes still on the table,
bills piled in the middle, you'd cover your face with your
hands—hands black from feeding the coal furnace. You'd say, "I
wish I could die." But then, in the next breath you might call us
outside, "Come on . . ." You'd smile. "Let's go sledding!"

Saturday nights while he worked on his sermon, you ironed
his white shirt and cleaned his Sunday suit with Energine. One
spring you took a class from County Extension and made us
identical coats using the cheapest wool you could find. ("Got to
stick to our budget," you reminded us.) That Easter Sunday you
buttoned us into them—coats the color of Easter basket grass
and the wool so coarse and prickly it made us itch. Before we'd
even stood for the opening hymn, we'd broken out in hives,
necks and wrists blooming as your proud gaze slid into dismay.

Mama: I loved the coat anyway.

Each weekend he drove the fifty miles home from Boston University to Myricks, where he preached his sermons and minis-
tered to the sick and poor in spirit. He brought back stories about
his classes, his professors. He described books to you, gave you
the names of Buber, Tillich, Nietzsche. Sometimes he saw movies
in the city or attended a concert. He told you how he and his
classmates from sociology class had taken a bus downtown to
observe a striptease show—"observe," as if it were some labora-
tory experiment. You listened—we listened—while he talked on,
grinning, warming his hands around a coffee cup. "Boston Garden," he said, and we imagined cool stone paths, lilacs, roses,
buttercups. And fairies—we felt sure about fairies. It seemed he
lived a magic life.

You'd written to him just before the two of you eloped on
Valentine's Day:

"Question:

What is a double petunia?"

"Answer:

A petunia is a flower like a begonia,
A begonia is a meat like a sausage,

A sausage and battery, is a crime,
Monkeys crime trees,
Trees a crowd,
A rooster crowed in the morning
     and made a noise,
A noise is on your face like your eyes,
The eyes are opposite the nays,
A horse nays,
A horse has a colt,
You can catch a colt, go to bed and wake
     up in the morning with *double petunia*."

Sometimes he performed a marriage in the parsonage—a couple suddenly appearing, about to be separated by war, with no time for a proper wedding. This usually happened at night, after you'd tucked the baby into bed and told Jan and me to stay upstairs and keep still. You almost always acted as a witness. You stood behind the bride and groom. He stood before them. Cautiously, Jan and I crept to watch from the landing, seeing two strangers standing in our living room, sometimes catching the scent of a gardenia corsage, cigarettes, hearing nervous laughter, maybe tears. And always his voice drifting up to us: "Dearly Beloved, we are gathered together here in the sight of God and in the presence of these witnesses . . ." Huddled on the landing, the two of us nodded silently, waiting for the ring. "In token and pledge of the vow between us made . . ." Then we lifted our eyebrows and elbowed each other. Now. The kiss was coming. And on those nights of such unexpected and mysterious ritual, it never occurred to us that you had ever been that bride rushing off to marry, that you'd once given and received the ring, the kiss. It seemed you had always worn that gold band, always borne witness to his performance.

Then, come Monday, he'd be gone again—a student driving away in a black Ford, back to the city and school. He left you in that quiet village, the curve of a one-lane road overgrown with elderberries. Left you without a car, on foot. Nowhere to go. You kept house and fed us, fed the furnace, fed our clothes through the wringer of an old washing machine. Bed sheets flapped on the line, froze stiff in the winter.

Mama: I understand now, how it is possible to be abjectly alone but not alone, how a person can have so much to do and yet have nothing to do.

You were the girl he left behind, though he didn't go to war. Everybody hated the Germans, the Japanese—you could've blamed those enemies for his absence and never have felt the worse for it. But how could you hate God or the church? You loved God, sang, "A Mighty Fortress Is Our God," sat in a wooden pew every Sunday and prayed to God. Loved God, loved us, loved him. Still, it seemed not a day passed that you didn't feel the worse for it.

One fall, you answered an ad promising to earn you extra money at home. A few weeks later a cardboard box arrived full of seashells and mimeographed instructions. We stared at those instructions—now there were four of us—intrigued by diagrams of tiny shells glued into flower-shaped pins and earrings. We flanked you as you spread all the beautiful colored shells on the dining room table. "This is going to be something," you told us, opening the small tube of glue. As you began to work, we stayed very quiet, watching for the flowers to form. We saw how careful you were. You said you wished that you could find the tweezers. Then it seemed without warning you were shaking your head and cursing your fingers—fingers fumbling to make the flowers, the glue running onto everything—I can still smell it—and you stamping feet, your arm suddenly sweeping shells everywhere, all your young anger spilling over, your eyes startled with such surprise that you could feel such rage at us, and at him—called by God, forever called from home, from you.

Your breath rustles the white surgical mask as you speak. "Sing 'Wishing,'" you say to me. In my dream it's beginning to grow light. This night is almost over. I clear my throat to sing for you, then stop, leaning closer across the table. "Mama," I whisper, "tell me how it is." I glance away. I do not say "heaven," though that's what I'm thinking. "You know—tell me what it's like." You gaze at me, blue eyes blinking above the mask. "Oh, it's really quite nice," you say after a minute. "But it's very crowded."

On June 11, 1950, the *Taunton Gazette* reported in its news of the region:

PASTOR CALLED WEST . . . About 150 persons gathered Saturday night at the Myricks Methodist Church for a farewell party for the Rev. and Mrs. Pritchard and family, who are scheduled to leave today for Modesto, Cal., where Mr. Pritchard will serve as an assistant pastor. The farewell, held in the social hall, included a vocal solo by Miss Patricia Stetson, accordion solos by William Melesky, selections by 'The Harmony Grits,' a quartet, and to complete the program Mr. and Mrs. Pritchard sang 'May the Good Lord Take a Liking to You.' The Pritchards and their children will make the trip cross country by car . . .

With his studies behind him—finally a full-fledged, ordained member of the clergy—you believed things would "settle down," as you wrote to your mother. "It will be good to have Joe at home more. Maybe we can even pay off some of these debts." But in the times ahead, through continual moves to bigger and busier parishes and the addition of another child, your worries over money only increased and it seemed he was called away even more.

"The church called," you used to tell him when he'd return from visiting some ailing parishioner. Then you'd read all the messages you'd written beside the telephone. One day we came home from school and found you crying, tears falling into a bowl of popcorn you held in your lap. "The church bought our washing machine," you told us. And we cried, too, because you'd been so happy to have that automatic machine, and proud to make the monthly payment—payments you finally couldn't afford. So the church took over, and though the washer remained in the house—the house and all its furniture, everything, owned by the church—the wonderful machine was never as wonderful again.

You compiled lists of all you planned to do—"When things settle down." Those words echoed through our house, the refrain of decades. Even now, I hear your voice, that phrase. It was a promise you made to yourself, to us. "Just wait," you'd tell us, "when things . . ."

Later, you made another promise—one I carried with me for twenty-seven years—a vow meant only for me. This was no refrain. You said it just once, although I might've seen it coming, I'd been asking for it—all your rage suddenly scalding me. "Joanne Marie," you said, your voice rough behind the bedroom door I'd slammed shut in your face, "someday I'll be dying—just mark my words." "Well, I wish you would," I shot back, my chest so tight. I would not cry. Across the room, my prom dress hung from the closet door—you'd helped me make it, sewing yards of white net to taffeta. In three hours I'd wear that dress. In a pol-

ished, festooned gym, I'd be crowned queen and carry a sheaf of
red roses. You'd stand in the crowd, then give me a hug and a
kiss for everyone to see. We'd enact this ritual exactly as we did
every Sunday in church—the preacher's smiling wife, his smiling
children, a model family. A Christian family. *Act as if,* our unspoken motto. Who could know that by then our house was no
church parsonage but a hostile camp where lines had finally been
drawn and sides taken. Not long into adolescence, I'd fled your
side to take his. "Just go ahead and die!" I shouted that afternoon. I sank onto my bed, flinging a white satin shoe at the
sound of your voice. "Mark my words," you said loud through
the door, "I'll be dying, and you'll come and ask my forgiveness,
but I won't forgive you. I will never forgive you. Never!"

Mama: These are the words that stick forever, that circle round
and round. And now there are times, when I ask my own children—"Why do you always, *always* remember only the bad
things?"

You would never forgive my sullenness, my rebel anger, my
arrogant ridicule. I would leave home for college. I'd marry, bear
three children, one after another. And with every passing day, I'd
tell myself I wouldn't ever be like you. I would be him, no matter
what. Because he loved his life, because he always seemed to
have more fun and performed important work—dedicated himself to the sick and poor in spirit.

"Dear Joanne," you wrote to me one spring in 1975. "Yesterday
some women from our church, along with a few from other
churches here in town came over to the house. We've formed a
coalition to end world hunger. While we were in the living room
deciding where to begin, a pipe burst under the kitchen sink,
and we had to stop everything. Of course, we couldn't figure out
how to fix it, so we had to call your father. But by the time he
got here the whole kitchen was flooded . . . ."

Dear mama, I have learned to fix the broken pipes. Two weeks
ago, I installed a light dimmer in our dining room. I've repaired
the old dishwasher. But I could never be him. I am you, standing
in a high school auditorium saying, "Mr. Buster, school board
members . . . I come before you to humbly offer my ideas on
forging an adequate system of defense." I am you, meeting in a
cramped living room in a tract house in a small town in Nevada,
trying to decide just how you and a handful of other women

will end world hunger. I am you chanting, "When things settle down . . ."

Here on yellow legal paper, I find a brief autobiography written in ballpoint for a club you joined: ". . . we had five babies—twin girls, two other daughters, and a son. I've always kept busy at home and in church work. I enjoy our children and grandchildren and all the people we have known. I also like to try new recipes (not always successfully!). For forty-three years, we served churches in Texas, Ohio (Joe's home state), Massachusetts, California and Nevada. Joe retired in 1982. My mother lives with us . . ."

The church held a retirement party. They gave you a yellow rose corsage. He wore a white carnation. You stood at a lace-covered table with two sheet cakes shaped like open Bibles. White sugar doves spread their wings at the corners, the frosted pages read: "Rev. Joe and Mary, Because of you, Our lives are richer." We watched you cut the cakes, all of us grown up and smiling, and our children smiling, too. Genuine smiles now, no act as if. Then you grabbed his hand and led him around the table, in front of the crowd. At this farewell, the two of you sang "Side By Side." And you meant those words.

Some time later, I asked you how it happened—how, after all the years, you'd come to feel so contented and happy with him. And you answered, "I think it was when I finally realized he was a good person."

But I believe there might be more to it—your children leaving home, leaving you with more time for yourself and fewer financial worries, more income. (Sad, that family income should almost always reach a maximum just at that point when we least need it.)

Or what might've happened was this: maybe you realized that you were a good person—you, yourself. Finally, *you*.

Regardless, it still seems such a long hard road to reach that place—too many mornings, covering your face with your hands, crying, "I wish I could die . . ."

(Why do you remember only the bad things? I hear you saying.)

"Someday," you told me, "I'll be dying . . . I will never forgive you . . ."

* * *

And then, too soon, you were. Dying. Three years after his retirement, August 17, 1985—your 65th birthday—he drove you to the Emergency Room. They took you into Surgery. They said, "It doesn't look good." Six weeks later, after you'd recovered from that operation in which nothing could be done, you started chemotherapy. Throughout those days, fear shot us scrambling—so much happening very fast—cancer like quicksilver beaded everywhere inside you, slippery, nobody could catch it. We lost all track of hours, whole weeks. Except now, time didn't escape you.

You *lived* those days. It appeared that nothing—not even death—could take you by surprise anymore. The look of astonishment I'd seen so often never once crossed your face. Instead, your blue eyes softened. Your gaze leveled, steady and straight ahead—you, who'd cringed, hardly able to look when one of us so much as nicked a finger. They told us, "It doesn't look good." You said, "It isn't so bad." Watching and listening, it was all I could do not to ask: What in the world's come over you. But I think I already knew.

On the last weekend of October, you asked me to give you a home permanent. I hesitated, wondering if this was such a good idea, considering your chemotherapy treatments. What about those solutions—the developer, the neutralizer—wouldn't they cause more damage to your hair? But you didn't seem the least concerned. So on Saturday afternoon, I draped a towel over your shoulders and began parting the damp strands. You held the flimsy endpapers, handed them to me one by one.

Your hair had thinned, but even in health it was never what you'd call thick. The nape of your neck appeared downy as an infant's. Your scalp looked very pink and new, and I tried to be careful with the comb. I kept extra cotton balls handy, dabbing at your forehead and temples, so the developer wouldn't run into your eyes.

You talked about what a good garden you'd had that summer, about what kinds of Trick or Treat candy you'd buy for Halloween. You said there was just so much going on at the church. You said, "When things settle down . . ."

While you leaned at the kitchen sink, I ran the water soft, rinsing your hair. I said, "I sure hope it takes."

Later, I fixed supper. He wouldn't be home. A friend from the church had taken him to San Francisco to watch a 49ers game—his first weekend away.

Somewhere you'd come across a pamphlet of special recipes for cancer patients undergoing chemotherapy. You showed me the dishes you wanted to try. While you rested in the other room, I cooked. The pamphlet looked typewritten and Xeroxed, hand-stapled. I studied the recipes, wondering just where the little booklet had come from. Still, I followed the directions exactly. I made everything from scratch.

"This is supposed to be good for me," you said as we sat down.

But I could not, for the life of me, imagine. We filled our plates with macaroni and cheese, pureed carrots, creamed corn and stewed apple chunks.

I swallowed hard. "In a couple of days," I said, "I'm pretty sure your hair will relax."

You nodded. "Honey, this is just delicious." You lifted a limp, syrupy slab of apple. "Really," you said.

The next day, after a lunch of scrambled Egg Beaters, mashed yams, and blended broccoli soup, I prepared to drive the sixty miles back to my own home and family.

As we walked to the car, you said, "If I remember where I got those recipes, I'll let you know."

"Well, if you think of it—" I mumbled. For a moment I looked away.

Someday, you said, *I'll be dying* . . .

Then you were holding me tight. Your hair smelled of curling solution. My eyes stung, but you said not to cry.

"Okay," I said, my face streaming as I climbed into the car.

I started the engine and you stepped back a moment. Then suddenly you leaned, reaching through the open car window. You grabbed my hand, as if some last words had just come to you . . . you remembered.

You said, "I wish I could give you everything."

Mama: Today, in my waking hours, I am making another end to my dream. What I do after I find you downstairs in the kitchen—after I sing all the songs—is prepare you a spectacular feast. I smooth a napkin in your lap and untie the surgical mask from your face. I pull off your blue cap. Your hair looks nice and relaxed. Things have finally settled down, no crowds, nothing taking our attention, which is—you must admit—amazing. It's no exaggeration when I say that a day scarcely passed when you weren't called upon to minister to the sick and poor in spirit. As I mention this, your sigh holds a little smile. "Oh yes," you say. "I did do that." And then we sit back. We gab on and on. Until the light over our heads softens and dims, and the candles burn low. Until after a while, I unfold the letter I've been writing.

But first, let me tell you this: during those last weeks, you showed me just how much living there is in dying.

And then let me read you this ending, which is only the beginning . . .

Dear Mama, You gave me everything.

Joanne

Mary Moore

Mary Moore and her mother, Idamae Siegel Loewe
Southern California; c. 1949

Mary Loewe Moore was born November 14, 1945, in Pasadena, California. Married in 1967, she migrated to the San Francisco Bay area. Their only child, Damara, was born June 25, 1971. Moore worked for a time in voluntary health organizations and in corporations as a technical writer. She now holds a Ph.D. in Renaissance poetry from the University of California, Davis, and teaches at Marshall University in Huntington, West Virginia. Her poetry has appeared in *Poetry, Mockingbird, Field, Prairie Schooner, New Letters, Nimrod,* and others. Her forthcoming collection, *Book of Snow,* is due out from Cleveland State University Press in 1997.

Idamae Siegel Loewe was born in St. Louis, Missouri, on June 29, 1910, and died March 5, 1995, in Brookshire, Texas. Raised in St. Louis, she married Dominic Arthur Loewe on May 29, 1945, and moved to California, where their only child, Mary, grew up. Although she held jobs in banking and retail, Idamae Siegel Loewe never saw herself as a career woman. She did love poetry: during her adolescence and twenties, she transcribed many of Edna St. Vincent Millay's and Dorothy Parker's cynical love poems, but she also read Kipling.

Lively in Her Soul

I
ELEGY

Mama, you ate ham sandwiches laced
with green olives for lunch and drank
Jack Daniel's, watered,
after six. Don't deny it. Your hair, silver-shot,

stayed black until you were eighty-four. You died not
of cirrhosis but of suicide:
you just quit
eating. Stoic, bones porous as pumice,

you couldn't go home again—said you'd
just as soon eat dust as

live like that—doled cigarettes
at someone's whim, nursed. Guaranteed:

freed. You made up your mind to mind
nobody. Agoraphobic,
self-confined,
perched in the mother-in-law suite

over the kitchen, you'd occupied
yourself, solitary
as the hermit crab whose house is
another's. Yours was your niece's. Wary

of men, hating trees, horses, all
animals
but dogs, you'd constructed
a life outlined by

Dutch-boy blue walls, old photos,
and a TV
console. You'd called me every Sunday
for thirty years to say "hello"

although your news was all your niece's—
her dogs' illnesses
and cousin John's politics, your own
life dwindled and eventless.

But inside that minuscule willful room
was freedom
you'd cultivated, a drummed-up plum
of a life flecked iridescent gold—

alizarin, mauve—as if Persian
rugs hid under
the floorboards. There, a connoisseur
of doubt, you hoarded worries

like gold. Imagine: in San Francisco,
a germ-armed
psycho might take the Presidio,
the San Andreas

flatten the city, the sky itself
collapse

in poignards and shards of blue glass.
All was precarious, suspect.

Myopic, not overjoyed by Freud,
you kept secrets that mystify
me even now;
I was forty-eight before you revealed,

with alliterative Victorian flourish,
relishing
the fricatives, "Your father
was a philanderer."

All those secrets buzzed in the white noise
of the phone lines. My distance
hurt, but drink
blinded you so, I was part mystery

anyway. Cut lace cuffs and peter pan
collars suited
other daughters, not yours; I was doubt
personified. I flouted

expectations as our hounds shook
off baths—in sprays
of mud and fur. At piano,
my fingers were bananas;

I tap-danced like a fiend, knock-kneed
and splay-footed;
my left side didn't mind my
right; my hands were unmatched sleight-

of-hands, their tricks a magic I
never mastered. Oh, you
got yours back allright. When I brought my
college boyfriend home, you

got drunk and said, "Fry your own
damn chicken";
I didn't but my goose was cooked anyway: he'd
never seen a woman drunk and useless.

I saw him see and was relieved
of his desire.

He told me "it" might be genetic.
He was right: heretics

run in families like poets, liars,
and drunks;
we'd rather die than be
foot-stools; we don't follow orders

well or mind the rules. We have odors
and ideas.
Unbridled fools and half-hysteric
ideologues,

sly dogs or loose cannons; we Siegel
women are not to be
ignored. Not regal
or brave, you died, refusing to be

what someone else ordained.
Unpoetic, unconsoled
for what life doled
out, you died, lively in your soul.

II
POST SCRIPT

Three thousand miles by car, I drove East,
carrying your ashes wrapped in brown
funerary paper, anonymous as porn.
I told no one you were there, lodged
behind the seat, humble as groceries.
What were you anyway? what
burned off, quirky as fireworks, sparking up
the mortuary chimney? Humor, worry,
your love of words—*copacetic, diffident,*
knurl, flange—words whose use alone inspired
laughter—so oddly could sound accord with sense.

Now in a strange city, in a rented house,
you sit on a closet shelf, hidden from
the vase of roses, the books of poems,
the pictures you took of my daughter, her smile
a posie for you. Hidden, you still attract

sparks of attention like an ingenue.
You told me you were so small at birth they
carried you on a lace pillow, like a jewel.
Your mother took to her bed—as Scarlett's
milder sister might have—with the vapors.
You're smaller now. Part Edwardian,
you weren't at ease with bodies anyway,
bought me a book to convey the odious
facts of life.

       Still, complex as myths
of twins, a Gemini besides, you were part
worldly, loved Dorothy Parker and Millay.
Your copy-book of poems included this:

> So praise the gods, at last he's away!
> And let me tend you this advice, my dear:
> Take any lover that you will or may
> Except a poet. All of them are queer.
>
> It's just the same—a quarrel or a kiss,
> Is but a tune to play upon his pipe.
> He's always hymning that or wailing this;
> Myself I much prefer the business type.
>
> That thing he wrote, the time the sparrow died—
> (Oh, most unpleasant-gloomy, tedious words!)
> I called it sweet, and made believe I cried;
> The stupid fool! I've always hated birds . . .

That was copied in St. Louis, a southern city
where the cicadas buzz louder than
children playing combs, on and off, on
and off, following a rhythm of sevens
like waves, or is it no rhythm, a rhymeless
meter grounded in chitin and the inhuman
tides of fluids. They're here too, lodged
in the maples and oaks downtown, invisible
voices, energies. Everywhere I face
feels South.

Here as there, fireflies, rise and fall, kindling
on the up draft, darkening on the down,
neon chips or ashes of chartreuse, eerie
but lovable, as if they refracted
the light from the other world into this;

but it's all myth-bio-luminescence, sex's
chemical attractant, a trick.
By day they're gnat-sized, frail and Puritan-
brown, butt-ends shaped like lightbulbs. You probably
hated them, like trees, "Nature," clouds and dirt.

Still, your ashes must go somewhere to earth.
Maybe you're already in the thick of things—
in the lilac nettles of stars, prickly
with light; in the spurs of flowering chicory
on the ground swells of Kentucky or
Virginia; or you ride the fireflies' spirals
up and down, up out of this world and back
as you believed, to be born again—not
as Whitman proposed, part of that enduring
green, but as Parker might have it, under
Jupiter, human again but luckier.

Love,

Mary

Nora Naranjo-Morse

**Rosarita (Rose)
Cisneros Naranjo,
in front of the bread
oven at her house**
Santa Clara Pueblo,
New Mexico; c. 1994

**Nora Naranjo-Morse,
in front of the
fireplace in the
studio she built
on the Reservation**
Santa Clara
Pueblo Reservation,
New Mexico; c. 1994

Nora Naranjo-Morse was born October 28, 1953, in the county hospital a few miles from the Santa Clara Pueblo Reservation. *Mud Woman,* a selection of poems and photographs of Nora's clay sculptures, was published by the University of Arizona Press in 1992. In 1993, the Children's Boston Museum Modern Curriculum Press Inc. published Nora's first children's book, *Kaa Povi's First Clay Gathering.* At the age of twenty-seven Nora gave birth to twins and from that moment on became a Gia.

Rosarita (Rose) Cisneros Naranjo was born in the Pueblo of Santa Clara, New Mexico, June 16, 1915. "People outside of the Pueblo know my mother as Rose; however, in the language of her people, the Tewa, she is known as Aah khong Povi (Meadow Flower), and for most of her life she has been called Gia (mother). Gia is the matriarch of seven daughters, two sons, twenty-two grandchildren and twenty-one great-grandchildren. My mother lives in the same house she was born in eighty years ago. Gia spends most of her time creating clay vessels and waiting for the endless stream of children that pass through her door every single day; this is the life she knows and loves."

Every Mother Knows a Coyote

My dear mother,

Did you know
  that at times
    I am tempted to let dust balls collect under the couch
      where I swear there is a small
        but highly efficient factory
          producing pesky reminders of my inability to keep up with
          chores
            you've instructed me to manage

Have you guessed
  That I'm the kind of woman who wonders
    What it would be like to cram chocolate-coated Bon-Bons in
    my mouth
      Three at a time
        While doing the Disco to Pueblo Turtle songs.

Have you ever suspected
  I long to experience
    Being the kind of woman
      You've warned me against
        A human coyote
          Washed in mischief
            Drenched in life's ironies
              And filled with the juices of passion fruit
                Grown in fertile ground.

Dear mother
  I'm curious
    Have you ever soaked in your desires
      And watched as ripples of consequence color your cheeks
    with a shameful blush
      Have you ever nagged the old man
        The same way bad boys shoot their sling shots
        Just because
          And has there ever been a handsome he coyote
          That corralled you into playful ecstasy
          Just because

Dear mother
  Are you aware
    Your doubts
      Became my traditions
        Your sorrows and misdirected angers
          Have multiplied effortlessly under my couch
        Nameless phantoms
          Who quote Bible scriptures
            Littered with "Thou Shall Nots."

I've been coated in this fashion of frustration for most of my
life
    I've worn it for the both of us
    And now it no longer fits.

How do I break with tradition
  Confessing to you that
    Coyote woman has been reincarnated
      In your daughter's forty two year old
        Slightly sagging body

Savvy and certain
   With enough audacity to speak openly of passion
   Mine
      Yours
         His
            Theirs.

My dear
  If not for coyote
    And her courageous insistence to live life
     I'd already be packaged in
       Antiseptically doused standards
        Ironed to a starchy stiff
         And appropriately fearful.

My precious woman
  You know coyote and her magic don't you
    She is the one who teased you
      the one you warned me against
        Years before my time
          The one you said would call saying
            "Come my child we've got some mischief to make."
              And I want to know mother
                Did you ever listen.

Dear mother
  I'm sure you've guessed by now
    I won't be coming to suffer over Sunday dinner
      I've got a date with trouble
        And Damn if I can't stop smiling
          When those Pueblo Turtles do the Disco.

Your Daughter

Nora

Naomi Shihab Nye

Miriam Shihab and her daughter, Naomi Shihab Nye
Dallas, Texas; 1995

MICHAEL NYE

Naomi Shihab Nye was born March 12, 1952, in St. Louis, Missouri, and grew up in St. Louis, Jerusalem, and San Antonio, where she presently lives. She graduated from Trinity University. Her books include *Words Under the Words: Selected Poems, Red Suitcase, Sitti's Secrets,* and *Benito's Dream Bottle,* and she edited the anthologies *This Same Sky, The Tree Is Older Than You Are,* and *I Feel a Little Jumpy Around You.* She was featured in a segment of *The Language of Life* with Bill Moyers. She is married to photographer Michael Nye, and they have one son, Madison.

Miriam Naomi Allwardt was born August 22, 1927, in Decatur, Illinois, and grew up in St. Louis. She received a fine arts scholarship to Washington University and married Aziz Shihab, a Palestinian student from Jerusalem in 1951. She raised two children, Naomi and Adlai. Although she has worked in various fields including Montessori teaching and retail sales of international products, she considers her family her "real work." She currently lives in Dallas.

Everything You Said, Stayed

Dearest Mommy,

Once you told me that a deer held the same kindness and gentility in its shy step that we indicate with "dear" in a letter. Later, I thought of a "deer" as a mother, standing off quietly by the side of the road as cars & trucks whirl by.

Everything you said, stayed.

Each year on the first day of school, just after your birthday, I am still holding your hand, not sure if I can let loose & face that large polished doorway, even if I am the parent now & our son holds on to me.

Did you know how long your arms would be?

As usual, I have brought no gift big enough. I always thought I would feel readier for everything. He has his fresh reams of lined paper & sharpened pencils in the white canvas bag.

This year he wants us to drop hands outside the foyer so nobody will see. The spear! He will not accept a kiss. Feel how the air trembles with kisses looking for a place to land!

Once, right before I married, I brushed away your hand. I have never stopped regretting it.

After our son enters his new hallway & I walk slowly back to the car alone, I realize my hand still feels full & it is yours, from hundreds of miles north. You give a little squeeze—*you can do it*—& I am off, tentative, across the gleaming floor. What does this mean to a life?

That a mother stood by us when we were young and unformed, believing already we carried everything we needed in the secret place under our skin. I smiled at my teacher. I imagined what you told us—that she was scared too.

These mornings I watch a sad mother shout her daughter out of their car. She pitches the girl's book bag out so hard it hits her in the back. I keep pulling up, unluckily, beside them in the school parking lot. The yelling penetrates our car, even with the windows closed. Once the mother felt my eye gripping them & looked away. I do not know her story. But what is it like for a girl walking into school after that? Can she pay attention? To what is she pledging allegiance?

Never, ever, did we doubt our ground.

I have kissed him enough already, to last. Is it possible? Some part of me will always be kissing him. Until he was born, I did not feel a part of history. The vast transmissions from parents to children needed to be *passed on,* somehow, for them to be *recognized.* Sometimes in the least breeze, I feel your cool lips on my forehead. They help me close my eyes.

Someone asked me recently if I consider myself a good mother. Of course a door opened that was bigger than the door to a school, and the hall with its wide throat looming held a hundred small cabinets, each filled with something as small as a glass of freshly squeezed orange juice or swirling as a tornado. *(That poor interviewer, with her skinny paper and pen! But I wasn't talking about me, I was talking about you.)*

You sang the lullaby of leaves, the long curl of comforting song. You stood beside our beds, brown ponytail cascading down your back. I gripped your hand, thinking, if my mother dies, could I keep her hand?

In a picture of you taken in the St. Louis vegetable market before you married, a grocer in a white apron turns his face away. A perfectly balanced mountain of oranges sits on a wooden crate. The mystery of strangers with their backs turned. The mystery of a mother's face before she becomes a mother. The mystery of your distant, mournful gaze—where did you want to be looking?

I have inherited the curse of lying awake in bed. I have felt that day when he will leave us as the loss from which I will never recover. Already! And he is still sleeping calmly in the next room!

How did you stand it? We wouldn't leave, so you and Daddy moved out. (That was how I told it.) Actually, he took a job in another city. By that time we had "our own lives," so we couldn't follow. I sat on my bed after the two of you drove off, impossibly, *drove off and turned the corner,* thumbing through *The Important Book* by Margaret Wise Brown which you had read with me years before. I argued with Margaret, I thought everything was as crucial as everything else. I fell into the spoon. And the important thing is, *you will have one another forever.*

These words won't sit still. They tumble through our skins. *Who? Me? I thought that happened to your mother.* In each cabinet a mother was standing or sitting or stroking. She was knotting a dull darning thread in a pool of tired light. She was sighing the terrible sigh. Even now it was hard not to dry her stray tears, not to turn the phrase inside out and repeat to her—in the way that every question contains a mirror—you have always been a good mother to me.

So, I talked about you, I left things out. Sometimes you were too sad to tell us why. Did other mothers cry? Sometimes the shadow of doubt rode your back and you could not shake it off. *You can do it.* The words went both ways. Were they ever enough? Who was the shadow? The self you might have been, without us?

When I was twelve, I found one of your giant oil paintings from art school tucked behind my grandma's dresser stuffed with

powder puffs & support hose & geranium hankies. A splendidly
gloomy portrait of a man with his hand over his mouth—was he
stunned? shouting?—& a whirligig stuck in his hand. You had
scrawled a title on the back. I HAD TEN HEARTS AND EACH
WAS BROKEN. This was before you knew us.

Did we help any one of them to heal?

Years ago our son was mad at me because I would not let him
eat frosted mini-wheat cereal before dinner. He was carrying the
small red box around the house, mumbling. He could smell the
rice cooking & the beans cooking, but as usual I was talking on
the phone. How many people were there to talk to? I had been
talking forever. I had been talking since he was a baby in diapers
lying on the green quilt on the floor & now he was four. I was
talking long-distance and business, making the NO signal with
my finger, the X in the air, so he went to his room & pulled out
a large poster board from behind his dresser & wrote on it with
black márker a sign that he held in front of my face. It said in
perfect crooked letters—LOVE HAS FAILED.

Did our love ever fail? What would love be without the stum-
bling?

Once you said Get out of my sight & I got out through the front
door & began walking far down the street to the place where the
drainage ditch began. Greens melted into telephone poles. I had
forgotten what a big green mass everything could be, how a person might lose her bearings & feel the leaves inside her bones &
know no one could see her. Now I had gotten to the age where
everyone could see me & it was not going to be easy.

The girl had to walk back inside the house & find something to
say to her mother which would soften the air. *I made a mistake*
or *Excuse me, you were right, I was not right.* Even if telling right
from right felt as hard as distinguishing one yard from another
now, the green swoop of hedge welded to the droopy magnolia,
the fig fastened onto the plum.

Now that I am a mother myself I know those mad words bubble
up unexpectedly, not meaning very much sometimes. *Don't you
dare! How could you?* Like loose air, they don't even feel like they

started in your own body. But it's different from the mother in the car. She's mad every day.

I lay on the floor as you ironed Daddy's white shirts, as the steam puffed up in clouds, as you scraped long strips of peel from the peaches, devouring your small red leather diary, reminding myself of the girl inside my mother. *Went to movie, ate popcorn, wore yellow dress. First hot day.* Layers of phrases. I wished you had written in complete sentences. What movie WAS it? *How would I know? Do you think I can remember everything?*

I started writing because I wanted to remember everything. Your codes, your hidden stories, your halfway hurts. My own diary was a run-on sentence, an endless essay, a mixed metaphor of gigantic proportions. I stood on the cliff staring out to sea, on the tracks of the train, on the lip of the volcano. I was hanging on to each slim stalk of waving grass.

What did I do that made you angry? I say it to our son now. But did I ever say it enough to my mother? Let's go back. Let's slow down. Put one part together with the other. Let's sit close together in the swing the way we do when we read books. Let's fix it. Already he had forgotten what made him so mad, nor could I begin to remember. No wonder people feel affection for waves in the sea!

When I was eighteen, I began dreaming of a boy who came from the forest & followed me, the pockets of his overalls stuffed with leaves, his hair tousled & thick. He handed me sticks & seed pods. He skipped into shadows. I told you about him & shivered. But how will we ever find one another? I worried. You consoled me. *That's how I felt about you.* Sixteen years later when I carried him inside my body, I smelled the rich scent of pine.

He lay in his cradle. Delicate yolk of an egg. Small head shining. He lay on his side, fingers curled, night-blooming cereus. Because of him, the evening news took on sharper dimensions.

> This was happening to children & mothers out there. His long cry
> threaded our world to every other & the pull of every mother answering.
> There were worlds without money, without sun, without
> presidents, but there were no worlds without mothers.

Then I was able to observe you more clearly, as if my eyes had finally clicked into focus, & see how demanding I had been. How many times I had called *Come!* & expected you to be there.

And you were there. Where else could you be?

You held us up. When the organizer for the Girl Scouts promised to make me a leader, you said, *Follower, please.* When I wrote: *Harvey Street was a song you weren't always sure you wanted to sing,* you said, *Could you just leave me out of it? Write anything but leave me out?*

I cannot leave out the foundation of the house.

Holidays were hard for us. Things didn't fit. Too many wishes tipping the air. The year two of us gave you clothespins & you cried. The year you stitched bouquets of flowers onto white cotton pillowcases for me. Your note said: *Not very much inside, but made for you with love.* I cried.

Your 66th birthday was the best ever, more interesting than the many years in which you said *Oh, no presents please, I don't want anything but your love,* because you requested specific gifts: a hand-painted Mexican gourd with a curly blue stem on its top, a new Baldwin piano, & a book called *Maybe, Maybe Not.* This seemed promising somehow: to grow more particular rather than blurrier.

Our son made the card because he could draw faces on which all the features—eyes, nose, ears—were somebody's new age. The eyes read "66"—that gave a quizzical look. The nostrils were easy. "66" was the best age he had ever done.

When you opened your presents you were genuinely glad to see each one. We all went out together for a lavish breakfast in the first restaurant we had ever visited in this city, before we lived here, an elegant room rich with polished woods & fresh flowers. How had we managed to stumble into such a good place that long-ago day? We sat in a dark corner, trying to remember it. We had ordered lemonade in tall, frosty glasses. We did not know we would return to live in this city or that we would ever feel like natives here.

Love you, Nini

Joyce Carol Oates

Carolina Oates and her daughter, Joyce Carol Oates
Millersport, New York; May 14, 1941

Joyce Carol Oates was born in Lockport, New York, on June 16, 1938. She is the author of a number of works of fiction, poetry, drama, and essays. Her most recent novel is *Zombie* and her most recent story collection is *Will You Always Love Me?* She has been a member of the American Academy of Arts and Letters since 1978 and is a past recipient of the National Book Award as well as numerous prizes for her short stories. She is the Roger S. Berlind Distinguished Professor in the Humanities at Princeton University.

Carolina Oates was born in Lockport, New York, on November 8, 1917. She has lived in Millersport, New York, on the same plot of land since the age of nine months; she is the wife of Frederic Oates, whom she married in 1937, and the mother of three children—Joyce Carol, Fred Jr., and Lynn Ann. Her favorite activities have been sewing and gardening; she enjoys swimming, walking, and traveling.

A Letter to My Mother Carolina Oates
on Her 78th Birthday
November 8, 1995

Dear Mom,

I've always meant to tell you . . .

I've long rehearsed telling you . . .

I've meant so many times to tell you, and Daddy . . .

How the human world divides into two: those who speak unhesitantly, smoothly saying *I love you*—and possibly not mean it; and those too shy or constrained by family custom or temperament to utter the words *I love you*—though they mean it. To the depths of what's called the soul.

How deep inside me, imprinted in infant memory, the sight of my young parents leaning over me, gazing at me smiling, lifting me in their arms. The wonder, the unspeakable mystery. Radiant unnamed faces of first love.

For this I've long believed: we carry our young parents within us, so much more vivid and alive, pulsing-alive, than any memory of ourselves as infants, children. We carry our young parents within us everywhere, through life. No wonder is ever quite equivalent to that first wonder. Blinking up from a crib, gaping in absolute trust and amazement lacking words to stammer, even to *think Who are you? Why do you care for me? What does it mean, we are here together? Only hold me, hold me. Only feed me, love me, forever.*

An inventory of our lives. The back fields shimmering in sunshine, humming with summer insects, iridescent dragonflies' wings. The countryside, farm region of western New York State, northern Erie County near the Niagara County border, near the Tonawanda Creek and the Erie Barge canal. Waking to such days, a succession of days—what happiness! To a child, eternity is this morning, this hour. Forever is now. Permanent.

Into the pear orchard: a harvest of greeny-yellow Bartlett pears. How hard they've seemed, like stone, green stone, for weeks. And now ripe, ready to be picked. That ripe sun-warmed smell. Picking pears, a single pear, a single gesture. Placing, not dropping, the pear into the bushel basket. You taught me patience: Like this! Daddy was the one who used the ladder. A harvest of pears—so many. At least it seemed like so many. Some of the pears were for us to eat then, some were for canning; most were sold by the roadside, in quart baskets, pecks, bushels. We sold apples, too—not so many, since we had only a few apple trees. And black cherries (sweet) and red cherries (sour). And tomatoes—those juicy plump red First Lady tomatoes, pole climbers, with their strong tart smell. And sweet corn, peppers, onions.

But it's the pear orchard I remember most vividly. Beyond the swing that seated four people, an old-fashioned metal-and-wood swing Daddy painted blue, the orchard, to the very rear of our property, the fragrance of pears, the perfect shapes of pears, smooth skins sometimes touched with a russet-red blush as with a delicate watercolor brush like the petals of your favorite rose, Double Delight.

Those long summer days. Cicadas screaming out of the trees. *Listen to those crazy things!* you'd say, laughing. The very music of the country, of deep intransigent summer; like crickets at dusk, the cries of owls in the near distance, a faint dry rustling of leaves. Flashes of lightning—"heat lightning"—silent nervous rippling-veins of flame renting the sky and disappearing in seemingly the same instant. *You look, it's already gone.* How nature, how the world surrounding us, *is* us; yet shrouded in mystery. You and I are in the back field picking corn, tomatoes. We're in the barn, we're feeding chickens in the mottled pecked-at dirt surrounding the chicken coop, tossing grain, what childish pleasure in tossing grain, and the chickens come clucking, fretting, plumping their wings, and the big rooster, his lurid-red comb, his mad yellow eye, that look of male impatience to all roosters, and I'm squealing, shrinking back to avoid the rooster who pecks at feet when he's in a bad mood, and where is my chicken?—my pet chicken—Happy Chicken, so-called? A reddish-brown bird, with a bad limp. *If you pet a chicken the right way, if you show you're not going to hurt it, it will go very still and crouch down.* We're in the kitchen, upstairs in the farmhouse, you're cooking tomatoes, simmering them slowly into a thick ripe sauce in a large pan on the stove beneath the bright yellow plastic General Electric clock (bought with stamps from Loblaw's, pasted assiduously into a little booklet, the accumulation of months) with its shiny black numerals and red hands moving slowly, imperially, unswerving through the days. Those long summer days I believed, as a child, would never end.

I've always meant to tell you how in awe I am of . . .

How hypnotized, entranced I've been by . . .

Since I became mature enough, in high school perhaps . . .

Most powerfully, painfully since I've become of the adults of the world, like you . . . though so much older now than you were through my childhood, girlhood, my luminous and fascinating memories . . .

Dedicating how many of my books to you. How many times *Again, for my parents Carolina and Frederic Oates, and in memory of that world, now vanishing, that continues to nourish.*

That vanishing world. Before I was born. So vast, so mysterious falling away like a seeming edge to the horizon that shifts into shadows even as we push eagerly forward, hoping to illuminate, to see.

I've always meant to tell you though it would have been impossible to tell you, impossible to choose the words, for such words embarrass, such words make self-conscious what must remain unconscious or at any rate unspoken, always I've meant to tell you how in awe I am of the lives you and Daddy lived; your strength, your resilience, your good humor; your utter lack of self-pity; never complaining, except perhaps jokingly as if to indicate *That's the way the world is, you might as well laugh.*

The yearning, the wonder. I've always believed that some secret must reside in you, and your world, before I came into being, let alone into consciousness. My birth, June 16, 1938. When you were twenty years old. And Daddy was twenty-four. In our old precious snapshots, some of them a bit mangled, what an attractive young couple you are: you, with your bushy-springy hair and sweet smile, a look of girlish hope, openness, Daddy with his swarthy features, stiff-crested dark hair and heavy eyebrows, easy smile. Radiant faces of first love, romance.

What a precious hoard of twenty or so snapshots, old family snapshots, scattered across my desk.

The earliest is of Blanche Oates, later Blanche Woodside, Daddy's mother, an attractive dark-haired young woman in her early or mid-twenties. When was this picture taken, and by whom? I can only guess, about 1914. (The year of Daddy's birth.) No one living could even hazard a guess who might have taken it.

Most of these precious pictures are of you, Daddy, my brother Fred, and me, taken in the 1940s and 1950s. All have a much-thumbed, much-contemplated look.

How unknowing we are, taking pictures! The very concept— "taking a picture." Unable to guess what significance this fleeting moment among a vertiginous ceaseless cascade of similar moments will acquire in later years; how *representative.* For such images give distinct, visible, daylight shapes to our ever-shifting and ever-precarious memories.

These snapshots are of the early 1940s. My favorites. There's quite a dramatic shot of Daddy kneeling, very handsome with sleek thick dark hair and a look of some solemnity for the camera, with me, a child of perhaps four? five? on his knee. We're in the leafy backyard near one of the pear orchards. I'm in a pretty floral dress, my curly, inclined-to-snarl hair beribboned, wearing white anklet socks, no doubt new white shoes. Daddy's and Mommy's little girl, dressed for some special occasion.

Can it be—over fifty years have passed?

Fifty years.

Well, here we are, in that long-ago lost time, as in a region of Time itself, oblivious of our circumstances. You are a pretty young mother in your midtwenties, with springy-curly hair, a white flower in your hair, slender, smiling, in an elaborately buttoned dress, very likely a new spring dress, and white spring shoes. In one of the snapshots we're standing in the very spot Daddy had posed with me, I seem to be clowning for the camera, what a show-off spoiled child I must have been, firstborn, enjoying sovereignty as a child in the farmhouse in Millersport among adults for five years before my brother Robin was born. (In fact I was clowning for Daddy wielding the blue box Kodak camera I wasn't allowed to play with, that in later years would be a household relic whose interior workings, subtly distorting magnifying lenses, and very smell, impossible to describe, would fascinate me. How moon-faced I am, at the age of four or five; how rather plumpish, like one of those luxury dolls with "real"-seeming skin. I don't recognize myself at all, feel no kinship with that child at all, the kinship I feel is with you, my mother gazing down at me so sweetly with what motherly indulgence and patience. *Who has been secure in his mother's love,* Freud has speculated, from his narrowly masculine perspective, *will be secure through life.*

In other pictures taken that day or at that general time you and I are similarly posed in that leafy space, a world of trees it seems, childhood's green world. In one of my favorite pictures, you and I are sitting together in the grass, you're holding a tiny black kitten in your hands and I'm in the crook of your arm, this is in fact May 14, 1941, as you've noted on the back of the snapshot. Is this kitten my first? (We had so many kittens, so many cats on the farm! I think I must have loved them all!) Behind us is what appears to be a cherry tree, long vanished from my memory as from that landscape. (Where, decades later, miraculously it seems to one who has moved so often, of a generation of Americans who have moved yet more often, you still live. Almost seventy-eight years on the same land.) And beyond the cherry tree is the farmhouse owned by my (adoptive) grandfather John Bush and my (adoptive) grandmother Lena Bush with whom we lived, one not-large, fairly typical farm family, for all the years of my childhood and adolescence. The farmhouse is always old in my memory, built in 1888, in any case its foundations laid in 1888, but it doesn't look particularly old in these snapshots, a durable woodframe two-story steep-roofed house like many others in rural western New York, then and now. In the snapshots, the house appears about to dissolve in light; in my memory, and in other, subsequent snapshots, the house is sided with a gritty practicable gray, "simulated brick" made of asphalt. Did Daddy put the siding on the house? I suspect he did. And there's the outside cellar door, at an angle against the rear of the house. Gone forever, these cellar doors! A commonplace of a vanished America, like the hefty rain barrel at the corner of the house. Virtually every house, of a certain economic level at least, had rain barrels in those days, strategically positioned to collect rain running down roofs. Unfathomable to the inhabitants of that world, still recovering from the Depression, our contemporary indifference to "usable" water allowed to fall and drain away into mere earth.

If I could slip back into that instant, as the shutter clicks!

But I can't, of course. This species of time travel is wholly imaginary. Our lives are time travel, moving in one direction only. We accompany one another as long as we can; as long as time grants us.

My father was killed and I never knew why. No one would say. Now there's no one I can ask. My mother didn't want me, there were too many children I guess, nine children counting me, I was a baby when my father died, not a year old. My mother gave me to her sister Lena who didn't have any children. I felt so bad, I used to cry all the time . . . my mother didn't want me. It was so strange! I went to visit them, they had a farm in Pendleton, only about three miles away on the other side of the creek. They weren't really very nice to me. I don't know why, I guess they thought I was better off here with Aunt Lena and Uncle John, not so many children to feed I guess. My father's name was Steve and my mother's name was Elizabeth. I never knew my father of course. He was Hungarian, my mother was

Hungarian, she and her sister Lena married two brothers in Buda-
pest, Steve and John, and they all came over together. This must
have been 1900 or so. My mother never learned English, always
spoke Hungarian. She was a short, plump woman, a pleasant
woman, with curly hair like mine. She didn't want me, it was so
strange . . . she had so many children she had to give me away.
There was Leslie, he was the oldest; then Mary, I didn't get to know
too well; then Steve, who was kicked by a horse, wasn't ever quite
right in the head and always lived at home with Ma; then Elsie, I
came to be so close with Elsie; then Johnny; then Edith; then George,
I wasn't too close with George. It's a long time ago but I remember
crying a lot, when I was a little girl and my mother didn't want me.

It is a mystery how my (biological) grandfather Bush died, in or
near a tavern, in or near Lockport, who killed him, murdered
him, with what sort of weapon, and was the assailant arrested,
tried, sent to prison?—a family legend, yet blurred, dreamlike.
Now there's no one I can ask.

An eerie symmetry: my father's grandfather, too, died violently, in Hartland, New York, north of Lockport, a suicide.

Of these old tragedies, if tragedy is the right term and not
rather misadventures, sheer bad luck, no one ever spoke during
my childhood, girlhood, young adulthood. Now, old family secrets seem to matter less, even as their details have faded, their
very contours blurred as bad dreams recounted by others.

How ironic, as a writer I've been constantly queried why do
you write about violent acts? What do you know of violence?
And my replies are polite, thoughtful, abstract and even idealis-
tic. I might say that my entire life, indeed the lives of both my
parents, have been shaped by "violent acts"—yet that would not
be entirely accurate, since I knew very little of these old, near-
forgotten family tales, tales of the Bushes and the Morgensterns,
through most of my life. Only the past decade or so has been
illuminating in this regard—like a door opening to a shadowy
passageway, but only just opening a few inches, never to be
budged any farther.

Yet: what romance, in that world. Because you inhabited it,
you and Daddy, it's transformed.

You came, in 1918, an infant, to live with your uncle John and
aunt Lena on their farm in Millersport, never formally adopted,

that was how things were done in those days, no need for law-yers, government intervention, blood relatives in any case. Your uncle John, my "grandfather" Bush. He was a farmer, a black-smith, later a factory worker in Tonawanda. *So tough and strong, a hard-drinking man, a true Hungarian, what a character! A jug of hard cider on the kitchen floor beside his chair even at breakfast. Chewed tobacco, rolled his own cigarettes. His long underwear, his bristly chin, whiskers. Everyone had horses then, blacksmiths were in demand. John Bush was tough and strong, could practically lift a horse. If a horse acted up while he was shoeing it, tried to get away, he'd wrestle it down, sometimes he'd hit it with his hammer. Yes he was tough! And Lena, your grandmother Bush we called her—a plump, pretty woman when she was young, like her sister Elizabeth. She never learned to read English but she could speak it, in her way. She never learned to drive a car, and Ma didn't either, so the sisters didn't see much of each other. They only lived a few miles apart, and were sisters, from the old country, but didn't see each other much. That was how women were in the old days.*

And how you were, when you married.

Hardly more than a girl, when you and Daddy met. You'd gone to the one-room schoolhouse, Lockport District #7, to which I, and my brother Robin would later go, and you'd gone to a Catho-lic school in Swormville, about four miles away, dropping out after eighth grade to work at home and on the farm. Meeting Fred Oates, a brash young man, a boy really, hardly nineteen, one day in Lockport when you were with a friend of his, driving in the friend's car. *He stopped for a light, and somebody yanked open the car door and surprised us both—it was Fred! That was how we met, that day. He always did surprising things, things you couldn't predict, you know what Dad is like.* You fell in love, and swiftly I gather. Fred Oates was such a handsome boy, quick-tempered, volatile, possibly a little wild but good-hearted, kind and intelligent. He had an Irish father named Carlton Oates, a drinker, "no good"—a man who'd walked out on his young wife and child, years before, refusing to support them—but a beauti-ful, well-spoken mother. Blanche Oates *so dignified, so well-dressed and chic, I was afraid of her at first.* (In fact, no one knew at the time, in 1936, that Blanche Oates, formerly Blanche Morn-ingstar, had been born Morgenstern, the daughter of German Jews who had immigrated to rural western New York in the

1890s, changed their name in 1894, seemed to have hidden their Jewishness from their neighbors and even from their several daughters.) Fred Oates too had dropped out of school, worked for a Lockport sign painter and would shortly go to work at Harrison Radiator, the Lockport division of General Motors, where he would be a loyal and inventive employee, in the tool and dye design shop, for the next forty years. You were married in 1937, and your first baby was born in 1938, named Joyce Carol; your second, in 1943, Fred Jr., nickname "Robin"; your third, Lynn Ann, in 1956.

An inventory of our lives. The lost world of laundry: clotheslines, clothespins, sheets, towels, trousers, dresses, and underwear, socks flapping in the wind, a ceaseless wind it seemed, how crude by present-day standards, how primitive; yet there was pleasure in it, in even the repetition, the familiarity. Each item of laundry lifted by hand, smoothed and affixed to the line with wooden pins, in later years plastic pins. From my small room on the second floor rear of the house I could glance out at any time when the laundry was hanging on the line and see a reflection of our household, our family, like ghost-figures glimpsed in water.

Who taught me patience, if not you? The sometimes-consoling rituals of housekeeping, small simple finite tasks executed with love or at any rate bemused affection, cheerful resignation. You tried to teach me to knit, and to sew, for which feminine activities I demonstrated little talent if, at the outset, energy and hope. You had more success teaching me to iron, a dreamy mesmerizing task I seem to have liked, as girls will, in small intermittent doses. Though not so much as I came to like vacuuming, a more robust, even acrobatic activity: the very opposite, I've often thought, of the obsessive activity of "creating art." And I enjoyed cooking with you, cooking under your easygoing tutelage. Just the two of us, you and me, preparing supper together in the kitchen. *This is how you set the timer for the oven. This is how you use the Mixmaster—see the speeds? This is how you whip egg whites. This is how you stir the macaroni to keep it from sticking in the pan. This is how you make a Jell-O mold. This is how you set the table, paper napkin neatly folded in two at the left side of the plates. This is how you smile when you don't especially feel like smiling, this is how you laugh when you don't especially feel like laughing, this is how you prepare a life.*

Item: a large fringed knitted afghan of orange, brown, white
   wool
Item: a knitted quilt, of many brightly colored wool squares,
   predominately red, yellow, green
Item: a pale peach-colored sweater coat with a matching belt
Item: a crimson sweater coat with matching belt
Item: a turquoise jacket, matching skirt (light fabric)
Item: a dove-gray jacket, matching skirt (wool)
Item: a dark red jacket, matching skirt (wool)
Item: a fine-knit pale pink jacket-sweater with matching belt
Item: a jacket of soft autumnal brown-floral check with a rus-
   set-red skirt (wool)
Item: a camel's-hair skirt
Item: a lilac silk dress, long-sleeved, with lace trim
Item: a dark blue velour dress
Item: a crimson velour dress
Item: a long dark red cocktail skirt (light wool)
Item: a long purple velvet skirt
Item: a dark blue and black floral checked cocktail dress (silk)
Items: a white silk long-sleeved blouse (raw silk); a pumpkin-
   colored silk blouse; a pink blouse, ruffled; a raw silk deep-
   pink blouse with pleated bodice; a dark blue silk blouse,
   with tie; a maroon silk blouse, with tie; a dove-gray silk
   blouse with a fine-stitched collar; a dark gold blouse; plus
   shirts in cotton, rayon, flannel, some long-sleeved, some
   short.
Items: a black vest (rayon, wool), a beige vest (velour)
Items: summer dresses, summer skirts of various colors, fabrics

All of these, and more, you've made for me. How many hours
of effort, concentration, skill in these things so delicately fashioned, so exquisitely sewed or knitted. What infinite patience in
such creation. What love.
   An inventory of our lives.

The old farmhouse was razed years ago, the very site of its foundation filled with earth, all trace of its existence obliterated. Yet
I see it clearly, and the lilac tree that grew close beside the back

door, a child-sized tree into which I climbed in a crook of whose twisty sinewy limbs I sat, a dreamy child given to solitude in places near the house, near you. Within the range of your raised voice. *Joyce, Joy-ce!* Why is it always a misty-hazy summer day, that peculiar translucence to the light that means the air is heavy with moisture though the sky is cloudless, the sun prominent overhead? The house of my childhood is the house of recurring dreams yet subtly altered, the rooms mysterious, their dimensions uncertain, always there is a promise, alarming yet tantalizing, of rooms yet undiscovered, through a back wall, in the attic perhaps, or the cellar, rooms yet to be explored, beckoning. Your presence permeates the house, you are the house, its mysterious infinite rooms. You are the hazy light, the rich smell of damp earth, sunshine and grass, ripening pears. You are the humming buzzing not-quite-audible sound of fields, of distance. I see you pushing me on the swing, your hair reddish brown, you're wearing a shirt and pale blue "pedal pushers," I'm a lanky child of nine or ten on the swing Daddy made for me, the swing I loved, rough hemp rope hanging from a metal pipe secured between the branches of two tall trees in the backyard. I see you pushing me, I see myself stretching my legs upward, straining higher, higher, squealing with childish excitement, fearless, reckless, flying into the sky. So often I have wanted to tell you how in patches of abrupt sunshine hundred of miles and thousands of days from home I am pulled back into that world as into the most seductive and most nourishing of dreams, I'm filled with a sense of wonder, and awe, and fear, regret for all that has passed, and for what must be surrendered, what we can imagine as life but cannot ever explain, cannot possibly put into words for all our effort, cannot utter aloud, dare not utter aloud, this succession of small particular moments like the movement of the red second hand on the General Electric clock, moments linked together as pearls are linked together to constitute a necklace, linked by tough, invisible string, the interior mystery. We were lucky, and we were happy, and I think we've always known.

love, Joyce

Carole Simmons Oles

Helen Kampmeyer Simmons and her daughter,
Carole Simmons Oles
Central Park, New York City; c. 1953
PHYLLIS KLEIN

Carole Simmons Oles was born on January 7, 1939. "I was born at Women's Hospital in Manhattan: an infant so comical—with a shock of red hair oiled to spout up—that my godmother fell down the hospital steps laughing, and broke the birthstone in her ring. Much later I wrote poetry books, most recently *The Deed* and *Stunts*. Much later also, I had Brian and Julia, born in the age of the Beatles, and in their manner both with profusions of dark hair."

Helen Kampmeyer Simmons was born on December 29, 1911, in Van Horne, Iowa. "My first big thrill was winning the spelling bee; my greatest thrills of all were the births of my children and grandchildren. I should mention our wedding day, June 3, 1933. We made it forty-eight years and then Pop got his call. I'm sitting in the park writing. I just want you to know I am at peace with the world. I wish more of the world population could have this feeling."

Time Left

Oh Mama!

The first time I realized how beautiful you were, are, I had already become a mother twice myself. The family was assembled at your apartment in Watertown, Massachusetts, the foreign state and town where you had moved when Daddy's declining health coincided with an eviction notice from your landlord of over forty years, and you decided to leave The City (New York, the only one) and move nearer to me and my then family.

Daddy was dying of emphysema, the slow death of respirators and defeat by the smallest exertions: shaving, buttoning a shirt, pulling on a sock—and we were all assembled to look at old slides, batches of them pulled from battered cardboard boxes never opened since the move. Perhaps we thought we could really transport ourselves for an hour to happier times, when Daddy could walk and you two could have dinner at the Rialto on Friday nights.

Suddenly out of the darkness between slides, there was a gor-

geous woman—my mother!—on-screen. You, yes, because I
perched there on the arm of her chair, my aunts and cousins
variously disposed along the periphery. You, dazzling me with
a smile brilliant as any I saw those Saturday afternoons of my
childhood at the movies, on the romantic heroines whose lives
might forecast, I could only hope, my own. NO, don't change it
yet. I couldn't stop looking. Was this really you? and how had I
come only now to see what all those years had been concealed
from me? How had I not recognized?—me the frizzy-haired adolescent at your elbow . . . *Frizzy-haired. Why did you insist on
giving me those Toni home permanents, a misnomer because thanks
to a merciful God-mother they eventually did yield to the straight
hair which genetics ordained. Who was I to be molded into? You
were doing your utmost to get me the look that insured proper re-
wards to a female child of the 1950s.* Too close. Too dangerous: a
goddess I could never challenge. If the scenes I had witnessed in
our kitchen could happen to glorious you, what awaited me?

My mind flashes fifteen years ahead from that slide show to
your surgery last Christmas. In the birthday shot I took of you,
the self-destructing tape reflected light off the incision that ate
halfway down your cheek: melanoma. A procedure repeated now
for the third time, the other two efforts small and tentative, but
this so bold that the new surgeon could proclaim, "We got it all."
And still you smile, elegant in the white suit you made ten years
ago, your hair curled into nimbus clouds, your ears dangling the
fake pearls I found for you in one of the boxes under your bed,
an aquamarine ring on your pinky. I dressed you like my doll,
the way you Toni-ed me? and it seemed to please us both. Jan and
I laugh about the way you looked into the mirror, demanded a
comb to make yourself presentable just after heart surgery. In
that instant we knew you'd survive.

Back to my teenage years. I dismantle this grudge. Remember
when Aunt Viola's friend's son invited me to a weekend at his
fancy boarding school in Connecticut? The Kent School. Significance all in the *The.* You refused to let me go, said I "wouldn't
belong there." *Child of the working-class, I've heard these words
replay for years inside my head, whenever I stepped over that line.
I believe you only wanted to save me from . . . what? . . . potential
cruelty? shame at my homemade clothes?—but these fears were*

*yours, bestowed upon me. I wanted my children to think they be-
longed everywhere—my own equal and opposite error.*

Soon you'll be here in Vermont. You'll ride up with Jan, saying
of each small town as you read its name off the road sign "Never
heard of it," though you take the identical roads each summer.
Forgetful, or making it new? Several years ago I asked you to write
me stories about your early life and send them to me in Vermont.
I transcribed your handwritten notes and left most of them to
cure in a metal box in my closet until this winter. Here's a version
of one of your stories, back in a poem:

RUNNING AWAY WITH RALPH

Arthur kept pulling my braids
and it wasn't my fault.
Mama stood in the kitchen, canning
while the others all played that game
he said I couldn't, nanh-nanh.
I shuffled away.
They didn't care.
Ralph was stretched beside the pump.
I pulled his big fan of a tail
and he turned to lick
my hand, ready to follow
me anywhere. I whispered
and we both slunk away.
We could go to Bohemia
that place Mrs. Brabec came from
with her raspberry cakatchys.
It was getting hot. I yawned.
We came to the toolshed, a hideout
with just enough space
to crawl under and still see
through the X's if Arthur
or strange devils walked by.
Ralph curled up and I leaned
my head on him for a furry pillow
all smooth since Mama cut
out the burrs. I sniffed
his own pure dog smell

hoping I smelled to him
like no other child.
We slept there till dusk
and never knew how Mama
thought we'd got drowned or lost.
Seventy years later
when they sliced my heart valve
I would wake
from that heavy sleep calling
Ralph . . .

This shows how I long to know you, the earliest you before
she even thought of me or my father. You're with me always, in
the flare of my thighs and the flags I begin to wear on my skin; I
wish too for your capacity to outstare trouble. *You're with me
watching through blank heat the pool of silence where our girl in
purple floated . . . Brave legacy of the farm, the communal need,
observed in your mother and father.* Years earlier, you were with
me, wisely acting against the best judgment of the aunts when
you let me, age seven, visit the funeral home to meet for the only
time my week-old brother Gary. Robust and perfect, all I could
see; hidden, the flawed ventricle. Though you married a man
also a helper, you have stood where I think he would have fallen.
So the beauty on-screen is a woman of character, a lustrous
spirit. Mother-worship? Why not.

Last March, several nights after the dream in which an official
holds up a sign with the motto TIME LEFT, and I don't know if a
number must be written below, or it's a statement of fact, we had
this dream rendezvous:

I'm walking with you, slowly, into a fog bank and I urge us to turn around,
not walk where we can't see the ground. We face the other direction, a snow-
covered hill quite steep *can you climb it?* and dotted with black pots with fires
burning in them small and cozy; domestic, not threatening *out of Hardy, the
furzepots.* You're holding my arm as we proceed toward that hill, when across
the crest a herd of wild ponies streaks, ebony vaulters across the white sky,
stunning us both with their sure-footed grace. We begin to follow.

With love,

Carole

Linda Pastan

Linda Pastan (age three) and her mother, Bess Olenik (age twenty-seven)
New York City; c. 1935

Linda Pastan was born in New York City in 1932. She graduated from Radcliffe College in 1954, and received an M.A. from Brandeis University in 1957. She has published 9 volumes of poetry: *A Perfect Circle of Sun; Aspects of Eve; The Five Stages of Grief; Waiting for My Life; PM/AM: New and Selected Poems; A Fraction of Darkness; The Imperfect Paradise; Heroes in Disguise; An Early Afterlife. Carnival Evenings: Poems 1968 to 1998* will be published in 1998. Her awards include: the Dylan Thomas Award, a Pushcart Prize, the Di Castagnola Award (Poetry Society of America), the Bess Hokin Prize *(Poetry Magazine)*, and the Maurice English Award. *PM/AM* was a nominee for the American Book Award, and *The Imperfect Paradise* was a nominee for the *Los Angeles Times* Book Prize. Poet Laureate of Maryland from 1991 until January of 1995, Pastan has been on the staff of the Bread Loaf Writer's Conference and has taught at American University. She lives in Potomac, Maryland, with her husband; they have 3 children and 5 grandchildren.

Bess Olenik was born Bess Schwartz on January 18, 1907, in New York City. The daughter of emigrants from Eastern Europe, she was the eldest of four children. She lived in various parts of New York City until 1945 when she moved to Armonk, New York. As a young woman, she attended Evander Childs High School and Columbia College. In 1929 she married Jack Olenik, a physician, and devoted the rest of her life to taking perfect care of her family. She died in April 1987.

Notes to My Mother

1.
Your letters to me
are forwarded to my dreams
where you appear in snatches
of the past, wearing
appropriate clothes—
a 30's shirtwaist or the long
seal coat you wintered in.
And since your gravestone
is shaped like the front
of our old mailbox,

I'll try to leave my messages
of flowers there.

2.
"Feeling fine, having a good time."
I had to stamp those words
on postcards from camp,
though I was so homesick there
I'd read the nametapes on my socks
and handkerchiefs—scraps of my real self
you had sewn on by hand.
And so I write it now, though
I'm still homesick eight years after
you left me in my life for good:
feeling fine, having a good time.

3.
The roles of wife and mother
matched you with yourself

as perfectly as your shoes matched
your handbags. Therefore, for years

I couldn't understand my own failures
at order and optimism.

4.
How many autumns I've tried to pick my life up
like a dropped stitch and just get on with it,
tried to pretend the falling temperatures,
the emptying trees were not a synopsis:
so many losses behind me, so many
still ahead. The world is diminished leaf
by single leaf, person by person
and with excruciating slowness.
Sometimes I wish some wandering
comet would hit, as the newspaper
this morning warns or promises—some stray
pinball ricocheting through space.
Then we'd go up together in a lovely blast
of fireworks like the kind I watched

from our July 4th window light up
the sky with percussive neon ribbons.
And the dog, in his last month, hid
under the couch; and your great-grandchildren
couldn't decide whether to be frightened
or ecstatic, their laughter had that edge
of shrillness to it. They don't know
that danger is the shadow thrown
by every bright object; that even family love
can show this dull metallic underside,
as the leaves do which move in sudden gusts
of September wind all in the same direction,
like a school of panicked minnows
sensing a predator ahead.

5.
Though I learned to love
the woman you became
after the stroke,

I never quite forgave her
for hiding my real mother—you,
somewhere

in the drifted snows beyond
that unscalable
widow's peak.

6.
Everywhere
the stream
of life goes on,
and I try to
go with it,
non-swimmer,
paddler in a leaky
canoe.

7.
You taught me always
to write thank you notes, though

I never thanked you properly,
not even when you were dying. But
I thought our inarticulateness
in the face of love was as elemental
as the silence of stones
in the same streambed. I thought
you wanted it that way.

8.
As I grow older, I try
to draw the world in close
as if it were a shawl you had crocheted for me
from small indulgences—morning coffee
from the same cracked cup,
a stroll downhill past empty mailboxes
where only the weather may be different
or the seasonal colors of the birds.
And I try to think of loss as a salt sea
I'll learn to swim in later,
getting closer to you
with every overarm stroke.

9.
Things I refuse to think about
also come back in dreams:
the way my fingers have started
to fail as yours did, knuckle
by swollen knuckle. Last night
I dreamed of handcuffs,
amputation.
Or how even repented sins
are ours for good: they drift
down the exotic rivers
of medicinal sleep,
mewling like kittens.

So in the last moments of wakefulness
I recreate that lost world
whose textures are like braille
beneath my fingertips: the enamel

of the 40's stove where you taught me
to cook; the floral wallpaper you chose
whose roses had no thorns;
the strictness of starch against skin.
And here sleep comes
with all its complicated gifts
and treacheries to gather me
in its arms.

Linda

Marge Piercy

Bert Bernice Bunnin Piercy
Detroit, Michigan;
c. 1945

Marge Piercy, in the garden at her home
Wellfleet, Massachusetts; October 1993
IRA WOOD

Marge Piercy was born in Detroit, Michigan. She is the author of thirteen collections of poetry including *The Moon Is Always Female, Circles on the Water: Selected Poems, My Mother's Body, Available Light,* and *Mars and Her Children. Eight Chambers of the Heart,* a book of Selected Poems for the British and world markets, was published by Michael Joseph and a new volume, What Are Big Girls Made Of by Knopf. Her book of craft essays, *Parti-Colored Blocks for a Quilt,* is part of the Poets on Poetry Series of the University of Michigan Press. She has written thirteen novels, including *Woman on the Edge of Time, Vida, Braided Lives, Gone to Soldiers, Summer People,* and *He, She & It,* which won the Arthur C. Clarke Award for Best Science Fiction published in the United Kingdom in 1992 under the title of *Body of Glass, The Longings of Women* and, most recently, *City of Darkness, City of Light.* She is the poetry editor of *Tikkun.*

Bert Bernice Bunnin Piercy was born "perhaps in 1893, perhaps in the United States, perhaps in Philadelphia. She was the third of eleven children, nine of whom survived to grow up. When she was in the tenth grade, she had to leave school to go to work, as her family was desperately poor. Her father was a union organizer who knew nine languages fluently and had been trained as a doctor in Russia. He was eventually beaten to death because of his political work. My grandmother was the daughter of a Hasidic rabbi from a small town in Lithuania. After my grandfather was murdered, she kept kosher and returned to Orthodox practice, but she had a very womanly perspective on Judaism. She was my religious mentor. My grandmother lived mostly with my Aunt Ruth, but with us part of every year. She and my mother had an overheated and confrontational relationship. My mother was married quite young, had an annulment and an abortion around the same time. Then she was married to the father of my brother for some years, before she ran off with my father. It took her two years to get custody of my brother. She lived in Philadelphia, Pittsburgh, Cleveland, and then with my father in Detroit. The last twelve or so years of her life, she lived in Tequesta, Florida. She did not like Florida and would rather have stayed in Detroit, where she had many friends. She died of a stroke in 1981. I brought her back here."

Voices After Dark

Dear Mother,

I contemplate our long relationship and I see how it is shaped: peace at both ends, a loving early childhood, a loving middle age for me and old age for you, and in between, war, war, war. Why did we have to fight for so many years, wasting our potential intimacy?

It is now thirteen years since you died. They said you never regained consciousness after you lapsed into a coma after your stroke. It was supposed to be your first, but in your drawer, I found clippings about strokes that made me guess you had experienced some episode you kept to yourself. You lay on the floor for close to two hours. That time haunts me. You were still aware then. My father was napping. When he finally awakened and found you on the floor, he was angry because you had broken a fluorescent light when you fell. He picked up every piece of it before he called the ambulance. By the time they arrived, you were losing consciousness.

I felt you. I had an excruciating headache. I could barely function on the telephone when the call came. Then while we were still trying to get a flight south, I felt you die. The planes were crowded going down. Your yahrzeit is easy to mark, because you died on the first night of Chanukah. He chose to have you cremated. You had purchased a cemetery plot, but he had decided that was an unnecessary expense. He did not want the ashes, but I did. I brought them home on the plane. It was late the night of December 24th and the plane was almost empty and the ride very bumpy. I had to wait till spring to dig you into the garden. You are buried among my cats. Your ashes were singularly beautiful. They were not grey or black and white but multicolored, with bits of coral and aqua and pale yellow. I have never seen ashes like those.

In all this time, I have never stopped having the occasional thought, Mother would like this, I should tell her about this, I should show her this clipping or send her that scarf. I have most of the presents I gave you. You kept them wrapped in plastic like clothes back from the cleaners. They were too good to wear every day, you said, or apparently, any day. I was married to Ira under the chuppah made of a shawl I had given you, that you particularly liked and kept in tissue. I took the good dishes that you had all the forty-five years I knew you, and I used them for every day. Many of them are broken now. I did this intentionally. I enjoyed thinking of you as I ate from them and I wanted them used, as they should have been.

I promised you I would say kaddish for you. You and I both knew that Grant would not do it. He had converted to Catholicism, something he never told you or me, but that we had both guessed. I did say kaddish, and in so doing, became aware of my own ignorance. He had been bar mitzvahed, but that was never done for girls in your family. So I had never learned Hebrew. Thus I was every day saying blah blah blah, beautiful sounds actually, but with no meaning to the sounds uttered in compelling rhythm that fascinated me. This began to irritate me as the year wore on. The first piece of liturgy I ever wrote for the Reconstructionist Siddur I worked on was the Mourner's Kaddish. I had a passionate need to transform it to something in English that was real to me.

But I also decided as that year came to a close that I had to learn what I was saying. That it was not enough to resent having never had a bat mitzvah but was high time to change that and give myself one: a real one that began with my studying Hebrew, which I continued to do for the next six or seven years, not intensely but regularly. My Hebrew teacher, Shira, became a good friend. You would have liked her. You would also have been startled how much her daughter Ruth looked like your sister, my favorite aunt, Ruth. Everyone in our family looks alike. Even my niece looks astonishingly like you and me.

At my father's funeral, his brother called me by your name. Father himself, during the last two years of his life, called me Bert. He would try to order me around as he had always done with you. He thought I should be you. In many ways, we are similar, but in many ways, I have had and I have made for myself opportunities so different from yours that my life has been unreal to you since I turned seventeen and went away to college on a scholarship I had won without your permission, on money I had earned from summer and after-school jobs.

Physically we were obviously alike. Mentally, we are both stubborn, imaginative (overimaginative?), passionate, short-tempered, foul-mouthed, fast-moving and profoundly sexual. Some of the differences between us date to my catching German measles followed by rheumatic fever. That turned me from a street kid, bored by school and very physical, to an intellectual. I tired easily, was pale blue with anemia, fainted often and embarrassingly, and caught bad colds and sore throats at the first drop of rain. I went into the world of books because the physical world was scarcely open to me. I began to test years ahead in reading comprehension. Any test I took, I excelled in. I learned to use my brain as a tool of survival. It was my best weapon.

It was not that you were naive, given what you had been able to see of the world, or that you had lacked experiences. You had married three times (unusual for those years), had two children who lived. You had grown up in poverty. Hannah—your mother and my grandmother—gave birth to eleven children, and you helped deliver at least four of them. You had an immense amount of women's lore on herbs, home remedies, abortion, pregnancy, child rearing. Your father was a radical, a labor organizer, an intellectual and an activist, and he was murdered. You had seen plenty of violence close up. You had presided over birth and death. You were a natural mystic. You never doubted G-d was in you, although you did seem to think of G-d as male, as I never could. You were true to your radicalism. You espoused the left position on most issues, although you were afraid of Blacks. You did not think they should be mistreated, but you were terrified I would take up with a Black man. I had, after all, immediately acquired a Black boyfriend in kindergarten, one of the times I was most severely punished—although certainly I was knocked around plenty in my childhood. Both you and far more violently, my father, freely used your open hands, your fists, a wooden yardstick and in his case, his feet, to keep me in line. It never worked. I could be beaten but I would not give in. I simply grew cleverer in my transgressions. I made sure as I entered puberty that you knew as little about me as I could manage. It was my best protection—like Joyce from Ireland, the weapons of silence, exile and cunning.

Why did you become the cop in my life? I have often wondered at how women coerce themselves into coercing other women to stay in line. You were sure that it was necessary to pretend with men, to simper and flirt and then in your head (or to me) call them fools. You were terrified I would have sex with women, you were terrified I would have sex with men. All your fear did was point me in the directions of the possible. I was eleven when I had my first sexual adventure.

What you taught me inadvertently was that the most important thing for a woman was not to be economically dependent on a man. It was very clear by midchildhood that you would have left my father if you had not depended on him for support. I was already saying to myself overtly and clearly by the time I was thirteen that I must work and make enough money to survive on my own. I had no idea how to do this, but I knew it was necessary. I also considered it important (I have all this in my childish handwriting the one year I kept a diary) that I not want too much comfort, or I might be seduced into dependence and thus be trapped. I had a hostile analysis of marriage by the same age. You saw all the drawbacks, but you did not think there were alternatives. Women had to marry. There was no other option but dying in the gutter. You saw sexism clearly, but you imagined there was nothing that could be done to fight it, except for the usually futile attempts at manipulation and subterfuge.

The two of us, who had been partners, who had been allies against my father and against the world, were by the time of my puberty, at war. We did not really come to trust each other again until I was forty or so, when you began to confide in me again and you began to try to accept me. You tried very hard. It was easier on the phone than in person. We used to talk on Monday nights when Father was playing cards at the senior center. My life was so different from that of anyone you had ever known that it was difficult for you to understand, and I tried to give it to you in small doses, so you would not be too frightened. You learned a certain amount from my books. You always preferred the poetry to the fiction. The fiction offended you. You believed in talking about sex, but not putting it down on the page. That was shocking.

Part of it was the age difference, part the cultural differences. You had me at age forty-four. When I was that age and considered that fact, I was filled with sympathy. I realized what it would be like to have a child in middle age, how much harder those incessant demands would prove to be. A generation had passed between us. You had not really been out in the world but had been a housewife since late adolescence. By the time I was twenty, I had held far more jobs than you had ever experienced. When your first marriage failed you went back home. You did not leave your second husband till you had acquired your third.

I never again lived in your house after I was eighteen. I never visited for longer than a week, usually no longer than three or four days. It was too harrowing for both of us. You would start prying, start trying to control. You could not understand how I could go off to New York City between my junior and senior years, live in an apartment with two other students, get a job and play in the city. I organized a student housing co-op where I lived my junior year. My senior year I lived alone in a tiny apartment. All of that was incomprehensible to you. To you, a respectable life (and respectability had come hard to you, born in the slums) meant a little house, a husband, a lawn. I was always living in mixed neighborhoods (like the one I had grown up in) in aging places you had never been and could not imagine going to: Chicago, New York, San Francisco, Paris, Nice, London, Florence, Crete, the Peloponnesus, islands whose names you had never before heard. It always felt dangerous to you.

You had ambitions for me, but they were such narrow ones. I should get a job as a secretary. That seemed to you safe, respectable, clean. You could not imagine any higher calling for a woman than to have a nice secretarial job in an office with middle-class men to flirt with, wearing nice clothes to work and bringing home a little money. My grandmother Hannah—your mother—spoke to me of how the people back home in the shtetl could never understand what life was like in the New World. Until they were all murdered, every one, she kept in touch, writing occasional letters in Yiddish. I often thought of her telling me how they just couldn't imagine her life, couldn't begin to see it, when I tried to talk to you of mine. I also lived in a New World, one in which women were far more independent and had more options than you could imagine.

Everything about me was wrong. I had long hair when nobody did. I wore black. Who ever wore black but mourners and peasants? I was always with strange men I was not married to. I never had an engagement ring. I travelled alone. I got on planes by myself and went odd places and people paid me to come there. Why would they do that? What was really going on?

I was always being seduced by my desire to share with you. You had such avidity for life that I kept thinking somehow I could open up more of the world for you. You had been given so little to enjoy in your life, and you made the most of that little. You could make a celebration out of one rose, a bottle of cheap red wine, a few cookies and some supermarket ice cream. You taught me that if you want to enjoy, any celebration is better than none. Make rituals, you taught me, make occasions. Mark time passing with candies and sweets.

I liked to give you presents, even if you put them away, because you so much liked to be given nice things. It satisfied at least for a moment a hunger that was never satisfied, for a better life, a kinder life, something warmer, a life that would not grind your face in the floor every day.

You gave me a direct open sensuality that little in your life spoke to. Oh, you loved flowers. You always managed to grow them whenever you could find a tiny plot of ground. You understood compost years ahead of the organic gardening movement. We always had a compost pile in our tiny yard in Detroit. In the shadow of factories, you grew tomatoes, lettuce, beans, carrots, parsley. I see you with your face like a flower holding up a sheaf of lilacs or irises. You were always putting sugar on everything. You put sugar on lettuce, you put sugar on cantaloupe. Nothing was sweet enough but it must be made sweeter. You were always baking and you were always eating cake. As an adult I puzzled over how you and father would have cake and coffee before going to bed. If I did that, I wouldn't sleep for a week.

You had your generation's mistrust of vegetables. You liked them canned or cooked until they were slime. Rare meat was never served in your house. You believed in cooking everything and cooking it some more and then giving it a little extra time to get really cooked—whether we're talking about beef or peas or pears. When you were having trouble with your blood pressure, I kept giving you health foods, whole grain foods. After your death, I found them all stored on the top shelf of your cupboard where you would never have to look at them. They were simply not your idea of the edible. Their very being affronted and insulted you, but you would not throw them away. Out of politeness, you kept them—but well out of sight.

I have to smile when I think of our attempts to improve each other. "You'd look so cute if you'd cut your hair and curl it. They have electric curlers nowadays." "Why are you still eating eggs for breakfast? Didn't I get you some low-fat cereals in four different flavors? Is that cream in your coffee?" What a futile exercise, two cats each trying to groom and wash each other and ending up in a spat, hissing.

We could both communicate with cats; we loved and understood them. They recognized us as soon as they met us. Oh, it's you, they'd say, about time. Now scratch me right under here and let me into your lap.

You taught me how to handle birds that had been injured. You taught me about plants. We both could grow anything if we bother with it. I have learned not to fully indulge my penchant for bright colors; you never did. To the degree that either of us ever cared about jewels, we don't like diamonds or that sort of glittery thing, imitation or real. We like jade, amber, pearls. They speak to the body as the hard glittery stones never do. We think they speak only to acquisition. You had a gift as a palm reader that made some men call you a witch. Years ahead of feminism, you told me that witches were just wise women who had knowledge of herbs and got along with animals. How did you ever know that? I think you knew it instinctively. I got paid in college to be in an experiment because I came up totally negative on telepathy. I would not get one card right. I had mental defenses they couldn't even guess about.

It wasn't until I was studying Yeats that I discovered my weird portal. The Tarot works for me. I can't read cards on myself. Only a fool does their own. And I have no illusion I am reading the future. I am taking a clear view of all the forces in the moment. Nothing comes out because I wish it to be. Nothing will come out as I'd choose. My readings are often disturbing, for they are seldom trivial. My card reading, your reading of palms: one of those doors left unguarded between people who are after all never so separate as we are led to believe.

You believed in training the senses and in training the powers of observation. I have no idea where that came from. But you trained me very early to see exactly what was there, in a butterfly's wing, in a bird's eye, in a lily. Don't see what you expect to see: see what's really there. Is a white lily white? What's the shape of a cat's pupil? What color is dirt?

We played hide and seek mentally in other people's rooms. We played word games that nowadays some teachers play with students. I had to make up sentences using two odd words or stories incorporating three disparate objects. You were training me to be a writer, but that was not your intention. I have no idea what you thought you were doing. You had read it someplace.

You read omnivorously. Never having finished tenth grade but forced to go to work instead, you had no grand schemes in which to place the little glittering bits of history and fact you picked up. Your head was full of Amazing Facts and outright nonsense and shrewd observations, all jostling. You made me systematic, because it drove me batty that you weren't. I learned logic to withstand the flood of chaos.

You were a fine storyteller, even if your stories had a tendency to move toward the overly dramatic. Hannah, Grandmother, was an equally fine storyteller whose stories, even family stories from a few years before, tended to meld into folklore, Jewish myths, old tales. You two never told the same story the same way, and you fought bitterly over whose version was the best. Hannah could love me uncritically, as grandmothers can, as you never could, as she could never love you. You were jealous of our intimacy.

What wouldn't I give for us to have, not the five or six good years at the end of your life, but twenty good years in which to have shared all that we could share, in which to enjoy the ways in which we are alike and the ways in which we are strange to each other. I use the present tense but only the desire is present. You, my dear, are gone, except inside me, where you will always live, as long as I do.

Love,

Marge

Susan Power

Susan Power, Senior
(age sixteen)
North Dakota; 1941
FRED FISKE

Susan Power, Junior
(age nineteen)
Chicago, Illinois; 1981
WAYNE OLENICK

Susan Power (Jr.) was born October 12, 1961, in Chicago. She is a graduate of Harvard/Radcliffe, Harvard Law School, and the University of Iowa Writers' Workshop. Her first novel, *The Grass Dancer*, won the 1995 PEN/Hemingway award. She currently resides in Cambridge, Massachusetts, where she is at work on her second novel, *War Bundles*.

Susan Power (Sr.) was born January 22, 1925, in Fort Yates, North Dakota, on the Standing Rock Sioux Reservation. She was raised in a log cabin across from the site of Sitting Bull's original grave. She left the reservation in 1941 to pursue work opportunities in Chicago. She has been an active member of the National Congress of American Indians, and a founding member of Chicago's American Indian Center and American Indian Businessman's Association. She continues to live in Chicago but is making plans to move back "home."

Reunion

Mama, I am eleven years old, sitting in an empty corner of the school library, playing God. I miss my father, as I know you do, and so I return him to us with a few careful scrawls of my felt-tip pen. I rush back in time; carry us, all three of us, to the year 1935. I am not yet born, I am not dreamed of, so I tread the air a little above your heads and breathe softly through my nose.

You are standing beside Sitting Bull's grave, no, you are leaning against the marker—a small tower of stones—with your arms crossed and your eyes hidden beneath black bangs. You are ten years old, barefoot, wearing coveralls of an unknown color; and what looks to be a halo behind your lowered head is actually a cloud of dust, blown there by the drought.

A car is coming, you can see it from at least a mile away. Sioux children leap onto the wide running board, and two lean dogs snap at the belching smoke this noisy car trails in its wake. I stir them with a finger, these characters, knock them all to either side because I want you to be alone with the man in the car. My father leaves the car parked in the road and walks straight to

371

you. He doesn't know why. He doesn't know it is his unborn child telling him what to do.

My father is twenty years old and a Hamilton College man. His fraternity brothers must be looking for him right about now; they would never dream he is two thousand miles away, approaching an Indian grave in North Dakota.

You like to tease the white tourists by pretending you can't speak English. Sometimes they take your picture and offer you a nickel. You wonder what my father will do. He doesn't smile and he doesn't speak. He doesn't look the least bit warm in his heavy tweed jacket. He removes a pipe from an inside pocket and a leather pouch filled with fragrant tobacco. You have seen men smoke pipes before, but never one this small.

What can you possibly say to one another? I hold my breath and bite my tongue. I'm tempted to tease you young people, chuckle from the sky, saying: *Little girl, this is your husband. College man, this is your future wife. Twenty-five years from now you will give each other matching gold rings and you will promise to stay together and you will keep the promise until the day the college man dies.*

Finally I direct you both to speak. My father says: *Tell me about this beautiful country. I've never been here before.*

I make you speak English to my handsome father and I know you wish you could touch the thick brown waves of his hair. You tell him the stories you have already told me. You point in one direction and then in another. He gestures toward Proposal Hill with the gnawed stem of his pipe, and so you tell him other tales. You are bolder after so much talking and twice you have glanced quickly into his eyes. They are gray—silver storm clouds—and you laugh to yourself because your Dakota name is *Mahpiya Bogawin*, Gathering of Stormclouds Woman.

I whisper in your ear: *Yes, someday you will gather him in.*

Now it is my father's turn to speak and he describes his mother's home in Albany, New York. You cannot imagine his life, his summers at a lake cottage, and his Greek and Latin, his football injury and his Phi Beta Kappa key. His family is "old," you come to understand. His ancestors traveled to the North American continent in the early 1600s.

Years into your marriage you will say to his elderly mother: *Oh, your family is so old.*

And she will look up at you, up and up, because she is not quite five feet tall and you are a six-foot Dakota woman. *Yes, but yours is older,* she will tell you, firmly, graciously. As if you hadn't taught me that from the beginning.

My father is not a storyteller and hasn't much to say, but his reading voice could coax the stars from their bright positions, so I have him remove a slim volume of poetry from his jacket pocket. Emily Dickinson. You sit on the ground, your back pressed against Sitting Bull's marker, your knees drawn up to your chin. You trust this dapper young white man with a flair for the dramatic, I can tell. You scratch his name in the dirt with a thin crooked stick. You draw it with the right hand and he stands on your left, so he cannot see that you are adding your name to his.

I want to keep us all together at this gravesite, young as we are. But I know if I do that you will never meet my father and marry and give me life. You will spend your days listening to poetry.

Have to go, my father says, slapping the dust from his tweed.

You remain on the ground, hugging your knees. You are already afraid of losing him. My father slips his hand in the pocket of his stylishly baggy trousers.

Here you are, he says, cheerfully. He bounces a little on the balls of his toes.

I can see you are disappointed. What is it? A nickel, a dime, maybe a quarter. *Perhaps he isn't different after all? Perhaps he isn't special?* you're thinking.

But wait, I tell you. *Take a look.* My father has given you his Phi Beta Kappa key and it glints from the small page of your palm.

This should belong to you. These are the last words you hear my father speak. He waves from the car window as he drives away. The Sioux children and their lean dogs are waiting for him at the bottom of the road. They'll chase him to the edge of the reservation.

You admire the key; you hold it up to the light as if you could unlock the sun. You toss it and catch it, you press it to your lips, you squeeze it in the tight curl of your fist. You wonder why he's given you such a present, and I proceed to tell you, though you may not believe me. You say you aren't particularly smart, that you haven't done very much in life, but my father and I know that this is just another one of your stories.

You read so many books—you are my encyclopedia. You recite the history of my ancestors without pause, without forgetting a single detail—you are my memory. You speak up when others are afraid to—you are my voice. You notice what so many people would like to ignore—you are my vision. You imagine that I can do anything I decide upon—you are my dreams. You've shown me where the spirits hide—you are my imagination. You've challenged me to change my corner of the world—you are my conscience.

Mama, I am eleven years old, sitting in an empty corner of the school library, missing my father, who has been gone for six months. I place the cap on my felt-tip pen because I no longer need to comfort and distract myself by playing God.

After school I tell you how I managed this first meeting in my notebook, how I brought you and my father together on paper. We laugh at the unlikelihood of your union, smug in our knowledge that it all came to pass. You help me keep my father alive. You encourage me to tell my own stories. You say that I must have inherited the words from my father. But when I close my eyes, searching for inspiration, it is your voice I hear chanting in the dark.

Susan

Dawn Raffel

Dawn Raffel and her mother, Francine Goldfarb, at a family wedding
Wisconsin; c. 1984

Dawn Raffel was born in Wisconsin in 1957 and has lived all her adult life in and around New York. Her story collection, *In the Year of Long Division,* was published by Knopf. She is the fiction editor of *Redbook.*

Francine Goldfarb (née Bern) was born in 1927 in Illinois and moved to Wisconsin in 1947 when she married Mark Raffel. She graduated from college in her middle forties and for many years was an art teacher.

A Love Story

Dear Mother,

As I write this, I am three months pregnant with my second child, and I wonder whether this time I'll become the mother of a daughter. It exhilarates and frightens me, this thought, for while the lives of a mother and her son (this mother and her son) are tightly intertwined, while the feelings between the two are steeped in the deepest mysteries of the heart, I suspect that a mother and daughter are forever engaged in a more dangerous embrace.

You gave me my name: Dawn. The doctors told you I would not be born alive. You'd lost two unborn babies and had been warned you would never carry another baby to term. When I was born, no doctor was present. It was only you and me. And our parting was a terror: The umbilical cord was wrapped around my neck.

It was the first separation, this entry into the world, release and refusal, the body's unwillingness to let go. For the next year, I labored for breath. My cries sounded strange, you later told me, because one of my vocal cords had been paralyzed. I was expected never to have a normal speaking voice, not to be able to sing. What must you have thought of this newborn Dawn, damaged and greedy for life? My sister, seven years older, resembled more closely our father, but as time passed, I began to resemble you.

My voice, despite the expectation, healed—although to this day it is weak enough that I am told (urged, scolded) to speak up. But the rebellion, the rage to be free of the umbilical cord, was anything but weak. When you were effusive, I was contained. When you reached out, I withdrew. On days when you were sunny, I wanted to be the darkest Dawn around.

One day when I was four, we went shopping for clothes, whether for dresses for you or suits for my father I can't recall—only that it was essential to find the right look, and that while whoever tried on whatever, I became absorbed in finding myself (is that really me?) in a full-length mirror propped against a wall. The next thing I remember is lying in a bloody heap of shattered glass; I had pulled the mirror down onto myself and had been knocked unconscious. At the hospital, it took what seemed like hours to remove the glass slivers. I still have a scar on my leg—but I was lucky. In my rush to own my own image, I could have killed myself.

By the time the X rays revealed the absence of damage, your relief had turned to anger. How reckless I had been! What on earth was going on inside my head? You were angry, I think, not only at my foolishness but at the universal insult: When all is said and done we have little understanding of those whom we've harbored in our bodies and nourished with our blood.

Your mother came to visit. She often did. With her fingers, she found the many errors of our house. Our cupboards and crevices troubled her. She was a woman whose shoes matched her dresses, which matched her handbags; her hair was always pinned. She was a woman whose cooking was perfection, even when her ankles swelled over the tops of her shoes, and her eyes, behind glasses, betrayed her. And she was a woman who cried: in the kitchen, in the yard, in the closet, in the bedroom, in the dark, in the light, in the car when she waved good-bye. Her heart failed early, her death a greater blow, you told me, for the words unsaid. Still later, you told me she had been ashamed that we lived in a wooden house.

What must you have felt when you visited me, at twenty-two, in my tiny, crumbling walk-up apartment, seven flights above a crowded Greenwich Village street? No one in our family had left the Midwest, and the noise where I lived, the crowded living quarters, would have been unthinkable back home. We both pretended not to see the insects and the grime. You brought me household goods; you bought me clothes—sweaters and skirts you believed I wanted but could not afford. What I wanted was what I believed you had given away: A life of the artist, a life of the mind.

Your mother, you said, did not understand your need to make art. When my sister and I went to school, you did too—to study painting and sculpture and weaving. Your paints and clay and yarns were often on the kitchen table, for there was no room, it seemed, in our house for your work. On Sunday afternoons, you dragged me to local galleries. "What's this?" I would ask, standing before some modern creation. "What is this supposed to be?" And you would answer to my frustration, "It doesn't matter what it's supposed to be. Just look at the color and form. Just experience it."

I experienced it in a sulk. Years later, though, I believed that my father and sister and I had stolen from you. Our needs and wants, our very existence had robbed your life of a "real" artist. Now I don't know. I don't think you ever wanted that life. It was I who wanted it for you.

And I wanted it for myself. I became a writer of stories that often have their origin in visual images. I wrote about you and my sister, our family: I broke with traditional narrative in an effort to capture the weirdly lit landscapes of the inner life. Time became elastic. I married much later than you did, and waited to have children. "I hope you have children who treat you the way you treat me," you would say. Lord knows I didn't want that. For years, wars raged between us. As is the case with most wars, the reasons pale before the wreckage.

Some days, I think we've reached an accord. Other days you're angry with me: I don't call enough; I don't visit enough with my two-year-old son; I live so far away. And I'm angry with you: You want so much.

When I look in the mirror, I see your face.

A few weeks ago, you told me about a dream you'd had. In it, your mother, twenty years dead, appeared to you. "There is too little time," she said. And in the dream you'd answered, "No, there is too little love."

What I want to tell you, Mother, is this: There is enough love. It's just not the love we think we crave. It is quirky, angry, wistful, imperfect. It hurts and it heals, and it leaves us gasping for breath. We don't always recognize it. If I give birth to a daughter, perhaps I will tell her this—that this, too, this thing we shape between us, is a kind of art: It doesn't resemble anything. We are moved in ways we can never explain.

See, Mother, I was listening.

A ways back, you asked me whether I could write a love story. This is it.

Your daughter,

**Shirley Farley Ransom and her daughter,
Jane Reavill Ransom**
Boulder, Colorado; 1958

Jane Reavill Ransom was born in 1958 in Boulder, Colorado. Her first novel, *Bye-Bye* (New York University Press, 1997), won the Bobst Award. Her first book of poetry, *Without Asking* (Story Line Press, 1989), won the Nicholas Roerich Prize. Her second poetry book, *Scene of the Crime,* will be published by Story Line Press in fall, 1997.

Shirley F. (Ransom) Staton was born Shirley Farley in Belmont, Massachusetts, in 1929. The creator and editor of the college textbook *Literary Theories in Praxis* (University of Pennsylvania Press, 1987), she was a Professor of English at Purdue University-Calumet. She died of cancer at age 58.

Missed

Dear Mom,

Remembering you in your final months, emaciated and helpless, I've thought I should have stripped you naked and spitefully fondled you while I had the chance.

It's a harmless fantasy; I embrace my natural depravity, and welcome whatever righteous hostility it may invite. This is a thank-you letter, surely. They say loss feeds desire, and it's true I only love you more for leaving me at age 13 with an enraged alcoholic father and deranged older brother in order to marry one of my father's colleagues.

Because it was at that point I began to think for myself—to entertain violent sexual fantasies, paranoid suspicions and misanthropic cynicism—and this opening of my imagination helped make it possible for me to become a writer. Of course I'd always wanted to. You had hoped to be a writer, and like any love-struck daughter, my lifelong ambition has been to surmount and overthrow you. Thank you for being formidable. Thank you for teaching by mistake.

Talented and smart, at age 20 you got a scholarship to Iowa's graduate writing workshop. At 22, you married into a literary family. But it turned out that sex with your husband made you feel like a corpse. Soon you saw he was an emotional cripple. Soon you knew you didn't love him. Unable to admit the error of your marriage, you faked its success for 20 years.

Having children snared you tighter in denial. More and more, you despised my father; more and more, he ignored you. By nine I could survive by deflecting the tension of denial into my body: psoriasis, hemorrhoids, compulsive masturbation. I learned to keep these secret; keeping secrets was a skill that at the time made me lonely but would later serve me well. Besides, I was often happy, a much-adored girl living in the woods, with my own horses, rabbits, dogs and cats. My brother was less lucky. Ostracized at school as his expressions swung from scowling shyness to grinning hostility, at home his illness passed as if it were unseen. By the way, now he's medicated, friendly and bona fide insane. He thinks he's God. But that's another story.

As for your husband, after seven years toiling on a thesis disagreeing here and there with his famous-scholar father, he collapsed in guilty surrender. He never sent the book to the waiting publisher. He took to doodling airplanes, remained an undistinguished English professor. After the divorce, he passed out at work so often he was fired despite having tenure. Today he's just a derelict, although he hasn't had a drink since he burned down the house. But that, too, is another story.

You later claimed it was the marriage that made you give up writing fiction. You said the loneliness of it was paralyzing. And so—"no more little housewife"—you went back to school. And fell in love with another English professor, one you could look up to. In a stunning epiphany of courage and honesty, you left your family for him.

That was when the silent tension in our house collapsed into chaos. My father had been a secret drinker, my brother a disturbed introvert. But now my father was an all-out drunk. Now my brother was a violent psychotic. And now I was the only female, sole object of their animosity: Now, I was the star.

No longer playing blithe family, I could write my own script. My father and brother became villains I could scorn and outwit. Niceness lost its obligation, became a mere disguise. By day a good girl, I snuck out at night to get drunk and high, which in our small town was decadent. Distrust of others made me wise. Denial's curtain had cracked open to reveal the props behind reality, the expedient acts, the infinite cruelties. I had the little lead in a minuscule tragedy—but my vista through the curtain slit was vast.

Your bliss and my autonomy were not to last. Within a year, your second husband's death left you desolate. So, emotionally, you reclaimed me, had me stay on weekends, made me your confidante. Desperate to keep you, I was once again trapped. I fell back into stifling ugly insights, suppressing nasty thoughts. Sometimes I'd get drunk and lie down on the highway for several minutes in the dark, but mostly I suppressed my unhappiness. I began racking up school honors, smiling too much. I stopped wearing makeup, became ashamed to shoplift. I basked in the vanity of my hard-earned intolerance. We believed in our facades. I dutifully served as your surrogate living at my father's house: I cooked and cleaned and absorbed their rage. When my brother tried to rape me, you said to keep it secret. His sickness advanced ignored. I slept with my desk pushed against the door.

You became a feminist. I remained your apologist. You no longer needed a spouse to admire. You yourself were teaching English. Your graduate students looked up to you. One became your lesbian lover. It was the 1970s, redneck Indiana, when you and she moved in together. Another stunning metamorphosis, another fearless act.

And yet you retained your righteousness. Messy ambiguity got swept aside by feminist polemics. I moved far away, began to disengage from you, but mostly was too cowardly to question. Ten years later, weak with cancer, you loosened your defenses. You apologized, before you died, for having left me with my father. I demurred, volunteered that, at least, he'd never sexually molested me. "Oh, I always wondered," you half smiled. Yet you'd never asked.

Your lover recently rebuked me for insisting, years before, on calling you by your name instead of *Mom*. I tried to tell her that I had complained of the stress in our relationship; you'd written back denouncing my "misogyny" and from then on, signed your letters *Shirley*. I tried to tell your lover that many years earlier, you had asked to see my poetry, but when I mailed you a sad poem, you inexplicably took it as a personal indictment and shot back an aerogram expressing indignation and likewise signed *Shirley*. That first time, I apologized for having "sent something so depressing," and asked you please to reconsider, to "please sign yourself *Mom*." But the second time, I didn't protest, just went along, for two years until you changed your mind. We never spoke about it. When you stopped using *Shirley,* so did I. So why had you misled your lover into thinking this had all been my idea? To get her sympathy, did you frame me?

Just as, no doubt, here am I, in this letter framing you. Pretending you weren't trapped by history and circumstance. And maybe it's unfair of me to say—as I said to your lover—that you had deigned to be my mother so long as I feigned cheerfulness.

Your lover chided me that you yourself had been a stoic. Besides, she said: *"Your mother loved you."* Yes, but I don't know why love should have silenced us. Or why love turns into cowardice. Whom are selfless smiles for? I'm most grateful for your acts of open selfishness, for they helped free me from good-girl fealty. Writers often need to be traitors, but without lying to themselves. I suspect it was not my father's paltry company but your self-denying rectitude—first as wife, then as feminist—that made you give up writing fiction. The need to justify yourself deprived you of the psychic license that your role betrayals later gave me. By the way, I've slept with many women, surely in an effort to surpass you. And possess you. Competition feeds desire. And you continue to elude me.

Sincerely,

Jane

P.S. I love you, too.

Linda Raymond

**Lillian Robinson (age thirty-eight) and her daughter,
Linda (age four)**
Dayton, Ohio; 1956

Linda Raymond was born in Dayton, Ohio, on May 4, 1952. Her novel *Rocking the Babies* received the American Book Award. She lives in Northern California with her husband and children.

Lillian Robinson was born in Borderland, Kentucky, on March 1, 1918. She worked for thirty years as a clerk-typist at Wright Patterson Air Force Base, retired, then took up her second career as a Volunteer Grandmother. She lives in Dayton, Ohio, with her husband.

Between the Lines

MAY 1, 1995
SACRAMENTO
"SUNNY CALIFORNIA"

Dearest Mama,

"How Are You? We Are Fine."

I will not ask you how you are today. I already know the answer: You are not well. In fact, since your third stroke you seem hardly there at all, sitting slumped in your easy chair in front of the big screen TV, waiting. At seventy-seven, your eyes are bad, your concentration dilute, and you cannot read. Instead of writing, I talk with you on the telephone. Our conversations are broadcast through the big screen TV speakerphone. It works like this: Daddy picks up the regular telephone and greets me, "Hello, Second Born!" We chat, I ask for you, then he switches me to full blast Surround Sound. Your voice, traveling from the recliner to the microphone, then finally across wires to me, is small. The echo around our words heightens their importance, makes the conversation sound ludicrous. I wonder who on earth thought up such a device? "How are you feeling?" There is a long pause. "I'm all right," you say faintly. "Maybe I'm dizzy—my nerves are bad." I want to talk with you, to speak directly into your ear. Though I have nothing special to say, I want to say it only to

386

you. Far off clinking and running water mix with static on the line. Daddy must be washing the dishes. His voice rises from the background clatter. "We got cable," he calls out. "Thirty-six channels. Mommy is set. She's got everything she needs."

"The Sun Always Shines Here."

You have May sunshine in Dayton, but the weather has been strange here. We haven't yet unpacked our belongings from the flood cleanup—my sterling candlesticks and crystal fish plate are still in boxes along with lots of other stuff. Did I ever show you my salmon steamer, meant to hold an entire fish while it cooks pink? I bought it in case I threw a big party and would need a twenty-five pound fish decked out in thinly sliced cucumber scales, decorated to look as if it had jumped from the ocean onto my buffet. It is in a box, too. I never needed all that stuff anyway. In eighth grade my math teacher asked the class how many television sets we each had in our homes. One? Two? Three? Four? Only my hand remained up. Five? Six? We had a TV set for every room in the house. I was too embarrassed to publicly count the seventh set, the black and white portable with bad reception Daddy kept in the upstairs hall. Mostly we watched the big console in the living room. Remember how we used to lie on the couch in the evenings after you came home from work? I was five, you were in your late thirties. You'd curl on your side, holding me in the crook of your legs, my head buried in your behind and your knees. We'd chew Wrigley's spearmint gum and watch *Rawhide*. Sometimes you had just the one piece in your mouth, no more left in the pack; but if I asked, you'd give it to me. The gum didn't taste like much with all the sugar chewed out, yet it was the sweetest treat.

If I found you lying on your back instead of your side, I begged to comb your hair—straight, silky, dyed jet black—nothing like my own naps. Your hair could do anything—curl under, flip over or hang straight. I'd smooth it over the couch arm in one long, soft sheath. I'd comb it over my face, over my eyes. I'd sit beneath your hair, blinded.

Even back then I thought, "If anyone goes to Heaven, it will be my mother. She doesn't drink, smoke, or even dance. These are qualities God can appreciate. He will keep her in heaven for eternity." I, too, wanted to keep near you. You were large and soft, cleanly bathed in the bathroom sink every morning. In your bedroom, you'd tightly hook up your brassiere against deeply brown breasts, needing my help to zip your dress across your broad, rounded shoulders. In those days, alone in your room after you had gone to work, I'd find things fallen to the side of your bed—*True Story* magazine, lint and dust bunnies, and once, late in the evening when you were still at work and Daddy had suddenly woken up, showered and hurried out—I found seven one-hundred-dollar bills arranged, it seemed to me, to fall unstudied from the mattress to the floor. Though I was afraid to touch them, I picked one up, looked at the impossible number in the corners—one hundred—then replaced it just as I had found it. Another day, while you were standing at the bureau mirror combing your hair, I found a condom. It looked like an extremely plain, sticky balloon, and I tried to blow it up. You told me with amused disgust to get that nasty thing out of my mouth.

Sometimes when I visit I want to take you away from that house. I watch you channel-doze through the afternoon, then evening, while Daddy comes and goes on his way to the garage, to his broken lawnmower business. The summer before last we sat on the couch and dreamed: you could stay with me, in far-away California. I would talk to you; I would listen to your slow disjointed words, to your thoughts looping one into another. I would do the things I felt were not being done for you. I would save you. You said you would like that; then we both let it pass.

"I Have Been Busy—As Usual."

In high school when I learned who Emily Dickinson was, I dreamed she was you. You were the shadow passing swiftly by the door on your way to work. You were the sayer of cryptic lines, "Let the food stop your mouth," "A fool will *do*." Like reading her poetry—slant rhymes, angled meaning—you forced me to consider your perspective, though I wasn't good at it. When I was there the summer before last, relatives took turns visiting the house to see me and take me to dinner, leaving you to watch the big screen. The next day, you and I sat in your bedroom, stacks of folded laundry crowding us on the bed. As we waited for the iron to heat, you remarked to me, words coming slowly,

"I feel like a nobody," and my heart flew to yours. *I know,* I wanted to say, *I feel like a nobody, too.*

But I confess, I purposely brought that moment into being; its gestation period was longer than my adolescence. Maybe an adolescent daughter needs a mother to subdue, to defeat, to overcome with discouragement, to dishearten, to make the mother suddenly feel small, to feel less than the daughter. However, I was no longer an adolescent. I suppose my letting you see how newly popular I was with the cousins and aunts was a way to drag from you an acknowledgment that I was fine, capable, and that you had noticed. Did you ever notice me? I thought of you as passive, Mama. You laughed with your mouth closed; you never defended yourself against criticisms of your cooking, your gift giving, your taste in clothes. In your family, among your sisters and brothers, you were the oldest, but you were the unimportant one, and to them your children suffered from the same sickness. You would not defend us, and you would not praise us. You angered me. Yet how could I expect from you what you could not give anyone else, not even the most deserving person, the one most worthy of praise for strength, resourcefulness, hard work, and steadfastness: yourself?

"The Children Keep Us Hopping."
You told me, when you were in your sixties, that you wished you were like me, in your thirties raising children. I wondered why, feeling a lack of time for myself and a deep fear that this would never change. At times, I thought the demands my children made simply because they lived and breathed would bury me. Many years earlier, you had watched my first baby all day, every day while I finished twelfth grade, then you would put on your work clothes, comb your hair, and work a full second shift as a clerk-typist at Wright Patterson Air Force Base. But in your early sixties you had empty arms; you missed holding babies. I lived in Southern California with my new husband and two children; you had recently retired and now had your days free. Now that your two daughters were gone, truly able to take care of themselves, you went back to work rocking babies. You and I both worked in hospitals. You, in Dayton, riding the bus downtown three days a week to cuddle premature babies. Me, in Los Angeles, working in neonatal intensive care, handling babies for

medical reasons, no time for love. You, other women's babies in your arms, crooning, rocking. Me, evaluating their medical status, adjusting their oxygen, sucking mucus from their lungs.

Fifteen years later, your baby-rocking duties long finished, I sent a picture of myself and my second grandchild, held slung in one arm the day after his birth in San Francisco. I called to ask what you thought of his banana-shaped head. You responded, pushing out your words in breath and flat pauses, "He looks like any other baby." Our conversation halted. Listening to the hum of telephone static I wondered where your head was at. Suddenly I saw the blockages the last stroke had left, the misdirected nerve impulses, your mind maneuvering through the wreckage of your brain. Anatomy has redefined you. The shared memories, the good ones, the ones that comfort, are no longer available to inform your emotions. I didn't know what to do with this new version of you, and so pretending not to notice, I answered, "Oh."

"When Will You Come See Us? We Miss You."

You are different now. You now seem to be operating on Thoreau's dictum to simplify. You have pared down, drawn in, let fall away the unnecessary, and kept only what you need to go one more day. You are down to your essence, and you are sick. Stripped of your ability to help others, your usefulness gone, you wonder who will love you, who has need of you?

I miss being held by you; I miss the feeling of your arms containing me. What can a capable, accomplished woman gain from lying in the arms of her worn-out mother? When I held my own babies, I forfeited the ability to lose myself in the comfortable arms of another adult. Holding my children's new bodies against my breasts pulled from me promises of protection and love so powerful, promises so wildly dedicated and extravagantly loyal, so passionately, hopelessly impossible to fulfill (*I will never let anyone harm you, I will keep you safe, All good things will come to you, I will never hurt you*) that I knew I lied even as I spoke them. Yet I needed to believe I had the omnipotent power to protect. Just as children need do nothing to deserve the love of their mothers, mothers are forever needed in their primal, skin-to-skin protective role. No matter the age of the child or the lack of innocence, the need to be held by one's mother never goes away.

After months of talking with you through the speakerphone, I made myself a promise: The next time I saw you, in the early fall during a book-signing and reading tour, I would lie in your arms, and you would lie in mine. I would let myself need your love. I would give my love to you.

"I Really Enjoyed My Last Visit."

I have not seen you for more than a year. Sitting in your rocker-recliner, cable remote by your hand, you look more frail than your voice on the telephone has cautioned me. You now get around on a stick and by wheelchair. Immediately, I bend down to encircle you in my arms, my fingertips count the vertebrae in your spine, gently touch your ribs. You are too fragile to jostle, to rearrange into my arms for more than a lingering hug. When we talk, your eyes wander from mine, past my face, then back, roaming, determined not to drop the thought you are knitting with words. After a while, I get the peppermint foot lotion from my suitcase and rub your shiny, peeling feet. We watch the TV screen, big as the wall, and talk.

The night of the reading, Daddy parks the van in the large shopping center lot in front of the bookstore. He and Uncle Charles lift you into your wheelchair, your toes skimming the blacktop in their hurry to set you down before their strength gives out. Inside the bookstore they lift you again, this time onto the stage, two old men doing what they have to do, handling it. They won't permit strangers to touch you. I take my place behind the podium, my novel about grandmothers rocking babies in my hands, a familiar stance now. Behind me, a warm incubator holds a crazily redheaded Raggedy Ann doll as a patient. It is flanked by two padded wooden rockers, looking comfortable, as if the grandmothers might ease themselves down to rock "their" babies at any moment. Tonight Children's Hospital is honoring their volunteer grandparents, men and women, with my reading and a cake.

The store is full of people; more chairs are found to seat family, friends, volunteers, strangers. Daddy has asked your doctor to come, and he sits with his young family. I see cousins, neighbors, friends of friends. But you sit in front of everyone, straight before me. I have not lived in Dayton for twenty years; I know

I've Always Meant to Tell You

this assemblage of people is a testament to their regard for my parents.

I do not know what I will say before I begin to read from the novel. I have never enjoyed the sound of my own voice. There is a working microphone attached to the podium, and that helps ease my words forward. I thank you and Daddy jointly for giving me everything, giving me my life. I ask Daddy to stand, and he does so, smiling, enjoying this moment as much as I do. When I thank you, my mother, for being my inspiration, not just a model for one of my book characters, but for being my model as well, your face briefly convulses, then you quickly reorganized it into a closed-lipped smile meant to press back tears. I am the only person who sees your love for me destroy your composure. Standing before you, I feel as safe as a child.

"Well, Time to Close. I'll Write Soon."

Daddy has hooked up my call to the television set. There are rattles and clicks and long silences while he figures out what he is doing. "Okay, Second Born," he cries, always jovial. "Go ahead and talk to Mommy." I hear his footfalls diminishing in the background. "Hi, Mama," I begin. "How are you feeing?" I wait for your answer. "I'm fine. How are you?" you say. "I have my period," I announce to the room. "You know what that's like." We go back and forth like that for a while, not talking about anything important. I am enjoying the tenor of your voice, so familiar, a voice I have heard all of my life. Time passes. "Well," Daddy finally says, his voice growing louder with his footsteps. "I guess you're all done talking to Mommy." As he starts the button-pushing ritual that will disconnect us, I have just enough time to say, "Good-bye, Mama. I'll call soon. I love you."

Love,

Linda

"XXOO"
I am afraid of losing you.

Annie Reiner

Annie Reiner and her mother, Estelle Reiner
Beverly Hills, California; c. 1960

Annie Reiner was born in New York in 1949. She has lived in Los Angeles since the age of 10. She is the author of 2 books of poems, including *The Naked I* (Red Dancefloor Press); a collection of short stories, *This Nervous Breakdown Is Driving Me Crazy* (Dove Books); and 4 children's books, which she also illustrated. Her children's story, "Dancing in the Park," won Parents' Choice Gold Award for best audio for 1996. She also works as a psychotherapist.

Estelle Reiner (née Lebost) was born in New York in 1916. She has been a painter and more recently a jazz singer, in addition to raising 3 children. She has been married for 52 years to writer, director, performer, Carl Reiner.

To My Mother

I was born inside you once
but you have been born
and died a thousand times
inside my mind.
We've gotten used to each other in here,
you and me,
we have even begun to like me
after years fighting the octopus
of times past
and ancestors you carried
while you carried me.
But the child is inexorably free
in the arms of hope
and eternity.
I waited,
I played your heart,
rewrote your soul
till you could dare to see—
not a mirror of your dreams
or a clown to do the old dance

of disenfranchised families—
but me,
and now we have, yes,
begun to like me.

I am me
though I am always you
as every child is his mother
somewhere in the water of his deepest thoughts.
But the mother who dares to see her child,
to be him,
helpless and small
in his own universal ocean,
explorer of a new world
she has never known—
she is the mother of tomorrow's sun.
She shines so he can shine
orbiting together past the last frontier
into new times
where Time is a new dimension of Mind.
Here, children create their own world
inadvertently,
rebelling not against their parents
but against Time standing still.
It can't
and they can't.
They are made of light
and propelled to fly.

You have robbed me sometimes
of the things of which you had been robbed
but you were a child explorer too
and once
like an outlaw from your generation
you dared to enter mine
you dared to see me
here
in *my* world
destroying like Shiva
to create.
You dared to let me break your walls of Time,

to see me, not simply where I am
but where I'm going
and growing into another
and another world.
I can't take you with me there
where I become light,
protected from your mistakes by fire,
but I send you away with love
as your parents never did,
but would have
if they could have.

Upon my sometimes bitter truths
I have built the ground between us
to stand on
to stand up
to face each other once and for all.
In this harsh light you will see
forgiveness in my eyes.
Forgive us both our ignorance
which keeps love at bay
trying to stay safe
from its psychedelic beauty.
There are no good-byes inside
so I'll just thank you
for what colors and music you gave me
and the sound of distant bells you heard
to which I in my life
will have time
to get closer.

I love you,

Annie

Lynne Sharon Schwartz

Sarah Sharon in a typical summer pose, leading a chorus of amateur performers at Lansman's Bungalow Colony Woodbourne, New York; early 1950s

Lynne Sharon Schwartz, age twelve or thirteen New York; c. early 1950s

Lynne Sharon Schwartz was born in New York City on March 19, 1939. Her books include five novels—*The Fatigue Artist, Leaving Brooklyn, Disturbances in the Field, Rough Strife,* and *Balancing Acts,* as well as two story collections—*The Melting Pot and Other Subversive Stories,* and *Acquainted with the Night*—and *Ruined by Reading: A Life in Books* (Beacon Press, 1996) and *A Lynne Sharon Schwartz Reader,* an anthology of essays, stories, and poems.

Sarah Sharon was born in New York City on March 3, 1903, and died on November 17, 1986. She was the child of Eastern European Jewish immigrants and grew up in Brooklyn. She married Jack Sharon in 1925 and together they raised three children. A charismatic, highly articulate woman of generous impulses. A good mother.

Dear Mom,

You must be surprised to hear from me. I haven't written to you since I was living in Rome over thirty years ago and a trans-Atlantic call was something we'd never dream of. I remember I wrote you that I was pregnant, and you were very happy and wrote back that now I was truly and finally doing something creative, implying that being pregnant was more "creative" than my halfhearted efforts at writing, and I wrote back that I didn't see what was so creative about getting laid. Don't worry, though, I won't take that sassy tone now.

How to write to the dead? Are you interested in the news, or do you know it all even more thoroughly than I do, even the news of the future? I could tell you who's died since you left, but you never liked hearing about death, it frightened you too much. Long after you died, I learned that way back when you were in your twenties, you were so overcome by your favorite brother's death that you stayed in the house for a year. You couldn't even take care of your first child. Your mother and sisters helped— you all lived in the same brownstone. Nowadays they have names for such spells, even help, even medicines; maybe they did back then too, but you wouldn't have wanted that. I suppose you just waited for it to pass. In your last years you did everything you could to ward off death: you stayed very still, because the less active you were and the fewer places you went, the fewer dangers you would run. You slept on the edge of the bed, practically sitting up against the pillows, so you wouldn't be taken by surprise in the middle of the night. But although death didn't come at night, it did come while you slept, sitting up. You may not know how it happened because you were asleep. You had had a hard day, a bad cold and cough, so bad that you insisted on going to the hospital to be checked out—you were always slightly hypochondriacal, concerned about every inner flutter and flicker—and when they found nothing drastically wrong you were taken home and you sat in an easy chair in your room, wrapped in blankets. You were so tired, you said, so very tired. You fell asleep. Beverly called me and said she couldn't wake you. I packed an overnight bag and we drove up right away. I took the bag just in case you were dead and I needed to stay and help with the arrangements. I didn't understand that was my sister's way of telling me you were dead. I had the ghost of an expectation that when I arrived she would have succeeded in waking you. I saw you lying flat and still in the hospital where they'd brought you for the second time that day. You were not even cold yet. I touched your cheek.

If you were here now, in the room with me, I'd have many, many things to tell. To ask, also. Why, faced with the paper, have I nothing to say? Because it's all too private. I don't want the world listening in, especially on what has been left unsaid and will remain so. Which is exactly what I've been asked to do, write a letter to you, but a letter for the world to read, to listen in on our secrets and our tones of voice when we talk intimately. It goes against me, telling secrets to strangers. Writing stories is a different matter altogether. The privacy of the mind is what I love and won't ever forfeit. Few people understand that now, but I'm sure you'll understand.

I've written some poems, though, in which I bring you back a little bit. Would you like to read them? You loved attention, craved it, charmed everyone you met in order to get it. Well, here is my attention.

MY MOTHER'S REPORT WHEN I RETURN FROM WORK

So here you are. Everything's fine, she napped
in the morning and woke up happy to see me.

I gave her the jar of spinach with a soft-boiled egg,
she didn't take much of her bottle and I didn't force her,
but later, in the park, I got her a Dixie cup
from the man in the truck and she liked that very much—
she even tried to eat the wooden spoon.
She only wanted to go on the slide with the big kids
and cried when I wouldn't let her,
but I pushed her in the baby swings and she liked that.
You were short of milk, I noticed, so we stopped for some.

The ironing's on the bed. I pushed the vacuum around,
I hope you don't mind, the place looked like it could use it,
plus I did a load of diapers while she slept.
You had a few calls, I wrote all the messages down,
also the UPS man, looks like a book or something.
After the park we rested and played with her puzzle.
She's so smart, knows where all the pieces go,
she did it faster than I think I could.
When I read to her she pointed her finger at all the right pictures.
I gave her a bath, I knew you'd be tired after work—
boy, can she splash around, I mopped up the floor—
she's in clean pyjamas now, all ready for bed.
Oh, and I roasted a chicken—it's okay, to me that's nothing.
You'll have a head start with dinner
so your husband won't have to wait.

I'll tell you something, I always thought a woman
should stay at home and take care of her baby.
But in your case I see you can't. So all right,
it was a very nice day and I'll see you next week.
I suppose you'll manage till then?

MY MOTHER TELLS THE STORY OF THE RUBBER BAND BALL

When we were little we made things from whatever
came our way— there weren't fancy toys like now—
and one thing we loved to make was a rubber band ball.
First you balled up a bit of newspaper very tight,
rolled it around in your palms, got it nice and round,
bigger than a marble, not so big as a golf ball,

let's say a large strawberry if you could imagine that round—
and very tight was important.

You know how rubber bands keep turning up,
around lettuce or asparagus, brand-new pencils and envelopes,
in the old days a piece of fish in wax paper.
People save them, not knowing what to do with them,
but a rubber band ball is a wonderful thing.
We would wrap each one around the ball of paper,
doubling or tripling it depending on the size—
it was best to start out with a few strong fat ones—
and at first it looked like nothing, a clump of paper
with a few rubber bands around it,
then after a while—you needed time and patience—
there'd be less and less of the paper peeking through
till—here was the best part—you watched it
transforming into a real ball. The work
seemed to go faster once the thing took shape.
You kept on going, adding more and more. Suddenly,
there was a good firm ball you could bounce or throw.
It bounced very well, as high as you ever could wish,
such a lovely thing.

So I thought, here I am with time on my hands,
I'll make one for our little girl, your little one.
I started collecting rubber bands and wrapping them
around tinfoil—it's lighter and holds together better,
we didn't have it back then.
I imagined her playing with the ball I had made for her,
bouncing it on the sidewalk just as I used to do,
but then I imagined what if she dropped it
and it rolled into the street where the cars are?
She dashed out after it and a car was coming—
I tell you, my heart was racing, I couldn't watch . . .
So I didn't make the rubber band ball after all.
I couldn't, with what I had pictured in my mind.
I had to throw it away. I was so relieved
she wouldn't have it.

So, what do you think? Do you like them? You always loved
reading whatever I wrote, you would phone the minute you fin-

ished the last page to tell me how good it was. (Once I had the babies it was fine to be a writer too—as long as I did first things first.) I miss those phone calls. Maybe you don't know how I treasured them. No one else does that the way you did.

You may not like these poems as well as the books. You wanted attention, yes, but you wanted to choose exactly what you would display in order to get it. I understand, I'm the same way. Yet I've done something you may think is not so nice. I've made you into a character, a persona is the fancy word we call it. Maybe you don't want to be remembered the way I've presented you. Not so much the one about taking care of the baby. You'll probably like being remembered as generous and capable, even if there is an ironic edge. But the one about the rubber band ball—I worry about that. You don't like being remembered that way? Well, in that case you should have done differently. You should have conquered your fear and made her the ball.

Still telling you what to do. An awful habit, really. I know better now, really I do. Sometimes when my children look at me critically—lovingly but critically—scrutinizing and weighing, I remember looking at you the same way and I'm sorry, now that I see how it feels.

I don't want those to be my last words. They're only a small piece of the truth, not a very important piece. I'm thinking of the time, a year or so before you died, when you were staying with us for a few days and you sang "Santa Lucia," do you remember? My actress friend Florence came over, and you two really hit it off, both performers, both colorful, flamboyant characters. I'd told her how you used to sing torch songs and snappy songs, how people at parties would clamor for you to sing, how you were a natural, not only blessed with a low and strong and versatile voice, but you also knew how to make that voice pierce and penetrate deep in the hearts of your listeners so that the room was hushed and brimming with emotion and each person felt you were singing for him alone. We urged you to sing, Florence and I—I wanted to show you off, frankly, and also give you a chance to show off—and at first you said, Oh no, my voice isn't the same anymore, I can't do that anymore. But naturally in the end you did it. You stood by the piano in the living room exactly the way a torch singer in sequins and spangles stands—and I could remember you in your long-ago spangles—right in the bend of the magnificent grand piano you gave me as a high school graduation present, and sang "Santa Lucia," because it happened to be in the book and you knew the words and it was an easy song for me to play. It's a song I happen to like very much because the melody is simple and symmetrical, and because the reach up to the high notes feels like waves cresting. Each phrase imitates the rocking of the ocean evoked in the song.

Your voice was soft and velvety, full of feeling. You hadn't sung for a long time, and I didn't think you'd be singing again. It sounded so wondrous, your voice so low and rich, giving the simple words such tender and solemn attention, that I said to myself: Remember this, this moment and this sound, because you won't be hearing it anymore. It was one of those moments in which life becomes more than itself, so intense and fulfilled that we wish it could be that way always. But so keen a beauty for too long would shatter us like glass.

When I was a child and you sang in public in your sequins and spangles I was embarrassed at the spectacle you made of yourself. I was shy. I couldn't see how you could bear so much attention, like a hot light shining on you. Even though I was proud, I was embarrassed too, and you knew it and went right on singing. You weren't daunted by my embarrassment. Well of course not, why should you be? Probably I was envious; you must have understood that. Later on, when I could appreciate how well you sang, I was scornful that you never "did anything" with your talent: you should have pursued a career, I thought; you should have been aggressive about it, you would have been enormously successful. But instead you shrank back into domestic life out of fear and passivity and habit and convention. I thought of you as an example of unfortunate and benighted choices.

All of this, my changing and foolish attitudes about your singing, drifted through my mind as I listened to you, old and faded, singing "Santa Lucia," and then they drifted out and away into nothingness. No attitude was needed, only that I listen intently, a lifetime's worth, to remember the moment and the sound of your voice. And I do.

Lynne

Carolyn See

Kate Daly and her daughter, Penny Laws (later Carolyn See)
Los Angeles, California; c. 1938

Carolyn See was born in 1934 in Pasadena, California. She has most recently published *Dreaming: Hard Luck and Good Times in America, Making History,* and *Golden Days.* She has two daughters, Lisa See and Clara Sturak. She lives with John Espey in Topanga Canyon.

Kate Daly was born March 6 in 19? in New York. She has two daughters, Carolyn See and Maureen Daly. Lives alone in the California desert.

Dear Ma!

I've always meant to tell you that it didn't have to be this way; you made your own life by yourself. Yes, your own terrible childhood did occur; you nursed your mother to death of TB. You were so poor you had tea-and-toast three times a day. And when you were really still a child, you hooked up with my dad, who—because of his own mother's suicide—had a strong agenda of getting back at women. Because you were fitful and depressive, he put you in the perfect bind. He teased you out to be mean, then he declared you intolerably mean and left you flat.

Flat, flat, flat, with only a high school education and a little kid. Of course, it's easy, from outside a person's life, to see a structure, a turning point, a place where you had the choice to embrace life or kick it. You chose the latter. I think that from the age of thirty-five on, you constructed your own life with devilish care, the way a little kid constructs a tantrum and just keeps *on* with it, when she could get up and wipe her nose and eyes, sniff a little and go outside to play. That kid is so into the tantrum that she can't give it up. What I'm saying is you didn't have to live the last two-thirds of your life that way. (But what the hell do I know? Maybe you like it. Maybe you think it's what sets you apart and makes you sparkle.)

It's strange writing "to" you, although God knows I've written "about" you enough. "On Mothers Who Hate Their Children." Or *Rhine Maidens,* a whole novel. Or, finally, recently, *Dreaming: Hard Luck and Good Times in America,* nonfiction, where I talked about your throwing me out of your house for good when I was sixteen, and about my sister Rose, and how you did the same thing to her. So I guess it's pretty clear to anyone who gets around to reading that stuff that you hated me and—it took me a long time to admit this, because I'm always pretty intent on defining myself as "good"—I was never too crazy about you either.

To you, I always was an idiot, "slow on the uptake," as you put it. It took me *forty-one* years after my father left us when I was eleven to get it through my head that it wasn't working out, you couldn't stand me. And yet, you expected to be loved. Just as the kid throwing the tantrum, and so into the rare beauty of the tantrum, never considers that her parents might walk out of the room, and get into a car, and drive far away and never come back.

By 1989 I'd had enough and said we could only see each other in the company of friends or a therapist. I was still so scared of you, because the truth is, there is always some truth in what you say, and if you hate me, there must be something there to hate. Ah! I can see your face now, with its spiteful smile, hear your manicured nails drumming on the table. You're not even *here,* and you've got me where you want me, once again.

This is the part where I say all the good things you've done, and say that if it weren't for you I wouldn't be where I am today. So: You worked very hard at being a mother. You "sacrificed everything," you've told me many times. You once went into a screaming rant about how you hand-scraped cooked carrots because you didn't want to give me commercial baby food. I'm *sorry,* Ma! I would have told you to go for the Gerber's, but I couldn't talk yet. I know you did a lot of ironing and washing. You ironed all my clothes until my dad left, you ironed his underwear, you hand-ironed the sheets.

You never sent me away to boarding school, although you threatened it every day. You never killed yourself, although you threatened it every day. You always kept a very clean house, and drove me to parties and back. You took me to the library once a week and church once a week . . . you had some good things you liked to cook, like peach cobbler and all-day spaghetti and apple brown betty. While my dad was still around there was always chocolate pudding in the refrigerator. And in the summer you made Coke floats.

The best thing you did, and the bravest, because you were shy within all that rage, was to take me on the streetcar to downtown Los Angeles—even after my father had gone!—to hear Nellie Lutcher at a matinee, or watch Josephine Baker swan about the stage in different outfits, or you took me to the Philharmonic or to the Ice Capades. You wanted to give me what you never had, you said, and Josephine Baker would fall into that category. But you couldn't give me what you *really* never had, and that was love.

You cleaned my ears with olive oil. You scrubbed my scalp. You took me to the doctor. But you were always so mean! When Sister Edith down at St. Dominic's Elementary said I had a 165 IQ, you made sure to tell me that a "genius" in the third grade was actually a moron in adult life! You made fun of all my boy-friends . . . well, you know all that. And for every awful thing you said, if you could see that it hurt me, you'd shine that smile: *"What's the matter? Can't you take a joke?"* Actually, no. But I could hold a grudge.

So if it weren't for you I wouldn't be where I am today. Except for the fear that my daughters will die before me, I have no real fear. I went through the worst that life has to offer from the time I was eleven until I was sixteen. The physical stuff was bad; the emotional stuff was very bad. But when that was over, *I knew* life would only get better, and it did. I also had a clear map of how to proceed. You wanted me to be a secretary; I got a Ph.D. You hated my second husband; I married him. You scorned John Espey; I adored him. You detested my children; I was crazy about them. (I guess the only three things I finally agreed with you about were avocados, curly hair, and Mexican music. All very nice!)

And your meanness has had a bracing effect. My daughter Lisa, a few years ago, was bullied over the phone by some East-Coast-bitch-editor used to reducing writers to tears, just for the fun of it. Lisa met her bullying with cutting contempt and then later flew into a rhetorical rage: "Who does that slut think she's *talking* to? Who does she think she's pushing *around*? Doesn't she know I grew up with GRANDMA KATE?"

*   *   *

Now there are those who say you have "borderline personality disorder, that you're not responsible for what you do." I don't buy that. I've seen you with your friends, and you're a wonderful friend. You just can't stand your family. That's why I say you brought the second two-thirds of your life on yourself. (Boy, I can see you now, tuning up to scream.) Scream away, Ma! Throw those plates and tear your hair and totter about and threaten to faint and resort to weeping! Go for it. When I was on the road touring with *Dreaming* I ran into cousin Steve. I hadn't seen him in fifty years, not since he was a baby on a blanket, but I recognized him because he looked just like his dad. There we were looking at each other and I had to say, "I was rough on your grandma in the book, I'm sorry . . ."

And Steve, silver-haired and trim, said, "Well, Grandma was bad, I admit, but my God, YOUR MOTHER!" And his wife said, "That's why we moved up here, to get away from those people."

One by one they bailed on you. Daddy left, and your boyfriend killed himself when you dumped him, and my step-dad—who thought he was tough until he met you—keeled right over. My sister went away so far that none of us saw her for twenty years. I stayed around ("slow on the uptake," maybe, or maybe just as stubborn as you were, living on a stern diet of no-love, and that's what I gave back to you, contributing to every blighted holiday maybe just as much as you).

Until that day in 1989 when you came to that lecture John and I were giving to 400 people. You came up like some mean witch in a fairy tale and said, "You're bullshit, you're bullshit, and everything you do or say is bullshit," and, slow as I am on the uptake, I finally got it: This lady doesn't have my best interests at heart. And even though you said several times after that, *"What's the matter? Can't you take a joke?"* the answer, this time, really was: No, I can't.

You hated your life because you had to type, you told me forty million times (although it was your dearest wish for me). But a mile away from where we lived there was a junior college where at that time you could take classes for 2 dollars and 50 cents a semester. Why didn't you take some classes in travel-agenting or bar-tending or social-working or *anything*? How come you never joined a women's club or a women's group? We went to church; how come you didn't get some help from them? I think that yes, our childhoods "happen" to us, but that after a while we get the leading role in our lives, and we're the ones who set the tone. (Don't I sound prissy? And can't I just *see* your smile?) Honestly, Ma, you're the world's oldest living juvenile delinquent. You and James Dean, except you're 85. Still got that throwing arm, though.

What I'm telling you is this. All the time you were tearing your hair and breaking dishes and whaling away at us and screaming until your throat got hoarse and tottering and staggering and flailing and howling, *all around you there was a beautiful world.* A beautiful world, and two out of three men who wanted to be your husband, and two little girls, who early in their lives wanted you for a mother, believed you were their mother.

You got caught up in the beauty of the tantrum. And everybody walked out.

Your daughter,

Carolyn

Ntozake Shange

Ntozake Shange
c. 1996

JEFFREY ST. MARY

Ntozake Shange was born in Trenton, New Jersey, to a physician father and social worker mother. Later they moved to St. Louis where they counted Miles Davis, Ike and Tina Turner, and Dizzy Gillespie among their friends, as well as W.E.B. DuBois, who would often put Ntozake to bed. She holds degrees from Barnard College and the University of Southern California; she received the Guggenheim, Chubb, and the National Endowment for the Arts for Playwrighting fellowships, and a MacDowell Colony fellowship. Other awards include the Houston International Festival Prize, the 1993 Lila Acheson Wallace *Reader's Digest* Award, and the 1994 Philadelphia Mayors Arts & Culture Award. Her play, *for colored girls who have considered suicide/ when the rainbow is enuf,* received the Obie Award, the Audelco Award, and a Tony nomination; another play, *Mother Courage and her Children,* received the Obie Award. She has published several collections of poetry including *nappy edges, A Daughters Geography, Ridin' the Moon in Texas,* and *The Love Space Demands.* Her novels include *Sassafrass, Cypress & Indigo; Betsey Brown;* and, most recently, *Liliane.* She has been the Taos Heavyweight Poetry Champion of the World for three years running.

MAMA

by the mirrors near the windows
opening to flowers reaching toward
heaven yr smells danced
with blossoms i had no name for
even in winter i cd smell you
deep in lingerie drawers
& i cd pull a satin breast to
my cheek quickly before mae
or grandma came looking for me
always a liar/***** i'd say
i was doing nothing in your room
alone again i traced your face
veiled just married surrounded in
excited bronze smiles a halo
   grace
love in the hands of yr brand-new husband
who never looked at me
quite that way but it was enough
to grow up knowing

just to close my eyes
   your scent wells my body
& my eyes glaze every which way
tossing pillows at shadows

II MOMMY

"at this stage in your life
there are some very important
things you need to know"
that's what you said to me after
my period came twice & i thought
Christ was calling me to be a saint,
then i changed my mind & thought
i was dying of melancholia
you know like Camille and Liza
any way here's information you
have to have before you enter the
next phase.

1) you don't have to be a virgin.
   use tampons.
2) sucking dick is an acquired taste
   and can become a useful skill.
3) nobody cares about respect
   after a one-night stand.
   only was the sex good.
4) uncircumcised men are not dirty.
   they are an exquisite treat
   only a really exotic french
   tickler can approximate the tickle
   at yr g-spot. Yes, you have one.
5) men who really like women love
   to eat pussy, but you've got
   to tell em how fast & slow,
   nearer the clit or round about
   the vulva. yr pleasure is your
   responsibility & any man eating
   your pussy is down there to
   give you pleasure. so help him.
6) pussy's don't dry up ever. least
   check yours once in a while with
   a standard vibrator or a finger
   any one's will do.

7) just cuz you give somebody a lil/
   don't mean yr in love.
8) it is not a good idea to hide
   how smart you are from any man.
9) never let any one tie up your hands.
   ain't no dick worth all that.
10) daddy knew all this.

ELOISE

I knew you were pushed along too fast
New York is like that & shoved a tiny girl
ahead & ahead. why not? smart colored
children belong with a p t barnum or hunter.
but eloise you don't have to catch up
keep up with those big girls in fur coats
striver's row addresses
anecdotes from berlin barbados
not any more, ellie, the youngest
tiny tow head sitting at thomson's in
harlem folks staring at you
teasing you like ignorance demands
cloaking fears "can i do it can i do it
i'm just a girl from fulton ave
can i do it can i do it do i know how am i enuf"

ellie you can still those haunting taunts,
seditious
echoes of envy
remember i am constantly at your heels
troubling you for answers not jus cuz
on accountta you my ma what 'birth' me
ellie you a wise woman
and i know you don't know you never thought
anybody'd come chasin after you
ma you jus to goddamn quick tempered

i don't come to you jus for lovin arms

Dani Shapiro

Irene Rosenberg Shapiro lifting her daughter,
Dani Shapiro
New York City; c. 1962

Dani Shapiro was born April 10, 1962, in New York City. She grew up in New Jersey, graduated from Sarah Lawrence College, where she also received her M.F.A. She is author of the novels *Playing with Fire, Fugitive Blue,* and most recently *Picturing the Wreck.* Her short fiction, essays, and book reviews have appeared in *The New York Times Magazine, Story, People, Glamour, New Woman,* and others. She teaches creative writing at Columbia University and in the Graduate Writing Program at New York University.

Irene Shapiro (née Rosenberg) was born June 10, 1923, in Brooklyn. She was raised in Tom's River, New Jersey, spent most of her adult life in northern New Jersey, and has lived on the Upper West Side of New York City for the past ten years, where she is a psychotherapist in private practice.

Mother, I Am Listening

NOVEMBER 22, 1995
CAMBRIDGE, NY

Dear Mom,

As I write this I know exactly where you are—in the backseat of a Chrysler LeBaron whizzing up the Taconic Parkway, with my boyfriend's father behind the wheel, my boyfriend's mother beside him in the front passenger seat. I can picture you easily, sunk deep into the plushness of the seat, the late autumn scenery a blur through the window. The trees along the highway are bare, the ground wet with the last of the fallen leaves, but still, it is very beautiful. In the trunk, next to that twelve-pound turkey my boyfriend's mother has insisted on bringing for Thanksgiving, you have placed a Zabar's shopping bag packed with a home-baked pecan pie, cookies from a local café, and some lox for Sunday brunch. In fact, there's hardly any need for me to cook for the holiday. Between the three of you there is a feast: brussels sprouts (apparently my future husband likes them), cranberries, raw vegetables, hummus, cheese.

415

It is a relief to know where you are, tucked safely into the back of a car like a little kid. I try to imagine the conversation the three of you are having during the long drive. After all, you don't have much in common; what brings you together is the fact that their son is with your precious daughter. A fact you are none too happy with.

Admit it. You don't think he—anyone!—deserves me.

Your precious daughter. After three miscarriages, at the age of forty, you had me. *I hit the jackpot,* you like to say. You poured enough love and longing for a brood of children into me, your only child, and expected that love to be exponentially returned. I was always more important to you than I had any idea what to do with, certainly more important than any one child ought to be. As a teenager, I developed a fear of flying because one day, on a particularly rough flight, I suddenly imagined we would crash and wondered—what would happen to you? How would you survive the loss of the child into whom you had poured everything? Later in life, I heard the following definition of what it means to be a co-dependent: *"You're about to die, and somebody else's life flashes before your eyes."*

When I was twenty-three, the tables turned. You almost died, and my life flashed before your eyes. You and Daddy were whizzing down another highway, one of those four-lane-wide New Jersey highways, and Daddy passed out at the wheel, his foot heavy on the gas. As your Audi 5000 made wild, mad circles across the grass divider and all eight lanes, as you screamed *Paul! Paul stop! Wake up!*—it was my face you saw superimposed on the concrete wall. My face coming at you seventy miles an hour.

You lived to tell me this, which is how I know. I will never know what my father thought, if in fact he was conscious at all. Newly widowed you opened your swollen eyes in the hospital and saw me hovering there. You pulled my head down until our cheeks touched. It was I, you whispered, who pulled you through.

At the moment your car hit the divider, I was on the other side of the country, on vacation, at a spa. Until then, I had always believed in movie clichés: That the hair on the back of my neck would stand up, a chill would go down my spine, and in a Technicolor instant I would know a terrible thing had happened to someone I loved. Instead, I spooned a low-fat gazpacho into my mouth and debated whether to take yoga or tai chi after dinner. That night I slept like a baby. It wasn't till morning, when the phone's ring pierced the air and I groggily answered, that I was hurled into the reality of how truly separate all of us are: You spent the night on a hospital gurney with eighty broken bones while, across the country, your only daughter, light of your life, lay sleeping.

By now, you must be about halfway to our house on the snow-covered back roads. Perhaps you're listening to Benny Goodman on the car stereo, or maybe you're telling them about your upcoming trip around the world—Tibet, Rangoon, Bali, Australia, Marrakesh, Turkey—the trip of a lifetime. I know, as you watch my boyfriend's parents' heads bobbing in the front seat, that you miss Daddy. I know you resent spending these last ten years going on blind dates with retired ophthalmologists, attending the opera alone. That you resent my new extended family simply for the fact they're still alive and together. Perhaps you even resent me, just a little, for having the whole of my life still in front of me: Marriage, kids, family, home—all cards I am only now being dealt. And I am still younger than you were when you married my father.

Soon, you will pull up to the front door of the farmhouse where my boyfriend and I spend weekends, and you and your shopping bags will descend upon us. Within milliseconds, you will do something to irritate me: Maybe you'll begin singing off-key, or you'll look around the house at the threadbare rugs and flaking walls and through your own gaze I will find fault with this place I love. You will tell me how to cook the turkey or refrigerate the pie. I will watch the way you look at him out of the corner of your eye, not as my boyfriend, but as competition—someone who has grabbed a sizable portion of the discrete amount of love you think I have to offer. The phone rings. You are calling me from town, a few miles away. You're running late, the roads are icy—you don't want me to worry. What you don't realize, what I need to tell you, is this: I listen carefully now, Mother. I listen for the silent scream in the night, the tingle shooting up my spine, the way the world can be eclipsed in a split second. I am warm and toasty in this New England farmhouse under a dusky gray sky, and the patter of sleet on the roof is comforting. All the while, another self, a shadow self, the daughter who has enough love to make up for all those other children you never had, waits for you.

Love,

Dan

Carol Shields

*Carol Shields (age eleven), beside her mother, Inez
Sellgren. Brother Bob and sister Babs are at left*
Summer cottage at Lake Lawn, near Delevan, Wisconsin; 1946

Carol Shields was born in Illinois in 1935. She grew up in Oak Park, Illinois, and has lived since the fifties in Canada. Her Canadian husband and she have five grown children, a son and four daughters. A professor at the University of Manitoba and Chancellor of the University of Winnipeg, she writes fiction, poetry and plays, and in 1995 was awarded the Pulitzer Prize for *The Stone Diaries*, a novel.

Inez Adele Sellgren was born in 1902, the youngest of eight children of a Swedish immigrant family farming near Cortland, Illinois. She and her sister Irene were identical twins, and this twin-sistership was one of the joys of her life. She attended DeKalb Normal and later taught school in the Chicago area where she and three other teachers boarded at the Hemingway house. She married in 1927 and had three children, a boy and two girls. She died in 1971.

How Your Life Fascinated Me

Dear Mother,

You told me once—I must have been eleven or twelve—that my conception was "an accident." I suppose I could have been crushed, but I wasn't. The way you said it, the look on your face and the girlish way you rolled your eyes, told me that it was one of the good accidents of your life. It was an easy birth, too. "You slipped out like a lump of butter," you used to say. I can't think now why I found this announcement so mortifying. Was it the image of butter? Or the unimaginable bloody process and that most intimate of connections?

You said all kinds of things, and many of these sayings are available to me on the long-playing record inside my head. All I have to do is press a button and your voice comes on. "Always give to the Salvation Army, they do good work." "Never light candles in the daytime, and never have candles on the table if you don't intend to light them." "Always buy from the Fuller Brush Company, they're a fine old company." "Don't make promises you can't keep." "Add a few drops of strong coffee to chocolate cake." "Never let a boy put his hand on your knee."

"Crossword puzzles keep your mind active." "Your skin will turn to leather if you stay out there in the sun." "If you put good things into a casserole, it will turn out good." "Be sure to get your teaching license, so that you'll have something to fall back on." "When you make a tailored wool suit or dress, send it out afterward to be professionally pressed." "Pastry toughens if you roll it out more than twice." "Feed your husband nutritious meals, that way he'll live longer and support you."

Sometimes what you said and what you did were in conflict. "The human body is a beautiful thing," you said before each visit to the Art Institute, preparing us for the sight of nude statues. But you yourself dressed and undressed in your closet. I understood though, even as a child, that there was no hypocrisy involved here, that you were only trying to puzzle out your own feelings.

President Roosevelt was a bad man, you said. He was a threat to America. My brother and sister and I grew up thinking this was true, that Franklin Delano Roosevelt was in the same camp with Hitler and the devil. And so, when the news came crackling over the radio that he had died—I was nine, my twin brother and sister were eleven—the three of us set up a rousing cheer. You spanked us all on the spot, the only real spanking I can remember. Something was amiss here, something not quite logical. And yet an underlying logic made itself instantly known.

You can be anything you want, you told us, even president. Part of me believed this, or at least believed that you believed it. But there was a gap always between how you saw yourself and how you were seen by others. You were pretty, you went to teachers college, you lived most of your adult life in a Chicago suburb, you were innovative in the way you cooked and dressed—that red gabardine pantsuit circa 1946!—but you never got over the feeling that you were a gawky girl from the sticks.

You grew up on an Illinois farm, you and your twin sister being the youngest in a family of eight children. I never saw that farm. It was only fifty miles from Chicago where we lived, and I can't help wondering why, on a family outing, we never drove by and paid a nostalgic visit. I can only guess the reasons. It was probably poor—your parents had immigrated from Sweden at the beginning of the century—and it may have held memories you preferred to forget; not every rural family is as jolly and cohesive as the Waltons.

I'm not sure why I know so little of your childhood. You were not, of course, one of those jolly storytelling mothers, and I was not, sad to say, curious enough to demand information. For your first eight years of schooling you went to a one-room school-house, and for a number of those years your teacher was your own older sister, our Aunt Edna (the difficult one, as she came to be called in the family). This teacher/sister coincidence seemed wildly improbable to me as a child, the sort of twisted unlikelihood one comes across in ancient folktales.

You went to a nearby town for high school—I believe it was called Villa Park—and while at that school you failed Latin. You told us this, sitting one day at the kitchen table. Your tone and your timing were deliberate. We paid attention. "I want you to know that I failed Latin in high school," you said to me and my brother and sister. Of course we understood why we were hearing this: so we wouldn't be afraid of our own failures. None of this had to be explained.

Your twin sister was your best friend—you told us this often—but sometimes you mentioned other girlhood friends. There was Grace, brave Grace, who had to be pushed to school in a wheelchair. Grace grew up, married a man named George, and the two of them lived like a pair of sparrows in a tiny house in Sycamore, Illinois. One day George went down to the basement and shot himself. It was said that his eyes were failing and that he didn't want to be a burden to poor crippled Grace. I found this story deeply poignant as a child, but didn't quite believe it. Why not, I wonder.

You had another friend called Lily. She signed her letters "Lovingly, Lily," one word swimming above the other, the L and y linked with inky tendrils. I never knew anything else about Lily, but this feat of penmanship seemed all I needed to know.

There was Helen, there was Hap, there were the Betchlor sisters (who never married). You kept up with these friends all your life, writing back and forth, dropping in when you were in the neighborhood. And, later, there was Mary Organ, your Catholic friend, who cried all night long when Al Smith was defeated for the presidency in 1928. Teaching school in Chicago, Mary Organ got pregnant and in desperation leapt from the top of an upright piano—but this story is oddly unfinished, or have I simply forgotten the ending? Did she succeed in aborting the baby, did she die? In my mind she is still suspended in that still parlor air, her destiny unknown.

You and your sister Irene, finished high school and enrolled in college. Who paid for this education? Who offered encouragement? (You almost never spoke of your parents.) You lived at home, taking the new Interurban back and forth to DeKalb Normal School, and two years later, your diploma in hand, you arrived in Chicago where you had secured a teaching job.

Then followed what I have always thought of as a great adventure. You and Irene and two other young teachers roomed in the Hemingway house in Oak Park. At this time Ernest had not yet begun to publish. He was in Paris, living what his parents considered to be a dissolute life—if only he had gone into medicine or into the educational field! The Hemingways were proud; they wouldn't have dreamt of turning over their third floor to roomers if it weren't for the expense of their daughter Sunny's college education. Mrs. Hemingway informed you four young women that you were not to entertain your boyfriends in the house. You could have only two inches of hot water in the bath, and that only twice a week—this was all the Hemingways allowed themselves. Noise would not be tolerated after ten o'clock since Dr. Hemingway was a light sleeper.

The Hemingways seldom referred to their son. "Is he an artist?" you once asked. "He is a time waster," Dr. Hemingway replied.

A year later Ernest Hemingway published *The Sun Also Rises* and became famous, but by that time you and the others had moved to a more congenial apartment on the west side. This has always seemed to me a tragedy of timing, your near-brush with celebrity. I remember badgering you. "Couldn't you have lasted one more year?" "Oh, that drafty house," you said, "we had colds all the time, and Mary Organ came down with pneumonia."

You never read Hemingway. I think his reputation intimidated you. You read the *Reader's Digest* instead, and the *Ladies' Home Journal* and *Better Homes & Gardens*.

You quit teaching when you settled down with my father and began to raise a family. (Somewhere along the way you took the train to California to visit your sister, Edna, and this journey was always spoken about with epic resonance: *the time you traveled all the way to California, and by yourself.*)

After a year or two of marriage you had a miscarriage, a little boy. "I think of him as Jack," you told me once. "And I think of him every year on his birthday." Then came the twins, my brother and sister; eighteen months later I was born.

You went back to teach after the war, and I have no idea how you felt about that. (Teaching always seemed to be what you did, rather than what you wanted to do.) You ran a Girl Scout troop for years. You sewed for me and my sister, beautiful clothes, though you always told us not to tell anyone they'd been made at home.

On Saturday afternoons you played bridge with your school-teaching cronies; these bridge parties took place in a local restaurant called The Spinning Wheel, and always, before you drove off for the afternoon, you sat down in the living room and did your nails, spreading your hands out on a dish towel to dry. I never smell nail polish, even today, without thinking of the enchantment those afternoons must have offered—you were always rushing to get ready, you were excited, looking forward to being with old friends. One day you were on your way out the door when you noticed a water stain on the pink shantung dress you had just finished making. You started to cry a little, and then you cried harder and in the end you telephoned your regrets and went to bed.

This happened more often as you got older. It was your nerves, you said, or maybe someone else said it. You had bad nerves. Sometimes, when under stress, you broke out in hives. Once or twice you were hospitalized for reasons that were never revealed to me, but I think it must have been that old problem of nerves.

And I think, too, that you had an artist's side to you that was never fully expressed, though everyone admired your flower arrangements. Your centerpieces—you lived in the great age of centerpieces, the forties, the fifties—were cleverly concocted from whatever was at hand. You could slipcover a chair in an afternoon and always with an eye for texture and color. I used to watch you canning peaches on hot August afternoons, how you would turn each peach-half with a fork so that the curve, round as a baby's cheek, gleamed lustrous through the blue glass. Now why would anyone go to all that bother? I didn't understand as a child, but now I do.

You would be surprised, and also baffled, to know that your birthday, March 8, is the official date for International Women's Day. "International what day?" you would ask.

This event involves celebrations, and also protests, all over the world. Women march in the streets on this day, picket porn shops, storm their various legislatures, hold candlelight vigils for women who have been murdered. Not everyone, though, participates in this active and public way. Some of us have found other means to focus our thoughts. As one of my colleagues says, we also serve who only sit and write.

You died when I was thirty-five. I was married then, and a mother myself, but I had not yet begun to publish. I regret this terribly, not because I feel needy for your praise, but because you were uniquely enthusiastic about the awful poetry and stories I wrote as a child. One of these poems began:

> Spring is here, horray, horray.
> Come on, boys, come out to play.
> Put away your scarves and hats.
> Grab your baseballs and your bats.

On and on it went through the four seasons, yards of it. Never mind. You carefully copied down these execrable words, validating them with the nib of your pen, and thereby demonstrating your belief in the act of creativity, and, by extension, the notion that your own child could be a writer. I would have told you how important this was to me, but—and this is what hurts my heart—it's only recently I've been able to articulate it to myself. I've only just begun, twenty-five years after your death, to know who you are and how much I need to reach out and touch your hand.

Your loving

Carol

Enid Shomer

Enid Shomer and her mother, Minnie Steine, near their row house
Washington, D.C.; 1951

Enid Shomer was born in Washington, D.C., in 1944. Her stories and poems have appeared in *The New Yorker, The Atlantic, Paris Review,* and other magazines. Recent books are *This Close to the Earth* (poems; U of Arkansas) and *Imaginary Men,* winner of the Iowa Short Fiction Prize as well as the *Southern Review/LSU* Fiction award for the best first collection by an American. A new poetry book, *Black Drum,* is forthcoming from Arkansas.

Minnie Steine was born in Boston, Massachusetts, on April 15, 1913, and has lived most of her life in the Washington, D.C., area. She has three surviving children, eight grandchildren, and nine great-grandchildren.

Vigil Without Words

After a decade of strokes, then three days
of grand mal seizures, you lie gowned
in faded cornflowers, a frostbitten garden
surrounded by hospital white.
The bed absorbs your sobs. You want to leave
for home, ready to die at the same age

as your own mother. Hospitalized in her dotage
after breaking a hip on her birthday,
she bossed the nurses, conducted her leave-
taking not in jewels and silks, but gowned
like you, in the regalia of illness, white
plastic tubes draping the ruined garden

that birthed four. We paid our last regards
to a machine. Now I watch old age
divide your body into parts like white
light through a prism. You're aphasic, dazed.
My voice can't penetrate the gown
of silence you wear even while thrashing to leave.

Recently, I began to say *love, I love
you.* But it's only love the way a garden
might be called an absence of weeds instead of a gown
of flowers and fruit. Look at us: 82 and 50, ages

of silence between us! All those days
I cowered under the piano, wishing the row of white

teeth above me could bite. Father was like white
water, always raging, always leaving
us to play the horses. Even the day
he pawned your wedding ring and ruby ring-guards
you loved him more. I never said *hostage*
but paid your ransom with dread and prom gowns

prim enough to avert his wrath. He's gone.
Bad mother, I could say now, *coward*. You white-
washed his every cruelty. But we're beyond that age.
Your paralyzed hand curls in like a dried leaf.
The other presses my arm to your lips, soft gardenias.
I recognize the blank space you inhabit today

from the days whited-out in your closet, that garden
of shoes and gowns where I played at leaving, at aging
into the mother I never had. The mother I am for you now.

Enid

Louise Farmer Smith

***Virginia Storm Farmer with her daughter, Louise
Farmer Smith***

Aberdeen Maryland Proving Ground; early 1941

Louise Farmer Smith was born in 1940 and educated at the University of Oklahoma and Yale University. A 1995 PEN/New England Discovery and the 1996 winner of the *Antietam Review* Fiction Prize, she is currently working on a memoir of her mother. In 1997 her work will appear in the *Virginia Quarterly Review*.

Virginia Storm Farmer was born in Clinton, Oklahoma, in 1913, the daughter of a painter and a writer. She received a B.F.A. from the University of Oklahoma in 1936 with a major in drama and minor in violin. She presently lives with her husband in a military retirement community near Washington, D.C.

Supper Alone

Dear Mother,

Wasn't that a scene last night! When Daddy and I ran into each other at the elevator, I said, "Ah, the changing of the guard," because I thought he was leaving. Silly me. Except for a quick swim he had sat beside your bed all day—been there with your guests, been there for each of your phone conversations, been there when the nurses rolled off your surgical stocking to check your incision. I showed up early, thinking I would do your hair and help you dress for your debut in the dining room. I must have forgotten I would have to compete with my father for custody of the hairbrush.

You've always been elegantly groomed, a woman with her chin lifted who grew in beauty as she aged. You never went in for hair dye or face lifts, but you also never went out unless your heavy graying hair was professionally teased up or even lay in a hospital room without your big sapphire and diamond ring. I knew you'd want a little help.

Later going home in the car I laughed, but at the time I was furious. I tried to stand in front of you as though to shield your body from the eyes of your own husband. I couldn't get rid of him. You, bless your heart, were in a passive mode, as though the property we were vying over was just some lawn chair. And I'll be darned if he didn't follow us to the dining room, telling me all the way how to push your wheelchair. "Am I going to get to eat alone with Mother?" I asked. "That was the plan."

"Oh yes," he said. But that evidently meant that we could be alone only when the food was actually going into our mouths.

Finally, he left after getting us completely settled in the dining room. The young waitress, delighted to be serving so bright and responsive a patient as yourself, brought us the menu for people who could both feed themselves and chew. Before I could glance at the menu, you looked me in the eye and said, "Once you told me I taught you something too well. I want you to tell me what that was?"

Frankness is not a virtue in our family. I'll say here that it has been much confused with rudeness or selfishness. What gets a great deal of credit is sweetness. Of course, if an Oklahoma girl had her choice of characteristics, she would choose beauty, that being prized above all else. You won't admit it, but the first thing you tell me about any woman is whether or not she's beautiful: "Walter's new wife isn't beautiful, but she is sweet."

But frankness is a flaw. "Well," you'll say, "one always knows where Maude stands."—meaning Maude should keep her thoughts to herself.

All of this is to say that, close as you and I have been all my life, I have trouble telling you hard things. Even as a teenager I could never bring myself to criticize either you or Daddy. But last night I felt time running out. General Holden sat at the next table, his back still straight, his sad eyes gazing onto some distant battlefield as his wife brought each spoonful to his wobbly mouth. I must answer you while you still care about the meaning of answers. But more than urgency, I felt the great slamming demand of what your courage deserved.

A week ago you were rolled into the operating room for knee replacement—only a local anesthetic and enough Valium so that you could stand the sound of the saw. You had decided you would rather try this than sit down for the rest of your life. You have never shrunk from pain, and last night at the age of 81 you deserved to have your oldest child answer your question.

I look now at this old snapshot of us. Unsmiling, you hold the baby on your knee as though you will be the backdrop, and she will be the star. But it was you who were trained to be the actress. As a little girl you stood before huge crowds in western Oklahoma—the stunning little actress whose tender performance made the grown men cry.

You tried to train me to perform, patiently taught me all those "readings"—a performance style outmoded even when I was a child. You showed me how to do the flirting eyes, the haughty toss of the head, and I could imitate, but it was too late. By the time you took my dramatic education in hand, the fiery creature I'd been as a baby was stone cold.

My father, a young army officer with a degree in engineering, did not allow temper in a two-year-old girl. You stood by and let him hit me until I promised to be good. It was a test of wills. If I had not been so stubborn at two and three, I would not have been so inhibited at nineteen and twenty. But I know how you felt, standing by mumbling your pleas. Maybe you were afraid of him, but it was more than that. You were making choices.

Neither of you had been out of Oklahoma before he joined the army. Two greenhorns, you found yourselves living at Aberdeen Maryland Proving Ground, a gracious old post on the banks of the Chesapeake Bay. Every day was a test. Daddy, a second lieutenant in a bomb disposal unit, had a short temper and no social graces. He was attempting to make a career in the Old Army in which the rules of tradition and protocol were writ in stone. His career, his success, was as much a figment of your optimistic imagination as it was a result of his own hard work. You were the one who buoyed him up, advised him, read aloud to him from Dale Carnegie's *How to Win Friends and Influence People*. If he'd had a rough, uneducated wife, he never would have made it. You told him every day what a promising young officer he was. Therefore you could not be the one to stay his hand, to deny him the fundamental authority to discipline his own child. Besides, unruly children could hurt an officer's career. The stories of such things were rife in '42 and '43 as our nation stood tough in war.

Now you say no one knows who you really are, and I believe it, for you have pretended all your life. After you married, you never performed again except to give a tea or a coffee to celebrate someone else. A small-boned redhead with a degree in theater, you had enough social grace for a whole officers' club and sweetness beyond any old man's dreams. But you submerged yourself and harnessed your rich imagination to the cart of his career.

You lost your first baby. I was the second and for some reason was born believing that I was entrusted with the safekeeping of this bad marriage, believing that I alone was commissioned to bind together the oil and water of your personalities. As a little girl I ran back and forth between you, witnessing to the other's needs. I learned to soothe and insinuate, to help the dreamer dream and the engineer focus on the project. I learned to protect you from each other. And I counted as my own the daily failure, the wounds and disappointments. I sat in the backseat of the old blue Dodge, carried along in the wreck of the marriage like a little ambulance attendant pressed with urgency into service—to bind up the wounds, to placate each enemy, to make it all better.

But I could not fix the fact that he never measured up to your dream. In recompense I left off shielding you, and joined you in protecting him from your disappointment. I swallowed you whole. I didn't learn the flirty eyes and haughty toss of the head you tried to teach me. I learned your endurance, our little escapes, your artful lying to yourself and to your children. I learned to lie down in mute despair and let my *own* children grow up around me, to look into the eyes of my concerned little girl and *lie to her about her father.*

Perhaps it is a necessity of civilization that mothers lie to their daughters. "He does not wound me. See, I'm laughing."

This is the answer, what you taught me too well: that above all else, the woman must protect the man's authority, must collude with him in the daily smoothing and mending of this thin garment. See how *he* protects it with his fiery temper? We must also protect it with the balm of forgiveness and encouragement. We must be sweet.

You would think that sitting there in the backseat I would have learned a lot about marriage, learned how to avoid the kind of noiseless collision that does so much damage to the internal organs. But I was not capable of saying, *This will never happen to me; I won't be this kind of sucker.* I couldn't achieve any distance.

Last night you drank down every bitter thing I said and didn't flinch. I think you and I agree that the sweetest thing in the world is to be understood. But before we were able to finish, Daddy returned to take charge. "Daddy!" A rare complaint out of my mouth. He stepped back, blinking. "Oh, we're so glad you're back, sweetheart," you said to him before I could say another word. You didn't need to hush me. You did it long ago. The two of you. It was partly his hard hand, but it was the fundamental fact of your love for me that nailed it. For I knew how important I was to you, and if you sacrificed me to the cause of male authority, then that must be the ultimate cause.

He's old now. You're both old. I can't fix it. You taught me to protect him, and I will go on doing it, even though I learned from my own marriage that I was not valued for it. My compliance and selflessness and all my scurrying about to provide support only resulted in a poverty of self and in being a disappointment to my husband.

Remember the little beaded Indian moccasins you gave me? You told me an old squaw named Standing Bent made them. I ran all over the neighborhood in those things when I was three or four, traipsing up and down the sidewalk beating my little tom-tom. Phoebe and Larry did the same thing when they grew into them. Yet, not one bead ever came loose; the soles never wore through. Those moccasins are framed now in a shadow box on the wall of my study. They used to be a sad reminder of the fiery child I felt I'd been born to be. But not anymore. These days I look at the little moccasins and at the picture of you and me, and I know I have reclaimed my self. I was late. Got to admit that. My revolution came after the white streak in my hair, but it came.

"How did you do it, Weeze?" you whispered. My heart thumped. The waitress whisked away our plates. The empty table lay between us. "I never asked you," you pressed on, "but I watched you all those years when your kids were little, and what I saw in your face broke my heart. Then, somehow a few years ago things seemed to get better for you two."

"Yes," I said, "they did get better. My only regrets are about the way I failed my children."

"Those are my only regrets too, but—" You waited. Your eyes searched once across my face, but you didn't ask your question again. Even with the Tyrant Time hard on your heels, you allowed me leisure with my disclosure, for yours is a most disciplined heart.

We will talk again. I'll bring this old snapshot. You may not have seen it in awhile. Rest well and heal.

Love,

Weeze

Donna Baier Stein

Donna Baier (Stein) and her mother, Dorothy Baier,
on vacation
New Mexico; 1955

Donna Baier Stein was born January 5, 1951, in Kansas City, Missouri. She now lives in Lexington, Massachusetts, with her husband, son, and daughter. Her work has appeared in *Prairie Schooner, Kansas Quarterly, Florida Review, South Carolina Review,* and other journals. She has been a Bread Loaf Scholar and a Johns Hopkins Writing Seminars Fellow. She is at work on a novel and is also an award-winning direct mail copywriter with a book, *Write on Target!,* from NTC Publishing in 1996.

Dorothy Rathbun Baier was born April 24, 1923, in Kansas City, Missouri. She was a Navy WAVE during World War II and lived for a short time in Seattle, Washington, before returning to Kansas City, where she lived most of her life. She now lives in Wintergreen, Virginia, with her husband of 48 years in a beautiful mountain home she designed and decorated.

My Vocation

How to even start? Dear Mom, Mommy, Mother, Dorothy, Sister, Child? Truly beloved, target of all need and rage!

You and I are the two who most want to heal each other and are least able to do so. I remember you telling me the story of how I sleepwalked as a child, opening the refrigerator in the house on Fair Acres Drive, asking plaintively, "Mom, are you in there?" We've laughed about this for years, but do you understand how it's haunted me? I must have found you cold, Mom; I did find you cold, until finally, *finally,* I knew you were *your* mother's child.

We rarely spoke the truth. I think *that* is why I was so sad, so long, and why I became a writer. I had to say it somewhere.

Remember my story "Melissa in Book World," about the little girl going under water, into a world of books? You nurtured that mysterious, drowning love in me—in afternoons spent side by side, reading *The Pink Motel* and *Mrs. Piggle-Wiggle, Simple Spigott* and *The Merriweather Girls.* Remember writing our first mystery together? What a fast typist you were, and that, too, nurtured my love of words, of writing—seeing your nimble fingers fly over the keys, hearing the soft clicks of *t*'s and *n*'s and *o*'s and feeling bound with you as I never would with anyone again. Remember the summer reading programs you signed me up for in the old brick library in Burlington, Iowa, the stacks of books we brought home and the wonderful, wonderful smell that rose from their bindings?

Now, like Melissa before me, I've discovered this really *is* an ocean, a big ocean of life and love, and all of us swim through the unseen the best we can. Holding on to each other would be the best way, I think. You show me your wounds; I'll show you mine, and together we can push forward on a new boat, to new lands.

So bound up in you I was. I remember standing in the family room in the house in Apple Valley (you've built three houses now, each one better than the last). The wood-paneled walls; the cuffs of your crisp white shirt loose on your thin, strong wrists; that mysterious constellation of freckles above your knee. Even then, I was so big and ungainly next to you! You held a small white envelope, the one we'd been waiting for from Bryn Mawr, and inside it said, as those from Vassar and Wellesley had before, that I'd been accepted. I stood next to you, felt your excitement as my own. What if we'd known then what would follow? How hard it would be for me to leave your side to enter the world? For that was the problem, of course, that I hadn't separated from you, ever, and so my journey to the East was filled with struggle—the kind some kids take care of at sleep-away camp.

I couldn't live without you, hadn't even needed to until I left home for college. So many nights I cried, gulping, hysterical. To everyone's shame, I came home and oh, I remember you driving me in the car from the Kansas City Airport, hardly even speaking to me; you were so mad I had failed us.

Abandonment was the issue, and you did abandon me, disdainful of my hippie friends and always silently asking, whatever happened to my little star? A few years later, when I tried to kill myself, I killed you, too, of course. How it hurts to remember you sitting by my bed as I woke up after having my stomach pumped. I can imagine myself sitting there as the mother I now am and know how deep that pierced inside you, wounding you forever and numbing whole parts of yourself as if they'd been amputated.

Twenty years later, I think, Look, now, how far I've come—to a life of spirit, words, children, and other good fortunes—and, of course, I know that that, too, I owe in part to you. Your grit. In the office where I write, I finger the dry, torn pages of the little book, bound with brown yarn, that you wrote at age fourteen: "My Vocation, by Dorothy Rathbun." Inside, a photo of you in a white hat, a yellow blouse with a black anchor pointing to your heart, a calm but full smile, eyes gazing left to the future.

"A nurse can perform valuable services for others," you write, "reading to people who are sick and trying in other ways to entertain them, doing things that are of service to others when they are unable to do it themselves, fixing appetizing meals and attractive trays.

"But," you continue, "she must not let her nerves get the better of her; a nurse has to learn how to control them. She mustn't put too much faith in some of the advertisements that say 'Samco cigarettes quiet your nerves.'

"I am not very adept at meeting people," you admit, "I am not very calm in a crisis. But I am cooperative and accurate. I also possess willingness to learn. Honesty is one of the most necessary characteristics to have in any place in life. My weakest traits are those which have been least developed: courage, perseverance, and endurance."

Sometimes I think if you and I had found a way to cling together more—without drowning each other—we might both have been stronger women, going after what we wanted and getting it. Mama, *I love you*. I want you happy. I think Jonathan has been a joy to you, and I'm glad you found that love with my son.

Sometimes I think I learned from you to look for a distant man, some ghostly lover, but he's not there and never was. The men in our lives have brought some problems; their presence too often overshadows ours. They're so much more talkative, aggressive, *there* in the outer world than you or I. But oh, how they ground us. *Love* is here and paradise, too—do you know that now, too? You are so smart and so strong, Mama, and I am proud of you in so many ways.

Sometimes it is hard for you to give love, and it is hard for me, too—the body stops, pulls back in fear, even from hugs—but still we do the best we can. Even when we fail, I know love's there, flowing from you to me and back again.

I've told you recently that the times when you visit our busy, overstimulating household are some of the times I feel most happy in all that hubbub because I know someone is there watching out for me, caring about *me*. But have I ever been able to show you I am there for you as well?

At the writers' retreat I went to recently (you baby-sat so I could go), Beth and Sally led us in a guided imagery one morning that went like this:

Imagine you are a little girl, age four, cooking in the kitchen with your mother. She tells you she has to go into her bedroom for just a moment and will be right back. You follow her and look through the keyhole of her closed door. She is standing at her dresser, taking out a cigar box that is filled with the important things of her life. What do you do?

And I wrote:

I see you sitting on the bed, and you look calm and happy. The cigar box is next to you, and what's in it? Little treasures, but for Mama, what ever would they be? I know you're glad I'm out here, waiting for you, and that there's something cooking on the stove. Your dress is full and belted; you're neat and tidy and pretty. The bedspread is unwrinkled except where your small form makes an impression. What's on the bedspread? The things from the box don't make any dents; they're very small and light. One is a picture of me in a gold frame. You look at this and kiss it, keep it tight in your hand. Another is a red, red jewel that means something to you from your past, but I don't know what. There must be something blue in there, too, but I can't see it. Why, why not? What *are* your treasures? Why do you keep the door closed anyway? Why won't you let me into the room with you to sit on the bed? Because you're afraid I'll mess it up. I'd rather be with you than looking through this keyhole. I knock, knock, knock, knock. "Mama, let me in." You get up in your full-skirted dress and walk to the door and open it. I don't know what to say, but you take me by the hand silently and lift me up to sit on your bed. "Look, Donna, see what I have." And you show me the photo of me in a frame and the red jewel and say, "This I got from my father." And you finger it and hold it tight in your palm. What else, Mama, what else? I look around on the bed; there are other little things—there is a key. And then I'm blocked, I don't know. It's like I'm blind, and so I close my eyes and say, "Put these in my hand, and tell me what they are." You kiss my forehead and my closed eyes. You put something in my hand, and it's cold and slightly heavy, and you say it's a charm, a medal you won in school. And here is a silver tube of bright red lipstick and a small tortoiseshell comb and a little book, the yarn-bound one from the room where I write. "I know there will always be something I do not know." And there's a star and a piece of blue felt. We look at all these things, and then you put them back in the cigar box and put that in your dresser drawer. And then we go cook.

Here is my wish: That we cook and cling together for many years to come, take what we need from that damn cold refrigerator and warm it up. That we feel God's breath on the hair of our arms, which we will wrap so tightly around each other that this time, this time, we will never, ever let go.

Love,

Donna

Susan Straight

Susan Straight and her mother, Gabrielle Watson
Riverside, California; 1995

Susan Straight was born in 1960 in Riverside, California, where she still lives with her husband and three daughters, a few miles from her mother. She has published four novels—*Aquaboogie* (Milkweed Editions, 1990), *I Been in Sorrow's Kitchen and Licked Out All the Pots* (Hyperion, 1992), *Blacker Than a Thousand Midnights* (Hyperion, 1994), and her most recent novel, *The Gettin' Place,* published in June 1996 by Hyperion. She has also published a children's book, *Bear E. Bear* (Hyperion Books for Children, 1995).

Gabrielle Watson was born in 1934 in France, of Swiss parents who moved back to Switzerland a year later. She immigrated to Canada in 1950, and then to California in 1954. She raised three children, numerous foster children, and has been employed in banking and finance for many years. She has six granddaughters whom she loves dearly.

Not Skin Deep—Heart Deep

Dear Mom,

It wasn't ugly. I don't recall you using that word. The way I remember it, you used to say, "Well, you're plain, and you're never going to make a living on your looks. You might not even get married, and that's why you'd better learn to use your brain . . ."

Had your stepmother told you that? I know your mother died when you were ten and lived in Switzerland, and the woman your father married treated you terribly. She must have told you much worse. We're both small, sturdy, and tough.

I know I was homely, back when I was thirteen or so and you gave me this talk. Remember my blue cat-eye glasses? And the gap between my front teeth, along with the high-placed fang I had instead of a left incisor? Remember when I was the shortest, skinniest girl in every class? And my legs—they were painfully thin and slightly bowed until the car accident broke my left thighbone and the traction straightened it. Then they didn't match—I had one leg curved and one spindle straight. Of course, you were right. I wasn't going to catch any modeling jobs or men looking like I did.

I had plenty of beautiful friends, girls I watched at school.

They made cheerleader, leaned against the eucalyptus tree trunks with guys, wore hip-hugger jeans with their curves swelling out and baby-doll tops with scoop necklines showing pillow-soft shadows. The football players, who were the best for status, always went for them.

But I liked watching the game of football as much as the guys, because during all those weeks of traction, I'd combined reading, studying, and watching sports on that little hospital TV, waiting for your daily visits. Remember? We'd already had the plain talk, I think. Because I decided I wanted to be a sportswriter instead of a cheerleader. With my face and legs and glasses, I'd never get a cheerleader spot anyway. Use my brain, right? I started observing the plays, keeping stats on the sidelines, and I practiced writing sports stories at home, in secret.

You thought being a female sportscaster was a great idea, because there weren't many and it was a professional-type career. You'd emigrated from Switzerland to Canada and then America, barely getting to finish high school, having to work, and then when my father left, having to work and leave babies with sitters. But you loved sports—remember, you always told me you'd learned your American English from listening to Vin Scully and Howard Cosell broadcasts?

When my pretty friends got married or had babies or partied, I went to college and became a sportswriter. I still thought I was plain; I still do, even though Dwayne has been telling me for almost fifteen years that I look okay to him. And then I moved from sportswriting to stories and novels.

Now, the "ugly" story is my favorite tale to tell on you when I give a reading. You know that, because you came to the author festival in Long Beach to hold Delphine when she was four months old. You didn't hear what I said about you and the talk you'd given me, because you were outside walking with her. But after the presentation, a "plain" woman, meaning she was un-adorned, un-madeup, unpermed, approached us. She said, "Is this your mother? The one who called you plain and said you'd better use your brain?"

I nodded, embarrassed. You looked at me, embarrassed, too.

She said, "My mother told me something similar. And I'm a chemist."

We were about to take this further, to tell each other why we were glad we'd been told our brains were far more important investments than our faces, but several other women crowded around to say that was an awful thing to tell a daughter, something certain to have ruined her self-esteem and confidence and femininity. But that's not what the words were intended to do. The words built me up, in an unusual way.

Hey, I thought, but I couldn't tell them, I've got a job. I've still got that brain. I'm not on the street. And that's because of my mother's words, in a way.

Because so many of my lovely friends you remember from when I was in high school, the ones who traded on their looks and didn't go to class and laughed at brainiacs like me, who went for guys who had good looks, too, or who were dangerous and wild and infamous, those friends are on the street. I see them almost every day, Mom. One has no teeth. She's a prostitute. And teeth get in the way of what she has to do now for a living. Someone knocked them out for her. Remember D, whom I've known since kindergarten, who wore glasses like me, and who took them off a few years later so she could be beautiful even though she couldn't see? She lived in the barn on Jeff's land last year, Mom. I didn't tell you. She's lost her three kids because she does speed; she trades herself for drugs.

I have three kids now, too. Three girls you love. Three daughters who are so startlingly lovely that they get modeling offers every week, along with compliments and stares and comments from total strangers on their gorgeous faces and eyes and skin and hair. No one ever calls them plain. But I work on their reading and writing every day, with your help, Mom. And whenever anyone says to them, "Look at how beautiful they are!" their father and I always add, "And they're smart."

Sometimes at night, I whisper to them that looks fade away and brains never do. I let them type on this typewriter. The little blue one you bought me for high school graduation, the Smith-Corona the exact shade of blue as my cat-eye glasses, finally wore out. But I keep it nearby now, and I never forget what you taught me.

With love,

Susan

Joan Swift

Joan Swift and her mother, Lorraine Anderson Angevine—first day of school
Rochester, New York; September 8, 1931

Joan Swift was born November 2, 1926, in Rochester, New York, and now lives in Edmonds, Washington. Her most recent book of poems, *The Dark Path of Our Names*, won a Washington State Governor's Award. She is the recipient of three National Endowment for the Arts Creative Writing Fellowships (1982, 1990, 1995), grants from the Ingram Merrill Foundation and the Washington State Arts Commission, as well as a Pushcart Prize. For decades during her adult life she was accustomed to writing to her mother each week. "Letter from Hilo" describes, in part, an automobile accident in Hawaii four years after her mother died.

Lorraine Angevine was born Laurina M. Anderson on May 14, 1904, in Antrim, Pennsylvania, the fourth and youngest daughter of Swedish immigrant parents. She later moved to Rochester, New York, married, had one child, and divorced to raise her child alone during the Depression. Still single, she died in Rochester in 1991.

Letter from Hilo

Dust among stars, dear Mother, blind space
without words when words were the typed story
of my life, here's my last epistolary
news. Remember the two of us
at the black caldera, its precipice
and charred ohia trees in a slurry
of lava below, then the hard sea?
Of course you can't. It's your darkness
I drive through trying to find my way back.
Someplace on this road we saw orchids
growing from cinders the volcano
left behind: pale lavender like a flock
of imagined birds here where my car skids
and the pavement slips away and then *no*.

You always said I was like my father so
I've wondered my whole life what that meant.
He threw me down the stairs. Was I violent?

I tongued a small cake made from tar-dough
melting in the street and with a bellow
through whiskey breath he smacked me. A temperament
like his might be inherited. I can't
forget your scared eyes and the two-pronged blow
near the hat tree where he cornered you. But
once in his Ford roadster, winter twilight
and the rumbleseat shut, you don't know how
ice spun us in a circle or of the vow
I made to keep secret our hi-jinks whirl.
It was fun. I was only a little girl.

There is a gorge above the hospital
where the Wailuku River slithers green
through rocks palmed smooth by the devotion
of water to a calm clear pool.
Nobody else did but I swam the crawl
all the way up under African
tulip trees and mango, crimson
petals above me slow and aerial.
You worried I would drown. A cousin did.
You imagined a family curse. Your sleep
pulled quick currents over my blank stare.
So I never wrote you about my slide
down the river's stony curves and the deep
plunge. Strange it was not water but a car.

In the dark under the dense clouds somewhere
alone dreaming the water buffalo dream
over and over again the same
ghost dream, the last Royal Bengal tiger
left in the Panaewa Zoo, feather
of peacock, bray of burro around him,
sadness or sun, sway of hala and palm—
is that extinction what I'm looking for?
The chain-link fence, the electric wire,
small paths in drizzle, tortoises, a pygmy
hippo, the turnstile box—*we are in dire
need*. Mother, it was nineteen thirty-three

when you divorced him—screech of a tire—
called yourself free.

If you had an address. If I could see.
My vanished lens invents anthuriums,
maile, plumeria, orchids, hau blossoms,
a whole tropical botany
swirling where the doctor's shirtsleeve should be.
They're like the flowers whose sway your arms
imitated as I watched from our room's
bed, you trying a hula from a movie.
He took you no place, jealous that your blonde
hair, teased and ratted to a summer cloud's
gift for changing light, might unhinge a crowd's
gaze. That's why I brought you to the black sand
of Kapoho, the last jungle, the sea's
ten thousand thousand glittering eyes.

In the gloom a woman—Japanese
I think—so far off. I'm calling, calling.
Her skirt is busy reading her legs' long
Braille under the flow of wherever she's
going. Gravel, asphalt, each of the trees
a lava-sooted 'alala wing
come down from the mountain the way a thing
near-extinct can be near. A man shadows
behind her there and then not there like points
of a star clouds race to unilluminate.
And no one hears. He glides to her once,
they link their arms, they drift, they separate.
It could be some kind of veiled dance
of yours and his. I slump in the car, wait.

Unconsciousness. Morning shines on my hurt—
eye, knee, wrist, rib—to show me a flaw
like his after all. Nothing I say will draw
you from your star's chaste orbit,
untangle the dust from your soul to right

me. I remember the clench of your jaw
once when he brought me back, eyes swollen, raw
from sobbing. If you could take me like that
now—. Past the window a courtyard, a gulch
full of hapu'u fern you'd lose your face
in if you were here. Did I want so much
to contain the life you missed? Look. Across
the ravine sways a purple-berried branch
of sorrow. It's for both of us.

Joan

Shari Thurer

Lilly Lehrer and her daughter, Shari Thurer
New York; c. 1947

Shari Thurer was born on October 9, 1947, in New York, and currently resides with her husband and daughter in Boston. She is author of *The Myths of Motherhood: How Culture Reinvents the Good Mother* (Penguin, 1995). A practicing psychologist, she is also a professor at Boston University.

Lilly Lehrer was born on April 28, 1922, in New York, where she spent most of her life. She is a retired secretary who currently resides with her husband of fifty years in Florida. Besides Shari, Lilly had two other children, both boys, one of whom died in childhood. Her son, Gary, lives in New York.

The Impossibly Good Mother

SUMMER 1995

Dear Mom,

People tell me that it's hard to believe that we're mother and daughter—we're so different. You have your feet planted firmly in the ground; mine reside permanently in the air (along with my head in the clouds). You buy low-maintenance polyester and wear sensible shoes. I disdain unnatural fibers and insistently clomp around on clunky heels. You love details, schedules, itineraries. I wish they'd go away. You regard modesty as a virtue; I'm an irrepressible exhibitionist. You mind your own business. I'm in the business of minding others'—I'm a psychologist, after all.

Yet, scratch the surface, and we're so much alike. Both of us are flustered by machines. We're resourceless in the kitchen, neat to a fault, trustworthy. Nothing makes us happier than spending a day shopping for bargains, searching for the perfect accessory to match some garment or other. We're crazily obsessed with matching. But at bottom, I'm driven and achievement-oriented, while you're content with your lot . . . though you always tolerated my ambition.

It never occurred to me that mothers could be jealous, or

needy, or mean-spirited, or competitive with their daughters. It was never part of my experience. You were always so nice! I was flabbergasted to hear from patients of mothers who sabotaged their daughters' vocational success, who envied their youth or opportunities, who clung and manipulated. I never knew mothers could come in malevolent form. It was my reading about selfish, grasping mothers in books like *Portnoy's Complaint* or *Sons and Lovers* that enabled me to appropriately empathize with my patients.

You always make me feel loved and important to you, but when the time came, you were able to let go. I recall once, when you were en route to a visit with me, the flight crew announced that your airplane might have to crash-land. Though the crash landing never happened, I asked you later what had gone through your mind. You replied, "I thought how you'd never forgive yourself for inviting me." Because of you I assumed mothers were born self-sacrificing.

Of course, your niceness isn't entirely a blessing. You're a hard act to follow. It was precisely your lack of conflict about mothering that made me, with all my ambivalence, feel so abnormal, so guilty. How could one be both ambitious (like me) and a good mother (like you)? Surely I would damage my child! It was that very guilt that fueled my desire to research the nature of good mothering, out of which I wrote *The Myths of Motherhood: How Culture Reinvents the Good Mother.* I found, to my relief, that there are many effective ways to parent, and that maternal ambivalence is quite ordinary, and not necessarily deleterious to one's offspring. Whew!

Sure, there were times I wished you were more like Simone de Beauvoir or Jackie Kennedy. (My own daughter once lamented that I was not Diana Ross!) Conflict is inevitable between mothers and daughters, I guess. But in the end, I regard myself as tremendously fortunate to have you as my mother, with your remarkable capacity to both treasure my visits, and overlook the times I don't find time to visit. No one else asks so little of me—and gives so much.

Love Always,

Shari

Alma Luz Villanueva

**Alma Luz Villanueva
with her grandmother,
Jesus Villanueva**
San Francisco,
California; 1949

**Lydia Villanueva,
birth mother of
Alma Luz Villanueva**
Tucson, Arizona; 1918

Alma Luz Villanueva was born October 4, 1944, in California. Author of novels *The Ultraviolet Sky* (Doubleday, American Book Award, 1989), *Naked Ladies* (Bilingual Press, PEN Oakland Award, 1994), and *Planet*, poetry (Bilingual Press, Latin American Writers Institute Award, 1994), and *Weeping Woman: La Llorona and Other Stories* (Bilingual Press).

Jesus Villanueva was born on June 11, 1886, in Sonora, Mexico. Trained by her mother to be a dreamer and healer, she was a full-blood Yaqui Indian. She married Pablo Villanueva, a poet and Baptist minister, in 1906 and crossed the border into Tucson, Arizona, when she was thirty, giving birth to Lydia, my womb-mother. She left the body in 1955.

Madre de Mi Alma

"Love is not mere impulse;
it must contain truth,
which is law."
—RABINDRANATH TAGORE

Mamacita, Little Mother, Mother of my soul
who named me Alma, Soul:

Querida Mamacita,

I write you, formally, nearly forty years after your soul, your spirit, left your body. You see (of course you see), you took your soul, but left a generous piece of your spirit with me. At eleven it was too much to bear, to understand. To accept. That I had to let you go, physically. That your spirit never left me, completely. That your strength continued to live in me, and that you were my mother, as well as my mother's mother.

You know how stubborn I was. How I dressed in a bright red blouse for your funeral. How I refused to cry. How I threw a single red rose onto your casket as they lowered it. You also know how much I needed you. You returned that night, sitting at the foot of the couch I slept on. You were entirely made of a glowing white light that comforted me once my terror subsided. You stayed with me for the longest time, and when I finally fell asleep, struggling not to, when I woke you were gone. Your light. Your soul.

You know my life wasn't easy. I had three children at fifteen, seventeen, and twenty-one, and during those years of strict survival all the words welled up in me. Then finally, in the safety of a farm in a town called Sebastopol (away from my childhood memories of you and San Francisco), I wrote this poem.

TO JESUS VILLANUEVA,
   WITH LOVE

My first vivid memory of you
Mamacita,
we made tortillas together—
yours perfect and round,
mine irregular and fat—
we laughed
and named them: oso, pajarito, gatito.
My last vivid memory of you
     (except for the very last
     sacred memory
     I won't share)
Mamacita,
beautiful, thick, long, gray hair,
the eyes gone sad
with flashes of fury
when they wouldn't let you
have your chilies, your onions, your peppers.
     —What do these damned gringos know of *my* stomach?—*
So when I came to comb
your beautiful, thick, long, gray hair
as we sat for hours
     (it soothed you
     my hand
     on your hair)
I brought you your chilies, your onions, your peppers.
And they'd always catch you
because you'd forget

*Translated from Spanish; she refused (and pretended not to be able) to speak English.

and leave it lying open.
They'd scold you like a child,
and you'd be embarrassed like a child,
silent, repentant, angry,
and secretly waiting for my visit, the new supplies.
We always laughed at our secret—
we always laughed
        you and I.

You never could understand
the rules
at clinics, welfare offices, schools
any of it.
I did.
You lie. You push. You get.
I learned to do all this by
the third clinic day of being persistently
sent to the back of the line by 5 in the afternoon
and being so close to done by 8 in the morning.
So my lungs grew larger
and voice got louder

and a doctor consented
to see an old lady,
and the welfare would give you the money
and the landlady would remember to spray for cockroaches
and the store would not charge the food till the check came
and the bank might cash the check if I got the nice man this time
and I'd order hot dogs and Cokes for us
at the old "Crystal Palace" on Market Street
and we'd sit on the steps
by the rear exit, laughing
        you and I.

Mamacita,
I remember you proudly at Christmas
time, church at midnight services:
you wear a plain black dress,
your hair down, straight and silver,
        (you always wore it up
        tied in a kerchief,
        knotted to the side)

your face shining, your eyes clear,
your vision intact.
You play Death.
You are Death.
You quote long stanzas from a poem I've long
forgotten;
even fitful babies hush
such is the power of your voice.
Your presence
fill us all.
The special, pregnant
silence.
Eyes and hands lifted up
imploringly and passionately,
the vision and the power
offered to us.
Eyes and hands cast down,
it flows through you
to us,
a gift.

Your daughter, my aunt,
told me a story I'd never
heard before:
      You were leaving Mexico
      with your husband and two
      older children, pregnant
      with my mother.
      The U.S. customs officer
      undid everything you so
      preciously packed, you
      took a sack, blew it up,
      and when he asked about
      the contents of the sack,
      well, you popped it with
      your hand and shouted
      MEXICAN AIR!*

aiiiiiiiiii Mamacita, Jesus,
I won't forget my visions and reality.

To lie, to push, to get,
just isn't
enough.

I didn't know it, but it was my way back to you. To your voice, the voice of death/transformation. The voice of poetry, and your spirit crouched, waiting, always waiting, in my memory.

And I remembered *dreaming* as you taught me. I remembered poetry as you taught me. I remembered joy, food, laughter, anger as you taught me. Now, nearly fifty-one, I remember you were my true mother. Mother of my soul.

Did you know your first great-grandchild, my daughter Antoinette, was born on your birthday, June eleventh, when I was fifteen? Do you know she's a healer, an R.N., the way you were a healer in Mexico, and for a while in Los Angeles until your minister husband began to worry about the whispers of *bruja*. You stopped healing others with your herbs and flowers. But I remember how you healed me as a child. I remember your hands, your eyes.

I had three more children, three sons (Ed, thirty-three, and Marc, twenty-nine, beautiful men), and the youngest, Jules (who's fourteen), has the eyes of your people, the Yaquis, (dark, gentle deer eyes; dark, fierce eagle eyes). His father is Yaqui/Spanish, and of course you know all of this, but it seems I must write this here on paper; so blank it looks lonely until I fill each line with what lives in my daily mind, my heart's desires, my dreaming body, my ancient soul: memory.

And your great-great-granddaughter, Ashley (who's fourteen), has eyes the color of the sea at noon when it's most tempting (how you loved the sea). Your great-great-grandson, Cody (who's eleven), has eyes the color of the sky in summer when the sun is closest to the Earth. Now, they call me Mamacita.

All of this I offer you, if it's mine to offer. And if all these words, and people who I love, aren't mine to offer, then know I'm grateful for this moment. That I exist. To wonder what is mine, and what isn't. Who I love and don't love. Who I forgive, and don't forgive.

The truth.

Your daughters: my birth mother, Lydia; my aunt, Ruth. The women who were left to me. Certainly there were other women who sustained me, or I wouldn't have survived intact. But I speak here of family.

My birth mother, Lydia, the light-skinned one with European features (the Spanish ancestor from her father). My aunt, Ruth, the dark-skinned one with Yaqui features (from you and your mother's mother). I remember Lydia crossing the street when she saw us; you, an old Indian with a tiresome child. I remember Ruth's stories: "Lydia was the prettiest, the most talented, so our father chose her to play for Sunday services: Lydia was the better pianist, she was his favorite: She traveled with him for revivals, I stayed home with mi mamá: She tried to get rid of you, but the doctor just gave her aspirin, and here you are."

Your beloved daughters, Lydia and Ruth.

CHANCE

Yes, I've told you,
"You are a royal fucking pain in the ass,"

and you are my mother. I do not
forgive you for leaving me at

the Emporium in downtown San Francisco
when I was five. I do not

forgive you for betraying
my seven-year-old trust when we lay

in bed talking after I caught
my molester: "It's your fault he's gone

to jail, you know." The years when
you neglected my existence or tortured

me to rage (the time I broke the
window with my hand, the tiny scar

on my right hand baby finger still
hurts if it's bumped just so). Or when

you shook my daughter's crib violently
as she cried for her mother at seven days

old, and I slept through it at fifteen;
I woke up and saw you, screaming, "SHUT UP!

SHUT UP!" I leapt to my feet,
grabbed you, threw you against

the wall and yelled, "If you ever
touch my baby again, I'll kill

you!" And then you tried to give
her away—I escaped

to a flea-trap over a bar with
loud music, with a friend; she

and I (15 and 16) and my daughter
slept in the same bed. The time

you left me with a ten-year-old
friend and her mother, who didn't have

much to eat, and you didn't return
for days, and they took me to

the place where unloved children
are taken to be among strangers

(and as, when you left me at five,
I took care of myself and called

your sister, the one who lives in
a trance, while you dance,

while you dance. I have done
both: the trance of the unloved:

the dance of the unloved).
I could go on and on and on—

the time you refused me food,
"I fucked him for this food!"

I could go on and on and on—
but I won't. Well, what is

it? I ask myself. What is it
about this woman that moves

me? (At 78 you refuse self-pity—
you walk through the mall

making friends with all the sales
people—they know you by name;

you rise for work at 4 A.M. to shower,
apply your makeup, dress in bright

colors that tend to clash; your retirement
party from full-time work will be

celebrated on the Cinco de Mayo, Mexican
Independence Day, birthplace of your

mother and father, your people; you,
with your beautiful, light skin, who

always avoided the sun, your blonde
wig—at 78 you don't look your age—

privately, you tell me, "It's my
Indian blood, the Yaqui de mi

Mamá.") A story, a memory stored
in my body, in my childhood cells:

When I was three you refused
to let my father's racist family keep

me; when you carried me on a hot Louisiana
dirt road; when your mother's voice rang

true in your mind: "Bring the child home
to her people." And you did.

And so, at the very beginning of my life, then,
and the end of yours, now,

I'll take this chance (no trance,
no dance) and say I love

you, knowing full well who you are,
and who I am.

Mamacita, I know it wasn't easy for you. Your minister husband, Pablo, died when you were only forty-one, leaving you
stranded (financially, culturally, emotionally, spiritually) in the
United States. You came here at thirty, your mother's teachings
ringing in your head: "Heal, heal." She was also a healer, and

then you stopped. And you never married again. You were sure
your suitors wanted your almost grown daughters. And the
death of your grown son, Reuben (he could play entire composi-
tions on his violin from memory), broke your heart. Ruth (the
one with the memory) told me he was banned from the house
for cross-dressing, and that he died from pneumonia, the streets.
I think you never forgave Pablo for that.

And you refused to go home. To Mexico. Too much pride.
Too many conflicting loyalties. Too strong for your own good (I
remember your outrageous sense of humor, how you danced to
the *corridos* on the radio, lifting your skirt above your knees,
laughing; how you sang as you cooked and ironed).

Mamacita, I remember how happy you were when I told you
I'd flown in my dreams. And when I had falling dreams you told
me to spread my wings and use them. You also told me to not
talk about my dreams to anyone else, because people "over here"
think you're *locita*. (I wonder, now, if Pablo forbade you to teach
your children *dreaming*.)

Mamacita, I am grateful for this moment. That I exist. To wonder. To dream.

The truth.

DAZZLED

I sit next to a daring
beautiful trapeze artist—
we watch as the others
fly over our heads—

these women are strong,
their arms supple with muscle—
every inch of them ready
for flight—and they

fly, they fly over our
heads wearing rainbows,
millions of suns that shine
and dazzle—she waits

her turn, sullen, anxious—
she longs for her place where

millions of suns shine
day and night, night and day—

there is nothing else she
wants more, I see, I feel,
I know—I ask cautiously,
"When did you first want

to fly?" "It's none of
your business," she mutters
and turns her back
to me. I watch

the women fly over
our heads—I could
watch them forever and
ever, and I know this woman

next to me is Lydia, my
mother, dazzled by the millions
of suns, her longing
to fly. She does

not see me. She does
not hear me. She waits
her turn, forever.
And ever.
                    From a dream

    (To Lydia, my mother, awake)

I stand to leave.
I'm tired of waiting for
the right words to set
you free to fly, to turn
and answer my question,
to see the one miraculous
sun that rises, daily.
It is hard to love the night,
but I do, I do,
as much as the light
of a million
suns.

This dream allowed me to see Lydia's great beauty, longing, spirit. She could've composed her own music (she won a professional prize for composing music for the piano when she was seventeen, the year her father died). She could've flown through the air with greatest of ease, after the discipline of practice and hard work (what died with her father?). She could've been dazzling.

When she turns to me, in the dream, and says, "It's none of your business," I realize it really isn't. Any of my business. It has nothing to do with me as a person. Or as a daughter. I just can't compete with a million suns, no matter how hard I try (publishing books, winning prizes). I am unable to fulfill her expectations (I don't write for TV, a movie hasn't been made of my novels, my novels aren't in the checkout aisle of the supermarket . . . If it were so, would it matter?). She simply doesn't see me. Her beautiful face is turned up, always gazing up, dazzled by the dreams she failed to dream, and live by the hardest of work. Her own dark soul.

In spite of the blonde wig, her Irish last name (from her brutal second husband), her perfect English—she was your beloved Mexican daughter. She crossed the border from Sonora, Mexico, to the United States within the sweet darkness of your womb. She entered this country between your legs. Yes, she was your beloved Mexican daughter. I see the beautiful two-year-old girl in the photograph clutching her bouquet of silk roses. She could be my daughter, but she was yours.

You see, Mamacita, I never knew your beloved Mexican daughter. I never knew the darkness of her soul, and she never knew mine. (She took the ruby earrings from your dead ears—meant for me—and paid her son's baby-sitter with them, leaving me nothing tangible to hold; but the soul, you always knew, is not tangible.)

Mamacita, the night of your funeral when I awoke to darkness, after the comfort of your glowing light-filled presence, I followed you into darkness, dreams. Into the landscape of my soul. I am grateful for this moment. That I exist. To wonder. To dream. To know the truth. And to be able to say it, nearly forty years later.

My soul to yours.

Beyond all the women who have mothered me (and I them):

Lydia, Ruth, Demerce, Judy, Faith, Cathy, Irma, Anna, Erica, Gondola, Leslie, Linda, Adele, Laura, Ril, Janine, Little Wolf, Carmen, Antoinette . . .

You were my mother.

Amor, siempre jamás,
(Love, forever and ever,)

Joyce Wadler

Mildred Wadler and her daughter, Joyce
RAFAEL TORRES, ORMOND BEACH, FLORIDA

Joyce Wadler is a New York City journalist and screenwriter, the author of *My Breast* and *Liaison: The M. Butterfly Affair*. If you know a guy, write her.

Mildred Wadler grew up in the Catskills and "from the age of ten knew I had to get out of there." She succeeded after her three children were grown, now lives in Daytona Beach, Florida, and travels extensively.

My Hang-up

Here I am on the telephone, long-distance, with Ma. My dime, New York–Daytona Beach, but hey, I'm forty-four, I can handle it. I can handle conversation with Ma, too. Though who would call this a conversation I don't know. A twenty-minute monologue on her visit to Michigan, with one of her five million suitors, where his children couldn't have been nicer and everybody loved her. Wherever she goes, Ma says, people love her.

"I don't know why it is people think I'm so wonderful," says Ma, in a tone you might believe if you were dead. "*I* don't know if I'm so wonderful, what I think is, most people lead very uninteresting lives."

I got a theory on this if I could get a word in, but getting a word in takes muscle and sometimes it's easier to just let the words go by.

But what the hell, maybe I'll take a shot:

"I've been meaning to tell you, Ma, there's this thing called conversation. You talk, then after a while, you give the other guy a chance to talk—"

"—No kidding, how about that?" Ma interrupts.

"Then, here comes the money part, you listen," I say.

"Haha, you're so funny," laughs Ma. "How come you're not writing for television? Some nice little animal stories. Everybody likes an animal story. Because what they have now is *drek*. A hundred and three channels, not one thing to watch. Which reminds me. Did I tell you how much weight I lost this week—"

I hang in.

"—So what I'm gonna do now is tell you about my life," I say,

468

"and you're gonna listen. If this is too much to handle at once, you can just pretend to listen."

"I gotta *pish*," says Ma.

"How come you suddenly gotta *pish* when it comes to my life?" I say.

Ma laughs.

"Why is that?" she says. "Okay, I'm happy to talk about your life. Next time. Now I gotta go to the bathroom."

Ma, I've been meaning to tell you, I'm serious here. Ma, I've been meaning to tell you, growing up with the world's reigning power-talker may have made me a good reporter, but it's getting on my nerves. Ma, I've been meaning to tell you, you're a colorful personality, but you soak the oxygen out of the room, and that person lying on the floor gasping for air is your kid.

The world, (Ma), may be a stage, (Ma), but that does not mean everyone in it exists to be your audience. Especially when they have paid ninety bucks a pop to see the real thing. That moment in *Traviata* after Germont sings God gave him a daughter, *pura siccome un angelo,* and the house goes silent because their collective hearts have been torn out, that's the *singer's* moment, Ma. It is not intended for you to announce "Some voice" or "That Joe Green can sure write 'em." They're trying for a *mood* up there, Ma, the moment is fragile, much like myself.

"Ma, I've been meaning to tell you, the market for forty-something writers in L.A. is not so hot . . ."

"Ma, I've been meaning to tell you, Ma I've been meaning to tell you, early menopause seems to be changing my body . . ."

"Ma, I've been meaning to tell you, I haven't had a serious boyfriend for three years and I'm really worried I'll never get married. I mean, really worried."

"Marriage isn't for everybody," Ma says. "I miss your father, but there's a certain satisfaction to being on your own. I go when I want to go, I stay when I want to stay—"

A deep breath, here, concentration, and a great push. VROOOOOOMMM!!! Wadler the Younger charges into the airwaves at warp speed. And up ahead, can it really be? YES! A space of small, but finite, verbal opportunity, and I am about to seize it.

"—That's you, Ma," I say. "What we're talking about is me.

Y'know, there was a cord, the doctor cut it, and you got a new, independent life-form: your daughter."

"Y'know, somehow I don't think of you as my daughter," says Ma. "I think of you more as a sister. Why is that, do you think? I don't know what this thing is everybody has with marriage. I can't walk down the street here with some man without everybody in the synagogue *hocking* me: What's going on? Are we serious? Are we gonna get married? You know what I tell 'em? What do I need marriage? Some old *kocker* lying like a lump on the couch? Whose idea of a big event is going to the toilet? No, thank you."

"Me, Ma, that's what this discussion is about," I say. "The one who does not want to be sitting home alone New Year's Eve in the Year 2000. The one who would like to get laid one more time before she dies."

"I hear Boca Raton has the fastest growing Jewish population in the country," Ma says. "If you're really serious about this, you should go to Boca."

"I don't know a single person in Boca Raton," I say.

"Then there are services, Friday night, which you repeatedly refuse to go to—"

"I'm an agno—" I say.

"Join a radio club. It's all men in my club, and I'm talking nice men. I had to put up a satellite dish, they're falling all over themselves to help me. They love me, those men. They would cut off an arm for me."

"We've been over this, Ma," I say. "You're the one who likes shortwave radio. The synagogue, the radio, they're all things you're involved in."

It doesn't matter. The verbal opportunity is passed. She's over-powered me again.

"You've got to go where the men go," Ma is saying. "I've been telling you for years. Your problem is, you don't listen."

Joyce

Constance Warloe

***Constance (Bower) Warloe (age six) and her mother, Mary
Bower Knowles***
Albuquerque, New Mexico; 1951

HARLAN BOWER

Constance Elizabeth Bower Warloe was born December 25, 1944, in Charleston, West Virginia. She is the author of a novel, *The Legend of Olivia Cosmos Montevideo* (Atlantic Monthly Press, 1994), and the contributing editor of *I've Always Meant to Tell You: Letters to Our Mothers* (Pocket Books). Married, the mother of twin sons and the stepmother to three daughters, she lives in Sacramento, California. She holds degrees from the University of New Mexico and California State University, Sacramento, and will receive the M.F.A. degree in June 1998 from the Bennington Writing Seminars, Bennington College. She is at work on her second novel, *The Autobiography of Annie Rose Denim*.

Mary Elizabeth Brown Bower Knowles was born June 3, 1915, in Summersville, West Virginia. She graduated from Glenville State Teachers College with a B.A. in education and pursued graduate work at both West Virginia University and the University of New Mexico. She taught second grade at Whittier School and Eubank School in Albuquerque, New Mexico, for 27 years. Having always wanted to write, she began writing memoir and fiction at the age of 70; she became a popular columnist with the *Richwood (WV) News Leader*, and her work appeared in the journal *Rhododendron*. She was halfway through her first novel, *Four Women*, which deals with single mothers in the "family values" decade of the fifties. Married twice and divorced twice, she moved from northern New Mexico to Orangevale, California, to be near her only daughter, Connie, in 1995. She died on August 20, 1997.

Where'd You Come From?

AUGUST 15, 1995

Dear Mother,

How formal that greeting sounds in comparison to our daily phone calls, which begin with my "Hi, Ma," and your "Hi, Ca." But this letter marks, if somewhat belatedly, your 80th birthday, so a touch of formality does seem to be in order.

I want to tell you a story on this occasion because I'm quite certain that my storytelling vocation must be traceable, at least in part, to you. I remember our neighbor Alma Lee Dill one day in the mid-1960s, leaning over the tall fence between our houses and telling me how she loved the summers when you were not teaching and the two of you could fill up an afternoon with talk. "Good talk," she said. And I told her then, "My mother never really tells a short story, does she?"

You generally went back at least two generations if you considered a person's story at all worth telling, and that would have been the expected format if we had been living in the small town in West Virginia where you grew up and knew everyone. But we were not living in such a town at all. In fact, the two of us had come in 1950 to the southwestern equivalent of Ellis Island—Albuquerque, New Mexico. The migratory, postwar influx of which we were a part had its own oral traditions, one of which was to follow any introduction with a question: "Where'd you come from?"

Your women friends came from places like Ada, Oklahoma, and Tyler, Texas, and even Vancouver, British Columbia. The men you began to go out with were from Chicago, or St. Louis, or Philadelphia. All of your lives marked by that great divide—The War.

I suppose the geography of my life has its own generational divide. I have applied the breakthrough wisdom of what many call the Women's Movement to almost every major decision I have made in my adult life. From the shared responsibilities of my marriage and parenthood, to the dynamics of my teaching and writing career, I have been consciously and unconsciously benefiting from the new social and legal positions of women—and from your example.

Yet in spite of outward appearances, I have realized only this past summer the extent to which my life has also been marked by the great divide of your marriages. Try though I have to move on, I have never been able to reconcile the independent, adventurous woman you were during five years of single parenthood, with the long-suffering victim you were with my philandering father early in my life and, later, for forty years(!), with your verbally abusive second husband.

I asked you often enough, "Where'd you come from?" Often enough you told me: The West Virginia Stories. Your gentle father, whom I knew as my grandfather. Your solid and loving mother, my Granny. The senator grandfather who placed a high

value on education for men *and* women. The enterprising grandmother named Tillie, who sold pies to coal miners from her front
porch. I heard about the brothers and sisters, the aunts and uncles and cousins, the neighborly friendships of your early life.

From my childhood spent in the dry, wider spaces of the
American West, I was always able to take long looks—as well as
annual summer train trips—eastward. I was not at all deprived
of the quarterly seasonal shifts of your Appalachian origins. You
gave me plenty in stories: Blinding snow on winding mountain
roads. Gentle springtimes speckled with dogwood and lilacs.
Summer greenery so rich and deep the rains turned the hillsides
emerald. Autumn rainbows of leaf-color that are the best-kept
secret in America (Vermont has nothing on West Virginia!).
There will seemingly never be a shortage of the West Virginia
Stories—you are still writing them in your newspaper columns.

Yet what I wanted most to hear, I never heard—anecdotes,
even one anecdote, that would have explained the woman who
chose the men who dragged her down. Where did *that* woman
come from?

You have never given me an answer. From the ages of 10 to
20, I witnessed firsthand a man—your second husband—who
huffed his infantile rage into my life like a cloud of toxic fumes.
And, later, when I had moved as far away as I could get, I was
continually frustrated by phone calls when you recounted for me
the mean and inappropriate behavior of that second husband. In
one breath you were telling me of his nasty putdowns and day-
long sulks and irrational blowups; in the next breath you were
telling me that everything was "fine now," he was "over it" and
being "so nice" again. I wanted to shriek into the receiver: "What
are you, a Drama Queen? You must *like* this!" Other times, when
your chronic autoimmune disorder would flare up, I'd ask you
outright: "How much of this is stress?" "Well," you'd say, "I don't
know what I'd do without him!" Indeed.

Helpless, flailing around in my co-dependent Hell, I wanted to
help and knew very well that I could not. I spent all those years
trying to reconcile the paradox of your strengths and weak-
nesses, your visions and blind spots, your choices. I know now I
can never reconcile that paradox, any more than my 2 sons and
3 step-daughters will ever reconcile the paradox of my life.

But now has come this pivotal summer, the summer of 1995.

In this, your eightieth year, you have given me something better than a resolution of the paradox, better even than an answer to the question of where you come from. You have shown me who you are *today*, right now. What I want to tell you, my dear mother, is that you have become my heroine.

I must tell you in a story.

This is a true story, Ma, and like most stories that tell the truth, the facts are only secondary. Any resemblances to people, places and things we know, is purely intentional but probably happened by accident. What's true is that in June of 1995, without any prompting from me, you reached across the great divide of your life and mine, and decided it was time to divorce your second husband. It was the single most empowering, soul-satisfying thing you have ever done for me. And the beauty of it is, the healthiness of it is, that you did it for yourself. So sit back and enjoy, Ma. Oh joy and lamentation! This is Mary's story, a heroine's tale if ever there was one.

MARY'S STORY

Once there was a girl who was riding on a train with her mother and father. The girl was keeping watch on her mother, who had just had chest surgery a few weeks before. That night the mother asked the girl to rub alcohol on the c-shaped scar on the mother's side where the doctors had taken out a rib and a piece of her lung.

The girl said, "There's scabs there!"

"It's still healing," the mother said. The girl hoped her mother did not tear open, and her mother did not.

Soon, the father got off the train and the mother and the girl rode on.

When the train stopped the next morning, the mother and the girl got off. The sun was bright and the buildings at the train station were tan and softly rounded. The mother said the buildings were adobe.

The mother and the girl found a house to live in, and they began to walk a lot in the sunshine. They walked to the store, they walked to school and they walked home. The mother taught at the school and saved her money. She did not tear apart.

One day the mother told the girl that she was going to buy them matching red-and-white Fiesta dresses, and she did. Another day the mother told the girl that she was going to buy a piano, and she did. On yet another day, the mother told the girl she was going to buy a house, and she did. It was a little white stucco house with a red tile roof. It had tumbleweeds in the backyard.

The day after they moved in, the mother's friends came over. There were three women. Two of the girl's friends came over too. There were three girls. They all worked together. They painted the inside walls of the house chartreuse green. They hung green leafy curtains on the windows. They put the green sofa and chairs in the living room. They chopped the tumbleweeds out of the backyard.

That night the girl's mother served pinto beans and corn bread to all the women and girls. The job was done. The girl looked at her mother and thought, I want to be strong like my mother.

After a year or two, a man came to the house. He told the girl's mother that he had never had a house. He said his mother and her boyfriend had sent him to boarding schools when he was a boy. He said he liked the house she had. The girl's mother invited the man to live in their house and married him. She told the girl that she felt sorry for the lonely man.

Not long after the marriage, the man's cheek began to pulse. One day he was angry because the roast beef was too pink. Another time, he threw a dish of peas in the backyard because no one had put them away the night before.

Then came the day he was playing his Beethoven record on his record player in the back room. The girl and her mother were in the green living room. The mother was playing "Faith of Our Fathers" on the piano. She had not practiced the song; she was just playing it. The girl was sitting on the couch reading; she didn't notice her mother's mistakes. But the man was angry that the mother had made mistakes on the piano while he was listening to Beethoven. He told the mother, "Learn to play or give it up!"

The girl thought the mother would tell him it was her piano and she could play it however she wished. But the mother did not say a word. She closed the lid over the keys; soon she sold the piano. The girl was confused. This was not the same mother who had bought a piano and bought a house and painted the walls chartreuse. The girl was afraid and confused.

While she was growing up, the girl stayed confused. She would think one thing, and then her mother would do something else. She tried not to expect her mother to be strong. She tried not to make the man angry. But her trying did no good because he was cheerful for no reason and he was angry for no reason. Soon, the girl just put a mask across her face. The mask had eyes painted on it that either looked down or stared unblinking—the eyes in the mask never looked at the man.

When the girl grew up she married a man who did not have a disease of anger. He could talk things out. His cheek did not pulse when he was angry and he did not yell.

The girl visited her mother for only two or three days at a time. She stayed at a hotel with her husband and her children so that the man could never have a chance to be angry at her children.

Years went by. The mother grew very old. The mother told the girl that the old man was angry less often than before. But one time when the girl came to visit, both the old man and her mother had been sick, so the girl did not go to a hotel.

This is what happened: In the place where the mother lived with the old man, they had to keep their cat indoors. One day while the girl was visiting, she left the screen door ajar and the cat ran outside. "Damn cat," the old man said.

The mother looked at the girl. Then she looked at the old man. "Oh, she'll come back," the mother said.

The girl felt a knot in her stomach. Under the same roof, everything felt the same as when she was young. She had made a mistake and the man's pulse had throbbed in his cheek. Yet the girl knew now she had done nothing bad. The confusion was back again, but it was not her confusion. It was her mother's.

Soon the phone rang. The old man answered the phone. "Go to hell," he yelled into the phone.

A neighbor was complaining about the cat. The old man sat in his chair and did not talk. Before long, the girl's mother saw the cat at the door. She let the cat in. The cat walked in with her tail straight in the air, proud as a mischievous child. She walked straight over to the old man's chair and leaped to his lap. The old man would not look at the cat and pushed her down.

He treated the cat the way he had treated the girl and her mother—except he had not shouted at the cat. The girl was no longer confused. The girl went home to her own place.

Soon the mother broke a bone in her back. She could no longer cook or clean. A nurse came to give the mother daily baths. One day after the nurse had given her a bath, the girl called her mother and the mother told her, "When the nurse left, he said, 'It stinks in here. Full of stink.'"

"What did you say?" the girl asked her mother.

"I said, 'The stink will soon be gone.'"

"What did you mean?" the girl asked, hoping her mother did not wish to die.

"I meant I'm ready to go and live in peace. Will you help me?"

The girl was proud of her mother. She felt the same feelings she had felt when her mother had bought the house and painted the inside walls chartreuse.

"Of course I'll help you!" the girl said.

And she did.

Early one morning, when the sun had turned the mesa pink and little puffs of clouds were glowing golden above the mountains and a slight breeze rustled the waxy blooms of the yuccas, the girl went to the place where her mother lived with the old man.

The old man was sitting in his chair. The girl did not look at the old man with her real eyes or with the eyes of her mask. She did not look to see if his cheek was pulsing.

The girl went straight to her mother's room. She helped her mother into a wheelchair and wheeled her to the door. The cat jumped in her mother's lap.

"I'm taking my mother for a ride," the girl called out. Her heart was beating. Her stomach was in a knot.

Carefully, she wheeled her mother to the car. The cat stayed on the mother's lap. The old man did not come to the door.

The mother got in the car. The cat jumped in. The girl put the wheelchair in the backseat. As they drove away, the girl held her hand up to her mother. "Gimme five!" she said, laughing.

Her mother held up her hand as they turned east toward the

mountains. The sunlight on her mother's skin made it shiny. The girl could see her mother's twisted finger bones, arthritic and brittle beneath the shiny thin skin. It did not matter, she thought; the skin would not tear.

Their palms met in mid-air as the sun rose higher and the new day began.

Your loving daughter,

Lynna Williams

Dorothy Williams holding her daughter, Lynna, one year ("Taken so relatives could see a true phenomenon: an infant Williams with curly hair. For the record, my hair hasn't curled since.")
Belleville, Texas; 1952

Lynna Williams was born March 26, 1951, in Waco, Texas. A former newspaper reporter and political speechwriter, her short fiction has been published in *The Atlantic* and *Lear's*. Her first collection, *Things Not Seen and Other Stories*, was published by Little, Brown. She is an Associate Professor of English and Creative Writing at Emory University in Atlanta.

Dorothy Williams was born February 24, 1927, in Prairie Hill, Texas. She is the mother of two children, a son and a daughter. In 1970, after a lifetime in Texas, she and her husband moved to St. Louis, Missouri. Williams, who retired as a vice president of a St. Louis bank, now lives on 15 acres outside Kansas City, shared with her husband of 49 years, three horses, three dogs and two cats named for Henry V.

Everything I Know

Dear Mother:

You'll be surprised, of course, that there's anything left to tell.

In our regulation Southern-family-of-four—Daddy, big brother Marty, and me—I have always been the designated loudmouth, the one who tells all, and then some. This was true even in my preschool years when a speech impediment kept me from being understood by anyone but my famously taciturn brother, who was stuck with interpreting me to the world. Remember when Marty and I went on a kiddie show together in Fort Worth? I was summoned to the microphone for an interview by the oily host, and my red-faced brother followed to repeat my answers in English. Anyone tuning in the program halfway through saw a tall boy in a navy suit from JC Penney solemnly intoning: *My favorite color is pink. I like bunnies best. My Betsey Wetsey doll has a sister named Elaine, Elaine Wetsey.* Marty resigned as my interpreter that night. A year of speech therapy before first grade shaped me up, and the family legend goes, I haven't shut my mouth for five minutes since then. Which is why, I suppose, that all the while you were teaching me the fundamental rules of decent living (Sit with your legs together; don't wear rayon in summer; don't use *language*; the stinkier the gift the sweeter the

481

thank-you note), it seemed to me that what you wanted me to learn above all was this: *You don't have to tell everything you know.* I can't count the number of times you said that to me when I was growing up. You were talking, I know now, about discretion, and privacy, and circumspection. All fine things. But what I heard, almost from the beginning, was not *Don't tell*, but *Don't tell me*. So I didn't. Oh, I went on telling stories, around the dinner table, in the car on the way to church, in the stands at the Little League games, but they were never the stories that mattered.

The stories I told you depended on facts, on literal event, on who, what, when, where, and why. *Patty Bailey brought a shrunken head to social studies today; Mr. Pitts moved me down another chair in the flute section; Coach Gipson can't pronounce* bourgeois. A lifetime later, when I was learning to write fiction instead of newspaper stories, I figured out that it was your house where I learned to lie. The stories I told growing up were true in a literal sense: The shrunken head, like Patty Bailey, was a big fake. I was last chair flute—and the chair was practically in the lunchroom. Coach Gipson, condemned to teach fourth-period history after a loosing football season, announced one afternoon that no matter what the snotnosed-hippies-against-the-Vietnam-War-said, it was the bur-goy-see who made the world run. What I wouldn't learn until I wrote fiction, not facts, is how little real truth has to do with literal truth. To quote the novelist Tim O'Brien, who's turned out to be more use to me than any advice about ladylike deportment, "A thing may happen and be a total lie; another thing may not happen and be truer than the truth." So I lied all those years by not telling the stories that were true to me, by not telling what was important: how I felt, what I saw, what I was afraid of, what I wanted and didn't want.

So here's a story you've heard before, but not quite the way you've heard it. You recognize the event, which did happen; you probably know more facts about it than I do. But the truth lies in what I haven't told you, until now.

I am eight years old, riding the bus home to Fitzgerald St. after another day at S. S. Dillow Elementary School. I need no help with reading, my flowery cursive writing makes even my book reports look like poems, and I see no real reason to linger in

third grade. Usually I spend the twenty-minute ride home playing Go Fish with my best friend, Missy Tucker, and praying that
fourth grade will be better. But today is different. I've been to
church every Sunday since I was born, so I know exactly what
I'm looking at outside the bus window; Noah saw the same thing
from a porthole of the ark: a straight-out, no-joke Biblical flood.
The world outside is only rain; I can see shapes from the window
I share with Missy, but nothing distinct. I'm not sure where we
are. It's never occurred to me before that I could be lost in a
familiar place, and I feel sweat collecting in the hollow between
my shoulder blades.

The bus stops, once, twice, three times, and three groups of
kids get off, only to disappear inside the rain. There are only
seven of us left on the bus, which means Missy and I are the next
stop. The rain is coming down harder, and next to me Missy is
crying, softly, without hope. I have been through two summers
of church camp with Missy; between us, we have failed the basic
swimming test five times. It is six long blocks from the bus stop
to my house, and we both come from one-car families where
Daddy, and the Rambler station wagon, are at work; no one is
coming to rescue us. I don't have to look at Missy to know what
she's thinking. We're going to drown. We'll never see fourth
grade, or long division, or the Tri Delt house at Baylor. Missy, at
least, has accepted Jesus as her personal Lord and Savior; I've
failed at becoming a Christian more times than I've failed to learn
to swim, and so I'm going out in the rain completely unprotected.

The bus sloshes to a stop, and I push Missy to the front of the
bus. "Just hold my hand," I say. "Don't let go of me." She gulps,
like a fish, and then the two of us are standing in the rain. We
start to run, but we haven't gone half a block before I know we
can't make it home. The water is too high on the ground; it's too
cold; we're too little. I don't know anyone who lives on this
street, but it occurs to me suddenly that I am eight years old, a
child, and this is an emergency. I think of the Good Samaritan
in the Bible, and in the next instant I'm imagining Missy and me
in front of a roaring fire, being tended to by a sweet-faced woman
who looks like Mrs. Claus.

"Come on," I scream at Missy, and my mouth fills with water.
I pull her up a concrete driveway to a brick ranch house, and

pound on the front door, but Mrs. Claus isn't home. Instead of running to the next house, I propel Missy toward the carport door. No one I know locks their carport door, and with one turn of the knob, we're inside, out of the rain.

Missy is frozen in place on the kitchen tile, convinced that we're going to jail for breaking-and-dripping. "We have to go," she says.

I tell her she can go, but I'm staying until it stops raining. I don't tell her the rest, which is how much I want to be in this house. My friends live in houses like mine, but this is a different place, almost a separate country, and I am glad to be here. There is a skinny white phone on the kitchen counter—I would be even more charmed if I knew the word for it is princess—and I think briefly of picking it up to dial ED 5-3346, the number written in indelible marker inside the white cotton slip stuck to my skin. But the thought slips away, because I've never seen a phone like that, or a real cuckoo clock like the one above the sink, or breakfast dishes that have been left all day in the sink.

Missy pushes aside the red-and-white-checked cafe curtains, and tells me the rain has almost stopped. "This isn't our house," she says. "We can't stay here."

I nod, and walk her to the door.

This is how the story ends, at least the story you know. Missy goes home, her mother calls you, and you borrow a car to come get me. You're a block away when you see me walking down the street, a "borrowed" afghan over my head. You stop the car, pull me into it, and later that night, the two of us take the afghan back where it belongs. The couple who own the house are exactly the same height; side by side they look like salt and pepper shakers. They are childless, they whisper to you, and I am not even half-way through my apology before they interrupt. They call me sweetheart, and feed me poppyseed cake on a crystal plate, and in the car going home, you tell me that you hope I don't expect this treatment from everyone whose house I break into.

After that, I tell the story once or twice a year, at family gatherings where there are adults I know will think it's funny. You leave the room usually, and afterward, you tell me, again, that I don't have to tell everything I know.

* * *

The thing is, I didn't tell everything I knew.

This is the rest of it.

Missy left, and I dried my hair with a kitchen towel embroidered with a curly capital *G*. I wrung out the towel, hung it on a hook to dry, and then I went through every room in their house. It was as if I had a schedule to follow, a sense of what to do next. I sat on the bed; I closed my eyes and put my hand into dresser drawers; I reached into pockets of coats hanging on the hall closet; I tried on women's hats in the full-length mirror in the hallway. I drank milk from a glass with grapes clustered on the sides. I opened the center drawer of a desk in the living room, and sounded out the words written on a yellow legal pad. *Miriam dear: We are fine here. It is not a bad place; Samuel jokes we are cowboys now.* I could only guess at Miriam and Samuel, but the rest I understood. I turned to the next page, but that was all there was. The handwriting was spidery and faint, and I knew suddenly that the words were too much for me; they had to do with a grown-up sadness, and I was eight years old, trying out a different house like I was Goldilocks. I put the legal pad back in the drawer, and shut it, carefully, without sound. I picked up a burgundy afghan off the brocade sofa and went out the carport door. I didn't need the afghan; I took it because I knew you'd bring me back to the house to return it. I was a block away when I saw you coming toward me in a borrowed station wagon. You slowed down, and I got in, and you asked me how I'd feel if someone we didn't know walked into our house and made themselves at home. "I don't know. Is it raining?" I asked, and you covered your mouth with your hand. That night after dinner, we drove back to the house with the afghan, and some soggy flowers from your garden.

"Just tell the truth," you told me at the front door, and I stared at you. The front door opened, and Mr. and Mrs. Gerlach invited us into their home. I sat on the same sofa again, listening to the soft tinkle of Mrs. Gerlach's voice, and there was no way to tell them what I had done. I wanted to tell them I was sorry they were old, and alone, and that was impossible, too. In the end, all I could do was eat a slice of poppyseed cake, and say good-bye.

You came into my bedroom that night, but I never thought of telling you the rest of it: what I'd done in the Gerlach's house, that I might not have left at all except for those shaky words on a legal pad. I didn't tell you how exhilarating crime was, or how guilty I felt, or how scared I was running through the rain. You were already ashamed of me—*a girl who thinks she can just walk into someone else's house uninvited!*—and so I took that afternoon and turned it into an anecdote, another funny story about my failure to think before I acted.

I wish I had told the Gerlachs the truth. I wish I'd told you.

Love,

Lynna

Hilma Wolitzer

Rose Liebman
New York; c. 1917

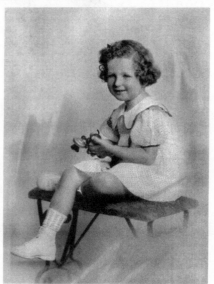

Hilma Wolitzer
(née Liebman)
("already using
the telephone")
New York; c. 1933

Hilma Wolitzer, born in 1930, is the middle daughter of Rose and Abraham Liebman. Born and raised in Brooklyn, New York, she now lives in Manhattan with her husband, Morton, a clinical psychologist. They have two daughters and two grandsons. Ms. Wolitzer is the author of six novels—including *Hearts, Silver,* and *Tunnel of Love*—and four books for children, the first of which was published when she was in her midforties. She taught for many years at the Bread Loaf Writers' Conference.

Rose Goldberg was born in Brooklyn, New York, in 1902, and she died in November 1995, just a few months after this letter was written. Although she wanted to become a dentist, she had to quit school after the eighth grade to help her ailing mother care for the younger children in the family. She worked as a typist and bookkeeper for several years. In 1924, she married Abraham Liebman, and helped him run a small dress factory. They have three children and several grandchildren and great-grandchildren.

The Oldest Orphan in America

Mother, Rosie, my dearest Ma Rose,

Ever since you began to lose the ability to speak three years ago, I've been keeping an involuntary mental record of some of the things you were still able to say to me in person and on the telephone. About getting new patchwork quilts; about watching a certain "literary" program on Channel 13; about coupons in the newspaper for Jell-O or canned peaches or something else you insisted I liked; about driving safely; about keeping warm (or cool, according to the season); and, mostly, worries about the children and grandchildren, whose names you faltered over, but finally managed to remember.

How your persistent phoning drove me mad toward the end—five, six, ten times a day! There was real cause for some of those calls. You'd suffered that disabling stroke a few years before and your body was continuing to fail in blatant and insidious ways. Your current home attendant was inattentive, or worse. And you needed things: stockings, new dentures, a replacement toaster oven, the canned salmon not sold anywhere in your neighborhood. Dad was failing just as quickly in his own ways—increasing blindness, deafness and those bouts of paranoia (he also phoned frequently, mostly to warn me of conspiracies)—and you were being besieged by those inscrutable bilingual letters from the City, repeatedly demanding proof that you were both still old and handicapped. But you kept repeating yourself, too, and I was trying to work, to live my own life. Now, of course, in predictable guilt and remorse, I often dream a ringing telephone and your singular voice, your entire active, chatty, adorable self back into my cluttered and bereft world.

Almost every time we spoke in earlier, better days, you began with the same preface, "The thing of it is, dear . . ." Maybe it was just a verbal tic, or a stalling tactic while you gathered your thoughts, or maybe it was merely part of your *style.* As a reader and writer of fiction, I pay a lot of attention to personal style. In addition to that sweetly distinctive "The thing of it is," yours included an annoying little introductory cough before you began speaking, and, of course, your famous malapropisms. "He dropped her like a baked potato," will always be my favorite. But then there was one small stroke after another, like the aftershocks of a major earthquake, and you lost a few more words each time, until, at last, you were completely silent. A kind of death before death.

I'm still talking, though, interrupting your quiet days with my persistent telephone calls. Earseline or Elizabeth holds the receiver to your ear while I shout "Hello, Ma!" across the growing distance between us, and "I love you, sweetheart!" and various other Hallmark sentiments. I'm told that you nod and smile, the way you still do whenever I visit. During those visits, I turn into the family ventriloquist and speak for both of us, answering what I choose to believe are your urgent, unasked questions. I'm fine, Morty is fine, the kids are all fine—the little ones growing bigger and more beautiful every minute. Here, look at these pictures. And Dad is doing just fine in the nursing home; he asks for you all the time. I don't mention that he simply bellows your name at night, and holds hands during the day with any old woman, or man, whose wheelchair happens to be next to his, addressing them one and all as Rose. And I don't mention that your empty leg brace standing in its shoe next to the bed is like the abandoned carapace of some extinct creature, or that I joke darkly with my friends about becoming the oldest orphan in America one of these days. I just go on as loquaciously and desperately as Scheherazade, not sure whose life I'm trying to save with my narrative.

The ironic thing of it is, Mother, I'm being asked now to tell you whatever I always meant to but somehow didn't during our salad days of conversation. But all I have to offer, it seems, are questions about the things you surely must have meant to tell me.

Can you understand me, Rosie?
Are you warm (or cool) enough?
Do you think about dying?
Do you want it all to be over?
Are you afraid?
Do you dream in language?
Do you live in the past, like Dad?
Do you know our names?
What's the recipe for the potato pirogen?
What is it like in there?

Your Hilma

Irene Zabytko

Irene Zabytko and her mother, Maria Zabytko
Humboldt Park, Chicago, Illinois; c. 1958

Irene Zabytko was born in Chicago in 1954. She is a writer and ESL teacher. A past recipient of the PEN Syndicated Fiction Award, she has published her fiction and nonfiction in various newspapers and anthologies. She resides at this time with her mother in Florida, and at other times in Vermont. Currently, she is at work on a travel memoir about her year teaching English in Ukraine.

Maria Zaraska Zabytko was born in Prusy, Ukraine, in 1913. She attended Lysenko Musical Institute in Lviv, Ukraine, for voice training (mezzo-soprano). In 1936, she married Stanley Zabytko, then followed him to America in 1937 and settled in Chester, Pennsylvania, with subsequent moves to Chicago, Illinois, and Florida. Stanley succumbed to Alzheimer's disease in late 1993.

This Should've Been Your Trip

(In 1993, I was among the first Americans invited to teach English to Ukrainian students in post-Communist Ukraine. My assignment was in the middle-sized town of Drohobych, in western Ukraine. My mother was born in a village near there and had attended schools in Drohobych. Since she hadn't been in Drohobych for nearly fifty years, I invited her to accompany me, but she preferred to remain in America and take care of my father, who was dying of Alzheimer's disease. My father has since died. This is the letter I tried to write then but could only write now.)

JULY 25, 1993

Doroha Momma,

I'm here. You told me to go. Tato in his delirium told me that as well. Remember, when I said good-bye to him, he said with some lucidity, "Have a good time." I'm not having a good time. Everyone I meet tells me how hard it is to live here. Economically, the times are such that everyone is complaining about the price of bread, of post-Communist confusion, of losing their jobs and apartments to foreigners. Seeing your family was the most difficult. They tell me their problems with inflation and how they don't trust the new "democratic" government, and then they look at me, ask about you, and I see the deep disappointment in their eyes because I am not you.

I stopped in Kiev earlier this week, before I arrived here in Drohobych. I had some time before my long train ride, which would take me overnight to the town where my eager students wait for me. I will try to teach them some English and they will learn enough to ask me how much I paid for my Reeboks and Levi's. In Kiev, I found a street with old Byzantine churches that were packed with old people. Many of the old *babas* stood begging in front of the iron gates. An old woman approached me. Her eyes were the same shade of intense turquoise yours become whenever you shed tears. She managed to open one of her thick arthritic hands toward me and I gave her some of the worthless Ukrainian money I found in my pocket. She stood alone, abandoned by Lenin and her family, but, still holding on to God, she muttered a blessing for my kindness. Inside, I heard the dissonant prayers of worshippers between the dark, cavernous walls of icons. I bumped into a waxy-skinned monk with a long reddish beard who watched me with great seriousness as I tried to light one of the thin orange candles. I said some prayers for you, and I was surprised I still remembered the Old Slavonic words I first learned from you.

The *baba* I gave the money to could have been you. You were the only one in your family who moved away to find a life in another country. I wonder now—if you had stayed and had never come to America, would you have been like that ancient woman? Would you have been abandoned by your daughter and left to care for your sick husband by begging in front of churches? As for me—how would I have turned out? Like so many of our family in Ukraine, would I have also embraced vodka and violence? Would I have been a fervent Communist; a factory worker; a dreamy poet (I'm that anyway); a lunatic, a charismatic Christian; an unhappy, overburdened woman who succumbs to a bad marriage because everyone has to marry in Ukraine? Would I have yearned to escape to America the way you once did?

When you left so many years ago, your own family had their hopes imprinted in your memories. Your parents sold their cow and vegetables to buy you and Tato boat tickets to New York. Over there, they reasoned, *only* there can you be a singer. When you were a student studying harmonics and scales, the Poles, who owned Ukraine before Hitler and Stalin, wouldn't let you graduate from the conservatory unless your parents converted to Roman Catholicism. In brave protest, you took your voice across the ocean and escaped with a man you hardly knew.

But America wasn't interested. Pity you didn't have a way to learn Italian or German in a public school—fascist languages in those days, but then you could have sung *La Bohème* or *Die Fledermaus* instead of the unknown operas only you learned by heart and no American opera companies needed.

You were never at home in America. You grew sick from the food and the stink of factory smoke in the cities Tato took you to. Worse, you were wearied by the hostile gazes from the already settled family members who housed you and Tato until he could find a job. Then your children came too fast, and your husband wanted you in the kitchen where all good Slavic wives disappeared. All of your talent went into humming the lullabies and somber folk songs you consoled yourself with at night before sleep rescued you from your loneliness and allowed you to run barefoot as a girl again; the girl with the wild yellow hair whose voice harmonized with the village church bells.

I remember you always singing to us children. Now, you sing solos to Tato, my father, whose glassy eyes sometimes sparkle in response to your clear voice. You sing to him and to God in hopes that Tato will stop this nonsense and walk again.

"What nice legs he had," you've often told me during his illness, now going on the fourth year. I watched you give him sponge baths. "See how much his legs have shrunken to twigs, poor man."

You hold in your resentment when the nurse's aides come, and you relinquish some of the burden as they scrub Tato's back, comb his sparse hair, swab his gums. They never realize that you were up hours before they came, and you had already made up his bed, changed his diapers, fixed the drawsheet beneath him and fed him yogurt and mashed fruit through a large syringe. "Why do they bother coming," you say in your exhaustion. "I don't need their help."

Take him to a nursing home, just for awhile, I beg. Come with me to Ukraine. You are defiant.

"No, as long as I live, I won't take him there to die." In a way, it's easier now that he doesn't walk through the night anymore. It was only a few years ago that he used to take his car keys and drive in circles, on sidewalks, and into fences before a cop would bring him back. Not anymore. Tato stays home these days. He is in the room next to mine, and I hear him sometimes sighing loudly, as though he is tired of it too. Sometimes when I can't sleep, I find you coaxing him to get up and walk. But he merely looks at the ceiling and whispers that he wants to go home, and calls you his mother. I hear you cry, and I have to leave the room before you discover my presence.

The night before I left, you asked me to make sure I visit Hrushiv, a village near your old home. You told me to go to the church where you and Tato met. You were singing in the church choir. ("Och, Maria Zaraska what a voice, a natural *soloveyka*—a nightingale.") Your mother told you to go home early and light the stove before the holiday visitors arrived. "I don't want to walk alone," you said. A dark handsome man said, "I'll walk you." He was a dandy; a well-dressed farmer's son from the same village. He had a walking cane and an American passport and he loved to hear you sing . . .

Hrushiv—the small village where the Virgin Mary made an appearance. Eyewitnesses report that she was dressed in black veils and stood on the balcony of the church. Outside the wooden church, I take some of the well water and pour it into a thick green jar. "Bring back the holy water," you told me before I left. "It might cure Tato." But I will not bring it back to you because I cannot watch you bathe him in this water, only to see that there are no miracles.

In Drohobych, I visit the school you attended. Every morning you came on the early train, far from your little village. Your father was a conductor, and you rode for free. But when you missed the train, you walked in deep snowdrifts, red-faced and chilled. You always told me how, on Christmas Eve, it was you who was sent into the forest to cut down the best tree for your family. You strapped the tree on your broad back and trudged back to your home. How strong you were! Not even your brother could lift a tree as high as you. I think of this as I sit in the building where I am about to teach my first English class. This is the school where you were taught your first songs. I look out the window, recognize nothing, and I am wondering what I am doing in this strange place.

On Sunday, I finally manage a visit to your village—Dorozhiew, a place that is barely on a map. Your sister and brother are polite when they greet me, but they are shy with me because, after all, I am an American. You still belong to them. They have no memories of me growing up amongst them.

Your brother, Slavko, and his wife live on the land where you grew up. Dorozhiew is an ugly village compared to others. You can't see the Carpathians because the land is so dry and flat. The river is dried up and the mill is closed. Only the village store, a converted barracks, is filled with people. They line up for milk and bread and stare at the few overpriced cosmetics that sit out of reach on a bare shelf. They are curious if I will buy the garish lipstick or crumbly face powder from Lithuania.

The house you were raised in is now a barn. A cow nudges me and moos when I enter the yard, angry that I snubbed her and didn't thank her for the cheese my aunt has made only that morning.

Everyone gathers at the table, and talks about you. "Oh, she was something," they tell me. "You should have seen her when she was young. Blonde hair like the sun!"

"And her voice . . . her voice. The mass couldn't start without her. If she was late, everyone, even the priest waited . . ."

A legend.

I am aware that I am as much a stranger in your country as you are in mine. After fifty years, you still cannot speak in English comfortably to strangers without blushing and apologizing for your grammar. And here in *this* country, I am out of my own life. Nothing is connected to me.

How would you see this country of yours now? To combat flies hanging on the ceiling, would you savor the tickle of black walnut leaves framing your head on a pillow? Can you smell the burnt aroma of birch bark erupting in the woodstove, and the solitary warmth of the kitchen where you slept as a girl? Can you see red poppies growing aimlessly along the dirt roads, and the cows clomping out of the way of the sporadic buses, with windows that are stuck shut in the stifling heat? Do you remember the endless pots of gurgling, lush, ruby-colored beets bleeding their juices for the evening's soup?

Why did you dream about this place all those years during your loneliness in America, Mom? Was it the sonorous bells of the churches? The fat worms rolling around in the tilled black earth now drenched with the radiation from Chernobyl? The bazaars where old women sell bucketfuls of currants and tiny wild strawberries they picked for hours that morning in wet forests? The thick, creamy vanilla (always vanilla) ice-cream on wooden sticks that leave slivers in your mouth? The dark cafés with sticky-sweet cakes cut in diagonals, and the golden-toothed smiles of pretty young women whose seductive hips swish inside the rayon skirts they've found on the black market? Can you feel the velvet touch of goose-down feathers plumping up a new coverlet for the winter or taste the first batch of homemade, rose-petal vodka that swims in your head the minute you put the shot glass to your lips?

You left so long ago—before the hammer and sickle were imprinted on monuments and public buildings. Your own Ukrainian is archaic—no one in your village speaks the way you do anymore. Now, you alone speak your language to Tato, who no longer understands you.

Still, *you* should've been here, not me. I can't feel the thrill of recognition of seeing your family's worn faces; the old yellowed pictures of yourself as a child; the school where you had your first crush; the stage where you sang your first solo; the home of the tailor who made your first high-fashion dress (from a French design) that you wore with such grace on that one-way ship to America. Those are *your* memories.

As I write this, the only vision I have of you right now is of Tato being rocked in your arms. You are softly humming a song he used to know, and I think, in your separate ways, both of you are dreaming of home.

I dream of home, too.

Much love to you and Tato.

Ipka (Irene)

Mary Zeppa

Mary M. (Rose) Hunstock and her daughter,
Mary D. Hunstock (Zeppa)
Marshfield, Wisconsin; c. 1944

Mary Zeppa was born in Wisconsin in 1943. She is a singer and lyricist as well as a poet and literary journalist. Her poems have appeared in, among others, *Shaman's Drum, Zone 3, The New York Quarterly, Mixed Voices,* and *I Am Becoming the Woman I've Wanted.* For the last twelve years, she has served the Sacramento Poetry Center as volunteer board member, board president, and most recently as editor of *The Tule Review.* Zeppa is also one-fifth of Cherry Fizz, an a cappella quintet specializing in Doo Wop.

Mary M. Rose Hunstock was born in Wisconsin in 1923. She is the mother of five children, of whom Mary Zeppa is the eldest. A stay-at-home mother for most of her adult life, she has always found the time and energy to volunteer with her church, the Girl Scouts, the elderly and the developmentally disabled. As a young woman, she, too, wrote poetry.

I Grudge You the Mothertalk

Dear Mom,

I grudge you the varicose veins, the striated belly and breasts,
the stretch marks. Though no child came out of this body,
   somehow,
it bears all those marks. Weight loss? heredity? time fabricating
the shadow woman I lost on that July day in '67 when I trusted
a stranger with $500 and my unstrung pregnant self. Seed
   planted,

I think, in Bob's vine-covered cottage. In that 2nd floor, tiny-
dark-kitchen-apartment where he wrestled me out of my girdle
and flashed his white teeth in the dark. How we savored
our sweaty condition, our lust-at-first-sight romance. Days

in that blue bed, tears on that pillow. Who knew when the sperm
hit the egg? We borrowed the money. Used Mastercard.
And Albert O. Lott, Episcopal priest, found us a moonlighting
nurse in the Berkeley hills. Miles, we drove. Al, at the wheel,
cracking jokes. Bob, with his arm tight around me, his whisper:

"You don't *have* to do this." Al spotted the place first:
   the dull-red

brick house where an overblown blonde in fuzzy, pink slippers
waited to beckon us in. To her kitchen: green, plastic
    grapes taped
to blue walls. To her white-washed livingroom where, over
    the sofa,

from black, nappy velvet, luscious black women looked
    down. "They
turn my boyfriend on," she explained. He, brown-skinned
    and muscular,
strut like a panther, said, "Hello." Raked-me-slow with his
    eyes. Al did
the talking. Money changed hands. We walked to their
    bedroom, just we
two women. And there, on that itchy, fake-leopard-skin
    bedspread, there

dressed in almost all of my clothes, I gave myself to her
    pink swollen,
fingers. She fumbled inside me, complained of her sore feet,
    left me alone
to teach myself pain. Afterwards, we drove back to the city.
    I wanted
to be clean, to bleed on alone. I sent Bob away and called
    the first doctor.

A black woman (Al's ex-wife's gyn) who, as I begged in my thin,
    paper gown,
drew back her hands at the mere word *Abortion*. But a friend
    got her
doctor to call me. A bass voice, in Al's hall, on Al's phone,
    said my name,
said his name. I froze. Then, croaked out the particulars.
    Our first
appointment, he touched and probed, looked up over my body
    to tell me:

"There's still some soft tissue. You might still be
    pregnant." Despair
like a black cloak. But drugs did the trick. In 10 days, a girl
    with her own

body back! One who "should have no trouble later. When you
    feel ready,"
he said. Emptiness swallowed me. My body screamed *Ready*.

Throat thick with crying, I begged Bob to come to me. And
    when he did,
I clung hard. "Do you know why you needed me? Do you
    know why
it had to be me?" And I did. And our romance turned
    serious. We
moved in together: Bob and I and the fill-me-up hunger. But
    we said,
"Narrow escape." We said, "Destiny." And, in November, we
    married.

On Veterans' Day, we drove to Carson City. Just us, a J.P.
    on auto-pilot,
his clerk and Milton standing beside us. Milton, our
    best man and
matron of honor, who said, "I feel like I'm marrying
    both of you." We
three kissed, we three signed our names. Drove to a casino
    for our

wedding supper. We three drank a mutual toast. That Christmas,
    Milton
made two stuffed animals. A woolly, Persian-lamb bear for Bob
(the hairy one: back, belly, toes). And for me, a brown velvet,
"motherly" creature: a wise, button-eyed kangaroo. He slipped
a poem in her empty pouch. Said he'd "make a baby when it
    was time."

But it was never time. Fertility specialists found nothing obvious.
"Slightly tipped uterus." "Sperm few but fleet." And so,
    it was years
of sex by the charts. Of the Ovulindex, of boxer shorts.
    And Mom, it
hurt so much, I couldn't tell you: the skull of barrenness,
    probable cause.

Mary

Feenie Ziner

Sophie Katz, at about the same age her daughter is now
Dobbs Ferry, New York; c. 1964

GENEVIEVE REZNIKOFF

Feenie Ziner
Windham, Connecticut; 1979

SANDY HALE

Feenie Ziner was born in 1921. She began as a writer of children's books. Her first adult book was *A Full House* (1967, Simon & Schuster), about having triplets. Her best book was *Within This Wilderness* (1978, W. W. Norton). She was a Professor of English at the University of Connecticut, Storrs, until her recent retirement. Married to Zeke Ziner, sculptor, she is the mother of five, grandmother of seven, and a resident of Branford, Connecticut.

Sophie Katz was born in 1891, in Palanga, Lithuania. She arrived in Brooklyn with her family in 1899 and never left. She married Morris Katz, a diamond dealer. They were the parents of three children: David Karr (now deceased), Florence (Feenie) Ziner, and Mort Katz, of Dallas, Texas. Sophie Katz died in 1978.

For the Time Being

If I never said good-bye, you would never go. In dreams I search for your number among tattered telephone directories, forget which train has red and white lights on the first car, take the Seventh Avenue to the long, cool arsenal at Grand Army Plaza Station where, at the top of the stairs, you occupy your post on a park bench, vanquishing the competition with photographs of my triplets. In dreams I knock on interminable brown-painted doors, wait while the bolt slides back, not surprised that you are sitting at a white porcelain-topped table, pretending to be my grandmother. As usual, I am late.

Now it is I, with my blue-veined hands: I am the grandmother. It is I who await the ringing of the doorbell. Where are you? Surely you could not have left until I said good-bye? Remember how you touched my arm and said, straight from the heart, "I never want to know when I'm about to die"? Surely you understood my absence, my silence, as obedience to your will?

Your picture above my desk—the very image of my present self—shows a smiling face above a pleated collar; for every yes a no.

* * *

503

Not for me, but for my innocent children, you drove each Friday morning to Sheepshead Bay for the freshest fish in Brooklyn. Flounder: a contrary fish, grey-brown on top and white below. All night you'd waited for the dawn, for the signal releasing you from Park Slope. At a quarter to eight you'd arrive, rosy and triumphant, at the door of my improbable house in Dobbs Ferry, your chariot the old green Chevrolet, object of my schoolboys' lust. You were the Queen of the Sea. Crowned by a proper felt hat, you'd commence frying the fish while the house was still asleep. As the odors mounted, the Natives would tumble down the stairs, one by one, to be sure of a piece of Grandma's fish before it was all gone. All gone? How could it be all gone, when you just got here?

"Won't you take off your hat?" I'd ask, falling for it, every time.

"No," you'd reply, "I'm not staying long. The conversation might get boring."

By which you meant that a truce might be declared in our long, thin warfare.

But what was it about?

I wake, as I awake so often, from a running dream. If I am quick enough I will find you in THIS kitchen, in THIS house, standing where I stand now. I pass you the flour, the butter, the can of pepper covered with thumbprints. Couldn't we be grandmothers together? I don't care if you win. I'll let you win. By now, everything's been deplored, defined, belittled, understood, predicted. I promise to reserve my foolish celebrations for an indefinite future.

Yes, everything's been said a thousand times.

Only one word has never been said, nor will I speak it now, because you are alive in me: my irritant, my critic, my goad. My venerable, beloved, imperishable Mother.

Wait for me.

Jeenie

Postscript

September 4, 1997

Dear Reader,

My mother died on August 20, 1997. It seems appropriate to say here that during her last days, and during the weeks afterward, I have been accompanied by the letters in this book:

When she was dying, I remembered Susan Griffin's discussion of the sweetness she and her mother found at the end of their previously difficult relationship.

The morning I went to arrange for her cremation, I remembered Marge Piercy's description of the lovely colors of her mother's ashes and the fact that she put them in her garden.

And as I have arranged the program for her memorial service in the past few weeks, I have drawn on the way Carol Bly and Lucile Adler revealed their ongoing conversations with their mothers long after their deaths.

I also drew, as we all do, upon stories our family has told about the deaths of our loved ones who have gone on ahead. I have, of course, been sustained by the loving support of my family and friends. But this book dedicated to my mother, which was never more than a foot or two from her side from the day I first gave it to her, nurtured and sustained me. You should know that, I think. It seems such a completion of the circle of the written word: the telling of things that come from so deep inside us; the telling meant for our closest blood relative; then the expanded telling that ripples out toward others we never thought to reach.

505

I have received many letters and phone calls from readers who say they want to write a letter to their mothers, but they hesitate, don't quite know how to start. I have even written up guidelines to help you get started on your own letter. But I have to add now, from my own experience: Store up these letters already written, and keep them in your heart. They will give you remarkable strength and comfort at the most unexpected times.

With my best wishes,

Constance Warloe
Contributing Editor